RESEARCH METHODS IN HUMAN–COMPUTER INTERACTION

"This book by Lazar, Feng and Hochheiser is a must read for anyone in the field of Human-Computer Interaction. Their multi-disciplinarian approach, housed in the reality of the technological world today, makes for a practical and informative guide for user interface designers, software and hardware engineers and anyone doing user research. From the basics for doing usability studies to the challenges of doing diary studies or analyzing qualitative data, there is something in this excellent book from which anyone can benefit. I will personally go to this book whenever I am tasked with a methodology with which I'm not 100% confident!"

Dr Mary Czerwinski, Research Area Manager, Microsoft Research, USA

"Lazar, Feng, and Hochheiser have done a great job of collecting in one place everything you need to know to start using the wide variety of research methods employed in HCI. Because this topic draws from a broad range of other disciplines, it is difficult to find it all in one book.

They cover the spectrum of research methods from traditional controlled experiments to methods from sociology, ethnography, and usability testing, to new developments in physiological monitoring.

They also show how HCI has made transitions from the early days of user interface guidelines to controlled, performance-based experiments, to the "new HCI" of measuring lifestyle, satisfaction, and aesthetic and emotional qualities of interaction – all tied together by the continuing quest for scientific methods in this still-young field."

Professor Robert J.K. Jacob, Department of Computer Science, Tufts University, Medford, Massachusetts, USA

"The book is superb: comprehensive, clear, and engaging! This is a one-stop HCI methods reference library. If you can only buy one HCI methods book, this is the one!"

"How did these accomplished authors cram so much valuable HCI methods content in such a clearly written, well-organized, and streamlined book that employs examples, discussion questions, and hands-on exercises based on published research? It's simply amazing, this is an HCI methods reference book that students, researchers and practitioners will turn to again and again in their work."

"The examples, review and discussion questions, and exercises speed readers assimilation of valuable HCI methods, tools and plans, building their network of knowledge in this far-reaching domain."

Dr Clare-Marie Karat, IBM TJ Watson Research, USA, and recipient of the 2009 ACM SIGCHI Lifetime Service Award

"Research Methods in Human-Computer Interaction is an excellent book, and I am looking forward to using it with my students! In contrast to most books that I have used for teaching research methods, it discusses many problems specific to HCI, it covers all the main methods in the field (both quantitative and qualitative), and it is filled with examples that students love."

Professor Kasper Hornbæk, Associate Professor, Department of Computer Science, University of Copenhagen, Denmark

A much needed and very useful book, covering important HCI research methods overlooked in standard research methods texts, and focusing mainstream approaches on HCI research needs. Its balanced and fair coverage provides readers with a broad understanding of multi-method research. This book provides great support for making a sure start (and continuing!) in HCI research.

Professor Gilbert Cockton, School of Design, Northumbria University, United Kingdom

"The Lazar, Feng and Hochheiser book stimulates and guides quality research in HCI. Their combination of insight, good pedagogy and pleasant writing style achieves an excellent presentation of the main research methods used in the discipline. Their questions, discussion topics and exercises at the end of chapters will certainly contribute to waking up the talent of young scientists in HCI."

Professor Clarisse Sieckenius de Souza, Departamento de Informatica, PUC-Rio, Brazil

"Research methods in HCI is an excellent read for practitioners and students alike. It is comprehensive and clear, written in plain English and covers the entire spectrum of evaluation and analysis relevant for HCI. It discusses all the must-know theory, provides detailed instructions on how to carry out the research, and offers great examples. This is a superb book to introduce you to the investigation of all things HCI. I loved it!"

Professor Vanessa Evers, Assistant Professor, Human Computer Studies Lab, University of Amsterdam

RESEARCH METHODS IN HUMAN–COMPUTER INTERACTION

Jonathan Lazar
Jinjuan Heidi Feng
and
Harry Hochheiser

A John Wiley and Sons, Ltd., Publication

This edition first published 2010
© 2010 John Wiley & Sons Ltd

Registered office
John Wiley & Sons Ltd, The Atrium, Southern Gate, Chichester, West Sussex, PO19 8SQ, United Kingdom

For details of our global editorial offices, for customer services and for information about how to apply for permission to reuse the copyright material in this book please see our website at www.wiley.com.

The right of the author to be identified as the author of this work has been asserted in accordance with the Copyright, Designs and Patents Act 1988.

Reprinted with corrections May 2010
Reprinted September 2010

Library of Congress Cataloging-in-Publication Data

Lazar, Jonathan.
    Research methods in human-computer interaction / Jonathan Lazar, Jinjuan Heidi Feng, and Harry Hochheiser.
       p. cm.
    Includes bibliographical references and index.
    ISBN 978-0-470-72337-1 (pbk.)
    1. Human-computer interaction–Research.   I. Feng, Jinjuan Heidi.   II. Hochheiser, Harry.   III. Title.
    QA76.9.H85.L396 2010
    004.01′9–dc22
                          2009033762

A catalogue record for this book is available from the British Library.

Typeset in 11/13pt Bembo by Aptara Inc., New Delhi, India.
Printed in Great Britain by Bell & Bain, Glasgow.

To my mother, Libby
J. Lazar

To Hua, Enric, and my parents
J. H. Feng

To Judy, Elena, and Maia
H. Hochheiser

Contents

About the Authors

Dr Jonathan Lazar is a professor of computer and information sciences at Towson University. He is the founder and director of the Universal Usability Laboratory at Towson University and currently serves as director of the undergraduate program in information systems. He is interested in research issues related to user-centered design processes, web usability, and web accessibility for people with impairments. He is also very interested in the intersection of human-computer interaction and public policy. *Research Methods in Human–Computer Interaction* is Dr Lazar's fifth published book. Other recent books include *Web Usability: A User-Centered Design Approach* published by Addison-Wesley in 2006 and *Universal Usability: Designing Computer Interfaces for Diverse User Populations* published by John Wiley & Sons in 2007. Dr Lazar regularly publishes his research in journals including the *International Journal of Human–Computer Interaction, ACM Transactions on Computer–Human Interaction, Behaviour and Information Technology*, and *Interacting with Computers*. He currently serves as chair of the ACM SIGCHI US Public Policy Committee and also serves on the editorial boards of *Universal Access in the Information Society* and *Interacting with Computers*.

Dr Jinjuan Feng is an assistant professor of computer and information sciences at Towson University. She has taught both graduate and undergraduate courses including human–computer interaction, system analysis and design, and web analysis and design. She has conducted research in human–computer interaction and universal accessibility for nearly a decade. She has extensive experience in designing and conducting user studies and data analysis. She has published more than a dozen papers in top academic journals such as the *International Journal of Human–Computer Interaction* and *ACM Transactions on Computer–Human Interaction*.

Dr. Harry Hochheiser is an assistant professor of computer and information sciences at Towson University, where he teaches both undergraduate and graduate classes and conducts research into human–computer interaction, universal usability, computational thinking, computer security education, bioinformatics, and information visualization. He has also worked on a variety of issues at the intersection of public policy and computing, including privacy, security, accessibility, and electronic voting through his membership of the public policy committees of the US Association of Computing Machinery (USACM) and the ACM special interest group on computer–human interaction (SIGCHI).

Acknowledgments

It's almost a cliché for authors to complain about the difficulties of completing a book. In this case, the struggles of writing and revising were relatively minor, due to our mutual respect and strong working relationship. A top-notch editorial team helped as well: Jonathan Shipley, Claire Jardine, Georgia King, Sam Crowe, Nicole Burnett, and Céline Durand at John Wiley & Sons are phenomenal to work with, and we thank them for all of their work in moving this book through publication!

The chapters of the book have been reviewed numerous times and we thank the reviewers for all of their useful feedback, which helps strengthen the content of the book. In addition to the formal reviews from Angela Bah, Louise Barkhuus, Julia Galliers, Hilary Johnson and Joseph Kaye, collected through Wiley, our colleagues have provided informal feedback on specific chapters. We thank John Bertot, Beth Hanst, Kasper Hornbæk, Juan-Pablo Hourcade, Paul Jaeger, Jenny Preece, and Ben Shneiderman for their feedback on specific chapters. We would also like to acknowledge the support of the Department of Computer and Information Sciences at Towson University in the development and preparation of this manuscript.

Preface

Nobody wants to write a book that's already been written. Why bother, right? Many textbooks arise from a perceived need – in our case, the lack of a research methods book specifically focusing on human–computer interaction (HCI).

Both as doctoral students and now as academicians who both teach and conduct research, we have repeatedly faced questions on how to conduct research: which questions to ask, how to go about designing studies that will lead to answers, and how to interpret the results of those studies. As doctoral students, we took courses – from education, sociology, or psychology departments – or asked mentors. As professors, we find ourselves repeatedly returning to sources from outside our field to learn about research techniques that we have not yet had a chance to use.

Our examination of efforts from our colleagues in the field confirmed our suspicions that there was a void waiting to be filled. Recent trends towards the offering of courses specifically focused on research methods in HCI have not yet led to a specific textbook. Instead, instructors develop lists of papers and rely on texts from other fields.

What's wrong with resources from other fields? In some senses, nothing. HCI's history (see Chapter 1 for some highlights) owes a great debt to work in cognitive psychology, sociology, computer science, and many other fields that have informed work in this applied field. Over the past few decades, HCI researchers have built on this solid foundation, adding research techniques and perspectives that form the basis for a set of research methods that is both distinct from, and related to, techniques from other fields. Here's one example: while the methods used for survey research are generally the same in both HCI and sociology, non-random survey samples are considered valid in HCI, whereas they generally are not considered valid in sociology. It's not enough to just understand the methods from another field. You need to understand how those methods are applied in HCI, and what the acceptable standards are.

The evolution of technology has played a key role in the emergence of this new field of research methods. Online research, mobile devices, virtual worlds, and numerous other technological innovations have generated both opportunities and challenges for today's (and tomorrow's) HCI professionals.

The makeup of our profession has changed as well. The mixture of computer scientists and cognitive psychologists that formed the basis of the early HCI community has given way to a range of perspectives and backgrounds. Sociologists, librarians, educators, video game designers, artists, and those from countless other backgrounds now work in human–computer interaction. Work that was once done primarily in research labs and corporate settings has expanded to homes, schools, hospitals, cars, and practically everywhere in between, as product designers and system builders – often without formal HCI training – examine requirements and evaluate systems.

This explosion of the field led us to an inescapable conclusion: HCI needed a research methods book of its own. So, we've written it. We hope that you enjoy what we have built! And we hope that you use this textbook on a daily basis, as you are faced with the challenges involved in doing data collection. We hope that this book helps inspire you to do groundbreaking research, to change the way we all think about human–computer interaction, to do something different, something noteworthy, and something important.

Jonathan Lazar
Jinjuan Heidi Feng
Harry Hochheiser

Introduction

There is a general consensus that the field of human–computer interaction was formally founded in 1982. This is the date of the first conference on Human Factors in Computing Systems in Gaithersburg (Maryland, United States), that later turned into the annual ACM SIGCHI conference. So, at the publication time of this book, the field of human–computer interaction (HCI) is around 30 years old.

However, this is a deceptively simple description of the history of HCI. The field draws on expertise existing in many other areas of study. People were doing work before 1982 that could be considered human–computer interaction work. There is a fascinating article (Pew, 2007) that describes work on a project for the Social Security Administration in the United States starting in 1977. The work on this project could easily be described as HCI work, including task analyses, scenario generation, screen prototyping, and building a usability laboratory. Pew also describes presenting some of his work at the annual meeting of the Human Factors Society in 1979. Ben Shneiderman published *Software Psychology,* considered one of the first books on the topic of HCI, in 1980. The terms "office automation" and "office information systems" were popular in the late 1970s. At that time, you could find articles that could be considered HCI-related, in fields such as management, psychology, software engineering and human factors. In an interesting article on the history of office automation systems, Jonathan Grudin describes 1980 as the "banner year" for the study of office automation systems, after which, the number of people studying the topic dwindled, and many of them re-focused under the title of human–computer interaction (Grudin, 2006b). Still others point to seminal papers as far back as Vannevar Bush's "As We May Think," which looks surprisingly relevant, even today (Bush, 1945).

The field of human–computer interaction is really an amalgam of other fields, including computer science, sociology, psychology, communication, human factors engineering, industrial engineering, rehabilitation engineering, and many others. This is what makes HCI such a fascinating area of study and, at the same time, so complex. In the late 1970s and early 1980s, computers were moving out of the research laboratory and "secure, cooled room" into the home and the office. The use of mainframes was transitioning into the use of minicomputers, and the more popular personal computers were making their debut: Apple II series, IBM PC/XT, and the Commodore/Vic. It was this move, away from large computers in secure rooms used only by highly trained technical people, to personal computers on desktops and in home dens used by non-technical people in much greater numbers, that created the need for the field of human–computer interaction. Suddenly, people were using computers just as a tool to help them in their jobs, with limited training, and personal computers became a marketed product to home users, like stoves or vacuum cleaners. The interaction between the human and the computer was suddenly important. Non-engineers would be using computers and, if there wasn't a consideration of ease of use, even at a basic level, then these computers were doomed to failure and non-use. In the current context, where everyone is using computers, that may sound a bit odd, but back in the 1970s, almost no one outside of computing, engineering and mathematics specialists were using computers. Computers weren't in school classrooms, they weren't in homes, there were no bank machines or airline check-in machines, before this shift towards non-engineering use. This shift created the sudden need for the field of human–computer interaction.

1.1 Changes in topics of HCI research over time

The original HCI research in the 1980s was often about how people interacted with simple (or not so simple) office automation programs, such as word-processing, database, and statistical software. The basics of interfaces, such as widgets, dialog boxes, and error messages, were the focus of much research. Some of the classic HCI articles of the 1980s, such as Norman's analysis of human error (Norman, 1983), Carroll's "training wheels" approach to interface design (Carroll and Carrithers, 1984), and Shneiderman's work on direct manipulation (Shneiderman, 1983) are still very relevant today. Towards the late 1980s, graphical user interfaces started to take hold. In the late 1980s and early 1990s, there was growth in the area of usability engineering methods (and the Usability Professionals' Association was founded in 1991). But there was a major shift in the field of HCI research during the early to mid 1990s. As the Internet and the web gained wide acceptance, there was a need to research new types of interfaces and communication, such as web pages, e-mail, instant messaging, and groupware. This caused an increased number of research fields to be included under the umbrella of HCI, especially communication.

Around 2004–2005, the focus of research shifted more towards user-generated content that was shared, such as photos, videos, blogs, and wikis. On December 26, 2006, Time Magazine famously named "You" (the end users who generate content) as the "person of the year." The research focus is no longer on something as simple as task performance in statistical software, but is now focused on collaboration, connections, emotion, and communication. The focus isn't on workplace efficiency any more, but is now on whether people like an interface and want to use it. Terms such as "tagging," "friending," and "recommendations" are core components in today's HCI research. But, of course, that will change!

Every time there was a shift in the focus of research, there was a need to adapt or develop new research methods. HCI isn't a research area with a 100-year history. So whenever a new research approach is needed, it tends to be adapted from existing research methods in other fields, primarily the social sciences and engineering. Research methods in HCI are always changing, developing, and improving. And that's a good thing. But for those doing research that falls under the general umbrella of HCI, the question is, where to look for guidance on performing research?

Despite historic roots in the early 1980s, only in the last five years or so have individuals been able to graduate from universities with a degree that is titled "Human–Computer

Interaction" (and the number of people with such a degree is still incredibly small). Most people in the field of HCI have degrees in computer science, information systems, psychology, sociology, or engineering. This means that these individuals come to the field with different approaches to research, with a certain view of the field. Even students studying human–computer interaction frequently take classes in psychology research methods or educational research methods. But taking just an educational or psychological approach to research methods doesn't cover the full breadth of potential research methods in HCI.

Ben Shneiderman said that "The old computing is about what computers can do, the new computing is about what people can do" (Shneiderman, 2002). Since HCI focuses on what people can do, it involves multiple fields that involve the study of people, how they think and learn, how they communicate, and how physical objects are designed to meet their needs. Basically, HCI researchers need all of the research methods used in almost all of the social sciences, along with some engineering and medical research methods.

HCI research requires both rigorous methods and relevance. It is often tempting to lean more heavily towards one or the other. Some other fields of research do focus more on theoretical results than on relevance. However, HCI research must be practical and relevant to people, organizations, or design. The research needs to be able to influence interface design, user training, public policy, or something else. Partially due to the philosophies of the founders of the field, HCI has had a historic focus on practical results that improve the quality of life (Hochheiser and Lazar, 2007). At the same time, the research methods used (regardless of the source discipline) must be rigorous and appropriate. It's not sufficient to develop a new computer interface without researching the need for the interface and without following up with user evaluations of that interface. HCI researchers are often placed in a position of evangelism where they must go out and convince others of the need for a focus on human users in computing. The only way to back up statements on the importance of users and human-centered design is with solid, rigorous research.

Due to this inter-disciplinary focus, and the historical development of the field, there are many different approaches to research currently used in the field of human–computer interaction. A group of researchers, all working on HCI-related topics, often disagree on what "real HCI research" means. That is one of the reasons why Preece *et al.* (1994) provided interviews with leading HCI figures, all of whom come from different backgrounds and points of view. There are major differences in how various leaders in the field perceive the existence of HCI. Be aware that, as an HCI researcher, you may run into people who don't like your research methods, are not comfortable with them, or simply come from a different research background and are unfamiliar with them. And that's OK. Think of it as another opportunity to be an HCI evangelist. (Note: As far as we know, the term "interface evangelist" was first used to describe Bruce Tognazzini. But we really think that the term applies to all of us who do HCI-related work.) Since the goal of this book is to provide a guide that introduces the reader to the set of generally accepted research practices within the field of HCI, a central question is, therefore, how do we do measurement in the field of HCI research? What do we measure?

1.2   Shifts in measurement in HCI

In the early days of HCI research, measurement was based on standards for human performance from human factors and psychology. How fast could someone complete a task? How many tasks were completed successfully, and how many errors were made? These are still the basic foundations for measuring interface usability and are still relevant today. These metrics are very much based on a task-centered model, where specific tasks can be separated out, quantified, and measured. These metrics include task correctness, time performance, error rate, time to learn, retention over time, and user satisfaction (see Chapters 5 and 10 for more information on measuring user satisfaction with surveys). These types of metrics are adopted by industry and standards-related organizations, such as the National Institute of Standards and Technology (in the United States) and the International Organization for Standardization (ISO) (see http://zing.ncsl.nist.gov/iusr/ for more information).

While these metrics are still often used and well-accepted, they are appropriate only in situations where the usage of computers can be broken down into specific tasks which themselves can be measured in a quantitative and discrete way. However, many of the phenomena that interest researchers are not easy to measure using existing metrics or methods. Many of these phenomena cannot be measured in a laboratory setting using the human factors psychology model. These metrics for performance may not be as appropriate when the usage of a new technology is discretionary and about enjoyment, rather than task performance in a controlled work setting (Grudin, 2006a). After all, how do you measure enjoyment or emotional gain? How do you measure why individuals use computers when they don't have to?

Another example is that you may want to measure why people no longer use a specific interface; you can't measure them on using that interface. This is not just a theoretical question. Research has shown that many people start using the web but then lose interest or find it hard to use and stop using it; other people have the ability and access to the web but simply are not interested (Horrigan, 2007; Lenhart, 2003). You may not be able to use experimental laboratory research to learn why people don't use technology. If you want to examine how people use portable or mobile technology such as PDAs and cell phones, you can't study that in a controlled laboratory setting. If you want to study how people communicate with trusted partners, choose to perform business transactions with someone they don't know on another continent (as often happens with Ebay), or choose to collaborate, you need to find new ways of research and new forms of measurement. These are not research questions that can be answered with quantitative measurements in a short-term laboratory setting.

Consider Wikipedia, a collaborative, open-source encyclopedia. Currently, more than two million articles exist in English on Wikipedia (Reagle, 2009). At least 75 000 people, according to recent estimates (www.wikipedia.org), spend their own time creating and editing Wikipedia entries. What causes them to do so? What do they get out of the experience? Clearly, task and time performance would not be appropriate metrics to use. But what metrics should be used? Joy? Emotion? A feeling of community? Lower blood pressure?

While at first, some of these measurements might seem a bit odd, there are researchers currently examining how computer frustration impacts on pulse and blood pressure (Picard, 2000). Techniques from medicine, such as facial electromyography (EMG) and electroen-cephalography (EEG) are being adopted in HCI research (Grimes *et al.*, 2008; Hazlett, 2006). It's not surprising: if you have been trying to complete a task and have suddenly encountered a "blue screen of death," you know that there are some physiological impacts. Researchers are working on measuring these things. What about technologies that allow people to send a hug over a distance to someone wearing a vest that inflates to simulate the sensation of a hug (Mueller *et al.*, 2005)? How would you measure success? Emotion (Isbister *et al.*, 2006)? Feelings of love (Kaye, 2006)? How about technologies that provide information to you on energy usage, with the end goal of lowering your carbon footprint (Gustafsson and Gyllenswärd, 2005)? What's the measurement of success there? Your monthly electricity bill?

Note that there is no such thing as a perfect data-collection method or a perfect data-collection effort. All methods, all approaches, all projects have a flaw or two. One data-collection effort does not lead to a definitive answer on a question of research. In scientific communities, the goal is generally for multiple teams to examine the same research question from multiple angles over time. All of these efforts, if they come up with the same general findings over time, give evidence for the scientific truth of the findings. This is often known as "triangulation". One data collection effort, yielding one paper, is interesting in itself but does not prove anything. If you have 15 teams of researchers, looking at similar research questions, over a period of 10 years, and they all come to the same general conclusion about a phenomenon, then there is some scientific proof for the phenomenon. The proof is even stronger when multiple research methods have been used in data collection. If all of the research teams replicate the same research methods over 10 years, then there is the remote possibility that the methods themselves are flawed. However, the weight of evidence is strengthened when multiple research methods are used.

In HCI, there are some situations where the evidence over time supports a specific finding. One clear example is the preference for broad, shallow tree structures in menu design (see the "Depth vs Breadth" sidebar). Multiple research studies have documented that broad, shallow tree structures are superior (in terms of user performance) to narrow, deep tree structures.

Depth vs Breadth in Menus

Multiple research studies by different research teams, throughout the history of the HCI field, have examined the issue of the trade-off between depth and breadth in menus. Generally, tree structures in menu design can be implemented as narrow and deep (where there are fewer choices per level but more levels) or as broad and shallow (where there are more choices per level but fewer levels). Figure 1.1 shows three menu structures.

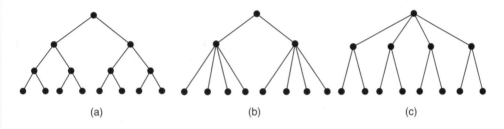

(a)   (b)   (c)

Figure 1.1 Types of tree structure in menu design: (a) Narrow–deep: three levels with two choices at each level; (b) broad–shallow: two choices followed by four choices; (c) broad–shallow: four choices followed by two choices.

The research has consistently pointed to broad, shallow tree structures as being superior to narrow, deep structures. There are many possible reasons: users get more frustrated and more lost, the more levels they must navigate; users are capable of dealing with more than the 7 ± 2 options often cited in the research literature (since menus deal with recognition, not recall), and strategies for scanning can lead to superior performance. Different research methods and different research teams, examining different users, have all come to the same conclusion. So over time, the superiority of broad, shallow tree structures has become well-accepted as a foundation of interface design. Some of the better-known articles on this topic include:

Kiger, J.I. (1984) The depth/breadth trade-off in the design of menu-driven user interfaces. *International Journal of Man–Machine Studies.* **20**(2):201–213.

Landauer, T.K. and Nachbar, D.W. (1985) Selection from alphabetic and numeric menu trees using a touch screen: breadth, depth, and width. *Proceedings of the SIGCHI conference on Human Factors in Computing Systems*, 73–78.

Larson, K. and Czerwinski, M. (1998) Web page design: implications of memory, structure and scent for information retrieval. *Proceedings of the SIGCHI conference on Human Factors in Computing Systems*, 25–32.

Miller, D. (1981) The depth/breadth tradeoff in hierarchical computer menus. *Proceedings of the Human Factors Society 25th Annual Meeting*, 296–300.

Snowberry, K., Parkinson, S., and Sisson, N. (1983) Computer Display Menus. *Ergonomics*, **6**(7):699–712.

Wallace, D.F., Anderson, N.S. and Shneiderman, B. (1987) Time stress effects on two menu selection systems. *Proceedings of the Human Factors and Ergonomics Society 31st Annual Meeting*, 727–731.

Zaphiris, P. and Mtei, L. (2000) Depth vs Breadth in the Arrangement of Web Links. *Proceedings of the Human Factors and Ergonomics Society, 44th Annual Meeting*, 139–144.

In contrast, other research topics in HCI still have no clear answer, with multiple studies that yield conflicting findings. For instance, what is the minimum number of people required for usability testing? See Chapter 10, where the debate still rages on, as there is no agreed answer (Lindgaard and Chattratichart, 2007). There may be some research questions to which the answers change over time. For instance, in the late 1990s, web users tended to find download speed to be one of the biggest frustrations (Lightner, Bose and Salvendy, 1996; Pitkow and Kehoe, 1996). User habits and preferences are fluid and there may be changes over, say, a 10-year period (factors such as increased availability of broadband Internet access may also play a role). The biggest frustration for web users right now would most likely be viruses or spam. When the web first became popular in the mid-1990s, web-wide subject lists and in-site navigation were popular methods for finding items; now, search boxes are far more popular methods for finding what you want (and it is possible that the introduction of Google played a role). When it comes to user preferences, there can be many different influences, and these preferences may change over time. This is yet another reason why one research project, at one point in time, does not make scientific fact.

You should never get disappointed or upset when you find out that another research team is working on a similar research question. You should get excited, because it means that both research teams are moving closer to the end goal of some definitive scientific answers. The chances are very high that your research method won't be exactly the same, your research questions won't be exactly the same, and your human participants won't be exactly the same. The fact that other research teams are interested in this topic shows the importance of the research area and strengthens your findings. Perhaps you should be more worried if no one else is interested in your research.

1.3 Inherent conflicts in HCI

It would at first seem that, with enough research, you could simply decide which design is best by optimizing some specific measurement, such as task performance or time performance. But HCI design and research is rarely that simple. Often, there are inherent conflicts in human–computer interaction research and design. We make trade-offs and accept "better solutions" rather than optimal solutions. We have multiple stakeholders and not all of them can be satisfied. Design is not simple and it's not an optimization problem. Good HCI research allows us to understand the various factors at play, which design features work well for which users, and where those trade-offs are, so that we can make an informed decision. That's not to say that we make perfect or optimal decisions.

For example, we can learn how to make interfaces that are far better than our current interfaces. However, users may not prefer those interfaces because they are so different from the current interfaces. So maybe we should modify our interfaces gradually, making only minor changes each time? Keyboards are a perfect example of this. We know how to make keyboards that are more ergonomic, with key layouts that allow for much faster typing. However, the keyboard layout predominantly used with the Roman alphabet is still the QWERTY key layout. Why? We have far superior designs. The QWERTY layout comes from the time of typewriters, when we had to worry about hammers striking each other. Clearly, that's no longer a problem. However, people have been comfortable with the QWERTY layout for years and the other key layouts have not caught on (despite their clear superiority from a design and usability point of view). So we still use the QWERTY layout. It's a trade-off. You want to make interfaces that are much better but users want consistency. In the short-term, a totally new interface lowers user performance, increases user error, and lowers user satisfaction. In the long-term, a newer interface may improve performance and result in higher satisfaction. Just researching a new interface isn't enough; you need to understand how users may or may not choose to adopt it. Of course, there are sometimes new interfaces, new devices, that just leap ahead with a totally different design and users love it, such as the Apple iPod device. You shouldn't create a totally new design, apparently, unless it's something so cool that users want to spend the time to learn how to use it. Well, how do you measure that? How do you decide that?

Another example of an inherent trade-off is at the intersection of usability and security (Bardram, 2005; DeWitt and Kuljis, 2006). We want interfaces that are 100% easy to use. People focused on computer security want computers that are 100% secure. By definition, many security features are designed to present a roadblock, to make users stop and think, to be hard. They are designed so that users may not be successful all of the time. The best way to make a 100% usable interface would be to remove all security features. Clearly, we can't do that. On the other hand, when success rates for users on security features are below 50%, we have a problem (Sauer *et al.*, 2010). Current techniques, such as passwords, human interaction proofs (such as CAPTCHAs), and security questions all leave a lot to be desired (from the point of view of both usability and security). What's the answer? Is it eye scans and finger scans? Are users ready for that? Right now, the typical user has so many passwords that they simply can't remember them or they choose easy-to-remember (and easy to crack) passwords (Chiasson *et al.*, 2008). Users may write their passwords on a sheet of paper kept in their wallet, purse, or desk drawer, or they click on the feature that most web sites have saying, "Can't remember your password? Click here!" and their password is e-mailed to them. And a password sent in e-mail isn't secure either! Research presented at the annual ACM Symposium on Usable Privacy and Security (SOUPS) attempts to address that inherent trade-off. Simply put, stakeholders may not be willing to value workplace efficiency over security of workplace data. So, lower workplace efficiency with some level of data security may be the acceptable trade-off. Again, HCI research addressing these trade-offs, these intersections of multiple priorities, is important, so that better decisions can be made.

Another consideration that has recently come to the forefront is the idea of sustainable interaction design (Blevis, 2007). While people working in the field of information technology may often be focused on new and better devices and design, faster machines, and faster processing, this can lead to high energy usage and a lot of waste. Sustainability means trying to encourage users to limit their energy usage (Chetty *et al.*, 2009), to keep using current devices, and to reduce the amount of technology waste by allowing current devices to be repaired or retrofitted, rather than just throwing the device out (Mankoff, Blevis *et al.*, 2007). It's possible that, with research, we could develop a new type of computer that would be incredibly easy to use and superior in many ways to our current computers. But would a better computing experience be worth it, if millions of current personal computers would end up in landfill, poisoning the earth and water?

Being user-centered, as HCI tends to be, also means being concerned about the impacts of technology on human life. In the past, this meant that HCI researchers were interested in repetitive strain injuries from computer usage, whether spending lots of time on the Internet made you depressed, and whether computer frustration could impact on your health. Currently, the issue is how all of our technology creation, usage, and disposal impacts on the quality of our life and the lives of future generations and on whether persuasive devices and social networking can be used to encourage us to lower our ecological footprint. (Gustafsson and Gyllenswärd 2005; Mankoff, Matthews *et al.*, 2007). So there's yet another trade-off: is optimal design sustainable design? If not, it's probably not the best choice. Let's go back to our keyboard example: if all keyboards in the English-speaking world were changed over to a different key layout (say, the DVORAK layout), there might be some initial resistance by users but, eventually, user performance might improve. However, how would those millions of keyboards in landfill impact on the quality of human life? This is a new point to evaluate when considering how we do research in human–computer interaction. What is the ecological impact of our research? What is the ecological impact of new interfaces or devices that we build? While it's likely that we won't know in advance what type of ecological impact our research work will lead to, it's an important consideration as we do our research, yet another inherent challenge in HCI.

1.4 Interdisciplinary nature of HCI research

While HCI has historically been inter-disciplinary, involving people from multiple fields, there have usually been one or two fields that have dominated the agenda alongside computer science (Grudin, 2006a). This might influence which research methods are considered to be most appropriate at a specific point in history. At the beginning, the dominant fields might have been human factors, engineering, and psychology (which, for instance, all support the experimental design model). Currently, the dominant fields may be leaning more towards library and information science, and art and design (Grudin, 2006a). More and more work in the area of HCI is now being done in design schools, information schools, and library schools (Olson and Grudin, 2009). As interface and interaction research moves away from desktop computers to portable devices, smart phones, tangible and wearable computing, audio, touch, and tactile computing, there is a natural involvement of the disciplines that have experience in these areas. Terms such as "information design," "information architecture," and "interaction design" are more prevalent. So, the combination of new disciplines that drive the HCI agenda and the current focus on enjoyable, discretionary (non-work-related) usage and users influence the use of new research approaches.

Shneiderman has named this new approach to research "Science 2.0." The idea is that to study today's research questions, there are so many variables involved (such as collaborations, empathy, and trust among individuals) that reductionist methods in the laboratory do not allow researchers to fully understand what is happening (Shneiderman, 2008). Multi-method approaches, possibly involving case studies, observations, interviews, data logging, and other longitudinal techniques, may be most appropriate for understanding what makes these new socio-technical systems successful.

The old methods of research are comfortable: hypothesis testing, statistical tests, control groups, and so on. They come from a proud history of scientific research, and they are easily understood across many different academic, scientific, and research communities. However, they alone are not sufficient approaches to measure all of today's phenomena. The same applies to the "old standard" measures of task correctness and time performance. Those metrics may measure "how often?" or "how long?" but not "why?" However, they are still well-understood and well-accepted metrics, and they allow HCI researchers to communicate their results to other research communities where the cutting-edge tools and research methods may not be well-understood or well-accepted. The field of HCI has begun to apply research methods from the social sciences, and we encourage the reader to start using some new research approaches that are not even in this textbook! Please be aware that people from other disciplines, as well as your "home discipline", will probably challenge the appropriateness of those research methods!

It is important to note that inter-disciplinary research, using multiple research methods, is not always easy to do. There are many challenges that can arise, in many cases due to the individual cultures of each of the disciplines involved. While the HCI community might be considered by some to be an inter-disciplinary community, many other conferences, professional organizations, and individuals keep the focus on their primary discipline. When inter-disciplinary research gets filtered through single-discipline evaluations, there are many challenges that can occur. Some of the challenges are well-known, such as how some disciplines (e.g. computer science) focus more on conference publications and others (e.g. management information systems) focus on journal publications (Grudin, 2006a). Some disciplines focus on single-author publications, while others focus primarily on group-author publications. Some disciplines are very open about sharing their results, while others keep their results more confidential. Some disciplines are very self-reflective and do research studies about their discipline (trends of research, rankings, funding, collaborations), while others do not. Some disciplines are primarily focused on getting grant money, while other disciplines are less interested, or can even be leery of the influences of outside sponsors. Even the appropriate dress at conferences for each discipline can vary widely. And inter-disciplinary researchers can sometimes have problems convincing others at their workplace of the quality and seriousness of their work. But all of these are primarily concerns with an individual's professional career or with administrative issues (Sears *et al.*, 2008).

There are more serious, but less well-known, challenges related to inter-disciplinary research. As discussed earlier in this chapter, no research method, approach, or discipline is perfect. In reality, a research project is a series of steps and decisions related to data collection. For instance, there is a theoretical foundation for the data-collection effort, there is a research method involved, often human participants are recruited and involved, there is data analysis, and then there is the discussion of implications involved. Different disciplines can sometimes be most interested in, and more focused on, different steps in the research process. While no one would ever say, "I'm not interested in the research methods," in many cases, there are steps that are considered of less interest to people from a certain discipline. And there may be historical roots for that. For instance, as described in Chapter 5, there are large data-collection efforts that use strict controls, in fields such as sociology, and those data sets are available for researchers internationally to analyze. However, no such central data sets exist for human–computer interaction and it's not considered a standard practice to publish your data sets or make them available to others. It's a very different model in other fields. That may lead to a focus on certain stages of research more than others.

(Note: We expect the following paragraphs to be a bit controversial; however, we do believe strongly, based on our experience, that they are true.) One discipline might have an expectation that a specific step (such as research design) is done "perfectly," but that it is acceptable to give more flexibility in other steps (such as the types of participants). The management information systems community of HCI researchers has a well-known focus on the theoretical underpinnings of any research. Computer-science-based HCI researchers have much less interest in theory and much more of an interest in the practical outcomes

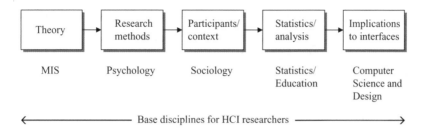

Figure 1.2 How disciplines focus on certain phases of the research process.

of the research on interfaces (although Carroll, 2003 is a noteworthy effort on theory in HCI). This distinction is seen, for instance, in the Technology Acceptance Model, which is core theory and has central importance for HCI researchers focused on management information systems, but is not well-known or of much interest to the HCI researchers focused on computer science (Davis, 1989; Venkatesh and Davis, 2000). While general computer science researchers have a great deal of theory in, say, algorithms, HCI research in computer science does not have a major focus on theory.

When having inter-disciplinary discussions and working on inter-disciplinary teams, it's important to be aware of these distinctions. Sociology-based HCI research tends to focus on the demographics of the research participants and determining if they accurately represent the population of interest, while this is not considered critical in computer science, where computer science students are often used as participants (even when not appropriate). Psychology-based HCI research tends to focus on an ideal and clean research design. HCI research based on computer science and on design is focused more on the implications for interfaces, although computer science may focus more on the technical underpinnings while design focuses more on the look and feel of the interface. Figure 1.2 provides an overview of which stage of research tends to be focused on most by different disciplines. These are just generalizations, obviously; all disciplines want excellence at all stages of research, but it is true that disciplines tend to focus more intensely on particular stages of research. The good news is that we want all of these different groups focusing on improving each stage of the research process. We WANT different groups looking at research through their different lenses. We want to get that triangulation, where people look at the same research questions, using different methods, different approaches, and different lenses, over time, with the goal of discovering some scientific truths.

1.5 Communicating your ideas

It is important, for a number of reasons, to become familiar with the research methods in different disciplines. You need to be able to communicate your research methods, and the reasons why you chose some and not others, in a very convincing way. When you submit journal articles, conference papers, or book chapters, you never know who will be reviewing your work. The chances are good that your work will be reviewed by people who come from very different research backgrounds. There really isn't one "HCI background."

The same is true of grant proposals. A large percentage of HCI research is funding-intensive. It involves graduate students, new equipment, and paying human participants to take part in research. Often, to get ground-breaking, large-scale research, funding must be available. Funding is secured through submitting multiple grant proposals to government organizations, NGOs, and private organizations. When you submit these grant proposals, you never really know the research background of the proposal reviewers. While many organizations strive to ensure that the reviewers are experienced and knowledgeable, this is no guarantee that the reviewers will come from a similar background to you. You need to be able to compare the different research methods available for your proposed research and explain why one method seems to be superior to another. Or, preferably, why you used a few research methods, but did not choose to include another specific research method.

1.6   Research and usability testing

We are often asked about usability testing, and whether or not it is considered to be "research." While the actual methods used in some types of research and usability testing are very similar, the goals of research and usability testing are very different. Both experimental research and usability testing may sometimes involve quarantining the user in a separate environment and asking them to perform a series of tasks without outside help, and they involve quantitative measurement of performance.

However, the goal of usability testing is simply to find flaws in a specific interface (or series of interfaces). A small number of users may take part in usability testing and it can be structured or unstructured. In usability testing, there is no claim that the results can be generalized – the goal is simply to find flaws in a specific interface to help the interface developers improve the interface. If that involves jumping in and helping a user or changing the tasks mid-process, that is acceptable. Usability testing can be messy but that's OK. See Chapter 10 for more information on usability testing.

Summary of Chapters

Given that the topic of research methods in HCI is so broad, we have tried to give approximately one chapter to each research method. However, the book starts out with three chapters revolving around the topic of experimental design. Whole books and semesters have focused on experimental design and, when you include all of the statistical tests, this simply can't be contained in one chapter. Chapter 4 can be useful for methods other than experimental design (for instance, statistical analysis is often used in survey research). For researchers using statistical software and advanced statistical analysis, additional reading resources are likely to be necessary.

Chapters 5 and 6 cover surveys and diaries, two key research approaches from the field of sociology. While surveys are used far more often than diaries in HCI research, there are some emerging research projects using the time diary method. Again, a number of textbooks have been written solely on the topic of survey design. Chapters 7, 8, and 9 are based on research approaches popular in the social sciences. Case studies, interviews/focus groups, and ethnography have also been popular approaches in business school research for years. The five research approaches in Chapters 5 to 9 – surveys, time diaries, case studies, interviews, and ethnography – are often useful for understanding "why?" questions, whereas experimental research is often better at understanding "how often?" or "how long?" questions.

Chapter 10 provides useful information on how to manage structured usability tests, in cases where usability testing is a part of the package of research approaches. Chapter 11 focuses on analyzing qualitative data, which might have been collected from case studies, ethnography, time diaries, and other methods. Chapter 12 and Chapter 13 focus on methods of collecting research data through automated means. One method is automated data collection indirectly from humans, through their actions on a computer, including key logging and web site logs. The other method involves data collection directly from humans through sensors focused on the body, such as facial EMG and eye-tracking. Chapters 14 and 15 focus on issues that arise in working with human subjects. Chapter 14 covers general issues, such as informed consent, and Chapter 15 deals with issues specific to participants with impairments.

We hope that you enjoy reading this book as much as we enjoyed writing it!

Jonathan Lazar

Jinjuan Heidi Feng

Harry Hochheiser

Discussion Questions

1. What were some of the major shifts in the topics of HCI research from the original focus on word-processing and other office-automation software? Discuss at least two shifts in the focus of research.
2. What are the standard quantitative metrics that have been used in HCI research since the early 1980s?
3. What are some newer metrics used in HCI research?
4. What is triangulation? Why is it important?
5. Why doesn't one published research paper equate to scientific truth?
6. Name four disciplines that have helped contribute to the field of human–computer interaction.
7. Describe three professional challenges of inter-disciplinary research.
8. Describe three research-design challenges in inter-disciplinary research.
9. How is experimental design different from usability testing?
10. Describe three inherent conflicts in human–computer interaction.
11. What do you think the field of HCI research will look like in 20 years?

Research Design Exercise

Imagine that you are going to be researching the topic of why people choose to take part in an online community for parents of children with autism. What are some of the reference disciplines that you should be looking into? What types of people might you want to talk with? What types of metrics might be appropriate for understanding this community? Come up with three approaches that you could take in researching this online community.

References

Bardram, E. (2005) The trouble with login: on usability and computer security in ubiquitous computing. *Personal and Ubiquitous Computing*, **9**(6):357–367.

Blevis, E. (2007) Sustainable interaction design: invention & disposal, renewal & reuse. *Proceedings of the ACM Conference on Human Factors in Computing Systems*, 503–512.

Bush, V. (1945) As we may think. *The Atlantic Monthly*, **176**:101–108.

Carroll, J. (ed.) (2003) *HCI Models, Theories, and Frameworks: Toward a Multidisciplinary Science*. San Francisco: Morgan Kaufmann Publishers.

Carroll, J. and Carrithers, C. (1984) Training wheels in a user interface. *Communications of the ACM*, **27**(8):800–806.

Chetty, M., Brush, A.J.B., Meyers, B., and Johns, P. (2009) It's not easy being green: understanding home computer power management. *Proceedings of the 27th ACM Conference on Human Factors in Computing Systems*, 1033–1042.

Chiasson, S., Forget, A., Biddle, R., and Van Oorschot, P. (2008) Influencing users towards better passwords: persuasive cued click-points. *Proceedings of the 22nd British HCI Group Annual Conference on HCI 2008: People and Computers*, 121–130.

Davis, F. (1989) Perceived usefulness, perceived ease of use, and user acceptance of information technology. *MIS Quarterly*, **13**(3):319–340.

DeWitt, A. and Kuljis, J. (2006) Aligning usability and security: a usability study of Polaris. *Proceedings of the Second Symposium on Usable Privacy and Security*, 1–7.

Grimes, D., Tan, D., Hudson, S., Shenoy, P., and Rao, R. (2008) Feasibility and pragmatics of classifying working memory load with an electroencephalograph. *Proceedings of the ACM Conference on Human Factors in Computing Systems*, 835–844.

Grudin, J. (2006a) Is HCI homeless? In search of inter-disciplinary status. *interactions*, **13**(1):54–59.

Grudin, J. (2006b) A missing generation: Office automation/information systems and human–computer interaction. *interactions*, **13**(3):58–61.

Gustafsson, A. and Gyllenswärd, M. (2005) The power-aware cord: energy awareness through ambient information display. *Proceedings of the ACM Conference on Human Factors in Computing Systems*, 1423–1426.

Hazlett, R. (2006) Measuring emotional valence during interactive experiences: boys at video game play. *Proceedings of the ACM Conference on Human Factors in Computing Systems*, 1023–1026.

Hochheiser, H. and Lazar, J. (2007) HCI and societal issues: a framework for engagement. *International Journal of Human–Computer Interaction*, **23**(3):339–374.

Horrigan, J. (2007) *A Typology of Information and Communication Technology Users*. Washington, DC: Pew Internet and American Life Project.

Isbister, K., Hook, K., Sharp, M., and Laaksolahti, J. (2006) The sensual evaluation instrument: developing an effective evaluation tool. *Proceedings of the SIGCHI Conference on Human Factors in Computing Systems*, 1163–1172.

Kaye, J. (2006) I just clicked to say I love you: rich evaluations of minimal communication. *Proceedings of the ACM Conference on Human Factors in Computing Systems*, 363–368.

Lenhart, A. (2003) *The Ever-Shifting Internet Population: A new look at Internet access and the digital divide*. Washington, DC: Pew Internet and American Life Project.

Lightner, N., Bose, I., and Salvendy, G. (1996) What is wrong with the world wide web? A diagnosis of some problems and prescription of some remedies. *Ergonomics*, **39**(8):995–1004.

Lindgaard, G. and Chattratichart, J. (2007) Usability testing: What have we overlooked? *Proceedings of the ACM Conference on Human Factors in Computing Systems*, 1415–1424.

Mankoff, J., Blevis, E., Borning, A., Friedman, B., Fussell, S., Hasbrouck, J., Woodruff, A., and Sengers, P. (2007) Environmental sustainability and interaction. *Proceedings of the ACM Conference on Human Factors in Computing Systems*, 2121–2124.

Mankoff, J., Matthews, D., Fussell, S., and Johnson, M. (2007) Leveraging social networks to motivate individuals to reduce their ecological footprints. *Proceedings of the 2007 Hawaii International Conference on System Sciences*, 87.

Mueller, F., Vetere, F., Gibbs, M., Kjeldskov, J., Pedell, S., and Howard, S. (2005) Hug over a distance. *Proceedings of the ACM Conference on Human Factors in Computing Systems*, 1673–1676.

Norman, D. (1983) Design rules based on analyses of human error. *Communications of the ACM*, **26**(4):254–258.

Olson, G. and Grudin, J. (2009) The information school phenomenon. *interactions*, **16**(2):15–19.

Pew, R. (2007) An unlikely HCI frontier: the Social Security Administration in 1978. *interactions*, **14**(3):18–21.

Picard, R. (2000) *Affective Computing.* Cambridge, MA: MIT Press.

Pitkow, J. and Kehoe, C. (1996) Emerging trends in the WWW population. *Communications of the ACM,* **39**(6):106–110.

Preece, J., Rogers, Y., Sharp, H., Benyon, D., Holland, S., and Carey, T. (1994) *Human–Computer Interaction.* Wokingham, England: Addison Wesley Publishing.

Reagle, J. (2009) Wikipedia: the happy accident. *interactions,* **16**(3):42–45.

Sauer, G., Holman, J., Lazar, J., Hochheiser, H., and Feng, J. (2010) Accessible privacy and security: A universally usable human-interaction proof. *Universal Access in the Information Society,* **9**(3).

Sears, A., Lazar, J., Ozok, A., and Meiselwitz, G. (2008) Human-centered computing: Defining a research agenda. *International Journal of Human–Computer Interaction,* **24**(1):2–16.

Shneiderman, B. (1983) Direct manipulation: A step beyond programming languages. *IEEE Computer,* **9**(4):57–69.

Shneiderman, B. (2002) *Leonardo's Laptop: Human needs and the new computing technologies.* Cambridge, MA: MIT Press.

Shneiderman, B. (2008) Science 2.0. *Science,* **319**:1349–1350.

Venkatesh, V. and Davis, F. (2000) A theoretical extension of the technology acceptance model: four longitudinal field studies. *Management Science,* **46**(2):186–204.

2

Experimental research

A variety of laboratory and non-laboratory research methods are available for human–computer interaction (HCI) researchers or practitioners to select when studying interfaces or applications. The most frequently used include observations, field studies, surveys, usability studies, interviews, focus groups, and controlled experiments (Shneiderman *et al.*, 2009). In order to study how users enter information into their mobile phones, a researcher may choose to observe mobile phone users in a natural setting, such as individuals who are using a cell phone in a company lobby, an airport, or a park. The researcher may write a survey that addresses questions that he'd like to have answered and ask mobile phone users to answer the survey. The researcher may interview a number of mobile phone users to find out how they enter information into their phones. The researcher may choose to recruit a couple of participants and run a usability test in a lab-based environment. Another option is to specify several conditions and run a strictly controlled lab-based experiment.

We can continue to add more options to the researcher's list: focus groups, field studies, and so on. Each of these options has its strengths and weaknesses. Unobtrusively observing users in natural settings may allow the researcher to identify the patterns that are most representative of the use of the mobile phone in natural settings, but observation studies can be extremely time-consuming. The researcher may wait for hours only to find that none of the individuals being observed has used the functions in which he is most interested. The survey approach may allow the researcher to reach a large number of users – say, over a hundred – in a short period of time, but the participants may misunderstand the questions, the data collected do not represent depth in understanding, and the participant sample can be highly biased. Interviews allow the researcher to clarify questions and dig deeper with follow-up questions when a participant provides interesting feedback. However, interviews cost significantly more time and money than surveys. Usability tests provide a quick and comparatively low-cost method of identifying key usability problems in an interface or application, but they cannot guarantee that all critical design problems can be identified.

Choosing which method to use is a highly context-dependent issue related to a variety of factors including the primary purpose of the study, time constraints, funding, the participant pool, and the researcher's experience. We discuss in more detail in Chapter 3 how to select the appropriate research method. This chapter examines experimental research in general and focuses on the very basics of conducting experimental studies. We discuss how to develop research hypotheses and how to test the validity of a hypothesis. Important concepts related to hypothesis testing, such as Type I and Type II errors and their practical implications, are examined in detail.

2.1   Types of behavioral research

Viewed broadly, all of the methods mentioned above are kinds of empirical investigation that can be categorized into three groups: descriptive investigations, relational investigations, and experimental investigations (Rosenthal and Rosnow, 2008). Descriptive investigations, such as observations, surveys, and focus groups, focus on constructing an accurate description of what is happening. For example, a researcher may observe that eight out of 10 teenagers in a class who frequently play a specific computer game can touch type while only two out of 12 teenagers in the same class who do not play the game can touch type. This raises an interesting observation. But it does not allow the establishment of a relationship between the two factors: playing the game and typing. Neither does it enable the researcher to explain why this happens.

Relational investigations enable the researcher to identify relations between multiple factors. That is, the value of factor X changes as the value of factor Y changes. For example, the researcher may collect data on the number of hours that the teenagers play the computer game per week and measure their typing speed. The researcher can run a correlation analysis[1] between the number of hours and typing speed. If the result is significant, it suggests that there is a relationship between typing speed and the time spent playing the game. The results of relational studies usually carry more weight than what can be learned through descriptive studies. However, relational studies can rarely determine the causal relationship between multiple factors (Cooper and Schindler, 2000; Rosenthal and Rosnow, 2008).

Using the same example, the significant correlation result does not allow the researcher to determine the cause of the observed relationship. It is possible that playing the computer game improves typing speed. It is also possible that teenagers who type well tend to like the game more and spend more time on it. To complicate matters even more, the correlation can be due to hidden factors that the researcher has not considered or studied. For example, it is possible that teenagers who read well tend to type faster and that teenagers who read well tend to like the game more and spend more time on it. In this case, playing the computer game has no impact on the typing speed of the teenagers.

How, then, can the researcher determine the causal effect between two factors? The answer lies in experimental research (Kirk, 1982; Oehlert, 2000). The researcher may recruit teenagers in the same age group and randomly assign the teenagers to two groups. One group will spend a certain amount of time playing the computer game every week and the other group will not. After a period of time (e.g., three months or longer), the researcher can measure each teenager's typing speed. If the teenagers who play the computer game type significantly faster than the teenagers who do not play the game, the researchers can confidently draw the conclusion that playing this computer game improves the typing skills of teenagers.

As shown in the above example and summarized in Table 2.1, the most notable difference between experimental research and the other two types of investigation is that experimental

---

[1] Correlation analysis is a statistical test designed to identify relationships between two or more factors. Details of correlation analysis are discussed in Chapter 4.

Type of research	Focus	General claims	Typical methods
Descriptive	Describe a situation or a set of events	X is happening	Observations, field studies, focus groups, interviews
Relational	Identify relations between multiple variables	X is related to Y	Observations, field studies, surveys
Experimental	Identify causes of a situation or a set of events	X is responsible for Y	Controlled experiments

Table 2.1 Relationship between descriptive research, relational research, and experimental research.

research enables the identification of causal relationships. Simply put, it can tell how something happens and, in some cases, why it happens. The ability of experimental research to identify the true cause of a phenomenon allows researchers to manipulate the way we do research and achieve the desired results. To give a few examples, experimental studies are widely adopted in the field of medicine to identify better drugs or treatment methods for diseases. Scientists also use experimental research to investigate various questions originating from both the macro-world, such as the impact of acid rain on plants, and the micro-world, such as how nerves and cells function.

The three kinds of research methods are not totally independent but highly intertwined. Typical research projects include a combination of two or even three kinds of investigation. Descriptive investigations are often the first step of a research program, enabling researchers to identify interesting phenomena or events that establish the cornerstone of the research and identify future research directions. Relational investigations enable researchers or practitioners to discover connections between multiple events or variables. Ultimately, experimental research provides the opportunity to explore the fundamental causal relations. Each of the three kinds of investigation is of great importance in the process of scientific discovery.

2.2   Research hypotheses

An experiment normally starts with a research hypothesis. A hypothesis is a precise problem statement that can be directly tested through an empirical investigation. Compared with a theory, a hypothesis is a smaller, more focused statement that can be examined by a single experiment (Rosenthal and Rosnow, 2008). In contrast, a theory normally covers a larger scope and the establishment of a theory normally requires a sequence of empirical studies. A concrete research hypothesis lays the foundation of an experiment as well as the basis of statistical significance testing.

Theory vs Hypothesis

The differences between theories and hypotheses can be clearly demonstrated by the extensive HCI research into Fitts' law (Fitts, 1954), one of the most widely accepted theories in the HCI field. It states a general relationship between movement time, navigation distance, and target size for pointing tasks in an interface:

In movement tasks, the movement time increases as the movement distance increases and the size of the target decreases. The movement time has a log linear relationship with the movement distance and the width of the target.

Fitts' law is a general theory that may apply to various kinds of pointing devices. It is impossible to validate Fitts' law in a few experiments. Since Fitts' law was proposed, hundreds of user studies have been conducted on various pointing devices and tasks to validate and modify Fitts' law. The research hypothesis of each of those studies is a much more focused statement covering a small, testable application domain.

For example, Miniotas (2000) examined hypotheses about the performance of two pointing devices: a mouse and an eye tracker. Movement time was shorter for the mouse than for the eye tracker. Fitts' law predicted the navigation time fairly well for both the mouse and the eye tracker, indicating the potential to apply Fitts' law to technologies that do not rely on hand-based control. Accot and Zhai (2003) investigated Fitts' law in the context of two-dimensional targets.

2.2.1   Null hypothesis and alternative hypothesis

An experiment normally has at least one null hypothesis and one alternative hypothesis. A null hypothesis typically states that there is no difference between experimental treatments. The alternative hypothesis is always a statement that is mutually exclusive with the null hypothesis. The goal of an experiment is to find statistical evidence to refute or nullify the null hypothesis in order to support the alternative hypothesis (Rosenthal and Rosnow, 2008). Some experiments may have several pairs of null hypotheses and alternative hypotheses. The characteristics of null and alternative hypotheses can be better explained through the following hypothetical research case.

Suppose the developers of a website are trying to figure out whether to use a pull-down menu or a pop-up menu in the home page of the website. The developers decide to conduct an experiment to find out which menu design will allow the users to navigate the site more effectively. For this research case, the null and alternative hypotheses[2] can be stated in classical statistical terms as follows:

- H_0: There is no difference between the pull-down menu and the pop-up menu in the time spent locating pages.
- H_1: There is a difference between the pull-down menu and the pop-up menu in the time spent locating pages.

From this example, we can see that the null hypothesis usually assumes that there is no difference between two or more conditions. The alternative hypothesis and the null hypothesis should be mutually exclusive. That is, if the null hypothesis is true, the alternative hypothesis must be false, and vice versa. The goal of the experiment is to test the null hypothesis against the alternative hypothesis and decide which one should be accepted and which one should be rejected. The results of any significance test tell us whether it is reasonable to reject the null hypothesis and the likelihood of being wrong if rejecting the null hypothesis. We explain this topic in more detail in Section 2.5.

Many experiments examine multiple pairs of null and alternative hypotheses. For example, in the research case above, the researchers may study the following additional hypotheses:

- H_0: There is no difference in user satisfaction rating between the pull-down menu and the pop-up menu.
- H_1: There is a difference in user satisfaction rating between the pull-down menu and the pop-up menu.

There is no limit on the number of hypotheses that can be investigated in one experiment. However, it is generally recommended that researchers should not attempt to study too many hypotheses in a single experiment. Normally, the more hypotheses to be tested, the more factors that need to be controlled and the more variables that need to be measured. This results in very complicated experiments, subject to a higher risk of design flaws.

In order to conduct a successful experiment, it is crucial to start with one or more good hypotheses (Durbin, 2004). A good hypothesis normally satisfies the following criteria:

- is presented in precise, lucid language;
- is focused on a problem that is testable in one experiment;
- clearly states the control groups or conditions of the experiment.

Good hypotheses normally come out of research investigations at an earlier stage, typically observational studies. In the early stage of a research project, researchers usually find themselves confronted with a broad and vague task. There are no well-defined research questions. There are no focused, testable research hypotheses. The common way to initiate a research project is to conduct exploratory descriptive investigations such as observations,

---

[2] Traditionally, H_0 is used to represent the null hypothesis and H_1 to represent the alternative hypothesis.

interviews, or focus groups. Well-conducted descriptive investigations help researchers to identify key research issues and come up with appropriate control groups to be manipulated as well as dependent variables to be measured.

2.2.2   Dependent and independent variables

A well-defined hypothesis clearly states the dependent and independent variables of the study. Independent variables refer to the factors that the researchers are interested in studying or the possible "cause" of the change in the dependent variable. The term "independent" is used to suggest that the variable is independent of a participant's behavior. Dependent variables refer to the outcome or effect that the researchers are interested in. The term "dependent" is used to suggest that the variable is dependent on a participant's behavior or the changes in the independent variables. In experiments, the primary interest of researchers is to study the relationship between dependent variables and independent variables. More specifically, the researcher wants to find out whether and how changes in independent variables induce changes in dependent variables.

A useful rule of thumb to differentiate dependent variables from independent variables is that independent variables are usually the treatments or conditions that the researchers can control while dependent variables are usually the outcomes that the researchers need to measure (Oehlert, 2000). For example, consider the null hypothesis proposed in the research case in Section 2.2.1:

> *There is no difference between the pull-down menu and the pop-up menu in the time spent locating pages.*

The independent variable is the type of menu (pull-down or pop-up). The dependent variable is the time spent in locating web pages. During the experiment, the researchers have full control over the types of menu with which each participant interacts by randomly assigning each participant to an experimental condition. In contrast, "time" is highly dependent on individual behavioral factors that the researchers cannot fully control. Some participants will be faster than others due to a number of factors, such as the type of menu, previous computer experience, physical capabilities, reading speed, and so on. The researchers need to accurately measure the time that each participant spends in locating pages and to relate the results to the independent variable in order to make a direct comparison between the two types of menu design.

2.2.3   Typical independent variables in HCI research

Independent variables are closely related to the specific research field. It is obvious that the factors frequently investigated in medical science are drastically different from those examined in physics or astronomy. In the HCI field, independent variables are usually related to technologies, users, and the context in which the technology is used. Typical independent variables that relate to technology include:

- different types of technology or devices, such as typing versus speech-based dictation, mouse versus joystick, touch pad, and other pointing devices;
- different types of design, such as pull-down menu versus pop-up menu, font sizes, contrast, background colors, and website architecture.

Typical independent variables related to users include age, gender, computer experience, professional domain, education, culture, motivation, mood, and disabilities. Using age as an example, we know that human capabilities change during their life span. Children have a physically smaller build and shorter attention span. Their reading skills, typing skills, and cognitive capabilities are all limited compared to typical computer users between ages 20 and 55. At the other end of the scale, elder citizens experience deterioration in cognitive, physical, and sensory capabilities. As a result, users in different age groups interact differently with computers and computer-related devices. Most computer applications are designed by people between 20 and 50 years of age who have little or no knowledge or experience in the interaction style or challenges faced by the younger and older user groups (Chisnell, 2007). In order to understand the gap created by age differences, a number of studies have been conducted to compare the interaction styles of users in different age groups (Zajicek, 2006; Zajicek and Jonsson, 2006).

Typical independent variables related to the context of use of technologies include both physical factors, such as environmental noise, lighting, temperature, vibration, and users' status (e.g. seated, walking or jogging) (Price *et al.,* 2006), and social factors, such as the number of people surrounding the user and their relation to the user.

2.2.4   Typical dependent variables in HCI research

Dependent variables frequently measured can be categorized into five groups: efficiency, accuracy, subjective satisfaction, ease of learning and retention rate, and physical or cognitive demand.

Efficiency describes how fast a task can be completed. Typical measures include time to complete a task and speed (e.g., words per minute, number of targets selected per minute).

Accuracy describes the states in which the system or the user makes errors. The most frequently used accuracy measure is error rate. Numerous metrics to measure error rate have been proposed for various interaction tasks, such as the "minimum string distance" proposed for text entry tasks (Soukoreff and Mackenzie, 2003). In HCI studies, efficiency and accuracy are not isolated but are highly related factors. There is usually a trade-off between efficiency and accuracy, meaning that, when the other factors are the same, achieving a higher speed will result in more errors and ensuring fewer errors will lower the speed. Consequently, any investigation that only measures one of the two factors misses a critical side of the picture.

Subjective satisfaction describes the user's perceived satisfaction with the interaction experience. The data is normally collected using Likert scale ratings (e.g., numeric scales from 1–5) through questionnaires.

Ease of learning and retention rate describe how quickly and how easily an individual can learn to use a new application or complete a new task and how long they retain the learned skills (Feng, Karat and Sears, 2005). This category is less studied than the previous three categories but is highly important for the adoption of information technology.

Variables in the fifth category describe the cognitive and physical demand that an application or a task exerts on an individual or how long an individual can interact with an application without significant fatigue. This category of measures is less studied but they play an important role in technology adoption.

2.3 Basics of experimental research

In order to understand why experimental research can allow causal inference while descriptive and relational investigations do not, we need to discuss the characteristics of experimental research. In a true experimental design, the investigator can fully control or manipulate the experimental conditions so that a direct comparison can be made between two or more conditions while other factors are, ideally, kept the same. One aspect of the full control of factors is complete randomization, which means that the investigator can randomly assign participants to different conditions. The capability to effectively control for variables not of interest, therefore limiting the effects to the variables being studied, is the feature that most differentiates experimental research from quasi-experimental research, descriptive investigations, and relational investigations.

2.3.1 Components of an experiment

After a research hypothesis is identified, the design of an experiment consists of three components: treatments, units, and assignment method (Oehlert, 2000). Treatments, or conditions, refer to the different techniques, devices, or procedures that we want to compare. Units are the objects to which we apply the experiment treatments. In the field of HCI research, the units are normally human subjects with specific characteristics, such as gender, age, or computing experience. Assignment method refers to the way in which the experimental units are assigned different treatments.

We can further explain these three terms through an example. Suppose a researcher is running an experiment to compare typing speed using a traditional QWERTY keyboard and a DVORAK keyboard.[3] The treatment of this experiment is the type of keyboard: QWERTY or DVORAK. The experiment units are the participants recruited to join the study. To achieve the goal of fair comparison, the researchers would have to require that the participants have no previous experience using either keyboard. If most participants

---

[3] A computer keyboard with a key layout different from that of the traditional QWERTY keyboard.

can touch type using the QWERTY keyboard but have never used a DVORAK keyboard before, it is obvious that the results will be highly biased towards the QWERTY keyboard. The researcher can employ different methods to randomly assign the participants into each of the two conditions. One well-known traditional method is to toss a coin. If a head is tossed, the participant is assigned to the QWERTY condition. If a tail is tossed, the participant is assigned to the DVORAK condition. Obviously, researchers are not busy tossing coins in their lab; more convenient randomization methods are used today. We discuss those methods in Section 2.3.2.

This case illustrates a simple between-subject[4] design with two conditions. There are much more complicated designs involving multiple treatments and both between-subject and within-subject[5] comparisons. No matter how complicated the design is, all experiments consist of these three major components.

2.3.2   Randomization

The power of experimental research lies in its ability to uncover causal relations. The major reason that experimental research can achieve this goal is because of complete randomization. Randomization refers to the random assignment of treatments to the experimental units or participants (Oehlert, 2000).

In a totally randomized experiment, no one, including the investigators themselves, is able to predict the condition to which a participant is going to be assigned. For example, in the QWERTY vs. DVORAK experiment, when a participant comes in, the researcher does not know whether the participant will be using the QWERTY keyboard or the DVORAK keyboard until he tosses the coin and finds out whether it comes up heads or tails. Since the outcome of tossing the coin is totally random and out of the control of the researcher, the researcher has no influence, whether intentionally or subconsciously, on the assignment of the treatment to the participant. This effectively controls the influence of hidden factors and allows a clean comparison between the experiment conditions.

Traditional randomization methods include tossing a coin, throwing dice, spinning a roulette wheel, or drawing capsules out of an urn. However, these types of randomization are rarely used in behavioral research and HCI studies nowadays. One method to randomize the selection of experimental conditions or other factors is the use of a random digit table. Table 2.2 is an abbreviated random digit table taken from the large random digit table generated by RAND (1955). The original table consisted of a million random digits.

There are several ways to use this table. Suppose we are running a study that compares three types of navigation schemes for a website: topical, audience split, and organizational.

---

[4]A between-subject design means each participant only experiences one task condition. The details of between-subject design are discussed in Chapter 3.

[5]A within-subject design means each participant experiences multiple task conditions. The details of within-subject design is discussed in Chapter 3.

Line	Random digits				
000	10097	32533	76520	13586	34673
001	37542	04805	64894	74296	24805
002	08422	68953	19645	09303	23209
003	99019	02529	09376	70715	38311
004	12807	99970	80157	36147	64032
005	66065	74717	34072	76850	36697

Table 2.2 An abbreviated random digit table.

We recruit 45 participants and need to assign each of them to one of the three conditions. We can start anywhere in the random digit table and count in either direction.

For example, if we start from the third number on the first row and count to the right for three numbers, we get 76520, 13586, and 34673. We can assign the first three participants to the conditions according to the order of the three random numbers. In this case, 76520 is the largest, corresponding to condition 3; 13586 is the smallest, corresponding to condition 1; and 34673 corresponds to condition 2. This means that the first participant is assigned to the design with the organizational navigation scheme, the second participant to the topical scheme, and the third participant to the audience split scheme. We can continue counting the numbers and repeating the process until all 45 participants are assigned to specific conditions.

Nowadays, software-driven randomization is also commonly used among researchers and practitioners. A large number of randomization software resources are available online, some of them free of charge, such as the services offered at www.randomization.com. Randomization functions are also available in most of the commercial statistical software packages, such as SAS, SPSS, and SYSTAT.

In a well-designed experiment, you will frequently find that you not only need to randomize the assignment of experiment conditions, but other factors as well. In a longitudinal study reported by Sears *et al.* (2001, 2003), the researchers investigated the use of recognition software to generate text documents. Each of the 15 participants completed a total of nine tasks on different days. During each task, the participant composed a text document of approximately 500 words in response to a pre-defined scenario. Nine scenarios were developed so that the participants could respond to a different scenario in each trial. Typical examples included planning a business trip, evaluating a peer at work, and asking for office supplies. The researchers found it necessary to randomize the order of the scenarios being used in the nine tasks. If the order of the scenarios were not randomized, it is likely that the characteristics of the scenarios would become a factor that influences the results. For example, if scenario A is easier to respond to than scenario B and scenario A is always used in the first task while scenario B is always used in the ninth task, the time spent on the first task would be biased toward a lower value and the time spent on the ninth task would be biased toward a higher value. The systematic bias would pollute the data and alter the learning curve that the researchers would like to observe. Randomizing the order of the scenarios cancels out the potential errors introduced by differences in scenarios.[6]

Other types of factor that need to be randomized include the types of task, items in a menu, web pages or links in an information task, and so on. We follow up on this topic in Chapter 3 when discussing between-subject design and within-subject design.

2.4 Significance tests

2.4.1 Why do we need them?

Almost all experimental investigations are analyzed and reported through significance tests. If you randomly pick up an HCI-related journal article or a conference paper, it is very likely that you will encounter statements similar to the following:

> *On average, participants performed significantly better ($F(1,25)=20.83$, $p < 0.01$) ... in the dynamic peephole condition ... rather than the static peephole condition. (Mehra, Werkhoven and Worring, 2006)*
>
> *A t test showed that there was a significant difference in the number of lines of text entered ($t(11) = 6.28$, $p < 0.001$) with more entered in the tactile condition. (Brewster, Chohan and Brown, 2007)*

Why do you need to run significance tests on your data? What is wrong with the approach of comparing two mean values of error rate and then claiming that the application with the lower mean value is more accurate than the other application? Here we encounter a fundamental issue in statistics that has to be clarified in order to understand the numerous concepts, terms, and methods that will be discussed in the rest of this chapter and in Chapters 4 and 5. Let us consider the following two statements:

1. Mike's height is 6'2". Mary's height is 5'8". So Mike is taller than Mary.
2. The average height of three males (Mike, John, and Ted) is 5'5". The average height of three females (Mary, Rose, and Jessica) is 5'10". So females are taller than males.

It should not be difficult for you to tell that the first statement is correct while the second one is not. In the first statement, the targets being compared are the heights of two individuals, both known numbers. Based on the two numbers, we know that Mike is taller than Mary. This is simple to understand, even for a child. When the values of the members of the comparison groups are all known, you can directly compare them and draw a conclusion. No significance test is needed since there is no uncertainty involved.

---

[6]Special attention was paid during the development of the scenarios so that they were similar to each other in the degree of difficulty in responding, which was confirmed by the reported results. However, it is good practice to randomize the order of the scenarios in case there are unanticipated differences between them.

What is wrong with the second statement? People may give various responses to this question, such as:

- Well, by common sense, I know males are generally taller than females.
- I can easily find three other males and three other females, in which the average height of the three males is higher than that of the three females.
- There are only three individuals in each group. The sizes of the comparison groups are too small.
- The individuals in both the male group and the female group are not representative of the general population.

All of the above responses are well grounded, though the last two responses have deeper statistical roots. The claim that females are taller than males is wrong due to inappropriate sampling. The distribution of the heights of the human population (and many other things in our life) follows a pattern called "normal distribution." Data sets that follow normal distribution can be illustrated by a bell-shaped curve (see Figure 2.1), with the majority of the data points falling in the central area surrounding the mean of the population. The further a value is from the population mean, the fewer data points would fall in the area around that value.

When you compare two large populations, such as males and females, there is no way to collect the data from every individual in the population. Therefore, you select a smaller group from the large population and use that smaller group to represent the entire population. This process is called sampling. In the situation described in statement 2, above, the three males selected as the sample population happened to be shorter than average males, while the three

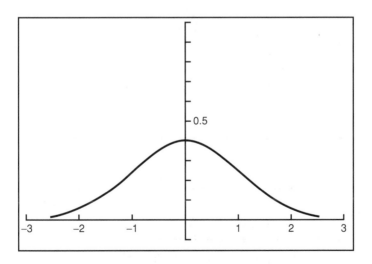

Figure 2.1 Normal distribution curve.

females selected as samples happened to be taller than average females, thus resulting in a misleading conclusion. Randomization methods and large sample sizes can greatly reduce the possibility of making this kind of error in research.

Since we are not able to measure the heights of all males and females, we can only sample a sub-group of people from the entire population. Significance tests allow us to determine how confident we are that the results observed from the sampling population can be generalized to the entire population. For example, a t-test that is significant at $p < 0.05$ suggests that we are confident that 95% of the time the test result correctly applies to the entire population. We further explore the concept of significance tests in the next section.

2.4.2 Type I and Type II errors

In technical terms, significance testing is a process in which a null hypothesis (H_0) is contrasted with an alternative hypothesis (H_1) to determine the likelihood that the null hypothesis is true. All significance tests are subject to the risk of Type I and Type II errors.

A Type I error (also called an α error or a "false positive") refers to the mistake of rejecting the null hypothesis when it is true and should not be rejected. A Type II error (also called a β error or a "false negative") refers to the mistake of not rejecting the null hypothesis when it is false and should be rejected (Rosenthal and Rosnow, 2008). A widely used example to demonstrate Type I and Type II errors is the judicial case. In the US justice system, a defendant is presumed innocent. This presumption leads to the following null and alternative hypotheses:

- H_0: The defendant is innocent.
- H_1: The defendant is guilty.

A Type I error occurs when the jury decides that the defendant is guilty when he is actually innocent, meaning that the null hypothesis is rejected when it is true. A Type II error occurs when the jury decides that the defendant is innocent when he is actually guilty, meaning that the null hypothesis is accepted when it is false. Table 2.3 illustrates these errors.

		Jury decision	
		Not guilty	Guilty
Reality	Not guilty	✓	Type I error
	Guilty	Type II error	✓

Table 2.3 Type I and Type II errors in the judicial case.

		Study conclusion	
		No difference	Touchscreen ATM is easier to use
Reality	No difference	✓	Type I error
	Touchscreen ATM is easier to use	Type II error	✓

Table 2.4 Type I and Type II errors in a hypothetical HCI experiment.

In the ideal case, the jury should always reach the decision that the defendant is guilty when he is actually guilty and vice versa. But in reality, the jury makes mistakes occasionally. Each type of error has costs. When a Type I error occurs, an innocent person would be sent to prison or may even lose his life; when a Type II error occurs, a criminal is set free and may commit another crime.

Let us further examine Type I and Type II errors, through a study in the HCI domain. Suppose a bank hires several HCI researchers to evaluate whether ATMs with a touch-screen interface are easier to use than the ATMs with buttons that the bank branches are currently using. In this case, the null hypothesis and the alternative hypothesis are:

- H_0: There is no difference between the ease of use of ATMs with touch screens and ATMs with buttons.
- H_1: ATMs with touch screens are easier to use than ATMs with buttons.

The possible Type I and Type II errors in this study are illustrated in Table 2.4. A Type I error occurs when the research team decides that touch-screen ATMs are easier to use than ATMs with buttons, when they are not. A Type II error occurs when the research team decides that touch-screen ATMs are no better than ATMs with buttons, when they are. Again, each type of error can induce negative consequences. When a Type I error occurs, the bank may spend money to switch to touch-screen ATMs that do not provide better service to the customers. When a Type II error occurs, the bank chooses to stay with ATMs with buttons and loses the opportunity to improve the service that it provides to its customers.

It is generally believed that Type I errors are worse than Type II errors. Statisticians call Type I errors a mistake that involves "gullibility". A Type I error may result in a condition worse than the current state. For example, if a new medication is mistakenly found to be more effective than the medication that patients are currently taking, the patients may switch to new medication that is less effective than their current treatment. Type II errors are mistakes that involve "blindness" and can cost the opportunity to improve the current state. Using the medication example, in a Type II error, the test does not reveal that the new medication is more effective than the existing treatment; the patients stick with the existing treatment and miss the opportunity of a better treatment.

2.4.3 Controlling the risks of Type I and Type II errors

When designing experiments and analyzing data, you have to evaluate the risk of making Type I and Type II errors. In statistics, the probability of making a Type I error is called alpha (or significance level, p value). The probability of making a Type II error is called beta. The statistical power of a test, defined as $1-\beta$, refers to the probability of successfully rejecting a null hypothesis when it is false and should be rejected (Cohen, 1988).[7]

It should be noted that alpha and beta are interrelated. Under the same conditions, decreasing alpha reduces the chance of making Type I errors but increases the chance of making Type II errors. Simply put, if you want to reduce the chance of making Type I errors with all other factors being the same, you can do so by being less gullible. However, in doing so, you increase the odds that you miss something that is in fact true, meaning that your research is more vulnerable to Type II errors.

In experimental research, it is generally believed that Type I errors are worse than Type II errors. So a very low p value (0.05) is widely adopted to control the occurrence of Type I errors. If a significance test returns a value that is significant at $p < 0.05$, it means that the probability of making a Type I error is below 0.05. In other words, the probability of mistakenly rejecting a null hypothesis is below 0.05. In order to reduce Type II errors, it is generally suggested that you use a relatively large sample size so that the difference can be observed even when the effect size is relatively small. If interested, you can find more detailed discussions on statistical power in Rosenthal and Rosnow (2008).

2.5 Limitations of experimental research

Experimental research methods originated from behavioral research and are largely rooted in the field of psychology. Experimental research has been a highly effective research method and led to many groundbreaking findings in behavioral science in the 20th century. Experimental research certainly plays an important role in the field of human–computer interaction. A large number of studies that explored fundamental interaction theories and models, such as Fitts' law, employed the approach of experimental research. To date, experimental research remains one of the most effective approaches to making findings that can be generalized to larger populations.

On the other hand, experimental research also has notable limitations. It requires well-defined, testable hypotheses that consist of a limited number of dependent and independent variables. However, many problems that HCI researchers or practitioners face are not clearly defined or involve a large number of potentially influential factors. As a result, it is often

---

[7]How alpha and beta are calculated is beyond the scope of this book. For detailed discussion of the calculation, please refer to Rosenthal and Rosnow (2008).

very hard to construct a well-defined and testable hypothesis. This is especially true when studying an innovative interaction technique or a new user population and in the early development stage of a product.

Experimental research also requires strict control of factors that may influence the dependent variables. That is, except the independent variables, any factor that may have an impact on the dependent variables needs to be the same under different experiment conditions. This requirement can hardly be satisfied in many HCI studies. For example, when studying how older users and young users interact with computer-related devices, there are many factors besides age that are different between the two age groups, such as educational and knowledge background, computer experience, common tasks, living conditions, and so on. If an experiment is conducted to study the two age groups, those factors will become confounding factors and may have a significant impact on the observed results. This problem can be partially addressed in the data collection and data analysis stages. In the data collection stage, extra caution should be taken when there are known confounding factors. Increasing the sample size may reduce the impact of the confounding factors. When recruiting participants, pre-screening should be conducted to make the participants in different groups as homogeneous as possible. When confounding factors are inevitable, specific data analysis methods can be applied so that the impact of the confounding factors can be filtered out. A common method for this purpose is the analysis of covariables.

Lab-based experiments may not be a good representation of users' typical interaction behavior. It has been reported that participants may behave differently in lab-based experiments due to the stress of being observed, the different environment, or the rewards offered for participation. This phenomenon, called the "Hawthorne effect", was documented around 60 years ago (Landsberger, 1958). In many cases, being observed can cause users to make short-term improvements that typically do not last once the observation is over.

However, it should be noted that the context of the Hawthorne studies and HCI-related experiments is significantly different (Macefield, 2007). First, the Hawthorne studies were all longitudinal while most HCI experiments are not. Secondly, all the participants in the Hawthorne studies were experts in the tasks being observed while most HCI experiments observe novice users. Thirdly, the Hawthorne studies primarily focused on efficiency while HCI experiments value other important measures, such as error rates. Finally, the participants in the Hawthorne study had a vested interest in a successful outcome for the study since it was a point of contact between them and their senior management. In contrast, most HCI studies do not carry this motivation. Based on those reasons, we believe that the difference between the observed results of HCI experiments and the actual performance is not as big as that observed in the Hawthorne studies. But still, we should keep this potential risk in mind and take precautions to avoid or alleviate the impact of the possible Hawthorne effect.

Empirical Evaluation in HCI

The validity of empirical experiments and quantitative evaluation in HCI research has been doubted by some researchers. They argue that the nature of research in HCI is very different from traditional scientific fields, such as physics or chemistry, and, therefore, the results of experimental studies that suggest one interface is better than another may not be truly valid.

The major concern with the use of empirical experiments in HCI is the control of all possible related factors (Lieberman, 2007). In experiments in physics or chemistry, it is possible to strictly control all major related factors so that multiple experimental conditions are only different in the states of the independent variables. However, in HCI experiments, it is very difficult to control all potential factors and create experimental conditions that are exactly the same with the only exception in the independent variable. For instance, it is almost impossible to recruit two or more groups of participants with exactly the same age, educational background, and computer experience. All three factors may impact the interaction experience as well as the performance. It is argued that the use of significance tests in the data analysis stage only provide a veneer of validity when the potentially influential factors are not fully controlled (Lieberman, 2007).

We agree that experimental research has its limitations and deficiencies, just as any other research method does. But we believe that the overall validity of experimental research in the field of HCI is well-grounded. Controlled experiments have allowed us to make critical and generalizable findings that other methods would not be able to provide. Simply observing a few users trying two interfaces does not provide convincing results on the performance and preference of the target population. The truth is, experimental research and significance testing is the only approach that enables us to make judgments with systematically measured confidence and reliability. The control of potentially influential factors is challenging but the impact of those factors can be reduced to acceptable levels through well-designed and conducted experiments, which we discuss in detail in Chapter 3.

Summary

Research in human–computer interaction examines human behavior in relation to computers or computer-related devices. There are three major types of research methods for studying human behavior: descriptive, relational, and experimental. The major strength of experimental research, compared to the other two types, is that it allows the identification of causal relationships between entities or events.

After a hypothesis is constructed, the design of an experiment consists of three components: treatments, units, and the assignment method. In an experiment, the process of sample selection needs to be randomized or counter-balanced, as does the assignment of treatments, or experiment conditions. Many methods can be used to randomly select samples or assign experiment conditions, including, but not limited to, the random digit table and software-generated randomization schemes.

Successful experimental research depends on well-defined research hypotheses that specify the dependent variables to be observed and the independent variables to be controlled. Usually a pair of null and alternative hypotheses are proposed and the goal of the experiment is to test whether the null hypothesis can be rejected or the alternative hypothesis can be accepted. Good research hypotheses should have a reasonable scope that can be tested within an experiment; clearly defined independent variables that can be strictly controlled; and clearly defined dependent variables that can be accurately measured.

Significance testing allows us to judge whether the observed group means are truly different. All significance tests are subject to two types of error. Type I errors refer to the situation when the null hypothesis is mistakenly rejected when it is actually true. Type II errors refer to the situation of not rejecting the null hypothesis when it is actually false. It is generally believed that Type I errors are worse than Type II errors, therefore the alpha threshold that determines the probability of making Type I errors should be kept low. The widely accepted alpha threshold is 0.05.

With its notable strengths, experimental research also has notable limitations when applied in the field of HCI: difficulty in identifying a testable hypothesis, difficulty in controlling potential confounding factors, and changes in observed behavior as compared to behavior in a more realistic setting. Therefore, experimental research methods should only be adopted when appropriate.

Discussion Questions

1. What is descriptive research?
2. What is relational research?
3. What is experimental research?
4. What is randomization in experimental research? Discuss several examples of randomization methods.
5. What is a research hypothesis? What are the characteristics of a good research hypothesis?
6. What is a dependent variable?
7. What is an independent variable?
8. What is a significance test? Why do we need to run significance tests?
9. What is a Type I error? What is a Type II error?
10. Discuss the practical implications of Type I errors and Type II errors.

Research Design Exercises

1. A research team is investigating three possible navigation architectures for an e-commerce website. Thirty participants are recruited to test the website, with 10 participants testing each architecture. How should the participants be assigned to the three conditions?

2. Read the following hypotheses and identify the dependent variables and independent variables in each hypothesis.

   H1.   There is no difference in users' reading speed and retention rate when they view news on a desktop computer or a PDA.

   H2.   There is no difference in the target selection speed and error rate between joystick, touch screen, and gesture recognition.

   H3.   There is no difference in the technology adoption rate between two speech-based applications with different dialog designs.

   H4.   There is no difference in the reading skills of children who used educational software for six months compared to those who have never used the software.

3. A spam filter assigns ratings to all incoming emails. If the rating of an email is higher than a specific threshold, the email is deleted before it reaches the inbox. Answer the following questions based on this scenario:

   (a) What is a Type I error in this scenario?
   (b) What is a Type II error in this scenario?
   (c) If the rating is assigned using a scale of 1 to 10, with 1 representing "definitely not spam" and 10 representing "definitely spam", what happens if the threshold is set to 1, 2, 3, ..., 10?
   (d) What do you think the appropriate threshold should be? Why?

References

Accot, J. and Zhai, S. (2003) Refining Fitts' law models for bivariate pointing. *Proceedings of the SIGCHI conference on Human Factors in Computing Systems*, 193–200.

Brewster, S., Chohan, F., and Brown, L. (2007) Mobile interaction: Tactile feedback for mobile interactions. *Proceedings of the SIGCHI conference on Human Factors in Computing Systems*, 159–162.

Chisnell, D. (2007) Where technology meets green bananas. *interactions*, **14**(2):10–11.

Cohen, J. (1988) *Statistical Power Analysis for the Behavioral Sciences*, 2nd edition. New York: Academic Press.

Cooper, D. and Schindler, P. (2000) *Business Research Methods*, 7th edition. Boston: McGraw Hill.

Durbin, C. (2004) How to come up with a good research question: Framing the hypothesis. *Respiratory Care*, **49**(10):1195–1198.

Feng, J., Karat, C-M., and Sears, A. (2005) How productivity improves in hands-free continuous dictation tasks: Lessons learned from a longitudinal study. *Interacting with Computers*, **17**(3):265–289.

Fitts, P.M. (1954) The information capacity of the human motor system in controlling the amplitude of movement. *Journal of Experimental Psychology*, **47**(6):381–391.

Kirk, R. (1982) *Experimental Design: Procedures for the behavioral sciences*, 2nd edition. Pacific Grove, California: Brooks/Cole Publishing Company.

Landsberger, H. (1958) *Hawthorne Revisited*. Ithaca, NY: Cornell University.

Lieberman, H. (2007) The tyranny of evaluation. Retrieved on November 16, 2007 at http://web.media.mit.edu/~lieber/Misc/Tyranny-Evaluation.html.

Macefield, R. (2007) Usability studies and the Hawthorne Effect. *Journal of Usability Studies*, **2**(3):145–154.

Mehra, S., Werkhoven, P., and Worring, M. (2006) Navigating on handheld displays: Dynamic versus static peephole navigation. *ACM Transactions on Computer–Human Interaction*, **13**(4):448–457.

Miniotas, D. (2000) Application of Fitts' Law to eye gaze interaction. *Proceedings of CHI 2000*, 339–340.

Oehlert, G. (2000) *A First Course in Design and Analysis of Experiments*. New York: Freeman and Company.

Price, K.J., Lin, M., Feng, J., Goldman, R., Sears, A., and Jacko, J.A. (2006) Motion does matter: An examination of speech-based-text entry on the move. *Universal Access in the Information Society*, **4**(3):246–257.

RAND Corporation (1955) *A Million Random Digits with 100,000 Normal Deviates*. New York: Free Press.

Rosenthal, R. and Rosnow, R. (2008) *Essentials of Behavioral Research: Methods and data analysis*, 3rd edition. Boston: McGraw Hill.

Sears, A., Feng, J., Oseitutu, K., and Karat, C-M. (2003) Speech-based navigation during dictation: Difficulties, consequences, and solutions. *Human–Computer Interaction*, **18**(3):229–257.

Sears, A., Karat, C-M., Oseitutu, K., Karimullah, A., and Feng, J. (2001) Productivity, satisfaction, and interaction strategies of individuals with spinal cord injuries and traditional users interacting with speech recognition software. *Universal Access in the Information Society*, **1**(1):4–15.

Shneiderman, B., Plaisant, C., Cohen, M., and Jacobs, S. (2009) *Designing the User Interface: Strategies for effective human–computer interaction*, 5th edition. Boston, Massachusetts: Addison-Wesley.

Soukoreff, W. and MacKenzie, S. (2003) Metrics for text entry research: An evaluation of MSD and KSPC, and a new unified error metric. *Proceedings of the ACM Conference on Human Factors in Computing Systems*, 113–120.

Zajicek, M. (2006) Aspects of HCI research for older people. *Universal Access in the Information Society,* **5**(3):279–386.

Zajicek, M. and Jonsson, I. (2006) In-car speech systems for older adults: Can they help and does the voice matter? *International Journal of Technology Knowledge and Society,* **2**(6):55–64.

Experimental design

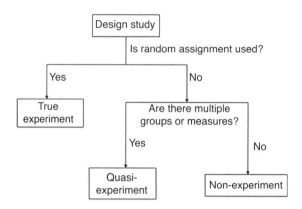

Figure 3.1 Defining true experiments, quasi-experiments, and non-experiments.

Experiments help us to answer questions and identify causal relationships. Well-designed experiments can reveal important scientific findings. In contrast, ill-designed experiments may generate results that are false or misleading. Experiments have been widely used in the human–computer interaction field to develop and modify user models or task models, evaluate different design solutions, and answer various other critical questions, such as about technology adoption.

Before we discuss specific experimental design methods, we need to differentiate three groups of studies: experiments, quasi-experiments, and non-experiments (Cooper and Schindler, 2000; Rosenthal and Rosnow, 2008). Figure 3.1 demonstrates the relationship among the three types of studies. If a study involves multiple conditions and the participants are randomly assigned to each condition, it is a true experiment. If a study involves multiple groups or measures but the participants are not randomly assigned to different conditions, it is a quasi-experiment. Finally, if there is only one observation group or only one measure involved, it is a non-experiment. True experiments possess the following characteristics:

- A true experiment is based on at least one testable research hypothesis and aims to validate it.
- There are usually at least two conditions (a treatment condition and a control condition) or groups (a treatment group and a control group).
- The dependent variables are normally measured through quantitative measurements.
- The results are analyzed through various statistical significance tests.
- A true experiment should be designed and conducted with the goal of removing potential biases.
- A true experiment should be replicable with different participant samples, at different times, in different locations, and by different experimenters.

In this chapter, we focus on the design of true experiments, which means that all the studies we discuss have multiple conditions or measures and the participants are randomly assigned to different conditions. We start with the issues that need to be considered when designing experiments, followed by discussions of simple experiments that involve only one independent variable. We then examine more complicated experiments that involve two or more independent variables. Three major types of experiment design are discussed: between-group design, within-group design, and split–plot design. Section 3.5 focuses on potential sources of systematic errors (biases) and guidelines for effectively avoiding or controlling those biases. The chapter ends with a discussion of typical procedures for running HCI experiments.

3.1 What needs to be considered when designing experiments?

We need to consider several issues when designing an experiment that investigates HCI-related questions. Some of these issues are universal for all scientific experiments, such as research hypotheses, the measurement of the dependent variables, and the control of multiple conditions. Other issues are unique to experiments that involve human subjects, such as the learning effect, participants' knowledge background, and the size of the potential participant pool. Detailed discussions of measurement and generation of research hypotheses are provided in Chapter 2. A complete review on conducting research involving human subjects is provided in Chapter 14.

Most successful experiments start with a clearly defined research hypothesis with a reasonable scope (Oehlert, 2000). The research hypothesis is generated based on results of earlier exploratory studies and provides critical information needed to design an experiment. It specifies the independent and dependent variables of the experiment. The number and values of independent variables directly determine how many conditions the experiment has. For example, consider designing an experiment to investigate the following hypothesis:

> *There is no difference between the target selection speed when using a mouse, a joystick, or a trackball to select icons of different sizes (small, medium, and large).*

There are two independent variables in this hypothesis: the type of pointing device and the size of icon. Three different pointing devices will be examined: a mouse, a joystick, and a trackball, suggesting three conditions under this independent variable. Three different target sizes will be examined: small, medium, and large, suggesting three conditions under this independent variable as well. Since we need to test each combination of values of the two independent variables, combining the two independent variables results in a total of nine ($3 \times 3 = 9$) conditions in the experiment.

The identification of dependent variables will allow us to further consider the appropriate metric for measuring the dependent variables. In many cases, multiple approaches can be used to measure the dependent variables. For example, typing speed can be measured by the number of words typed per minute, which is equal to the total number of words typed divided by the number of minutes used to generate those words. It may also be measured by number of correct words typed per minute, which is equal to the total number of correct words typed divided by the number of minutes used to generate those words. We need to consider the objective of the experiment to determine which measure is more appropriate.

Another issue to consider when designing experiments is how to control the independent variables to create multiple experiment conditions (Kirk, 1982). In some experiments, control of the independent variable is quite easy and straightforward. For instance, when testing the previously stated hypothesis, we can control the type of pointing device by presenting participants with a mouse, a joystick, or a trackball. In many other cases, the control of the independent variable can be challenging. For instance, if we are developing a speech-based application and need to investigate how recognition errors impact users' interaction behavior, we may want to compare two conditions. Under the control condition, the speech recognizer would be error free and recognize every word that the user says correctly. Under the comparison condition, the speech recognizer would make errors and recognize a percentage of the words incorrectly. This sounds straightforward, theoretically. But in practice, all speech recognizers make errors. There is no way to find a recognizer that would satisfy the requirements of the controlled condition. A possible solution to meet the needs of this experiment is the Wizard-of-Oz approach (Feng, 2005). That is, we can have a human acting as a speech recognizer, listening to what the user says and entering the user's dictation into the system. The truth would normally not be revealed to the participants until the end of the experiment. Therefore, all participants would believe that they are interacting with the speech recognizer when completing the task. The Wizard-of-Oz approach allows us to test ideal applications that do not exist in the real world. This approach is not without its limitations. Humans also make errors. It is very likely that the human "wizard" would make errors when listening to the dictation or when typing the words. Therefore, it is very difficult to control the independent variable to achieve the desired condition (Feng, 2005; Li, Welbourne and Landay, 2006). One approach that addresses this problem is the development of technical tools to assist the human wizard (Li, Welbourne and Landay, 2006) (see Chapter 10 for more information on the "Wizard-of-Oz" approach).

3.2   Determining the basic design structure

At the first stage of experiment design, we need to construct the experiment based on the research hypotheses that have been developed. This enables us to draw a big picture of the general scope of the experiment and, accordingly, come up with a reasonable estimation of the timeline of the experiment and the budget. The basic structure of an experiment can be determined by answering two questions:

- How many independent variables do we want to investigate in the experiment?
- How many different values does each independent variable have?

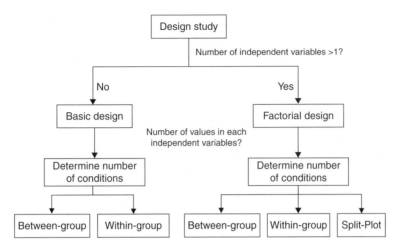

Figure 3.2 Determining the experiment structure.

The answer to the first question determines whether we need a basic design or a factorial design. If there is one independent variable, we need only a basic one-level design. If there are two or more independent variables, factorial design is the way to go. The answer to the second question determines the number of conditions needed in the experiment (see Figure 3.2). In a basic design, the number of conditions in the experiment is an important factor when we consider whether to adopt a between-group or within-group design. In a factorial design, we have a third option: the split-plot design. Again, the number of conditions is a crucial factor when weighing up the three options.

In the following sections, we first consider the basic design scenarios involving one independent variable and focus on the characteristics of between-group design and within-group design. After that, we consider more complicated designs involving multiple independent variables, to which understanding split-plot design is the key.

3.3 Investigating a single independent variable

When we study a single independent variable, the design of the experiment is simpler than cases in which multiple variables are involved. The following hypotheses all lead to experiments that investigate a single independent variable:

- H1: There is no difference in typing speed when using a QWERTY keyboard, a DVORAK keyboard, or an alphabetically ordered keyboard.
- H2: There is no difference in the time required to locate an item in an online store between novice users and experienced users.
- H3: There is no difference in the perceived trust towards an online agent among customers who are from the United States, Russia, China, and Nigeria.

The number of conditions in each experiment is determined by the possible values of the independent variable. The experiment conducted to investigate hypothesis H1 would involve three conditions: the QWERTY keyboard, the DVORAK keyboard, and the alphabetically ordered keyboard. The experiment conducted to investigate hypothesis H2 would involve two conditions: novice users and experienced users. And the experiment conducted to investigate hypothesis H3 would involve four conditions: customers from the United States, Russia, China, and Nigeria.

Once the conditions are set, we need to determine the number of conditions that we would allow each participant to be exposed to by selecting either a between-group design or a within-group design. This is a critical step in experiment design and the decision made has a direct impact on the quality of the data collected as well as the statistical methods that should be used to analyze the data.

3.3.1   Between-group design and within-group design

Between-group design is also called "between-subject design". Each participant is only exposed to one experiment condition. The number of participant groups directly corresponds to the number of experiment conditions. Let us use the experiment on types of keyboard as an example. As shown in Figure 3.3, three groups of participants take part in the experiment and each group only uses one specific type of keyboard. If the task is to type a document of 500 words, then each participant types one document using one of the keyboards.

In contrast, a within-group design (also called "within-subject design") requires each participant to be exposed to multiple experiment conditions. Only one group of participants is needed for the entire experiment. If we use the keyboard experiment as an example, as shown in Figure 3.4, the same group of participants uses all three types of keyboard during the experiment. If the task is to type a document of 500 words, then each participant types three documents, using each of the three keyboards for one document.

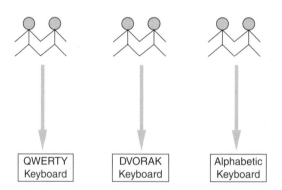

Figure 3.3 Between-group design.

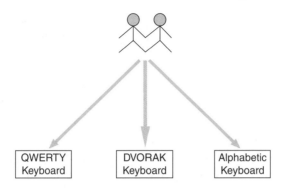

Figure 3.4 Within-group design.

Please note that different statistical approaches are needed to analyze data collected from the two different design methods. The details of statistical analysis are discussed in Chapter 4.

3.3.1.1 Advantages and disadvantages of between-group design

From the statistical perspective, between-group design is a cleaner design. Since the participant is only exposed to one condition, the users do not learn from different task conditions. Therefore, it allows us to avoid a learning effect. In addition, since the participants only need to complete tasks under one condition, the time it takes each participant to complete the experiment is much shorter than in a within-group design. As a result, confounding factors such as fatigue and frustration can be effectively controlled.

On the other hand, between-group design also has notable disadvantages. In a between-group experiment, we are comparing the performance of one group of participants against the performance of another group of participants. The results are subject to substantial impacts from individual differences: the difference between the multiple values that we expect to observe can be buried in a high level of "noise" caused by individual differences. Therefore, it is harder to detect significant differences and Type II errors are more likely to occur.

In order to effectively exclude the impact of noise and make significant findings, a comparatively larger number of participants is needed under each condition. This leads to the second major disadvantage of the between-group design: large sample size. Since the number of participants (m) in each condition should be comparatively large and approximately the same number of participants are needed for each condition (let n be the number of conditions), the total number of participants needed for the experiment ($m \times n$) is usually quite large. For example, if an experiment has four conditions and 16 participants are needed under each condition, the total number of participants needed is 64. Recruiting the number of participants needed for a between-group experiment can be a very challenging task.

3.3.1.2   Advantages and Disadvantages of Within-group Design

Within-group design, in contrast, requires a much smaller sample size. When analyzing the data coming from within-group experiments, we are comparing the performances of the same participants under different conditions. Therefore, the impact of individual differences is effectively isolated and the expected difference can be observed with a relatively smaller sample size. If we change the design of the experiment with four conditions and 16 participants from a between-group design into a within-group design, the total number of participants needed would be 16, rather than 64. The benefit of a reduced sample size is an important factor for many studies in the HCI field when qualified participants may be quite difficult to recruit. It may also help reduce the cost of the experiments when financial compensation is provided.

Within-group designs are not free of limitations. The biggest problem with a within-group design is the possible impact of learning effects. Since the participants complete the same types of task under multiple conditions, they are very likely to learn from the experience and may get better in completing the tasks. For instance, suppose we are conducting a within-group experiment that evaluates two types of ATM: one with a button interface and one with a touch-screen interface. The task is to withdraw money from an existing account. If the participant first completes the task using the ATM with the button interface, he gains some experience with the ATM interface and its functions. Therefore, he may perform better when he subsequently completes the same tasks using the ATM with the touch-screen interface. If we do not isolate the learning effect, we might draw a conclusion that the touch-screen interface is better than the button interface when the observed difference is actually due to the learning effect. Normally, the potential bias of the learning effect is the biggest concern of experimenters when considering adopting a within-group design.

Another potential problem with within-group designs is fatigue. Since there are multiple conditions in the experiment, and the participants need to complete one or more tasks under each condition, the time it takes to complete the experiment may be quite long and participants may get tired or bored during the process. Contrary to the learning effect, which favors conditions completed towards the end of the experiment, fatigue negatively impacts on the performance of conditions completed towards the end of the experiment. For instance, in the ATM experiment, if the touch-screen interface is always tested after the button interface, we might draw a conclusion that the touch-screen interface is not as effective as the button interface when the observed difference is actually due to the participants' fatigue. We might fail to identify that the touch-screen interface is better than the button interface because the impact of fatigue offsets the gain of the touch-screen interface.

3.3.1.3   Comparison of between-group and within-group designs

The pros and cons of the between- and within-group designs are summarized in Table 3.1. You can see from the table that the advantages and limitations of the two design methods are exactly opposite to each other. That is, the limitations of the between-group

	Type of experiment design	
	Between-group design	**Within-group design**
Advantages	Cleaner Avoids learning effect Better control of confounding factors, such as fatigue	Smaller sample size Effective isolation of individual differences More powerful tests
Limitations	Larger sample size Large impact of individual differences Harder to get statistically significant results	Hard to control learning effect Large impact of fatigue

Table 3.1 Advantages and disadvantages of between-group design and within-group design.

design correspond to the advantages of the within-group design while the limitations of the within-group design correspond to the advantages of the between-group design.

3.3.2 Choosing the appropriate design approach

It is quite common for experimenters to argue back and forth when deciding which of the two design approaches to adopt. Many times the decision is quite hard to make since the advantages and disadvantages of the between-group design and within-group design are exactly opposite to each other. It should be emphasized that each experiment is unique and the decision should be made on a case-by-case basis with full consideration of the specific context of the experiment. In some cases, a hybrid design may be adopted that involves both between-group factors and within-group factors. The hybrid approach is discussed in detail in Section 3.4.2. This section discusses the general guidelines that help us choose the appropriate approach for a specific user study.

3.3.2.1 Between-group design

Generally speaking, between-group design should be adopted when the experiment investigates: simple tasks with limited individual differences; tasks that would be greatly influenced by the learning effect; or problems that cannot be investigated through a within-group design.

The size of the individual differences is very hard to estimate. However, it is empirically confirmed that individual differences are smaller when the tasks are simple and involve limited cognitive process (Dillon, 1996; Egan, 1988). In contrast, individual differences are larger when the task is complicated or involves significant cognitive functions. For example, when the task mainly involves basic motor skills, such as selecting a target on the screen, the individual differences among participants might be comparatively small.[1] But when the task involves more complicated cognitive or perceptual functions, such as reading, comprehension, information retrieval, and problem solving, the individual differences have a much larger impact. When the task is simple, the impact of individual differences is limited and a between-group design would be appropriate.

Depending on the types of task, some experiments are more vulnerable to the learning effect than others. For example, in an experiment that compares the navigation effectiveness of two types of menu within a website, a participant that completes the navigation tasks under one condition would have gained a significant amount of knowledge of the website architecture. The knowledge would make a great impact on the participant's performance when completing the tasks under the other condition. Therefore, within-group design is highly inappropriate for this type of task and between-group design would have to be adopted.

There are many circumstances when it is totally impossible to adopt a within-group design. Taking hypotheses H2 and H3, previously stated, as examples:

- H2: There is no difference in the time required to locate an item in an online store between novice users and experienced users.
- H3: There is no difference in the perceived trust towards an online agent among customers who are from the United States, Russia, China, and Nigeria.

You can see that there is no way to compare the performances of novice users and experienced users through a within-group design because an individual cannot be both a novice user and an experienced user of the online store at the same time. For the same reason, a within-group design is not appropriate for H3 since any participant can only represent one of the four cultures. Under those circumstances, a between-group design is obviously the only option we have.

After choosing a between-group design for an experiment, we need to take special caution to control potential confounding factors. Participants should be randomly assigned to different conditions whenever possible.[2] When assigning participants, we need to try our best to counterbalance potential confounding factors, such as gender, age, computing experience, and internet experience, across conditions. In other words, we need to make sure that the groups are as similar as possible, except for the personal characteristics that are experimental variables.

3.3.2.2 *Within-group design*
Within-group design is more appropriate when the experiment investigates tasks with large individual differences, tasks that are less susceptible to the learning effect, or when the target participant pool is very small. As discussed previously, complicated tasks that involve

---

[1]Note that the individual differences in these types of tasks can be quite substantial when the participants come from different age groups or when individuals with motor disabilities are involved.
[2]We cannot randomly assign participants to different conditions in the cases of H2 and H3, obviously.

substantial human cognitive and perceptual capabilities generally encounter much larger individual differences than simple tasks. Therefore, when an experiment investigates complicated tasks such as reading, comprehension, information retrieval, and problem solving, a within-group design might be more appropriate since it effectively isolates individual differences from the main effects.

Most of the tasks that examine complicated or learned skills or knowledge – such as typing, reading, composition, and problem solving – are less susceptible to learning effects. For example, if an experiment investigates the impact of two fonts (such as, Times New Roman and Arial) on participants' reading speed, the learning effect between the two conditions would be very limited. Reading one text document of several hundred words is unlikely to improve an individual's reading speed. Therefore, a within-group design would be appropriate as long as the text materials presented to the participant under the two conditions are different in content but similar in levels of difficulty.

Difficulty in finding and recruiting qualified participants is a problem frequently faced by many HCI researchers. One typical example is the field of universal usability, which focuses on developing applications usable by diverse user populations. Numerous studies in this field examine how individuals with disabilities interact with computers or computer-related devices. The sample sizes are normally smaller than in studies examining users without disabilities. A reported experiment studied how individuals with high-level spinal cord injuries (SCI)[3] use speech-based techniques to generate text documents and correct errors (Sears *et al.,* 2003). Seven participants took part in the study. Although the total number of people falling into a specific disability or disease category is quite large, the number of such individuals living in a particular area is very limited.

Recruiting participants with specific disabilities is always a challenging task. For more detailed discussion on working with participants with disabilities, please refer to Chapter 15. The same problem also occurs when the target population is well trained, highly experienced, professionals, such as business executives or experienced project managers, simply because they are too busy to be bothered. Under those circumstances, it is almost impossible to recruit the number of participants needed for a between-group design, forcing the experimenters to adopt a within-group design.

Having decided to adopt a within-group design, you need to consider how to control the negative impact of learning effects, fatigue, and other potential problems associated with a within-group design.

One of the most effective approaches to controlling the learning effect is to randomize the order of the experimental conditions. For instance, in the experiment on three different types of keyboard, we can assign the order of the task conditions to a specific participant according to an order generated by randomization software. For example, the first participant can

[3]Spinal cord injuries (SCI) occur when the spinal cord (a collection of nerves extending from the base of the brain through the spinal column) is compressed, cut, damaged, or affected by disease (Stiens *et al.,* 1997). High-level SCI typically refers to injuries at or above the 6th cervical vertebrae that affect the motor functions in hands and arms.

Figure 3.5 Typical learning curve.

complete the typing tasks in the order QWERTY–DVORAK–Alphabetic and the second participant can complete them in the order DVORAK–QWERTY–Alphabetic. In this way, although the learning effect influences the performance of each individual participant (e.g., the first participant may perform better with the Alphabetic keyboard than with the QWERTY keyboard due to the learning effect), the learning effect of a particular participant is offset by another participant. Consequently, the entire data set is not significantly biased by the learning effect.

When the objective of the study is not initial interaction with the application, an effective approach to reduce the impact of the learning effect is to provide sufficient time for training. Research suggests that, for many types of tasks, the learning curve tends to be steeper during the initial interaction stages and flatter after that stage (see Figure 3.5). People achieve quicker progress in learning during initial stages, followed by gradual lesser improvement with further practice. Therefore, providing sufficient training time for users to get acquainted with the system or the task greatly reduces the learning effect during the actual task sessions. Of course, training cannot completely eliminate the learning effect. It only reduces the impact of it. This approach, combined with randomization of task conditions, is widely adopted in HCI studies to control the impact of learning.

To address the problem of fatigue caused by multiple experimental tasks, we need to design experiment tasks frugally, reducing the required number of tasks and shortening the experiment time whenever possible. It is generally suggested that the appropriate length of a single experiment session should be 60 to 90 minutes or shorter (Nielsen, 2005). When a session lasts longer than 90 minutes, the participant may get tired or frustrated. It is strongly recommended that a single session should not last longer than two hours. During the experiment, the participant should be provided with opportunities to take breaks as needed. Interestingly, even when the experimenter encourages the participants to take breaks, the participants may not realize that they are getting tired and tend to ignore the suggestion to take a break. Therefore, some researchers find it helpful to force the participants to take a break during an experiment. For more discussion regarding the benefit of breaks in HCI studies, please refer to Chapter 14.

3.4   Investigating more than one independent variable

3.4.1   Factorial Design

Factorial designs are widely adopted when an experiment investigates more than one independent variable or factor. Using this method, we divide the experiment groups or conditions into multiple subsets according to the independent variables. It allows us to simultaneously investigate the impact of all independent variables as well as the interaction effects between multiple variables.

The number of conditions in a factorial design is determined by the total number of independent variables and the level of each independent variable. The equation for calculating the number of conditions is:

$$C = \prod_{a=1}^{n} Va$$

where C is the number of conditions and V is the number of levels in each variable.

The best way to explain a factorial design and this equation is through an example. Consider running an experiment to compare the typing speed when using three types of keyboard (QWERTY, DVORAK, and Alphabetic). We are also interested in examining the effect of different tasks (composition vs. transcription) on the typing speed. This suggests that two independent variables are investigated in the experiment: types of keyboard and types of task. The variable "types of keyboard" has three levels: QWERTY, DVORAK, and Alphabetic. The variable "types of task" has two levels: transcription and composition. Therefore, the total number of conditions in this experiment is calculated according to the following equation:

$$\text{Number of conditions} = 3 \times 2 = 6$$

Table 3.2 illustrates the six conditions in this experiment. In the first three conditions, the participants would all complete composition tasks using different kinds of keyboard. In the other three conditions, the participants would all complete transcription tasks using different keyboards. When analyzing the data, we can compare conditions in the same row to examine the impact of keyboards. The effect of the tasks can be examined through comparing conditions in the same column. As a result, the effect of both independent variables can be examined simultaneously through a single experiment.

Either a between-group design or a within-group design may be adopted in this experiment. In a between-group design, each participant completes tasks under only one of the six conditions. As a result, six groups of participants would be required, one group for each condition. In a within-group design, each participant completes tasks under all six conditions. The advantages and disadvantages of between-group design and within-group design that we discussed in Section 3.3.2 also apply to factorial designs. No matter which design is

	QWERTY	DVORAK	Alphabetic
Composition	1	2	3
Transcription	4	5	6

Table 3.2 A factorial design.

adopted, it is important to counterbalance the orders and conditions in the experiment. In a between-group design, the participants need to be randomly assigned to the conditions. In a within-group design, the order in which the participant completes the six tasks needs to be counterbalanced.

3.4.2   Split-plot design

In experiments that study one independent variable, we can choose to implement the study as a between-group design or a within-group design. In a factorial study, we can also choose a split-plot design. A split-plot design has both between-group components and within-group components. That is, one or more independent variables is investigated through a between-group approach and the other variables are investigated through a within-group approach.

Table 3.3 illustrates an experiment that employs a split-plot design. The experiment investigates two independent variables: age and the use of GPS. The variable "age" has three levels: people who are 20 to 40 years old, people who are 41 to 60 years old, and people who are older than 60. The second variable has two levels: driving without GPS and driving with GPS assistance. Therefore, the total number of conditions in this experiment is six.

The impact of age is investigated through a between-group design since three groups of participants from different age ranges are studied. The impact of the use of GPS can be examined through a within-group approach. We can require each participant to complete the same driving task both with and without the assistance of the GPS. This gives us a typical split-plot design that involves both a between-group component (age analysis is based on the columns) and a within-group component (GPS use is analyzed by comparing condition 1 with condition 4, condition 2 with condition 5, and condition 3 with condition 6).

	20 to 40 years old	41 to 60 years old	Above 60
Driving without GPS assistance	1	2	3
Driving with GPS assistance	4	5	6

Table 3.3 A split-plot design.

Factorial Design in HCI Research

Factorial design has been adopted in numerous user studies in the HCI field. For example, Jacko *et al.* (2003) used a 7 by 4 factorial design in a study that examined the effects of multimodal feedback on the performance of older adults with differing visual abilities.

The between-group factor of the study was visual functionality. Four groups of participants took part in the study. The control group had no ocular disease and had corrected visual acuity of 20/20 to 20/40. All other participants had age-related macular degeneration (AMD). Those participants were further categorized into three groups based on best-corrected visual acuity (10/10 to 10/50, 20/60 to 20/100, >20/100).

The within-group factor of the study was the type of feedback. The following seven types of feedback were examined:

- auditory only;
- haptic only;
- visual only;
- auditory and haptic;
- auditory and visual;
- haptic and visual;
- auditory, haptic, and visual.

During the experiment, each participant completed 15 drag-and-drop tasks under all seven feedback conditions. This meant that each participant completed a total of 15 × 7 = 105 tasks.

Learning and fatigue would inevitably occur during the experiment. In order to address these two factors, the order of the condition under which each participant completed the tasks was counterbalanced using a 7 by 7 Latin square design that allows the control of the variation in two directions. Within each condition, the order of the location of the targets was also counter-balanced using a 15 by 15 Latin square design. Through this approach, the researchers effectively controlled the impact of learning and fatigue across multiple trials, allowing a comparatively cleaner examination of the factors of interest: feedback forms and target location.

3.4.3 Interaction effects

One advantage of a factorial design is that it allows us to study the interaction effects between two or more independent variables. According to Cozby (1997), an interaction effect can be described as "the differing effect of one independent variable on the dependent variable, depending on the particular level of another independent variable". When a significant interaction exists between independent variables X and Y, the means of the dependent variable Z would be determined jointly by X and Y.

Let us explain interaction effect through an example. Suppose we are conducting an experiment that investigates how types of device (mouse and touch screen) and experience impact the effectiveness of target selection tasks. Two types of user are studied: novice users and experienced users. Based on the data collected, we draw a diagram as shown in Figure 3.6. As you can see, novice users can select targets faster with a touch screen than with a mouse. Experienced users can select targets faster with a mouse than with a touch screen. The target selection speeds for both the mouse and the touch screen increase as the user gains more experience with the device. However, the increase in speed is much larger for the mouse than for the touch screen.

It is critical to study interaction effects in HCI studies since performance may be affected by multiple factors jointly. There are numerous studies that did not identify any significant effect in individual independent variables but found significant results in interaction effects.

Interaction effects may have important implications for design. For example, the interaction effect in Figure 3.6 would suggest that the touch screen performs better than the mouse during the initial interaction. But users can make greater progress in learning the mouse than the touch screen and eventually achieve higher efficiency with the mouse. This result may imply that a touch screen is a more appropriate input device when the interaction is normally brief and the opportunities for training are limited, such as an ATM interface. In contrast, a mouse might be more appropriate for long-term, frequent tasks, such as interacting with a computer desktop.

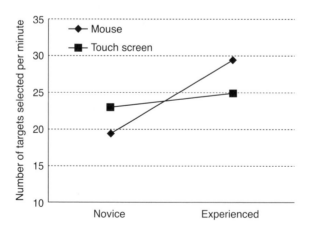

Figure 3.6 Interaction effects.

3.5 Reliability of experimental results

All experimental research strives for high reliability. Reliable experiments can be replicated by other research teams in other locations and yield results that are consistent, dependable, and stable. One big challenge in HCI studies is that, in contrast to the "hard sciences" such as physics, chemistry, and biology, measurements of human behavior and social interaction are normally subject to higher fluctuations and, therefore, are less replicable. The fluctuations in experimental results are referred to as errors.

3.5.1 Random errors

We may observe a secretary typing several text documents during five sessions and obtain an actual typing speed of 50 words per minute. It is very unlikely that we would get the same typing speed for all five sessions. Instead, we may end up with data like this:

Session 1: 46 words per minute
Session 2: 52 words per minute
Session 3: 47 words per minute
Session 4: 51 words per minute
Session 5: 53 words per minute

The general relationship between the actual value we are looking for and the observed values can be expressed as follows:

$$\text{observed values} = \text{actual value} + \text{random error}$$

Random errors are also called "chance errors" or "noise". They occur by chance and are not correlated with the actual value. Random errors push the observed values to move up or down around the exact value. There is no way to eliminate or control random errors but we can reduce the impact of random errors by enlarging the observed sample size. When a sample size is small, the random errors may have significant impact on the observed mean and the observed mean may be far from the actual value. When a sample size is large enough, the random errors should offset each other and the observed mean should be very close to the actual value. For example, in the typing task above, if we observe only Session 1, the mean would be 46, which is four words from the true value of 50 words per minute. If we increase the number of observed sessions to five, the mean of the observed values is 49.8, very close to the actual value. In reality, we can never claim that we are 100% confident that the observed value is the actual value. But we can be 100% confident that the larger our sample size, the closer the observed value is to the actual value.

3.5.2 Systematic errors

Systematic errors, also called "biases", are completely different in nature from random errors. While random errors cause variations in observed values in both directions around the actual value, systematic errors always push the observed values in the same direction. As a result, systematic errors never offset each other in the way that random errors do and they cause the observed mean to be either too high or too low.

Using the typing task example, the secretary might consistently under-perform during all five observation sessions, because of tiredness or nervousness, and we may collect the following data:

Session 1: 47 words per minute
Session 2: 44 words per minute
Session 3: 45 words per minute
Session 4: 42 words per minute
Session 5: 46 words per minute

In this case, the mean of the observed values is 44.8, five words lower than the actual value. Figure 3.7 illustrates the performance of the secretary in each case. Under the unbiased conditions, the observed values fluctuate due to random errors, but the fluctuations occur in both directions around the actual value and offset each other. However, under the biased condition, the systematic error consistently pushes all values down, causing the mean of the observed values to be significantly below the actual value.

Systematic errors can greatly reduce the reliability of experimental results, therefore they are the true enemy of experimental research. We can counter systematic errors in two

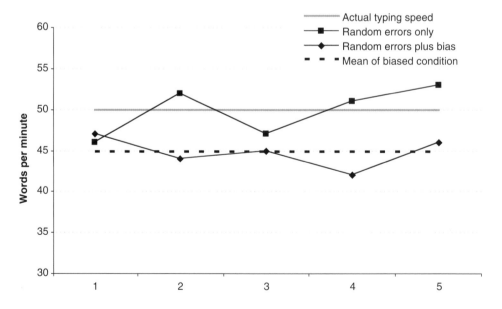

Figure 3.7 Comparison of random and systematic errors.

stages: we should try to eliminate or control biases during the experiment; when biases are inevitable, we need to isolate the impact of them from the main effect when analyzing the data. There are five major sources of systematic error:

- measurement instruments;
- experimental procedures;
- participants;
- experimenter behavior;
- the experimental environment.

3.5.2.1   Bias caused by measurement instruments

When the measurement instruments used are not appropriate, not accurate, or not configured correctly, they may introduce systematic errors. For instance, when observing participants searching for an item on an e-commerce website, we may use a stop watch to measure the time it takes to locate the specific item. If the stop watch is slow and misses five minutes in every hour, then we consistently record less time than the actual time used. As a consequence, the observed performance is seen to be better than the actual value. In order to control biases introduced by the measurement instruments, we need to carefully examine the instruments used before experiment sessions. Another approach is to use extensively tested, reliable, software-driven instruments. A bonus of software-driven instruments is that they can avoid human errors as well.

3.5.2.2   Bias caused by experimental procedures

Inappropriate or unclear experimental procedures may introduce biases. As discussed previously, if the order of task conditions is not randomized in an experiment with a within-group design, the observed results will be subject to the impact of the learning effect and fatigue: conditions tested later may be consistently better than conditions tested earlier due to learning effect; on the other hand, conditions tested earlier may be consistently better than later conditions due to fatigue. The biases caused by the learning effect and fatigue push the observed value in opposite directions and the combined effect is determined by the specific context of the experiment. If the tasks are simple and less susceptible to the learning effect, but tedious and long, the impact of fatigue and frustration may outweigh the impact of the learning effect, causing participants to consistently under-perform in later sessions. If the tasks are complicated and highly susceptible to the learning effect, but short and interesting, the impact of the learning effect may outweigh the impact of fatigue, causing participants to consistently perform better in later sessions.

The instructions that participants receive play a crucial role in an experiment and the wording of the experiment instructions should be carefully scrutinized before a study. Slightly different wording in instructions may lead to different participant responses. In a reported HCI study (Wallace, Anderson and Shneiderman, 1993), participants were instructed to complete the task "as quickly as possible" under one condition. Under the other condition, participants were instructed to "take your time, there is no rush". Interestingly, participants working on the no-time-stress condition completed the tasks faster than those working on the time-stress condition. This suggests the importance of critical wording in instructions. It also implies that the instructions that participants receive need to be highly consistent. When a study is conducted under the supervision of multiple investigators, it is more likely that the investigators give inconsistent instructions to the participants. Instructions and procedures on a written document or pre-recorded instructions are highly recommended to ensure consistency across experimental sessions.

Many times, trivial and unforeseen details introduce biases into the results. For instance, in an experiment that studies data entry on a PDA, the way the PDA is physically located may have an impact on the results. If no specification is given, some participants may hold the PDA in one hand and enter data using the other hand, other participants may put the PDA on a table and enter data using both hands. There are notable differences between the two conditions regarding the distance between the PDA screen and the participant's eyes, the angle of the PDA screen, and the number of hands involved for data entry. Any of those factors may introduce biases into the observed results. In order to reduce the biases attributed to experimental procedures, we need to:

- randomize the order of conditions, tasks, and task scenarios in experiments that adopt a within-group design or a split-plot design;
- prepare a written document with detailed instructions for participants;
- prepare a written document with detailed procedures for experimenters;
- run multiple pilot studies before actual data collection to identify potential biases.

A pilot study is not a luxury that we conduct only when we have plenty of time or money to spend. On the contrary, years of experience tells us that pilot studies are critical for all HCI experiments to identify potential biases. No matter how well you think you have planned the study, there are always things that you overlook. A pilot study is the only chance you have to fix your mistakes before you run the main study. Pilot studies should be treated very seriously and conducted in exactly the same way as planned for the actual experiment. Participants of the pilot study should be from the target population. Having one or two members from the research team completing the designed tasks is not a pilot study in its true sense (Preece *et al.*, 1994).

3.5.2.3   *Bias caused by participants*

Many characteristics of the participants may introduce systematic errors into the results. Potential contributors may be in a specific age range or have particular computer or internet experience, domain knowledge, education, professional experience and training, or personal interests. For instance, if we are running an experiment to test the user interface of a new mobile phone model, we might recruit participants by posting announcements on a popular blog on www.cnet.com. Since this website features highly technical news and reviews related to information technology, its visitors normally have a strong technical background and rich experience in using IT devices. As a consequence, the observed data would tend to out-perform what we would observe from the general public. The following guidelines can help us reduce systematic errors from the participants:

- Recruit participants carefully, making sure the participant pool is representative of the target user population (Broome, 1984; Smart, 1966).
- Create an environment or task procedure that causes the least stress to the users.
- Reassure the participants that you are testing the interface, not them, so they are calm and relaxed during the experiment.
- Reschedule a session or give participants some time to recover if they arrive tired, exhausted, or very nervous.

3.5.2.4 *Bias due to experimenter behavior*

Experimenter behavior is one of the major sources of bias. Experimenters may intentionally or unintentionally influence the experiment results. Any intentional action to influence participants' performance or preference is unethical in research and should be strictly avoided. However, experimenters may unknowingly influence the observed data. Spoken language, body language, and facial expressions frequently serve as triggers for bias. Let us examine the following scenarios:

1. An experimenter is introducing an interface to a participant. The experimenter says, "Now you get to the pull-down menus. I think you will really like them. . . . I designed them myself!"
2. An experimenter is loading an application for a participant. The response time is a bit long. The experimenter is frustrated and says, "Damn! It's slower than a snail."
3. An experimenter is loading an application for a participant. The response time is a bit long. The experimenter waits uneasily, tapping his fingers on the desk and frequently changing his body position as he stares at the screen impatiently.
4. A participant arrives on time for a study scheduled at 9 a.m. The experimenter does not arrive until 9:10 a.m. After guiding the participant into the lab, the experimenter takes 10 minutes to set up all the equipment. Once the experiment starts, the experimenter finds that the task list is missing and runs out of the lab to print a copy.

In Scenario 1, the experimenter is very demanding and his comment may make the participant reluctant to provide negative feedback about the interface in case it hurts the experimenter's feelings. Therefore, the data collected from the participant, especially the subjective data, is likely to be better than the actual value. In Scenarios 2 and 3, the experimenter's spoken language or body language reveals his negative attitude towards the application. Participants would register those cues and would form a negative perspective even before their first encounter with the application and the collected subjective ratings and feedback would be biased against the application. In Scenario 4, the unprofessional and slack style of the experimenter would give a negative impression to the participant, which may impact the participant's performance as well as the subjective ratings and feedback.

When multiple experimenters are involved in the experiment, bias is likely to occur due to inconsistency in instructions and training, as well as individual styles and attitudes. If one of the experimenters is very patient, offers long training sessions and demonstrates all related commands to the participants before the actual task, while the other experimenter is pushy, offers shorter training sessions, and only demonstrates a subset of the commands, the participants who complete the experiment under the guidance of the first experimenter may systematically out-perform the participants who complete the experiment with the second experimenter. In order to control possible biases triggered by experimenters, we need to:

- Offer training opportunities to experimenters and teach them to be neutral, calm, and patient when supervising experiments.
- Make sure that the experimenter arrives at least 10 minutes before the scheduled sessions and gets everything ready before the session starts.
- Whenever possible, have two experimenters supervise a session together, one as the lead experimenter and the other as the assistant experimenter. The lead experimenter is responsible for interacting with the participants. The assistant experimenter observes the session closely, fixes errors if noted, and takes notes when necessary.
- Prepare written documents with detailed procedures for experimenters and require all experimenters to follow strictly the same procedure.
- When appropriate, record important instructions before the experiment and play the recording to the participants during the experiment. In this way, we can guarantee that all participants go through the same training process and receive the same instructions.

3.5.2.5   Bias due to environmental factors

Environmental factors play an increasingly important role in HCI research due to the rapid development in mobile computing, universal accessibility, and recognition-based technologies. Environmental factors can be categorized into two groups: physical environmental factors and social environmental factors. Examples of physical environmental factors include noise, temperature, lighting, vibration, and humidity. Examples of social environmental factors include the number of people in the surrounding environment and the relationship between those people and the participant.

Both physical and social environmental factors may introduce systematic errors into the observed data. For instance, a study that examines the performance of a speech-recognition application may yield lower recognition error rates than the actual value if there is a significant level of ambient noise during the experiment session. Even when the study investigates applications other than speech, loud environmental noise may distract the participants or induce fatigue. Regarding social factors, a participant with a person watching over his shoulder may perform differently from a participant who is seated alone. Environmental factors may cause more problems when the experiment is not conducted in a lab, but in locations such as the participant's home or workplace. The following guidelines can help us avoid or control environment-induced biases:

- In a lab setting, make sure the room is quiet, the lighting is appropriate, and the chairs and tables are comfortable. The room should be clean and tidy, without notable distractions.
- Whenever possible, the participant should be seated alone and the experimenter can observe the session from another room via a one-way mirror or monitors.
- In a field study, the experimenters should visit the location before the scheduled time to confirm that the setting meets the requirements of the study.

Finally, it is important to realize that, no matter how hard you try to avoid biases, they can never be completely eliminated. A well-designed experiment with lots of consideration for controlling bias can improve the data, making the observed results closer to the actual values, but still subject to the impact of biases. Therefore, we should be careful when reporting the findings, even when the study results are statistically significant.

3.6 Experimental procedures

Experiments are conducted in dramatically different fields to answer a myriad of questions. Experiments in the HCI field, similar to many studies in sociology or psychology, typically involve human subjects. Studying human subjects is quite different from studying metal or plant reactions, or other animals, and introduces many interesting issues or challenges. It should be noted that, no matter how well an experiment is designed and conducted, bias and errors can never be completely eliminated. Therefore, we should be careful in interpreting the data and making claims, even when the results are statistically significant. The concerns and practices of working with human subjects are discussed in detail in Chapter 14. In this section, we briefly introduce the procedures for experiments that study human subjects.

In the lifecycle of an HCI experiment, we typically go through the following process:

1. Identify a research hypothesis.
2. Specify the design of the study.
3. Run a pilot study to test the design, the system, and the study instruments.
4. Recruit participants.
5. Run the actual data collection sessions.
6. Analyze the data.
7. Report the results.

Within a specific experiment session, we typically go through the following steps:

1. Ensure the systems or devices being evaluated and the related instruments are ready for the experiment.
2. Greet the participants.
3. Introduce the purpose of the study and the procedures.
4. Get the consent of the participants.
5. Assign the participants to a specific experiment condition according to the pre-defined randomization method.
6. Participants complete training task.
7. Participants complete actual tasks.
8. Participants answer questionnaires (if any).
9. Debriefing session.
10. Payment (if any).

Some experiments may require more complicated steps or procedures. For example, longitudinal studies involve multiple trials and we need to make sure that the tasks used in each trial are randomized in order to control the impact of the learning effect.

A number of open source platforms have been developed to help researchers design experiments, collect data, and analyze the results. One example is the Touchstone experimental design platform (Mackay *et al.*, 2007).

Summary

Experiment design starts with a clearly defined, testable research hypothesis. During the design process, we need to answer the following questions:

- How many dependent variables are investigated in the experiment and how are they measured?
- How many independent variables are investigated in the experiment and how are they controlled?
- How many conditions are involved in the experiment?
- Which of the three designs will be adopted: between-group, within-group, or split-plot?
- What potential bias may occur and how can we avoid or control those biases?

When an experiment studies only one independent variable, we need to choose between the between-group design and the within-group design. When there is more than one independent variable, we need to select among the between-group design, the within-group design, and the split-plot design.

The between-group design is cleaner, avoids the learning effect, and is less likely to be affected by fatigue and frustration. But this design is weaker due to the high noise level of individual differences. In addition, larger numbers of participants are usually required for a between-group design. The within-group design, on the other hand, effectively isolates individual differences and, therefore, is a much stronger test than the between-group design. Another bonus is that fewer participants are required. But within-group designs are more vulnerable to learning effects and fatigue. The appropriate design method needs to be selected based on the nature of the application, the participant, and the tasks examined in the experiment.

All experiments strive for clean, accurate, and unbiased results. In reality, experiment results are highly susceptible to bias. Biases can be attributed to five major sources: the measurement instruments, the experiment procedure, the participants, the experimenters, and the physical and social environment. We should try to avoid or control biases through accurate and appropriate measurement devices and scales; clearly defined and detailed experimental procedures; carefully recruited participants; well-trained, professional, and unbiased experimenters; and well-controlled environments.

Discussion Questions

1. Explain the differences among the three types of study: experiment, quasi-experiment, and non-experiment.
2. What are the major issues that need to be considered when designing experiments?
3. What is a between-group design? Explain the advantages and disadvantages of a between-group design.
4. What is a within-group design? Explain the advantages and disadvantages of a within-group design.
5. When should a between-group design be considered for an experiment?
6. When should a within-group design be considered for an experiment?
7. What is the benefit of a factorial design compared to experiments that investigate one factor at a time?
8. What is a split-plot design?
9. Explain the differences between random errors and systematic errors.
10. What are the major sources of systematic errors, or biases?
11. What can we do to reduce systematic errors in experiments?
12. Describe the typical procedure of an experiment that involves human subjects.

Research Design Exercises

1. Read the following scenarios. Identify actions or conditions that may induce systematic errors in each scenario and explain the direction of the impact (i.e., whether the observed data will be pulled up or down from the actual value).

   Scenario 1. In an experiment that investigates how novice users learn to use the T9 method to enter data into a PDA, a participant has actually used T9 for over a year.

Scenario 2. An experimenter is introducing a website to a participant. The experimenter says, "My team has spent six months on this site. The site is like our baby."

Scenario 3. In an experiment that examines how individuals with severe motor disabilities interact with computers using a brain–computer interface, all participants recruited are healthy individuals without any disability.

Scenario 4. In an experiment that examines speech-based dictation techniques, the experimenter forgets to switch the speech profiles between experiment sessions, so a participant used another person's speech profile to complete the dictation tasks.

Scenario 5. In an experiment that examines the design of an e-commerce website, participants complete multiple tasks to retrieve specific information on the site. However, the network speed is very slow and the participants have to wait significant amounts of time for each page to be loaded.

2. Read the following scenarios. Discuss the type of experiment design (between-group, within-group, or split-plot) that is appropriate for each scenario.

Scenario 1. A study investigates whether people who have attended a security training program generate and use more secure passwords than people who haven't received any security training.

Scenario 2. A research team examines the effectiveness of joysticks and trackballs for selecting static targets and moving targets.

Scenario 3. A research team examines whether the gender of an online agent affects the perception of trust for young users, middle-aged users, and older users.

Scenario 4. A research team examines whether virtual teams who use video instant messaging (IM) are more productive than teams who use text-only IM.

Scenario 5. A study examines the effectiveness of three menu structures. The first structure has two levels, with eight items in the first level and 64 items in the second level. The second structure has three levels, with four items in the first level, 16 items in the second level, and 64 items in the third level. The third menu has six levels, with two items in the first level and 2^n items in the nth level.

References

Broome, J. (1984) Selecting people randomly. *Ethics*, **95**(1):38–55.

Cooper, D. and Schindler, P. (2000) *Business Research Methods*, 7th edition. Boston: McGraw Hill.

Cozby, P.C. (1997) *Methods in Behavioral Research*, 6th edition. Mountain View, CA: Mayfield Publishing.

Dillon, A. (1996) User analysis in HCI: the historical lesson from individual differences research. *International Journal of Human–Computer Studies*, **45**(6):619–637.

Egan, D. (1988) Individual differences in human–computer interaction. In M. Helander (ed.) *Handbook of Human–Computer Interaction*, 543–568. North-Holland: Elsevier.

Feng, J. (2005) A power and reliability model for error prone technologies: Improving speech-based support for spatial navigation. *Doctoral dissertation.*

Jacko, J.A., Scott, I.U., Sainfort, F., Barnard, L., Edwards, P.J., Emery, V.K., Kongnakorn, T., Moloney, K.P., and Zorich, B.S. (2003) Older adults and visual impairment: what do exposure times and accuracy tell us about performance gains associated with multimodal feedback? *Proceedings of the SIGCHI conference on Human Factors in Computing Systems*, 33–40.

Kirk, R. (1982) *Experimental Design: Procedures for the behavioral sciences*, 2nd edition. Pacific Grove, California: Brooks/Cole Publishing Company.

Li, Y., Welbourne, E., and Landay, J. (2006) Novel methods: emotions, gestures, events: Design and experimental analysis of continuous location tracking techniques for Wizard of Oz testing. *Proceedings of the SIGCHI conference on Human Factors in Computing Systems*, 1019–1022.

Mackay, W.E., Appert, C., Beaudouin-Lafon, M., Chapuis, O., Du, Y., Fekete, J.-D., and Guiard, Y. (2007) Usability evaluation: Touchstone: exploratory design of experiments. *Proceedings of the SIGCHI conference on Human Factors in Computing Systems*, 1425–1434.

Nielsen, J. (2005) Time budgets for usability sessions. *Alert Box*, September 12. Retrieved on February 13, 2008 at http://www.useit.com/alertbox/usability_sessions.html.

Oehlert, G. (2000) A First Course in Design and Analysis of Experiments. New York: Freeman and Company.

Preece, J., Rogers, Y., Sharp, H., Benyon, D., Holland, S., and Carey, T. (1994) *Human–Computer Interaction*. Addison Wesley.

Rosenthal, R. and Rosnow, R. (2008) *Essentials of Behavioral Research: Methods and data analysis*, 3rd edition. Boston: McGraw Hill.

Sears, A., Feng, J., Oseitutu, K., and Karat, C-M. (2003) Speech-based navigation during dictation: Difficulties, consequences, and solutions. *Human–Computer Interaction*, **18**(3):229–257.

Smart, R.G. (1966) Subject selection bias in psychological research. *Canadian Psychologist*, **7a**: 115–121.

Stiens, S., Goldstein, B., Hammond, M., and Little, J. (1997) Spinal Cord Injuries. In B. O'Young, M. Young and S. Stiens (eds) *PM&R Secrets*, 253–261. Philadelphia: Hanley & Belfus.

Wallace, D., Anderson, N., and Shneiderman, B. (1993) Time stress effects on two menu selection systems. In B. Shneiderman (ed.), *Sparks of Innovation in Human–Computer Interaction*. Norwood, New Jersey: Ablex Publishing Corporation.

4

Statistical analysis

In Chapter 2, we discussed why we need to run statistical analysis on our data. Appropriate selection of statistical analysis methods and accurate interpretation of the test results are essential for user studies. After weeks, months, or even years of arduous preparation and data collection, you finally have a heavy set of data on hand and may feel the need to lie back and enjoy a hard-earned break. Well, it is a little too early to relax and celebrate at this point. With many studies, the data analysis stage is equally or even more labor-intensive than the data collection stage. Many critical decisions need to be made when analyzing the data, such as the type of statistical method to be used, the confidence threshold, as well as the interpretation of the significance test results. Incorrect selection of statistical methods or inappropriate interpretation of the results can lead to erroneous conclusions and waste high-quality data.

This chapter discusses general data analysis procedures and commonly used statistical methods, including independent-samples *t* test, paired-samples *t* test, one-way analysis of variance (ANOVA), factorial ANOVA, repeated measures ANOVA, correlation, regression, and chi-square test. The focus of this chapter is not on the mathematical computation behind each method or how to use statistical software to conduct each analysis. Instead, we focus on the contexts of use and the assumptions of each method. We also discuss how to appropriately interpret the results of each significance test. Through this chapter, we hope that you will be able to choose appropriate statistical methods for data analysis and accurately interpret the analysis results in your own studies. You will also learn how to justify the validity of the findings reported in academic articles based on the experimental design and the statistical analysis procedure.

4.1   Preparing data for statistical analysis

In most cases, the original data collected from lab-based experiments, usability tests, field studies, surveys, and various other channels need to be carefully processed before any statistical analysis can be conducted. There are several reasons for the need for pre-processing. First, the original data collected, especially when they are entered by participants manually, may have errors or may be presented in inconsistent formats. If those errors or inconsistencies are not filtered or fixed, they may contaminate the entire data set. Secondly, the original data collected may be too primitive and higher level coding may be needed to help identify the underlying themes. Thirdly, the specific statistical analysis method or software may require the data to be organized into a pre-defined layout or format so that they can be processed (Delwiche and Slaughter, 2008).

4.1.1   Cleaning up data

The first thing that you need to do after data collection is to screen the data for possible errors. This step is necessary for any type of data collected, but is particularly important for data entered manually by participants. To err is human. All people make mistakes (Norman, 1988). Although it is not possible to identify all the errors, you want to trace as many errors as possible to minimize the negative impact of errors. There are various ways to identify errors depending on the nature of the data collected.

Sometimes you can identify errors by conducting a reasonableness check. For instance, if the age of a participant is entered as "223", you can easily conclude that there is something wrong. Your participant might have accidentally pushed the 2 button twice, in which case the correct age should be 23, or he might have accidentally hit the 3 button after the correct age, 22, has been entered. Sometimes you need to check multiple data fields in order to identify possible errors. For example, you may compare the participant's "age" and "years of computing experience" to check whether there is an unreasonable entry.

For automatically collected data, error checking usually boils down to time consistency issues or whether the performance is within a reasonable range. Something is obviously wrong if the logged start time of an event is later than the logged end time of the same event. You should also be on the alert if any unreasonably high or low performance levels are documented.

In many studies, data about the same participant are collected from multiple channels. For example, in a study investigating multiple data entry techniques, the performance data (such as time and number of keystrokes) might be automatically logged by data-logging software. The participants' subjective preference and satisfaction data might be manually collected via paper-based questionnaires. In this case, you need to make sure that all the data about the same participant are correctly grouped together. The result will be invalid if the performance data of one participant is grouped with the subjective data of another participant.

After errors are identified, how shall we deal with them? It is obvious that you always want to fix errors and replace them with accurate data. This is possible in some cases. If the age of a participant is incorrect, you can contact that participant and find out the accurate information. In many cases, fixing errors in the pre-processing stage is impossible. In many online studies or studies in which the participant remains anonymous, you may have no means of reaching participants after the data is collected. Under those circumstances, you need to remove the problematic data items and treat them as missing values in the statistical data analysis.

Sometimes, the data collected need to be cleaned up due to inappropriate formatting. Using age as an example, participants may enter age in various formats. In an online survey, most participants used numeric values such as "9" to report their age (Feng *et al.* 2008). Some used text such as "nine" or "nine and a half." A number of participants even entered detailed text descriptions such as "He will turn nine in January." The entries in text formats were all transformed to numeric values before the data was analyzed by statistical software.

4.1.2 Coding data

In many studies, the original data collected need to be coded before any statistical analysis can be conducted. A typical example is the data collected about the demographic information of your participants. Table 4.1 shows the original demographic data of three participants.

	Age	Gender	Highest degree	Previous experience in software A
Participant 1	34	male	College	Yes
Participant 2	28	female	Graduate	No
Participant 3	21	female	High school	No

Table 4.1 Sample demographic data in its original form.

The information on age is numerical and does not need to be coded. The information on gender, highest degree earned, and previous software experience needs to be coded so that statistical software can interpret the input. In Table 4.2, gender information is coded using 1 to represent "male" and 0 to represent "female". Highest degree earned has more categories with 1 representing a high school degree, 2 representing a college degree, and 3 representing a graduate degree. Previous software experience is coded, with 1 representing "Yes" and 0 representing "No".

In various studies such as surveys, interviews, and focus groups, content analysis needs to be conducted in which text reflecting different themes or critical events is coded and counted (Stemler, 2001). Detailed discussion on content analysis is provided in Chapter 11.

Event coding is also quite common in usability tests or lab-based studies. For example, Feng, Sears and Karat (2006) used extensive coding schemes to analyze speech-based interaction data. In their study, they identified high-level events, such as direction-based navigation events (i.e., a navigation event such as "Move up") and target-based navigation events (i.e., a navigation event such as "Select book"). They further coded different events according to the navigation distance. This coding scheme allowed the authors to identify critical differences in interaction strategies between typical computer users and users with disabilities that hinder the use of the standard keyboard and mouse.

When coding your data, it is critical to ensure the coding is consistent. This is particularly challenging when the coding is completed by more than one person. If the coding is inconsistent, the validity of the analysis results will be greatly affected. Various statistical methods, such as Cronbach's alpha, can be used to assess the reliability of coding completed by multiple coders (Weber, 1990). Please see Chapter 11 for more details on this topic.

	Age	Gender	Highest degree	Previous experience in software A
Participant 1	34	1	2	1
Participant 2	28	0	3	0
Participant 3	21	0	1	0

Table 4.2 Sample demographic data in coded form.

4.1.3 Organizing data

Statistical and other data-processing software normally has pre-defined requirements for how data should be laid out for specific statistical analysis. In SPSS, for example, when running an independent-samples *t* test to compare two groups of data, the data of the two groups need to be listed in the same column. In contrast, when running a paired-samples *t* test to compare two means, the two groups of data need to be laid out parallel to each other in two separate columns. Similarly, other statistical methods such as ANOVA, repeated measures, and correlation all have different data organization requirements that need to be followed closely.

4.2 Descriptive statistics

After the collected data is cleaned up, you may want to run a number of basic descriptive statistical tests to understand the nature of your data set. For instance, you may want to know the range into which most of your data points fall; you may also want to know how your data points are distributed. The most commonly used descriptive measures include means, medians, modes, variances, standard deviations, and ranges.

4.2.1 Measures of central tendency

When we study a data set, we often want to find out where the bulk of the data is located. In statistical terms, this characteristic is called the "central tendency." Various measures can be used to describe the central tendency of a data set, including the mean, the median, and the mode (Rosenthal and Rosnow, 2008).

The mean is also called the "arithmetic average" of a data set. When multiple groups are involved in a study, comparing their means can provide preliminary insights on how the groups relate to each other. If you find that the mean of one group is notably higher than the other group, you may conduct significance tests, such as a *t* test, to examine whether that difference is statistically significant.

The median is the middle score in a data set. For instance, consider the following data set of typing speeds collected from seven users:

$$\{15, \ 19, \ 22, \ 29, \ 33, \ 45, \ 50\}$$

The median of the data set is 29.

The mode is the value that occurs with the greatest frequency in a data set. Suppose we collected the following data from seven participants about the number of hours they spend on the Internet every week:

$$\{12, \ 15, \ 22, \ 22, \ 22, \ 34, \ 34\}$$

The mode of the data set is 22.

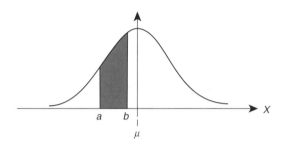

Figure 4.1 Normal distribution curve.

4.2.2   Measures of spread

Another important group of descriptive measures that we usually want to know is how much the data points deviate from the center of the data set. In other words, we want to know how spread out our data set is. Measures in this group include range, variances, and standard deviations.

The range measures the distance between the highest and lowest scores in the data set. In the typing-speed data set of Section 4.2.1, the range is $50 - 15 = 35$. The larger the range, the more distributed the data set is.

The variance of a data set is the mean of the squared distances of all the scores from the mean of the data set. The square root of the variance is called the standard deviation. As with range, higher variances or standard deviations indicate that the data set is more distributed.

A commonly used method for describing the distribution of a data set is the normal distribution, a special bell-shaped distribution that can be defined by the mean and the standard deviation (see Figure 4.1). The pattern of normal distribution is very important and useful for data analysis since many attributes from various fields of study are distributed normally: the heights of a population, student grades, and various performance measures.

Testing a data set to determine whether it is normally distributed is a necessary step when selecting the type of significance tests to conduct. Parametric tests assume that the data set is normally distributed or approximately normally distributed. If you find that the data collected is not normally distributed, you may need to consider transforming the data so that they are normally distributed or you may adopt non-parametric tests for the analysis.

For detailed calculation of each of the measures, please refer to statistical textbooks, such as (Hinkle, Wiersma, and Jurs, 2002; Newton and Rudestam, 1999; Rosenthal and Rosnow, 2008). Microsoft Excel offers built-in functions that allow you to conveniently calculate or count various descriptive values.

4.3   Comparing means

In user studies involving multiple conditions or groups, the ultimate objective of the researchers is to find out whether there is any difference between the conditions or groups.

Suppose you are evaluating the effectiveness of two search engines; you may adopt a between-group design, in which case you will recruit two groups of participants and have each group use one of the two search engines to complete some search tasks. If you choose a within-group design, you will recruit one group of participants and have each participant complete a series of tasks using both search engines. In either case, you want to compare the performance measures of the two groups or conditions to find out whether there is any difference between the two search engines.

Many studies involve three or more conditions that need to be compared. Due to variances in the data, you should not directly compare the means of the multiple conditions and claim that a difference exists as long as the means are different. Instead, you have to use statistical significance tests to evaluate the variances that can be explained by the independent variables and the variances that cannot be explained by them. The significance test will suggest the probability of the observed difference occurring by chance. If the probability that the difference occurs by chance is fairly low (e.g., less than 5%), we can claim with high confidence that the observed difference is due to the difference in the controlled independent variables.

Various significance tests are available to compare the means of multiple groups. Commonly used tests include *t* tests and the analysis of variance (ANOVA). A *t* test is a simplified analysis of variance involving only two groups or conditions. Two commonly used *t* tests are the independent-samples *t* test and the paired-samples *t* test. When a study involves more than two conditions, an ANOVA test has to be used. Various ANOVA methods are available to fit the needs of different experimental designs. Commonly used ANOVA tests include one-way ANOVA, factorial ANOVA, repeated measures ANOVA, and ANOVA for split-plot design.

Table 4.3 summarizes the major types of empirical study regarding design methodology and the appropriate significance test for each design. For studies with between-group design that only investigate one independent variable with two conditions, an independent-samples *t* test can be used. When the independent variable has three or more conditions, a one-way

Experiment design	Independent variables (IV)	Conditions for each IV	Types of test
Between-group	1	2	Independent-samples *t* test
	1	3 or more	One-way ANOVA
	2 or more	2 or more	Factorial ANOVA
Within-group	1	2	Paired-samples *t* test
	1	3 or more	Repeated measures ANOVA
	2 or more	2 or more	Repeated measures ANOVA
Between- and within-group	2 or more	2 or more	Split-plot ANOVA

Table 4.3 Commonly used significance tests for comparing means and their application context.

ANOVA can be used. When a between-group study investigates two or more independent variables, a factorial ANOVA test should be considered. For studies that adopt a within-group design, if the study investigates only one independent variable with two conditions, a paired-samples *t* test can be used. If the study's independent variables have three or more conditions, a repeated measures ANOVA test can be used. Finally, a study may adopt a split-plot design that involves both a between-group component and a within-group component. In this case, a split-plot ANOVA test can be used.

4.4 *T* tests

The most widely adopted statistical procedure for comparing two means is the *t* test (Rosenthal and Rosnow, 2008). Different types of *t* test should be adopted according to the specific design of the study. When the two groups being compared are presumably unrelated, an independent-samples *t* test can be used. When the two means are contributed by the same group, a paired-samples *t* test can be considered.

Suppose you want to investigate whether the use of specific word-prediction software has an impact on typing speed. The hypothesis of the test is:

> *There is no significant difference in the task completion time between individuals who use the word-prediction software and those who do not use the software.*

4.4.1   Independent-samples *t* test

You can test this hypothesis by recruiting two groups of participants and have one group type some text using standard word-processing software and another group use the word-processing software with word-prediction software. If a random-sampling method is used, the two groups are presumably independent from each other. In this case, the independent-samples *t* test can be used.

If you use SPSS to run an independent-samples *t* test, the data points of the two groups should be listed in the same column. You need to create an additional column to mark the group to which each data point belongs. In Table 4.4, each condition has eight participants. The Coding column marks the group information, with 0 representing the participants who completed the tasks without prediction software and 1 representing the participants who completed the tasks with prediction software. When using SPSS, only the third and the fourth columns need to be entered.

4.4.2   Paired-samples *t* test

An alternative strategy for the word-prediction software study is to recruit one group of participants and have each participant complete comparable typing tasks under both conditions. Since the data points contributed by the same participant are related, a paired-samples *t* test should be used.

Group	Participants	Task completion time	Coding
No prediction	Participant 1	245	0
No prediction	Participant 2	236	0
No prediction	Participant 3	321	0
No prediction	Participant 4	212	0
No prediction	Participant 5	267	0
No prediction	Participant 6	334	0
No prediction	Participant 7	287	0
No prediction	Participant 8	259	0
With prediction	Participant 1	246	1
With prediction	Participant 2	213	1
With prediction	Participant 3	265	1
With prediction	Participant 4	189	1
With prediction	Participant 5	201	1
With prediction	Participant 6	197	1
With prediction	Participant 7	289	1
With prediction	Participant 8	224	1

Table 4.4 Sample data for independent-samples *t* test.

If you use SPSS to run a paired–samples *t* test, the two data points contributed by the same participant should be listed parallel to each other in the same row. In Table 4.5, the two numeric values in each row were contributed by the same participant. When using SPSS to run the test, only the second and third columns need to be entered.

4.4.3 Interpretation of *t* test results

T tests return a value, *t*, with larger *t* values suggesting higher probability of the null hypothesis being false. In other words, the higher the *t* value, the more likely the two

Participants	No prediction	With prediction
Participant 1	245	246
Participant 2	236	213
Participant 3	321	265
Participant 4	212	189
Participant 5	267	201
Participant 6	334	197
Participant 7	287	289
Participant 8	259	224

Table 4.5 Sample data for paired-samples *t* test.

means are different. As stated in Chapter 2, we normally use a 95% confidence interval in significance tests. So any t value that is higher than the corresponding t value at the 95% confidence interval suggests that there is a significant difference between participants (for example, between users who use word-prediction software and those who do not).

SPSS generates a summary table for the results, containing both the t test results and additional test results that examine the data distribution. If we run an independent-samples t test using the data set provided in Table 4.4, the returned t value is 2.169, which is higher than the t value for the specific degree of freedom (df = 15) at the 95% confidence interval. In statistical terms, the result can be reported as:

> *An independent-samples* t *test suggests that there is significant difference in the task completion time between the group who used the standard word-processing software and the group who used the prediction software (*t *(15) = 2.169, p < 0.05).*

Note that the t value needs to be reported together with the degree of freedom and the level of significance. Presenting the degree of freedom helps readers to evaluate whether the data analysis is done correctly and to interpret the results appropriately.

4.4.4   Two-tailed t tests and one-tailed t tests

In some empirical studies, the hypothesis indicates the direction of the difference. For example, you may expect the use of word-prediction software to improve typing speed. In this case, the hypothesis of the study will be:

> *Individuals who use word-prediction software can type faster than those who do not use word-prediction software.*

How does this hypothesis differ from the original hypothesis? In the original hypothesis, the direction of the difference is not specified, implying that the use of word-prediction software may improve typing speed, reduce typing speed, or have no impact on typing speed. In the hypothesis above, we expect the use of the word-prediction software to either improve typing speed, or have no impact at all. In this case, a "one-tailed t test" is appropriate: a t value that is larger than the 90% confidence interval suggests that the null hypothesis is false and that the difference between the two means is significant.

4.5   Analysis of variance

Analysis of variance (ANOVA) is a widely used statistical method to compare the means of two or more groups. When there are only two means to be compared, the calculation of ANOVA is simplified to t tests. ANOVA tests normally return a value called the omnibus F. Therefore, ANOVA tests are also called "F tests."

4.5.1   One-way ANOVA

One-way ANOVA is appropriate for empirical studies that adopt a between-group design and investigate only one independent variable with three or more conditions. Let us revisit the word-prediction software study from Section 4.4.

You are also interested in a speech-based data entry method and would like to compare three conditions: text entry using standard word-processing software, text entry using word-prediction software, and text entry using speech-based dictation software. The independent variable of the study has three conditions. With a between-group design, you need to recruit three groups of participants and have each group complete the text entry task using one of the three methods.

The data layout for running one-way ANOVA using SPSS is similar to that for the independent-samples *t* test. Table 4.6 presents a data set for the one-way ANOVA test. The Coding column marks the group that each data point belongs to. Normally we use 0 to mark the control group (those who used the basic word-processing software); 1 and 2 are

Group	Participants	Task completion time	Coding
Standard	Participant 1	245	0
Standard	Participant 2	236	0
Standard	Participant 3	321	0
Standard	Participant 4	212	0
Standard	Participant 5	267	0
Standard	Participant 6	334	0
Standard	Participant 7	287	0
Standard	Participant 8	259	0
Prediction	Participant 1	246	1
Prediction	Participant 2	213	1
Prediction	Participant 3	265	1
Prediction	Participant 4	189	1
Prediction	Participant 5	201	1
Prediction	Participant 6	197	1
Prediction	Participant 7	289	1
Prediction	Participant 8	224	1
Speech-based dictation	Participant 1	178	2
Speech-based dictation	Participant 2	289	2
Speech-based dictation	Participant 3	222	2
Speech-based dictation	Participant 4	189	2
Speech-based dictation	Participant 5	245	2
Speech-based dictation	Participant 6	311	2
Speech-based dictation	Participant 7	267	2
Speech-based dictation	Participant 8	197	2

Table 4.6 Sample data for one-way ANOVA test.

Source	Sum of squares	df	Mean square	F	Significance
Between-group	7842.250	2	3921.125	2.174	0.139
Within-group	37880.375	21	1803.827		

Table 4.7 Result of the one-way ANOVA test.

used to mark the group who used the word-prediction software and the group who used the speech-based dictation software. When using SPSS, only the third and the fourth columns need to be entered.

Table 4.7 presents the summary report provided by SPSS for the one-way ANOVA analysis. The between-group's sum of squares represents the amount of variances in the data that can be explained by the use of text-entry methods. The within-group's sum of squares represents the amount of variances in the data that cannot be explained by the text-entry methods. The mean square is calculated by dividing the sum of squares by the degree of freedom. The returned F value of 2.174 is lower than the value at the 95% confidence interval, suggesting that there is no significant difference among the three conditions. The results can be reported as follows:

> *A one-way ANOVA test using task completion time as the dependent variable and group as the independent variable suggests that there is no significant difference among the three conditions ($F(2, 21) = 2.174$, n. s.).*

4.5.2 Factorial ANOVA

Factorial ANOVA is appropriate for empirical studies that adopt a between-group design and investigate two or more independent variables.

Let us continue with the data-entry evaluation study. You may also want to know whether different types of task, such as composition or transcription, have any impact on performance. In this case, you can introduce two independent variables to your study: data entry method and task type. There are three conditions for the data entry method variable: standard word-processing software, word-prediction software, and speech-based dictation software. There are two conditions for the task type variable: transcription and composition. Accordingly, the empirical study has a total of $3 \times 2 = 6$ conditions. With a between-group design (see Table 4.8), you need to recruit six groups of participants and have each group complete the text entry task under one of the six conditions.

If you use SPSS to run the analysis, the data layout for running factorial ANOVA is more complicated than that of one-way ANOVA. Table 4.9 shows part of the data table

	Standard	Prediction	Speech
Transcription	Group 1	Group 2	Group 3
Composition	Group 4	Group 5	Group 6

Table 4.8 A between-group factorial design with two independent variables.

Task type	Entry method	Participant number	Task time	Task type coding	Entry method coding
Transcription	Standard	Participant 1	245	0	0
Transcription	Standard	Participant 2	236	0	0
Transcription	Standard	Participant 3	321	0	0
...	...	...	...	...	...
Transcription	Prediction	Participant 9	246	0	1
Transcription	Prediction	Participant 10	213	0	1
Transcription	Prediction	Participant 11	265	0	1
...	...	...	...	...	...
Transcription	Speech-based dictation	Participant 17	178	0	2
Transcription	Speech-based dictation	Participant 18	289	0	2
Transcription	Speech-based dictation	Participant 19	222	0	2
...	...	...	...	...	...
Composition	Standard	Participant 25	256	1	0
Composition	Standard	Participant 26	269	1	0
Composition	Standard	Participant 27	333	1	0
...	...	...	...	...	...
Composition	Prediction	Participant 33	265	1	1
Composition	Prediction	Participant 34	232	1	1
Composition	Prediction	Participant 35	254	1	1
...	...	...	...	...	...
Composition	Speech-based dictation	Participant 41	189	1	2
Composition	Speech-based dictation	Participant 42	321	1	2
Composition	Speech-based dictation	Participant 43	202	1	2
...	...	...	...	...	...

Table 4.9 Sample data for the factorial ANOVA test.

for the factorial ANOVA analysis of the text entry study. The task completion time for all participants is listed in a single column. A separate coding column is created for each independent variable involved in the study. In Table 4.9, the column 5 shows whether a participant completed the transcription task or the composition task. Column 6 shows whether the participants completed the task using standard word-processing software, word-prediction software, or speech-based dictation software. When using SPSS to run the test, only columns 4, 5, and 6 need to be entered.

The SPSS procedure for factorial ANOVA analysis is the Univariate analysis. Table 4.10 presents the summary of the analysis results, with the first and second rows listing the information for the two independent variables respectively. The third row lists the information for the interaction effect between the two independent variables. The analysis result suggests that there is no significant difference between participants who completed the transcription tasks and those who completed the composition tasks ($F(1, 42) = 1.41$,

Source	Sum of square	Df	Mean square	F	Significance
Task type	2745.188	1	2745.188	1.410	0.242
Entry method	17564.625	2	8782.313	4.512	0.017
Task*entry	114.875	2	57.437	0.030	0.971
Error	81751.625	42	1946.467		

Table 4.10 Result of the factorial ANOVA test.

n. s.). There is significant difference among participants who used different text entry methods ($F(2, 42) = 4.51$, p < 0.05).

4.5.3 Repeated measures ANOVA

Repeated measures ANOVA is appropriate for empirical studies that adopt a within-group design. As stated in Section 4.5.2, the investigation of the text entry method and task type variables require six conditions. If you adopt a between-group design, you need to recruit six groups of participants. If 12 participants are needed for each group, you must recruit a total of 72 participants. It is quite difficult to recruit such a large sample size in many HCI studies, especially those that involve participants with impairments or specific expertise. To address that problem, you may decide to use a within-group design, in which case you recruit just one group of participants and have each participant complete the tasks under all conditions.

Repeated measures ANOVA can involve just one level or multiple levels. A one-way, repeated measures ANOVA can be used for within-group studies that investigate just one independent variable. For example, if you are interested only in the impact of the text entry method, a one-way, repeated measures ANOVA would be appropriate for the data analysis. If you use SPSS to run the test, the three data points contributed by each participant should be listed in the same row. Table 4.11 demonstrates the sample data layout for the analysis.

	Standard	Prediction	Speech
Participant 1	245	246	178
Participant 2	236	213	289
Participant 3	321	265	222
Participant 4	212	189	189
Participant 5	267	201	245
Participant 6	334	197	311
Participant 7	287	289	267
Participant 8	259	224	197

Table 4.11 Sample data for one-way repeated measures ANOVA.

Source	Sum of square	Df	Mean square	F	Significance
Entry method	7842.25	2	3921.125	2.925	0.087
Error	18767.083	14	1340.506		

Table 4.12 Result of the one way repeated measures ANOVA test.

Table 4.12 is the simplified summary table for the one-way, repeated measures ANOVA test generated by SPSS. The returned F value with degree of freedom (2, 14) is 2.925. It is below the 95% confidence interval, suggesting that there is no significant difference between the three text entry methods.

Multiple-level, repeated measures ANOVA is needed for within-group studies that investigate two or more independent variables. If you are interested in the impact of both the text entry method and the types of task, the study involves six conditions as illustrated in Table 4.13. A two-way, repeated measures ANOVA is needed to analyze the data collected under this design.

When using SPSS to run the analysis, the data need to be carefully arranged to avoid potential errors. The data points contributed by the same participant need to be listed in the same row. It is recommended that you repeat the same pattern when arranging the columns (see Table 4.14).

Table 4.15 presents the simplified summary table for the two-way, repeated measures ANOVA test. The task type has a significant impact on the time spent to complete the task ($F(1, 7) = 14.217$, $p < 0.01$). There is no significant difference among the three text entry methods ($F(2, 14) = 2.923$, n. s.). The interaction effect between the two independent variables is not significant either ($F(2, 14) = 0.759$, n. s.).

4.5.4 ANOVA for split-plot design

Sometimes you may choose a study design that involves both between-group factors and within-group factors. In the text-entry study, you may recruit two groups of participants. One group completes transcription tasks using all three data-entry methods. The other group completes composition tasks using all three data-entry methods (see Table 4.16). In this case, the type of task is a between-group factor and the text entry method is a within-group factor.

	Standard	Prediction	Speech
Transcription	Group 1	Group 1	Group 1
Composition	Group 1	Group 1	Group 1

Table 4.13 Experiment design of a two-way, repeated measures ANOVA.

	Transcription			Composition		
	Standard	Prediction	Speech	Standard	Prediction	Speech
Participant 1	245	246	178	256	265	189
Participant 2	236	213	289	269	232	321
Participant 3	321	265	222	333	254	202
Participant 4	212	189	189	246	199	198
Participant 5	267	201	245	259	194	278
Participant 6	334	197	311	357	221	341
Participant 7	287	289	267	301	302	279
Participant 8	259	224	197	278	243	229

Table 4.14 Sample data for two-way, repeated measures ANOVA test.

There are two benefits of this design as compared to a pure within-group design. First, it greatly reduces the time of the study and the participants are less likely to feel tired or bored. Secondly, it controls the learning effect to some extent. Compared to a pure between-group study, the mixed design allows you to compare the same number of conditions with a fairly small sample size.

Table 4.17 demonstrates the sample data table for the mixed design when running the test using SPSS. Note that one column needs to be added to specify the value of the between-group variable (types of task). Data points collected from the same participant need to be listed parallel to each other in the same row.

The results of a mixed design are presented in two tables in the outputs of SPSS. Table 4.18 provides the result for the between-group factor (task type). Table 4.19 provides the result for the within-group factor (text-entry method). From Table 4.18, there is no significant difference between participants who complete composition or transcription tasks ($F(1, 14) = 0.995$, n. s.). From Table 4.19, there is a significant difference among the three text-entry methods ($F(2, 28) = 5.702$, $p < 0.01$). The interaction effect between task types and text-entry methods is not significant ($F(2, 28) = 0.037$, n. s.).

Source	Sum of square	df	Mean square	F	Significance
Task type	2745.187	1	2745.187	14.217	0.007
Error (task type)	1351.646	7	193.092		
Entry method	17564.625	2	8782.313	2.923	0.087
Error (entry method)	42067.708	14	3004.836		
Task type * entry method	114.875	2	57.438	0.759	0.486
Error (task type * entry method)	1058.792	14	75.628		

Table 4.15 Result of the two-way, repeated measures ANOVA test.

	Keyboard	Prediction	Speech
Transcription	Group 1	Group 1	Group 1
Composition	Group 2	Group 2	Group 2

Table 4.16 Split-plot experiment design.

Task type	Participant number	Task type coding	Standard	Prediction	Speech
Transcription	Participant 1	0	245	246	178
Transcription	Participant 2	0	236	213	289
Transcription	Participant 3	0	321	265	222
Transcription	Participant 4	0	212	189	189
Transcription	Participant 5	0	267	201	245
Transcription	Participant 6	0	334	197	311
Transcription	Participant 7	0	287	289	267
Transcription	Participant 8	0	259	224	197
Composition	Participant 9	1	256	265	189
Composition	Participant 10	1	269	232	321
Composition	Participant 11	1	333	254	202
Composition	Participant 12	1	246	199	198
Composition	Participant 13	1	259	194	278
Composition	Participant 14	1	357	221	341
Composition	Participant 15	1	301	302	279
Composition	Participant 16	1	278	243	229

Table 4.17 Sample data for the split-plot ANOVA test.

Source	Sum of square	df	Mean square	F	Significance
Task type	2745.187	1	2745.187	0.995	0.335
Error	38625.125	14	2758.937		

Table 4.18 Results of the split-plot test for the between-group variable.

Source	Sum of square	df	Mean square	F	Significance
Entry method	17564.625	2	8782.313	5.702	0.008
Entry method * task type	114.875	2	57.437	0.037	0.963
Error (entry method)	43126.5	28	1540.232		

Table 4.19 Results of the split-plot test for the within-group variable.

4.6   Assumptions of *t* tests and *F* tests

Before running a *t* test or an *F* test, it is important to examine whether your data meet the assumptions of the two tests. If the assumptions are not met, you may make incorrect inferences from those tests. There are three assumptions, which apply to both *t* tests and *F* tests.

The errors of all data points should be independent of each other. If they are not independent of each other, the result of the *t* test can be misleading (Snedecor and Cochran, 1989). For example, in the text-entry method study, if two investigators conducted the study and one investigator consistently gave the participants more detailed instructions than the other investigator, the participants who completed the study with more detailed instructions might perform consistently better than those who received less detailed instructions. In this case, the errors of the participants who were instructed by the same investigator are no longer independent and the test results would be spurious.

The errors need to be identically distributed. This assumption is also called "homogeneity of variance." When multiple group means are compared, the *t* test or the *F* test is more accurate if the variances of the sample population are nearly equal. This assumption does not mean that we can only run *t* tests or *F* tests when the variances in the populations are exactly the same. Actually, we only become concerned when the population variances are very different or when the two sample sizes are very different (Rosenthal and Rosnow, 2008). In cases when this assumption is violated, you can use transformation techniques, such as square roots, logs, and the reciprocals of the original data (Hamilton, 1990), to make the variances in the sample nearly equal.

The errors should be normally distributed. Similar to the assumption of "homogeneity of variance," this assumption is only considered to be violated when the sample data is highly skewed. When the errors are not normally distributed, non-parametric tests should be used to analyze the data.

4.7   Identifying relationships

One of the most common objectives for HCI-related studies is to identify relationships between various factors. For example, you may want to know whether there is a relationship between age, computing experience, and target selection speed. In statistical terms, two factors are correlated if there is a significant relationship between them. The most widely used statistical method for testing correlation is the Pearson's product moment correlation coefficient test (Rosenthal and Rosnow, 2008). This test returns a correlation coefficient called Pearson's *r*. The value of Pearson's *r* ranges from −1.00 to 1.00. When the Pearson's *r* value between two variables is −1.00, it suggests a perfect negative linear relationship between the two variables. In other words, any specific increase in the scores of one variable will perfectly predict a specific amount of decrease in the scores of the other variable. When the Pearson's *r* value between two variables is 1.00, it suggests a perfect positive linear relationship between the two variables. That is, any specific increase in the scores of one variable will perfectly predict a specific amount of increase in the scores of the other variable.

	Computer experience	Standard	Prediction
Participant 1	12	245	246
Participant 2	6	236	213
Participant 3	3	321	265
Participant 4	19	212	189
Participant 5	16	267	201
Participant 6	5	334	197
Participant 7	8	287	289
Participant 8	11	259	224

Table 4.20 Sample data for correlation tests.

When the Pearson's r value is 0, it means that there is no linear relationship between the two variables. In other words, the increase or decrease in one variable does not predict any changes in the other variable.

In the data-entry method example, suppose the eight participants each complete two tasks, one using standard word-processing software, the other using word-prediction software. Table 4.20 lists the number of years' experience using computers that each participant had and the time they spent on each task. We can run three Pearson's correlation tests based on this data set to find the correlation between computer experience and task time under the standard word-processing software condition, between computer experience and task time under the prediction software condition, and between task times under the standard word-processing software condition and those under the prediction software condition.

Table 4.21 demonstrates the correlation matrix between the three variables generated by SPSS. The three variables are listed in the top row and the left column in the same order. The correlation between the same variable is always 1, as indicated by the three r values

		Experience	Timekeyboard	Timeprediction
experience	Pearson correlation	1	−0.723*	−0.468
	Significance		0.043	0.243
	N	8	8	8
timekeyboard	Pearson correlation	−0.723*	1	0.325
	Significance	0.043		0.432
	N	8	8	8
timeprediction	Pearson correlation	−0.468	0.325	1
	Significance	0.243	0.432	
	N	8	8	8

Table 4.21 Results of the correlation tests.

* Correlation is significant at the 0.05 level (two-tailed).

on the diagonal line of the table. The correlation between computer experience and the time using the standard software is significant, with r value equal to -0.723. The negative r value suggests that as computer experience increases, the time spent on completing the task using the standard software decreases. The correlation between computer experience and time spent using prediction software is not significant. The correlation between the completion times using the standard software and using the prediction software is also not significant.

In practice, the Pearson's r square is reported more often than the Pearson's r. The r square represents the proportion of the variance shared by the two variables. In other words, suppose we have two variables X and Y, the r square represents the percentage of variance in variable X that can be explained by variable Y. It also represents the percentage of variance in variable Y that can be explained by variable X. For many researchers, the r square is a more direct measure of the degree of correlation than the Pearson's r.

The most important thing to keep in mind about correlation is that it does not imply a causal relationship. That is, the fact that two variables are significantly correlated does not necessarily mean that the changes in one variable cause the changes in the other variable. In some cases, there is causal relationship between the two variables. In other cases, there is a hidden variable (also called the "intervening" variable, which is one type of confounding variable) that serves as the underlying cause of the change.

For example, in an experiment that studies how users interact with an e-commerce website, you may find a significant correlation between income and performance. More specifically, participants with higher income spend longer finding a specific item and make more errors during the navigation process. Can you claim that earning a higher income causes people to spend longer retrieving online items and make more errors? The answer is obviously no. The truth might be that people who earn a higher income tend to be older than those who earn a lower income. People in the older age group do not use computers as intensively as in the younger age group, especially when it comes to activities such as online shopping. Consequently, they spend longer and make more errors. In this case, age is the intervening variable that is hidden behind the two variables investigated in the correlation. Although income and performance are significantly correlated, there is no causal relationship between them. A correct interpretation of the relationship between the variables is listed in Figure 4.2.

Figure 4.2 Relationship between correlated variables and an intervening variable.

This example demonstrates the danger of claiming causal relationship based on significant correlation. In data analysis, it is not uncommon for researchers to conduct pairwise correlation tests on all variables involved and then claim that "variable A has a significant impact on variable B" or "the changes in variable A cause variable B to change", which can be spurious in many cases. To avoid this mistake, you should keep in mind that empirical studies should be driven by hypothesis, not data. That is, your analysis should be based on a pre-defined hypothesis, not the other way around. In the above example, you are unlikely to develop a hypothesis that "income has a significant impact on online purchasing performance" since it does not make much sense. If your study is hypothesis-driven, you will not be fooled by correlation analysis results. On the other hand, if you do not have a clearly defined hypothesis before the study, you will derive hypotheses driven by the data analysis, making it more likely that you will draw false conclusions.

4.8 Regression

Unlike correlation analysis, which allows the study of only two variables, regression analysis allows you to investigate the relationship among one dependent variable and a number of independent variables. In HCI-related studies, regression analysis is used for two main purposes: model construction and prediction. In cases of model construction, we are interested in identifying the quantitative relationship between one dependent variable and a number of independent variables. That is, we want to find a mathematical equation based on the independent variables that best explains the variances in the dependent variable. In cases of prediction, we are interested in using a number of known factors, also called "predictor variables", to predict the value of the dependent variable, also called the "criterion variable" (Share, 1984). The two objectives are closely related. You need to build a robust model in order to predict the values of the criterion factor that you are interested in.

Depending on the specific research objective, you need to choose different regression procedures to construct the model. If the objective of the study is to find the relationship between the dependent variable and the independent variables as a group, you can enter all the independent variables simultaneously. This is the most commonly adopted regression procedure (Darlington, 1968). Using this approach, you will find out the percentage of variances in the dependent variable that can be explained by the independent variables as a group. This percentage is presented in the form of R square. If the procedure returns a significant R square, it suggests that the independent variables as a group have significant impact on the dependent variable. This procedure is useful but is insufficient if you are interested in the impact of each individual independent variable.

If you want to create a model that explains the relationship between the dependent variable and each individual independent variable, the hierarchical regression procedure is appropriate. Using this procedure, you will enter the independent variables one at a time into the regression equation. The order of the entry of the independent variables is determined by the pre-defined theoretical model. The independent variables that are entered

Age	Computer experience	Target size	Target distance	Time
18	6	10	10	7
...	...	...	...	...
12	4	10	20	10
...	...	...	...	...
32	16	30	10	5
...	...	...	...	...
45	15	40	20	5
...	...	...	...	...

Table 4.22 Sample data for the regression analysis.

into the equation first usually fall into two categories. One category includes variables that are considered to be important according to previous literature or observation; in this case, you want to evaluate the overall impact of this variable on the dependent variable. The second category includes the variables (also called covariates) that are of no interest to you but have significant impact on the dependent variable; in this case, you want to exclude the variable's impact on the dependent variable before you study the variables that you are interested in. In other words, entering the covariates first allows you to remove the variances in the dependent variable that can be explained by the covariates, making it easier to identify significant relationships for the variables in which you are interested.

Suppose you conduct a user study that investigates target selection tasks using a standard mouse. One important dependent variable you are interested in is the task completion time and you want to know what factors have an impact on task completion time. There are a number of potential factors such as target size, distance, computer experience, age, etc. In order to find the relationships among the factors, you can conduct a regression analysis using task completion time as the dependent variable and the other factors as independent variables. Table 4.22 demonstrates a portion of the data from this study.

In this regression analysis, the dependent variable is the task completion time. The independent variables are age, computer experience (as represented by the number of years using computers), target size, and the distance between the current cursor location and the target. If you want to find out the relationship between task completion time and the independent variables as a group, simultaneous regression can be adopted. If you use SPSS to run the procedure, you enter task completion time into the dependent variable block and age, computer experience, target size, and distance into the same block for independent variables.

Table 4.23 shows the summary result of the simultaneous regression analysis. There is a significant relationship between task completion time and the independent variables as a group ($F(4, 59) = 41.147$, $p < 0.001$). The R Square indicates the percentage of variance in the dependent variable that can be explained by the independent variables. Age, computer

Model	R	R square	F	df1	df2	Significance
1	0.858	0.736	41.147	4	59	0.000

Table 4.23 Result for simultaneous regression procedure.

experience, target size, and navigation distance explain a total of 73.6% of the variance in task completion time. Please note that this percentage is unusually high since the data were made up by the authors.

If you are interested in the impact that each independent variable has on task completion time, the hierarchical regression procedure can be adopted. Suppose target size and navigation distance are the most important factors that you want to examine; you can enter target size in the first block for independent variables and navigation distance, age and computer experience into the subsequent blocks. Table 4.24 shows the summary result of this procedure. Since the four independent variables were entered separately, four regression models were constructed. Model 1 describes the relationship between task completion time and target size. It shows that target size explains a significant percentage of the variance (31.9%) in task completion time ($F(1, 62) = 29.054$, $p < 0.001$). The R square change column represents the additional variance in the dependent variable that can be explained by the newly entered independent variable. For example, Model 2 suggests that adding navigation distance to the regression model explains an additional 8.4% of the variance in task completion time. Navigation distance has a significant impact on task completion time ($F(1, 61) = 8.615$, $p < 0.01$).

4.9 Nonparametric statistical tests

All the analysis methods discussed in the previous sections are parametric tests that require several general assumptions. First, the data needs to be collected from a population that is normally distributed. Usually we consider this assumption as being met if the population has an approximately normal distribution. Second, the variables should be at least scaled by intervals. That is, the distance between any two adjacent data units should be equal. For

Model	R	R square	R square change	F	df1	df2	Significance
1	0.565	0.319	0.319	29.054	1	62	0.000
2	0.635	0.403	0.084	8.615	1	61	0.005
3	0.767	0.588	0.184	26.817	1	60	0.000
4	0.858	0.736	0.148	33.196	1	59	0.000

Table 4.24 Result for hierarchical regression procedure.

I am satisfied with the time it took to complete the task.

1	2	3	4	5
highly disagree	disagree	neutral	agree	highly agree

Figure 4.3 Likert scale question.

example, when examining the age variable, the distances between 1 and 2, 2 and 3, and 80 and 81 are all equal to each other. And thirdly, for tests that compare means of different groups, the variance in the data collected from different groups should be approximately equal.

In reality, you may encounter situations where one or more of the three assumptions are not met. Some studies may yield data that poorly approximates to normal distribution. Some variables may have to be measured through categorical or ranking scales that are not intervally distributed. For example, when collecting subjective satisfaction about an application, you may use a Likert scale question, as shown in Figure 4.3. In this case, the distance between the two adjacent data points can be unequal. The same problem exists for questions that require yes or no answers or ask participants to rank a number of options.

When the assumptions are not met, you need to consider the use of non-parametric analysis methods. Compared to parametric tests, non-parametric methods make fewer assumptions about the data. Although non-parametric tests are also called "assumption-free" tests, it should be noted that they are not actually free of assumptions. For example, the Chi-square test, one of the most commonly used non-parametric tests, has specific requirements on the sample size and independence of data points.

4.9.1 Chi-square test

In user studies, we frequently encounter situations where categorical data (e.g., Yes or No) are collected and we need to determine whether there is any relationship in the variables. Those data are normally presented in tables of counts (also called contingency tables) that can be as simple as a 2 by 2 table or as complicated as tables with more than 10 columns or rows. The Chi-square test is probably the most popular significance test used to analyze frequency counts (Rosenthal and Rosnow, 2008).

Let us explore the Chi-Square test through an example. Suppose you are examining the impact of age on users' preferences towards two target selection devices: a mouse and a touch screen. You recruit two groups of users. One group consists of 20 adult users who are younger than 65 and the other consists of 20 users who are 65 or older. After completing a series of target selection tasks using both the mouse and the touch screen, participants specify the type of device that they prefer to use. You can generate a contingency table (see Table 4.25) that summarizes the frequency counts of the preferred device specified by the two groups of participants.

As demonstrated in Table 4.25, more participants under the age of 65 prefer the mouse while more senior participants prefer the touch screen. In order to examine whether this

		Preferred device	
		Mouse	Touch screen
Age	<65	14	6
	≥65	4	16

Table 4.25 A 2-by-2 frequency count table.

result is merely by chance or there is indeed a relationship between age and the preference for pointing devices, you can run a Chi-square test. The test returns a Chi-square value and a p value that helps you determine whether the result is significant. The result for the data in Table 4.25 is ($X^2(1) = 10.1$, $p < 0.005$). It suggests that the probability of the difference between the rows and columns occurring by chance is less than 0.005. Using the 95% confidence interval, you reject the null hypothesis and conclude that there is a relationship between age and preferred pointing device.

The degree of freedom of a Chi-square test is calculated by the following equation:

$$\text{Degree of freedom} = (\text{Number of rows} - 1) \times (\text{Number of columns} - 1)$$

In the above example, the degree of freedom is $(2 - 1) \times (2 - 1) = 1$. If you have a contingency data with 3 rows and 3 columns, the degree of freedom of the Chi-square test will be $(3-1) \times (3-1) = 4$.

If you expand the study to three pointing devices and include children in it, you have three task conditions and three participant groups. Suppose the data collected are as demonstrated in Table 4.26. In this case, the Chi-square test result is $X^2(4) = 16.8$, $p < 0.005$, suggesting that there is significant difference among the three age groups regarding preference for the pointing devices.

As we mentioned before, non-parametric tests are not assumption free. The Chi-square test requires two assumptions that the data must satisfy in order to make a valid judgment. First, the data points in the contingency table must be independent from each other. In other words, one participant can only contribute one data point in the contingency table. To give

		Preferred device		
		Mouse	Touch screen	Stylus
Age	<18	4	9	7
	18–65	12	6	2
	≥65	4	15	1

Table 4.26 A 3 by 3 frequency count table.

a more specific example, you cannot have a participant that prefers both the mouse and the touch screen. All the numbers presented in Tables 4.25 and 4.26 have to be contributed by independent samples. Second, the Chi-square test does not work well when the sample is too small. It is generally suggested that, to acquire a robust Chi-square, the total sample size needs to be 20 or larger (Camilli and Hopkins, 1978).

4.9.2 Other non-parametric tests

Many parametric tests have corresponding non-parametric alternatives. If you are comparing data collected from two independent samples (e.g., data collected using a between-group design), the independent-samples t test can be used when the assumptions are met. When the assumptions are not met, the Mann–Whitney U test or the Wald–Wolfowitz runs test may be considered.

If you are comparing two sets of data collected from the same user group (e.g., data collected using a within-group design), the paired-samples t test is typically adopted when the assumptions are met. If not, the Wilcoxon signed ranks test can be used instead.

In cases when three or more sets of data are compared and the assumptions are not met, the Kruskal–Wallis one-way analysis of variance by ranks (an extension of the Mann–Whitney U test) may be considered when the samples are independent. When the data sets are dependent on each other, you can consider using Friedman's two-way analysis of variance test. For more information on non-parametric tests, please refer to sources, such as (Conover, 1999; Newton and Rudestam, 1999; Wasserman, 2007).

Summary

Statistical analysis is a powerful tool that helps us find interesting patterns and differences in the data as well as identify relationships between variables. Before running significance tests, the data needs to be cleaned up, coded, and appropriately organized to meet the needs of the specific statistical software package. The nature of the data collected and the design of the study determine the appropriate significance test that should be used. If the data are normally distributed and intervally scaled, parametric tests are appropriate. When the normal distribution and interval scale requirements are not met, non-parametric tests should be considered.

A number of statistical methods are available for comparing the means of multiple groups. A simple t test allows us to compare the means of two groups, with the independent-samples t test for the between-group design and the paired-samples t test for the within-group design. A one-way ANOVA test allows us to compare the means of three or more groups when a between-group design is adopted and there is only one independent variable involved. When two or more variables are involved in a between-group design, the factorial ANOVA test would be appropriate. If a study adopts a within-group design and involves more than two conditions, the repeated measures ANOVA test would be appropriate. For studies that involve both a between-group factor and a within-group factor, the split-plot ANOVA test should be considered.

Correlation analysis allows us to identify significant relationships between two variables. When three or more variables are involved and a quantitative model is needed to describe the relationships between the dependent variable and the independent variables, regression analysis can be considered. Different regression procedures should be used based on the specific goals of the study.

Non-parametric statistical tests should be used when the data do not meet the required assumptions of parametric tests. The Chi-square test is widely used to analyze frequency counts of categorical data. Although non-parametric tests have less strict requirements for the data, they are not assumption free and the data still need to be carefully examined before running any non-parametric tests.

Discussion Questions

1. What are the major steps to prepare data for statistical analysis?
2. What are the measures of central tendency?
3. What are the measures of spread?
4. What is normal distribution? Why is it important to test whether a data sample is normally distributed?
5. What statistical methods are available for comparing group means?
6. What statistical method can be used to compare two group means contributed by two independent groups?
7. What statistical method can be used to compare two group means contributed by the same group?
8. When should a one-way ANOVA test be used? Describe a research study design that fits the one-way ANOVA test.
9. When should a factorial ANOVA test be used? Describe a research study design that fits the factorial ANOVA test.
10. When should a repeated measures ANOVA test be used? Describe a research study design that fits the repeated measures ANOVA test.
11. When should a split-plot ANOVA test be used? Describe a research study design that fits the split-plot ANOVA test.
12. When should correlation analysis be used? What does Pearson's r square represent?
13. When should regression analysis be used? Describe a research study that requires regression analysis.
14. Name two regression procedures and discuss when a specific procedure should be used.
15. What are the assumptions for parametric statistical tests?
16. When should non-parametric tests be considered?
17. Is the Chi-square test "assumption free"? If not, what are the assumptions of a Chi-square test?
18. What are the alternative non-parametric tests for the independent-samples t test, the paired-samples t test, the one-way ANOVA test, and the one-way repeated measures ANOVA test?

Research Design Exercises

Read the following scenarios and select the appropriate statistical methods for each scenario.

1. Is there a difference in the time spent online per week for people who are single, people who are married without kids, and people who are married with kids?
2. Is there a difference between the weights of Americans and Canadians within the age ranges 20–40, 40–60, and above 60?
3. Is there a difference in the target selection speed between the mouse and the joystick for children who are five to nine years old? (Each child uses both the mouse and the joystick during the study.)
4. Use the distance between the current cursor location and the target location to predict the amount of time needed to select a target.
5. Is there a difference between users in the US and users in the UK when using three search engines? (Each user should use all three engines during the study.)
6. Do students in the English department have a higher GPA than students in the Education department?
7. Is there a relationship between the sales of Cheerios and the sales of milk in a grocery store?
8. Is there a difference between the blood pressures of people over 60 in the morning, at noon, and in the evening? (Each participant contributes three data points, each from a different time of the day.)

Team Exercises

Continue the design exercise that you completed in Chapter 3. Recruit 10 to 20 participants and collect a set of data. The participants can be your classmates, friends, or relatives. Complete the following steps to analyze the data:

1. Clean up the data and code it if necessary.
2. Describe the data using descriptive statistics.
3. Select the appropriate statistical method for analyzing the data.
4. Run a significance test using statistical software.
5. Write a report to discuss the findings of the significant test. Include graphical presentations to help illustrate your findings.

References

Camilli, G. and Hopkins, K. (1978) Applicability of chi-square to 2 X 2 contingency tables with small expected cell frequencies. *Psychological Bulletin*, **85**(1):163–167.

Conover, W. (1999) *Practical Nonparametric Statistics*, 3rd edition. John Wiley & Sons.

Darlington, R. (1968) Multiple regression in psychological research and practice. *Psychological Bulletin*, **69**(3):161–182.

Delwiche, L. and Slaughter, S. (2008) *The Little SAS Book: A primer*, 4th Edition. Cary NC: SAS Institute Inc.

Feng, J., Lazar, J., Kumin, L., and Ozok, A. (2008) Computer usage by children with Down syndrome: An exploratory study. Proceedings of ACM ASSETS 2008, 35–42.

Feng, J., Sears, A., and Karat, C-M. (2006) A longitudinal evaluation of hands-free speech-based navigation during dictation. *International Journal of Human–Computer Studies*, **64**(6):553–569.

Hamilton, L. (1990) *Modern Data Analysis: A first course in applied statistics.* Belmont, CA: Wadsworth Publishing Company.

Hinkle, D., Wiersma, W., and Jurs, S. (2002) *Applied Statistics for the Behavioral Sciences*, 5th edition. Houghton Mifflin Company.

Newton, R. and Rudestam, K. (1999) *Your Statistical Consultant: Answers to your data analysis questions.* Thousand Oaks, CA: Sage Publications.

Norman, D. (1988) *The Design of Everyday Things.* New York: Basic Books.

Rosenthal, R. and Rosnow, R. (2008) *Essentials of Behavioral Research: Methods and data analysis*, 3rd edition. Boston: McGraw Hill.

Share, D. (1984) Interpreting the output of multivariate analyses: A discussion of current approaches. *British Journal of Psychology*, **75**(3):349–362.

Snedecor, G. and Cochran, W. (1989) *Statistical Methods*, 8th edition. Ames: Iowa State University.

Stemler, S. (2001) An overview of content analysis. *Practical Assessment, Research & Evaluation*, **7**(17). Retrieved February 27, 2008 from http://PAREonline.net/getvn.asp?v=7&n=17.

Wasserman, L. (2007) *All of Nonparametric Statistics*. New York: Springer Science+Business Media.

Weber, R.P. (1990) *Basic Content Analysis: Quantitative analysis in the social sciences*, 2nd edition. Newbury Park, CA: Sage Publications.

5

Surveys

5.1   Introduction

Surveys are one of the most commonly used research methods, across all fields of research, not just human–computer interaction (HCI). Surveys are frequently used to describe populations, to explain behaviors, and to explore uncharted waters (Babbie, 1990). Surveys are also one of the most maligned methods. Surveys can be structured, well-tested, robust, and result in data with a high level of validity. However, surveys can be poorly done, resulting in data of questionable validity.

What is a survey? In short, it is a well-defined and well-written set of questions to which an individual is asked to respond. Surveys are typically self-administered by an individual, with no researcher present; because of this, the data collected is not as deep and in-depth as with other research methods (such as ethnography). The strength of the survey is the ability to get a large number of responses quickly from a population of users that is geographically dispersed. Surveys allow you to capture the "big picture" relatively quickly, of how individuals are interacting with a certain technology, what problems they are facing, and what actions they are taking. Surveys also allow you to make statistically accurate estimates for a population, when structured using random sampling.

One of the reasons why surveys may be maligned is that they are often used not because they are the best method but because they are the easiest method. There are a lot of bad research projects, in which professors or students quickly write a survey, do not do sufficient pilot testing of the survey questions, distribute it to first-year students, and then claim that the survey results can generalize to other populations. Unless the actual focus of the research is university students, then this research is misguided. An appropriate use of students was made in a survey study (Hanks et al., 2008), in which the goal of the research was to learn more about student perceptions of sustainable interaction design. It collected 435 surveys, from a cross-section of majors, not just computer science majors.

There are many research projects in which a survey is the ideal method; in which the survey is well-designed, strict controls are used, and the resulting data has a high level of validity. Since surveys primarily rely on users to self-administer, remember data from a previous point in time, and return the survey, without a researcher being physically present, there are a lot of background details that must receive attention for the data collected to be valid and useful.

Is a survey the same thing as a questionnaire? Well, many people do use the two terms interchangeably. Others differentiate between the "questionnaire", which is the list of questions, and the "survey", which is the complete methodological approach, including sampling, reminders, and incentives. For instance, Dillman states clearly that "the questionnaire is only one element of a well-done survey" (Dillman, 2000, p.149). While we acknowledge the difference, since the two terms are often used interchangeably, we use them interchangeably in this chapter.

5.2   Benefits and drawbacks of surveys

Surveys have many benefits and a few drawbacks. Using a survey, it is easy to collect data from a large number of people, at a relatively low cost. Surveys can be used for many different research goals. Because they allow access to a large number of people, surveys can be very useful for getting an overview, or a "snapshot", of a user population. Surveys, although they can be done using e-mail or web pages, do not require any special tools or equipment if done on paper. From a practical point of view, surveys are among the research methods most likely to get approval from an institutional review board because they are relatively unobtrusive (see Chapter 14 for more information on institutional review boards).

There are a few drawbacks to using surveys as a research method. A survey is very good at getting limited "shallow" data from a large number of people but is not very good at getting "deep," detailed data. Since surveys are typically self-administered (either on paper or by e-mail), if interesting phenomena start appearing, it is usually not possible to ask follow-up questions, or go back and change the original survey instrument to ask more detailed questions.

Another major drawback is that they can sometimes lead to biased data when the questions are related to patterns of usage, rather than clear factual phenomena. For instance, a question such as the user's age or gender is not subject to interpretation or memory. Clearly, on a given day, an individual has an age (say, 33 years old) and a gender (male). However, questions related to mood (e.g. "How were you feeling when you were using this software application?") are subject to recall bias if the event took place a significant amount of time earlier. Another example might be to ask people to recall how much money they have spent on e-commerce within a six-month period or how many times they completed a certain task. Their response might be biased and either overestimate or underestimate the amount (Andrews, Nonnecke and Preece, 2003). If data is of a factual nature and can instead be collected using the computer, it may be a preferred method compared to asking users to recall how many times they completed a task. In that type of situation, a combination of computer-collected data (see Chapter 12) and a user survey might make the most sense (see the Flickr sidebar). It is also possible that the individuals that you are most interested in studying may come from a culture that is more oriented towards oral (spoken) approaches to communication than written approaches. If that is the case, then interviews or ethnography might be a more appropriate research method than a survey.

Research
In
Practice

Researching Flickr

Nov, Naaman and Ye (2008) were interested in learning more about tagging behavior on Flickr (a website on which people can post pictures and notes ("tags") about those pictures).

The researchers were aware that it would not make sense to ask users how many tags they had created in a certain time period, as their responses were likely to be only a guess or an estimate, not an accurate count. However, there were a number of research questions that could best be investigated using a survey, so a combination of a survey and data logging, was used.

The researchers contacted a random sample of Flickr users who had posted at least five unique tags on pictures, in English (although this might have limited the sample to certain nationalities, the researchers wanted to make sure that the respondents understood the survey questions). A random sample of 1373 users was selected and e-mailed with an invitation to participate in a survey. At the end of the survey, respondents were asked to authorize the researchers to access data about tagging from their Flickr account (if the user gave permission, Flickr allowed access to data from a user's account).

Once the respondents filled out the survey and authorized access to their account data, the researchers were able to collect data on the number of tags. There were 237 valid survey responses and the average respondent had used 370 tags.

5.3   Goals and targeted users for survey research

Surveys are appropriate research methods for a number of different research goals. Since surveys are good for getting responses from large numbers of people, they are often used for collecting thousands, or even millions, of responses. The population of interest is also known as the "target population" (Couper, 2000) or, in the case of HCI research, the users. If it is a well-defined population of interest, the actual number of individuals in the population can be identified. It might be a group of 20 individuals or 300 million individuals. However, if it is a well-defined population, there will be a definitive number of people within the population and it will be clear who is and who is not part of the population (Couper, 2000).

Who are the targeted respondents for the survey? Why are these people of interest? It's rare that you can truly say "anyone can respond to the survey." Survey responses usually need to come from a specific population that is being studied – for instance, people of a certain age, users of a certain software application, people who work in a certain industry or company, or people who have a certain disability. You must first identify who they are and the limitations on this group. Do you limit responses to, say, people 30 years and older? People who are software engineers? People who have used the EndNote software application? People with a PhD in information systems? What demographic factors will decide whether a response from an individual is valid?

Once you have decided what qualities define someone who is of interest for this survey, the next question is how can you find contact information for these individuals? Is there a well-defined list or directory of who these individuals are? General sociological research tends to use phone books or e-mail lists for the general public. When a listing or set of listings is used to define the potential survey respondents, this is known as "defining the population frame" (Couper, 2000). It is important to note that phone surveys, while they used to be more frequent, are now used much less often in survey research. There are several reasons for this: due to telemarketing calls, people don't answer their phones as often; there are now several phones per individual; many people no longer have a landline phone; and government efforts in some countries have made it so that many individuals are placed on a "do not call" list because they do not want to receive many types of phone calls (Couper, 2005).

For research into human–computer interaction, the population of interest is generally a bit more focused. For instance, commonly used lists for HCI research are membership directories in professional organizations (such as SIGCHI or HFES), membership directories of organizations for people with a specific impairment (such as organizations for people with spinal cord injuries), lists of registered software users from a company, and list servers or e-mail distribution lists for people with a certain interest. All of these types of lists may provide information on postal mailing addresses, phone numbers, or e-mail addresses. There may also be monthly or annual gatherings at which surveys, or information about surveys, can be distributed (Lazar, 2006). It is also possible that an online community or social networking group might provide contact information for a group of potential respondents. However, these methods alone may not work well for a lot of HCI research.

If the population for a survey is not easily well-defined, then the goal may be either to get a response that is diverse and represents multiple sub-groups within the respondents or to get a survey response that matches what is known about the respondents (see Section 5.5).

5.4   Probabilistic sampling

The classic use of a survey in sociology is to make estimates for populations. The most accurate way to do this is by running a census, in which you attempt to get a survey response from every member of a population. Because a census is often very expensive and complex, they are not carried out very frequently. When a census is done, it tends to be sponsored by a large organization or governmental entity (see the US Census sidebar). If a population of interest is known and very small (say, up to a few thousand individuals), you might try to organize a modified census, in which everyone is invited to participate in the survey. However, it is not expected that everyone will take you up on it (Sue and Ritter, 2007).

Research In Practice

US Census—Counting Everyone

In the United States, a national census is taken every 10 years. Every person or family in the United States is supposed to fill out a paper survey. Responses to the Census Bureau are required by law, as the census count is used to distribute budgets and seats in congress and to make many governmental decisions. When a response is not received, individuals working for the Census Bureau visit residences to try and collect data from those who did not respond to the paper survey.

The Census Bureau tested a web-based form during the 2000 census. People who received the short form (five out of every six Americans) had the option of filling out the census form on the web. Each paper short form had an ID number. To ensure appropriate counting, the respondent had to enter the ID number on the web before filling out the actual survey.

Due to security and privacy concerns, the Census Bureau decided not to have a web-based form in 2010. However, the Census Bureau will use a web survey for "reinterviewing" those who have already submitted their primary census form. See www.census.gov for more information.

Instead of running a census, a structured method called "random sampling" (or "probability sampling") is often used. In a probability sample, it is known exactly how likely it is for a participant to be selected (Sue and Ritter, 2007). For instance, imagine that there are 10 000 members of a population of interest (the sampling frame). Perhaps 500 of these individuals are selected, at random, for requested inclusion in a survey study. All of these selected individuals must meet inclusion criteria (characteristics that they must have, such as being a non-smoker or male) and exclusion criteria (such as not being a native English speaker) (Sue and Ritter, 2007). See the Random Sampling sidebar for an example of random sampling of a population of users.

Research In Practice

A Study with Random Sampling

When users are required to log into networked resources (such as an e-mail system, intranet, or social networking site), random sampling methods can be used, since a detailed list of who is considered to be within the population of interest does exist. For instance, a research study focused on Beehive, an enterprise social networking system from IBM. At the time of the study, it was estimated that there were at least 38 000 registered users of the site. A total of 500 users were randomly selected and invited to participate in the research study, based on having logged into Beehive during the last week and having enough data in their account so that friend recommendations could be made. Each selected user received a personalized survey, asking them to respond to recommendations made by the social networking software. During the period of the research study, 415 out of the 500 users logged in, 258 responded to the survey, and when the data was cleaned (due to incomplete or missing responses), 230 users had submitted valid surveys (Chen et al., 2009).

It is important to note that the sample frame need not be individuals; it can also be organizations. A long-term survey has documented the level of Internet access in public libraries across the United States. See the Library Census sidebar for an example of a random sampling of organizations.

Use of Sampling Frames in Studying Internet Access

The American Library Association sponsors a survey on the implementation and use of the Internet in public libraries in the United States. The earliest survey was in 1994 and the survey has been repeated on an annual or biennial basis since then. The most recent survey was in 2009. The survey started out as a paper-based survey but, over the years, it has moved to a web-based survey.

Since the survey is used to make national population estimates, the research approach used must be highly structured and controlled. Data was recently collected using a web-based survey, with a paper letter mailed to public libraries to inform them about the existence of the survey. The letter included an identification code so that the survey data collected was identified to a specific library system or branch. The 2008 survey included 16 457 library outlets, a 6984 sample frame, and 5488 library responses (78.6%). The 2009 survey included 16 620 library outlets, a 5907 sample frame, and 4303 responses (72.8% response rate).

See www.iiicenter.org for copies of reports and (Bertot, 2009) for more information on methodological issues

5.4.1 Stratification

Sometimes a sample can be stratified. A stratified sample is when you ensure that you have an appropriate number of responses from each subset of your user population (Babbie, 1990). A simple example is a random sample of university students. A random sample of university students is likely to have freshmen, sophomores, juniors, and seniors represented. However, a stratified random sample would have an equal number from each of those subsets. For instance, a random sample with stratification was used in a study of how people use technology to keep in touch after they move (see the Stratification sidebar for more information).

Stratification

Shklovski, Kraut and Cummings (2008) were interested in studying how technology influences the maintaining of friendships after a residential move. A sample of 6000 individuals was chosen from the US Postal Service's Change of Address Database.

These were all individuals who had moved in the previous few months. The sample was stratified so that 1/3 of those selected had local moves, of 50 miles or less, while the other 2/3 selected had longer-distance moves, of 50 miles or more. This stratification was done because the researchers were interested in studying long-distance moves. However, it is implied in their write-up that a majority of moves are local moves. Of the 6000 people selected from the database, 1779 (32%) responded to the survey. Two follow-up surveys were sent to the 1779 individuals who responded to the first survey. The second survey received 1156 responses, and a third survey received 910 responses. This research shows a successful use of random sampling with stratification.

5.4.2 Response size

If it is feasible for random sampling to be used in the research, this is preferable. However, the next question that comes up most often is, "how many responses do I need?" The statistics on this are not as clear as in, say, statistics in experimental design, where there is a clear threshold of significance or non-significance. In probabilistic sampling, the number of responses required depends on what level of confidence and margin of error are considered acceptable. For instance, for a simple random sample, a sample size of 384 results in a 95% confidence level with a ±5% margin of error (Sue and Ritter, 2007). That means that, "if the survey were conducted 100 times, the true percentage would be within 5 percentage points of the sample percentage in about 95 of the 100 surveys" (Sue and Ritter, 2007, p. 30). To change the margin of error to ±4%, 600 responses are needed; for ±3% margin of error, 1067 responses are needed. The margin of error is only valid using a true random sample. And the actual size of the population sampled is irrelevant, since there is an automatic assumption that all populations being sampled are very large. (Babbie, 2009). If the sample is relatively large compared to the population size (more than 5 or 10%), then the margin of error may be smaller, and can be calculated using the "finite population correction," which is beyond the scope of this book. Another way to look at this, is that, in a small population size, a smaller sample may be needed. See (Sue and Ritter, 2007), (Babbie, 2009) or (Dillman, 2000) for more information.

5.4.3 Errors

Random sampling seems like an ideal method but it is subject to a number of potential errors and biases. Careful attention to these potential problems can increase the accuracy and validity of the research findings. For instance, sampling error occurs when there aren't enough responses from those surveyed to make accurate population estimates (e.g. if 10 000 individuals are surveyed but only 100 responses are received).

Coverage error occurs when not all members of the population of interest have an equal chance of being selected for the survey (for instance, if you use e-mail lists or phone lists to create the sample and not all potential respondents are on those e-mail or phone lists) (Couper, 2000). Measurement error occurs when survey questions are poorly worded or biased, leading to data of questionable quality.

Non-response error occurs when there are major differences (in demographics, such as age or gender) between the people who responded to a survey and the people who were sampled (e.g. if the sampling frame is split evenly by gender, but 90% of responses are from males) (Dillman, 2000).

5.5 Non-probabilistic sampling

The assumption in Section 5.4 is that the goal is to achieve a population estimate. In human–computer interaction research, population estimates are often not the goal. And so, users are more often recruited in a non-probabilistic manner.

Often, there isn't a clear, well-defined population of potential respondents. There isn't a list or a central repository of people that meet a certain qualification and could be respondents. That may just be the nature of the population. So strict random sampling cannot be done. However, valid data can still be collected through non-probability-based samples.

It is important to note that different academic communities have different standards in how they apply sampling techniques. For instance, there are many people in the fields of social science and statistics who believe that without strict random sampling, no survey data is valid (Couper, 2000; Sue and Ritter, 2007). On the other hand, the HCI community has a long history of using surveys, in many different ways, without random sampling, and this is considered valid and acceptable. Part of this difference may stem from the nature of research in different communities. In some research communities, large national and international data sets are collected using rigorous, structured sampling methodologies. The general social survey in the United States (www.norc.org/GSS+Website) and the National Centre for Social Research in the UK (www.natcen.ac.uk) are examples in the fields of sociology and public policy. Researchers can take these high-quality, probability-sampled data sets and perform analyses on the many variables in them.

This is *not* the model of research used in human–computer interaction. In HCI, researchers must, typically, collect the data themselves. No large, well-structured data sets exist. The HCI researcher must go out, find users to take part in their research, and collect the data, as well as analyze the data. Because of this difference, both probability samples and non-probability samples, are considered valid in HCI research. There are a number of techniques for ensuring validity in non-probability based samples.

5.5.1 Demographic data

One way of determining the validity of survey responses is to ask respondents for a fair amount of demographic data. The goal should be to use the demographic data to ensure that either the responses represent a diverse, cross-section of respondents or the responses are somewhat representative of already-established, baseline data (if any exists). For instance, even basic demographic data on age, gender, education, or computer usage can help establish the validity of survey responses when respondents are self-selected (Lazar and Preece, 2001). While this is not the same as a population estimate or random sampling, it is better than no check on the validity of survey responses.

5.5.2   Oversampling

When there isn't a well-defined list of users and strict random sampling is not possible, then the number of responses becomes increasingly important. For instance, in a non-probabilistic sample, 20 survey responses may not be sufficient. Even with demographic data present, there may just be too many biases present, relating to which users have responded. However, when the survey response reaches a certain number that is considered large in proportion to the estimated or perceived population size, this can help establish some informal validity. This is known as *oversampling*. While not all researchers agree that oversampling increases validity (Couper, 2000), simply having a large response can reduce the likelihood of excluding any segment of the population (Andrews, Nonnecke and Preece, 2003). However, the key is that the response must be large in the context of the population of interest. For instance, 500 survey responses would be a large number if the estimated total population of interest is around 5000 individuals. However, 500 survey responses would not considered large if the population of interest is a country, such as Australia or France. One researcher suggests that 30 responses should be considered a baseline minimum number of responses for any type of survey research (Sue and Ritter, 2007). Fogg *et al.* used both demographic data and oversampling to learn more about web credibility in 2001 (see Demographic Data and Oversampling sidebar).

Research
In
Practice

Demographic Data and Oversampling

Fogg *et al.* (2001) wanted to learn more about how different elements of design on a website impact on the user's perception of credibility. To do this, they recruited survey responses through charitable groups in the United States and a news media organization in Finland. They received over 1400 survey responses in one week. After discarding a number of responses due to inadequate information provided or responses that placed the respondent outside of the population frame, 1410 survey responses were considered valid.

The survey collected information on age, gender, country, education level, income, years on the Internet, average number of hours spent online per week, and average number of purchases online. The demographic information helped to confirm that the responses to the survey were, indeed, representative of the diversity of web users. The high number of responses helped to improve the validity of the study.

5.5.3 Random sampling of usage, not users

Another approach to sampling is the random sampling of usage, not users (Lazar and Preece, 2001). For instance, it may be that every 10th time a web page is loaded, the user is asked to fill out a survey. Often, this survey appears in a pop-up window. This sampling technique is also known as intercept sampling (Sue and Ritter, 2007). While this gets an accurate picture of usage, a subset of users (those who use the web page often) is over-represented and those who don't view the web page often are under-represented.

5.5.4 Self-selected surveys

Similarly, in a "self-selected" survey, there is a link on a web page every time that it is loaded and everyone visiting the website is invited to fill out the survey. So, it's less about a certain group of people being recruited to participate and more about inviting everyone to participate. (Yes, it can be a bit fuzzy sometimes in non-probabilistic surveys as to whether responses are invited or self-selected.)

If a self-selected survey is used, then both the number of survey responses and the demographic data on respondents become increasingly important in establishing the validity of the survey data. One of the earliest web-based survey studies came from the Georgia Institute of Technology. The entire population of web users was invited to participate. Banner ads about the survey, inviting people to participate, were placed on search engines, news sites, general advertising networks, mailing lists and newsgroups, and also in the popular press. Everyone was invited to participate in the surveys, which took place semi-annually from 1994 to 1998. In the final survey, 5022 people responded. See (Pitkow and Kehoe, 1996) and http://www.cc.gatech.edu/gvu/user_surveys/ for more information.

Finally, it is important to note that self-selected, non-probability-based surveys may be the most natural data collection method for investigating new user populations or new phenomena of usage. For instance, if no data exists about a certain user population or usage pattern, then a self-selected survey of users, asking about usage, might make the most sense. The population of interest can be informed about the survey by posting a message about the survey to a newsgroup, list server, chat room, or bulletin board where members of the population are known to congregate (Schmidt, 1997).

5.5.5 Uninvestigated populations

Surprisingly, there are user groups that have still not been investigated in much detail. For instance, people with certain types of cognitive impairments have yet to receive much attention, if any, in the HCI research literature. For these populations where no baseline data exists, not enough is already known to develop hypotheses, experimental design, or well-structured time diaries. Population estimates may exist on how many people are living with a certain impairment within a certain country, however, no data exists on how many individuals with a certain impairment are using computer technology. No baseline data exists, no estimate on the population size exists, no previous research exists, so all of the issues related to random sampling are really not appropriate. The goal of such a survey would be to establish the baseline data. In a case like this, the goal should be to simply get as large a response as possible. See the Computer Usage Patterns of People with Down Syndrome sidebar to see an example of where surveys were used to explore how young adults with Down Syndrome use computer technology.

Computer Usage Patterns of People with Down Syndrome

A search of multiple digital libraries and databases resulted in the determination that no research studies existed that examined how young adults with Down Syndrome use computers and the Internet. In fact, no published research studies existed in 2005 that specifically examined computer usage in individuals of any age with Down Syndrome.

Only one design case study, where a website was being built to assist children with Down syndrome in learning about computers, was known to exist and be moving towards publication (Kirijian, Myers and Charland, 2007). A large-scale survey was needed, simply to gather baseline data about this user population. A 56-question survey was developed, covering demographic information, usage patterns, interaction techniques, and use of other electronic devices. Because it could be challenging to get accurate survey data from young adults with Down Syndrome, it was decided that parents of children with Down Syndrome would be recruited to respond to the survey.

The survey was placed on the web using surveymonkey (a web-based tool), and responses were solicited through two organizations in the United States: the National Down Syndrome Congress and the National Down Syndrome Society. A total of 561 surveys were collected, which provides a rich foundation of data on which other studies and research projects can be built (Feng et al., 2008).

In communities where limited research has been done in the past, it may be challenging to find and recruit individuals to take part in the survey. There may be a lack of knowledge on the part of researchers, individuals may be reluctant to participate, or there might even be existing distrust.

Sometimes, snowball sampling can assist with getting survey responses. Snowball sampling is when individuals may not only respond to a survey, but also recruit someone else (usually a friend or colleague) to take part in the survey (Sue and Ritter, 2007). In a way, the role of contacting and recruiting participants shifts from the researchers to the survey respondents themselves. This method may work well when the population of interest is very small and hard to "break into," and individuals in the population of interest may know each other well. An outside researcher, coming into a community of individuals may not have a high level of credibility, but another community member suggesting participation in a survey may come with a high level of credibility.

5.6 Developing survey questions

Once the goal and strategy for using a survey has been decided upon, the next step is to develop a survey tool. As mentioned earlier, some describe the survey tool itself as a "questionnaire". The main challenge is to develop well-written, non-biased questions. The questions in a survey can often lead to answers that do not represent what the researchers were actually asking. Since a majority of surveys are self-administered, they must be easy enough to understand that users can fill them out by themselves. In a limited number of situations, an interviewer may ask survey questions. For more information on interviews, read Chapter 8.

It is important to understand that there are two different structures in a survey: the structure of single questions and the structure of the entire survey. More information on overall survey structure is presented in Section 5.7. Most survey questions can be structured in one of three ways: as open-ended questions, closed-ended questions with ordered response categories, or closed-ended questions with unordered response categories (Dillman, 2000).

5.6.1 Open-ended questions

Open-ended questions are useful in getting a better understanding of phenomena, because they give respondents complete flexibility in their answers. However, aside from the obvious drawback of more complex data analysis, open-ended questions must be carefully worded. Otherwise, they may lead to responses that either don't really help researchers address the root question, or responses that simply don't provide enough information. Consider the following open-ended question:

Why did you stop using the Banjee Software product?

This open-ended question provides no information about the possible causes; instead it requires the respondent to think deeply about what the causes might be (Dillman, 2000). The respondent may be too busy to come up with a complete response or may simply say something like "I didn't like the software." It is a very broad question. More specific questions might be:

How did you feel about the usability (ease of use) of the Banjee software?
Did the Banjee software allow you to complete the tasks that you wanted to complete?

These questions address more specific topics: ease of use and task completion. The respondents can't simply answer "I didn't like it," although they could just answer "yes" to the second question.

What is your impression of using the website for www.veggieland.com?
Please circle one number
Frustrating   Satisfying
1   2   3   4   5   6   7   8   9
(question from the QUIS, see http://www.lap.umd.edu/quis/)

Figure 5.1 A closed-ended question with an ordered response. (Source: QUIS, see http://www.lap.umd.edu/quis/).

5.6.2   Closed-ended questions

There are two types of closed-ended questions. One type has ordered response categories, and other type does not. An ordered response is when a number of choices can be given, which have some logical order (Dillman, 2000). For instance, using a scale such as "excellent to poor" or "strongly agree to strongly disagree" would be an ordered response. Likert scale questions, which often take the form of a scale of 1 to 5, 7, or 9, ask users to note where they fall on a scale of "strongly agree" to "strongly disagree." Typically, closed-ended questions with an ordered response request respondents to choose only one item (see Figure 5.1).

Closed-ended questions with an unordered response allow for choices that do not have a logical order. For instance, asking about types of software applications, hardware items, user tasks, or even simple demographic information such as gender or type of internet connection are unordered, but closed-ended questions. Figure 5.2 is an example of a closed-ended, unordered question.

With unordered, closed-ended questions, you can often ask respondents to select more than one choice. On paper, this is not a challenge. However, it is important to note that, if you are creating an online survey, different interface widgets must be used. Option buttons only allow one choice, whereas checkboxes allow for many choices. Figure 5.3 is an example of a question that allows multiple responses.

Which application do you use most often for text editing? (please select
only one)
__ MS-Word
__ WordPerfect
__ Notepad
__ Emacs
__ TextEdit
__ Pico

Figure 5.2 A closed-ended question with an unordered response (single selection).

> When using my computer on a daily basis, I use the following input devices
> or methods (Select as many as apply)
> __ Keyboard
> __ Mouse
> __ Trackball
> __ Touchpad
> __Voice recognition

Figure 5.3 A closed-ended question with an unordered response (multiple selection).

5.6.3   Common problems with survey questions

It is important to note that there are a number of common problems with survey questions. Researchers should carefully examine their questions to determine if any of these problems are present in their survey questions (Babbie, 1990):

- A "double-barreled question" asks two separate, and possibly related, questions. These questions need to be separated.
- The use of negative words in questions (e.g. "Do you agree that the e-mail software is not easy to use?") can cause confusion for the respondents.
- Biased wording in questions (such as starting a sentence with "Don't you agree that . . .") can lead to biased responses. If a question begins by identifying the position of a well-respected person or organization (e.g. "Oprah Winfrey [or David Beckham] takes the view that . . ."), this may also lead to a biased response.
- "Hot-button" words, such as "liberal", "conservative", "abortion", and "terrorism", can lead to biased responses.

5.7   Overall survey structure

Well-written questions are important, but so is the overall structure of the survey instrument. The questions don't exist in a vacuum, rather, they are part of an overall survey structure. For instance, a survey, in any format, must begin with instructions. These instructions must make clear how the respondent is to interact with the survey (Babbie, 1990). For instance, in a paper survey, are there ovals or checkboxes? Should a checkmark be placed in them, should an X be placed in the box, or should the box be filled in? Should items be circled? Are respondents to fill out all of the questions? These directions must be made clear. In addition, it is sometimes useful to put in a description, as a reminder, of who should be filling out the survey (for instance, you must be aged 65 years or older). If a survey is separated into multiple sections, then those divisions, and who should fill those different portions, must be made clear. Each section should be given an appropriate heading. Just as it is important to provide navigation on a website, a survey should provide navigation to the reader, whether the survey is paper, e-mail, or web-based. The user (respondent) needs to know where on the survey they should go, in what order. Sometimes, it is also helpful to provide contact information if the respondent has any questions (such as a telephone number or e-mail address). If the survey is a web-based survey, links are often provided directly in the survey, so that the respondent can click on the link and get a pop-up window with more detailed information. While pop-up windows are generally not good interface design, they work very well for giving short bits of information to users while they are in the process of responding to a survey.

If the survey is a paper survey, it is important to make sure that there is enough white space so that the respondent does not feel overwhelmed by the amount of information on a page (Babbie, 1990). Obviously, a balance needs to be struck. While respondents may worry if they see a 30-page survey, on the other hand, stuffing all of the survey questions onto two pages may prove to be problematic. Only white paper should be used, and a large enough font, in standard text, should be used (Dillman, 2000). Booklet printing (with two staples in the middle of the booklet) is preferred to one staple in the upper left hand corner, but that is still preferred to any type of unusual folding or paper shapes that users may have trouble understanding (Dillman, 2000). In addition, do not use abbreviations to cut down on the amount of space needed, as they may cause confusion among respondents (Babbie, 1990).

Survey questions generally may be asked in any order which makes sense in the context of the research. However, it is important to keep in mind that questions relating to a similar topic or idea should be grouped together (Dillman, 2000). This tends to lower the cognitive load on respondents and allows them to think more deeply about the topic, rather than "switching gear" after every question. Because some questions may require knowledge or details presented in other survey questions, it is generally hard to randomize the order of questions (Babbie, 1990). Rather, provide interesting questions at the beginning of the survey, to help motivate people to read the survey and complete it. Generally, it is a good idea to leave demographic questions until the end of the survey, as these are the least interesting (Babbie, 1990). Also, if there are any sensitive or potentially objectionable questions (relating to income, health, or similar), then they should be placed near the end, once the respondent has already become interested in the survey (Dillman, 2000). Note that survey length is an important consideration. While you want to include as many questions as possible on the survey, at some point, a survey becomes too long for many people to complete, and very long surveys can lead to very low response rates. Try to ask all of the questions that you need, but be reasonable when it comes to the amount of time that individuals need to set aside to respond to the survey.

The easiest type of survey is when all respondents should answer all questions. But frequently some questions do not apply to all respondents. For instance, imagine that you are running a survey to learn more about the e-mail usage habits of users over the age of 65. You may ask if they use Microsoft Outlook 2007. If the answer is "yes", you may

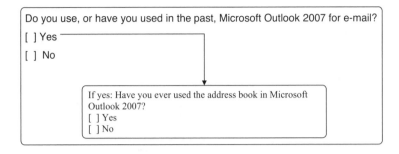

Figure 5.4 A contingent question on a paper survey.

want them to answer a set of additional questions; if the answer is "no", you want them to skip to the next set of questions. This is sometimes called a "contingent question" (Babbie, 1990) because the respondent's need to respond to the second question is contingent on their response to the first question. This can be cause for confusion: if the directions and layout are not clear enough, a respondent who does not use Outlook 2007 may start reading questions relating to Outlook 2007 usage and be unsure of how to respond. On a paper survey, there are a number of ways to manage this. Babbie suggests using an indented box, with an arrow coming from the original question (see Figure 5.4). For a web-based survey, it may be possible either to provide a hyperlink to the next section (e.g. "If you answered no, please click here to move on to the next section"), or to automatically make a section of the survey "disappear", so that the next question presented is the one relevant to the respondent. This is similar to the "expand and collapse" menus that exist on many web pages. On a further note, the first question of the entire survey should always be a question that applies to everybody (Dillman, 2000).

5.8 Existing surveys

It is important to note that there are many existing surveys that have already been tested and validated in the research literature in human–computer interaction. If a survey tool has already been developed, there is no need to create one from scratch.

For most research purposes, there will be a need to create a new survey tool. However, for tasks such as usability testing and evaluation, there are already a number of existing survey tools. Usually, these tools can be modified in minimal ways. For instance, one section of the survey tool can often be used independently of others. See Table 5.1 for a list of established survey tools.

For more information about existing surveys, the reader is encouraged to visit http://oldwww.acm.org/perlman/question.html or http://www.hcirn.com/atoz/atozu/usaques.php.

Tool	Citations
Computer System Usability Questionnaire (CSUQ)	Lewis (1995)
Interface Consistency Testing Questionnaire (ICTQ)	Ozok and Salvendy (2001)
Purdue Usability Testing Questionnaire (PUTQ)	Lin, Choong and Salvendy (1997)
Questionnaire for User Interaction Satisfaction (QUIS)	Chin, Diehl and Norman (1988) Slaughter, Harper and Norman (1994) http://www.lap.umd.edu/quis/
Software Usability Measurement Inventory (SUMI)	http://www.ucc.ie/hfrg/questionnaires/sumi/
Website Analysis and MeasureMent Inventory (WAMMI)	http://www.ucc.ie/hfrg/questionnaires/wammi/

Table 5.1 Survey tools in HCI.

5.9 Paper or online surveys?

An important question is to determine if you want to distribute surveys using paper, the web, e-mail, or a combination of the three. The traditional method is to use paper-based surveys. A benefit of this is that a majority of individuals can use a paper survey, however people who are blind, visually impaired, or have a reading impairment will not be able to use a paper survey (see Chapter 15 for more information on doing research with computer users with impairments). If you only use an electronic survey (web or e-mail), you are automatically cutting out any potential respondents who do not have access to a computer and a network, which may include users who are economically disadvantaged, or ethnic or racial groups that have lower base rates of computer access (Andrews, Nonnecke and Preece, 2003). In addition, if you are creating an electronic survey, you must make sure that the interface is usable by a wide range of individuals who may respond to your survey (such as users with impairments and older users).

In reality, the relative strengths and weaknesses of online and paper surveys generally do not influence which one is used. The greatest influence on which method (or combination) is used is how the researchers have best access to the user population of interest. In some cases, the best access is to visit individuals at a weekly meeting where paper surveys can be passed out. In other situations, if a list of postal mailing addresses exists for potential respondents, paper surveys can be mailed. If a list of e-mail addresses exists, e-mailed surveys may be best. If it's known that nearly all potential respondents have web access (Sue and Ritter, 2007) or if there is a website that attracts potential respondents, then a web-based survey is best!

Sometimes, a combination of paper and web-based surveys can be used to make sure that all portions of a target population are reached (Lazar, Tsao and Preece, 1999). It is also sometimes helpful to offer respondents a choice between a paper and an electronic version of the survey, as some recent research suggests that some people may simply prefer filling out surveys on paper (Schonlau, Asch and Du, 2003). These mixed-model designs, in which paper, e-mail, and web-based versions of a survey instrument are used together, can help improve the response rate, but caution must be taken to make sure that no biases are introduced into the data collection process (from three survey instruments that, in fact, do have minor differences) (Couper, 2005).Obviously, paper surveys must be used to study questions such as "why don't people go online?" and other research questions related to non-use of technology (Lazar and Preece, 2001). Another potential complication is that you may need to offer your survey in multiple languages. In countries where there are multiple official languages, this may be a legal requirement. In other cases, you may be interested in studying a group of computer users who do not share the same primary language. If so, you need to ensure that the surveys in two or three different languages are in fact asking the same questions and that there are no mistranslations.

There are benefits to electronic (both e-mail and web-based) surveys. Copying costs, mailing and related postage costs can be eliminated with electronic surveys. While the set-up costs may be high for a web-based survey, as the number of responses increases, web-based surveys may be the most cost-effective in terms of time and expenses (Sue and Ritter, 2007). In many cases, web-based surveys and even e-mailed surveys can automatically have responses saved in a spreadsheet or database, eliminating the need for time-consuming data entry and eliminating many data-entry errors (Lazar and Preece, 2001). While response rates in online surveys may sometime be lower, the speed of response is certainly higher (Sue and Ritter, 2007).

The question is often asked if the responses from electronic surveys are as trustworthy or valid as paper surveys. There is no evidence to suggest that people are more dishonest in online surveys than in paper surveys, as people can lie easily in both. However, there is evidence that people, when delivering bad news, are more honest in online communication than face to face (Sussman and Sproull, 1999). There is also evidence that people, when they care about a topic, are likely to be very honest. If the surveys can be submitted anonymously, this may also lead to an increased level of self-disclosure (McKenna and Bargh, 2000; Spears and Lea, 1994). Therefore, web-based surveys can sometimes be superior to e-mailed surveys (which clearly identify the respondent) for dealing with sensitive information (Sue and Ritter, 2007). In addition, respondents to self-administered surveys tend to provide more honest answers to sensitive questions than in interviews (Couper, 2005). Overall, the likelihood that someone will lie in an electronic survey is the same as the likelihood that someone will lie in a paper-based survey.

In traditional paper-based surveys, individuals may have to sign a "informed consent form" (also known as an institutional review board (IRB) form), acknowledging that they are aware that they are taking part in a research project and giving their consent. There is a question as to how individuals can give informed consent when they respond to a survey online. For more information on informed consent online, please see Chapter 14.

5.10   Testing the survey tool

After a survey tool is developed, it is very important to pre-test it, to help ensure that the questions are clear and unambiguous. There are really two separate types of survey testing: one type of testing focuses on the questions themselves. The other type of testing focuses on the interface of the survey. While the interface features primarily refer to web-based or e-mailed surveys, there are also interface features on paper-based surveys. For instance, on a paper survey, there should be an examination of issues such as the font face and type size, spacing, use of grids, and cover designs (Dillman, 2000). While these are theoretically different testing sessions for the questions and for the layout, in reality, they take place at the same time. See Chapter 10 for more information on usability testing of a computer interface.

Dillman (2000) suggests a three-stage process of pre-testing a survey, while noting that it is rarely done thoroughly. The three stages are:

1. review of survey tool by knowledgeable colleagues and analysts;
2. interviews with potential respondents to evaluate cognitive and motivational qualities in survey tool;
3. pilot study of both survey tool and implementation procedures.

The idea of this three-stage process is that you start first with people who are knowledgeable, but are not potential respondents. (Note that you start first with expert non-respondents, just as in usability testing (Chapter 10)). You begin with expert evaluations before involving any representative users. You then ask a few potential respondents about the clarity and motivation of the questions in the survey. Finally, you do a pilot study where actual respondents complete an entire survey and the researchers can note any flaws. While this three-stage process is ideal, in reality, most research in HCI involves either a few colleagues examining the survey tool or a few users reading over the survey tool and giving some feedback.

These efforts are aimed at determining the validity of the survey, that is, does the survey measure what it is claiming to measure? (Babbie, 1990; Ozok, 2007). When a few people respond to the survey in the pilot testing (Dillman's stage three), there are usually a few common problems to keep an eye out for. For instance, questions that were not answered; questions where multiple answers were given (when only one was expected); and questions where respondents filled out "other" (Babbie, 1990). All of these are signs that a question might need to be re-worded. In addition, respondents in the pilot testing should be encouraged to give direct feedback on the questions (Babbie, 1990).

A different type of evaluation can take place at a later time. When a survey instrument has been used to collect data multiple times, then the reliability of that survey can be established. Reliability is the determination of whether a survey measures constructs consistently across time (Babbie, 1990; Ozok, 2007). Methods for measuring the internal reliability of questions, such as having the same question asked multiple times in a different way, can be used. The Cronbach's Alpha Coefficient is often used in that situation (Ozok, 2007).

Another approach to evaluating survey questions after data is collected from multiple people, especially if the survey has a large number of questions, is *exploratory factor analysis*. In factor analysis, statistical software creates an artificial dimension that would correlate highly with a set of chosen survey question data (Babbie, 1990). Researchers then determine how important the specific survey question is, based on the factor loading, which is the correlation level between the data item and the artificial dimension. Survey items with high factor loadings have high correlation, and are likely to be more predictive, and therefore, more relevant (Babbie, 1990). Exploratory factor analysis can help to cut down the number of questions in a survey (Ozok and Salvendy, 2001). For instance, in the research project described in the Flickr sidebar, the survey questions were validated using an exploratory factor analysis of 193 users. "Items showing factor loading higher than 0.6 and cross-loadings lower than 0.4 were retained, and others were dropped" (Nov *et al.* 2008, p. 1098).

5.11 Response rate

A good sampling method and a well-written survey tool are important. However, those steps alone do not guarantee a sufficient number of responses to a survey. One of the main challenges of survey research is how to ensure a sufficient response rate. Other research methods tend to have fewer users taking part and higher incentives for taking part, than in survey research. For instance, If 70 people take part in an experimental research study, they may each be paid $100 for their participation. Obviously, this is not feasible when thousands of individuals are responding to a survey. Also, surveys are generally self-administered, regardless of whether they are paper, e-mail or web-based. Individuals often need to remember where the survey is located (the URL or where they have put the paper) and complete it in a timely manner, with the caveat being that they may not receive any major incentive for doing so. So it is important to motivate people to respond to surveys.

There are a number of tried and tested ways to increase the response rate to a survey. For all types of survey (paper, e-mail, web-based), there should be some type of introductory letter, letting individuals know that they have been selected for inclusion in a survey study. The letter should tell people: who is sponsoring the research study, why it's important, what the expected timeframe is, and hopefully establish some authority or credibility. This is not the same thing as an informed consent form, this is all about establishing the importance and credibility of the survey study, to motivate people to respond. For instance, if an individual that is a trusted authority within the community of individuals helps to introduce the survey, this may help increase the response rate. Or if the survey comes from a well-respected government source, this should be clearly identified to help establish authority.

Aside from establishing the credibility of a survey, another method for increasing the response rate is to increase the ease in returning a survey. For instance, a paper survey should be accompanied by a self-addressed return envelope with postage included.

A multi-step contact process tends to increase the response rate. Researchers should make multiple contacts with respondents. For instance, (Dillman, 2000) suggests the following process for paper surveys, but it could easily be modified for e-mail or web-based surveys:

1. Send a pre-contact letter (usually with information from a trusted authority, as stated above), before the actual mailing.
2. Send a postal mailing, which includes the actual survey.
3. Send a thank you postcard (which thanks people for their time and serves as a reminder).
4. Send a replacement survey to non-respondents 2–4 weeks after the original one was sent.
5. Make a final contact using a different mode. If the original survey was sent using postal mail, then maybe a phone call or e-mail should be used. If the survey was electronic, maybe a postal letter or phone call should be used. The idea is to have a different delivery method for the final contact that gets the attention of the respondent.

Depending on how the researchers have access to the potential respondents, different methods of postal mail, e-mail, phone calls, or even instant messaging, may be interchanged.

A common question, mentioned earlier in the chapter, is the question "How many survey responses are enough?" This is not easy to answer, as it has to do with a number of different issues: What is the goal of the survey? What type of survey? What sampling method has been used? What level of confidence and margin of error is considered acceptable? The reader is referred to Sections 5.4 and 5.5 for more information on an acceptable response.

5.12   Data analysis

There are several ways to analyze survey data. The analysis chosen will depend, in large part, on:

- whether it was a probabilistic or non-probabilistic survey;
- how many responses were received;
- whether a majority of questions were open-ended or closed-ended questions.

Generally, the quantitative and qualitative data is separated for analysis. The data is "cleaned," meaning that the researchers look through and make sure that each survey response is valid, and that none of the responses are either repeats (where the same person submitted more than one response), incomplete (where most questions weren't answered), or invalid (due to a respondent not meeting the qualifications). The quantitative data is ready to analyze, whereas the qualitative data must first be coded (see Chapter 11 for more information on content analysis).

Often, the goal of quantitative data analysis is simply to have a set of "descriptive statistics" that simply describe the data collected in a manageable way (Babbie, 1990). No one but the researchers will read through every survey response so the descriptive statistics are simply a short, high-level summary of the data. Most often, descriptive statistics involve percentages, ratios, or matrices. Inferential statistics involve a higher level of understanding of the data, by understanding the relationships between variables and how they impact each other. For more information on statistical analysis, read Chapter 4.

Summary

Surveys are a very powerful tool for collecting data from many individuals. However, for survey data to be valid, there must be a number of different steps that take place. Survey questions must be well-worded and the survey design should make it easy for respondents to understand and use. Appropriate sampling methods, even if they are non-probabilistic, must be used to ensure a representative response. There must be a sufficient number of responses for the data to be considered valid. The key is to use surveys when they are appropriate to the research questions. However, other methods can also be useful in conjunction with surveys, such as focus groups, interviews, or time diaries.

Discussion Questions

1. Is a survey the same thing as a questionnaire? If not, how are they different?
2. What is the difference between the target population and the population frame?
3. Why are censuses done rarely? What is often used instead when population estimates need to be made?
4. What is the defining characteristic of a probability sample?
5. What is a stratified random sample? How is it different from a traditional random sample?
6. What is one of the major reasons that non-probabilistic sampling is considered appropriate in human–computer interaction research but not in other research communities?
7. What is oversampling and why might it help improve validity of the research?
8. What is the difference between an open-ended and a closed-ended question?
9. Why might you want to use existing survey questions, when possible?
10. What is a double-barreled question and why is it not a good idea?
11. What is a contingent question and how might you deal with one in a survey layout?
12. What are two methods for testing a survey tool?

Research Design Exercise

Consider that you want to learn more about how people use USB portable storage, as compared to network-based storage (in web-based e-mail accounts) or storage on their computer hard drives. More specifically, you want to learn how children, aged 10–18, and older users, aged 65–85, use these storage devices. You want to learn more about which devices individuals prefer and in what situations they use them. Would you use probabilistic or non-probabilistic sampling? What questions might you ask? Come up with at least five questions. How would you structure the survey? Would you use contingent questions? How would you pre-test the survey? How would you ensure that you receive a sufficient number of responses?

References

Andrews, D., Nonnecke, B., and Preece, J. (2003) Electronic survey methodology: A case study in reaching hard to involve Internet users. *International Journal of Human–Computer Interaction*, **16**(2):185–210.

Babbie, E. (1990) *Survey Research Methods*, 2nd edition. Belmont, CA: Wadsworth Publishing.

Babbie, E. (2009) *The Practice of Social Research*. Belmont, CA: Wadsworth Publishing.

Bertot, J. (2009) Web-based surveys: Not your basic survey anymore. *Library Quarterly*, **79**(1):119–124.

Chen, C., Geyer, W., Dugan, C., Muller, M., and Guy, I. (2009) " Make new friends, but keep the old": Recommending people on social networking sites. *Proceedings of the ACM Conference on Human Factors in Computing Systems*, 201–210.

Chin, J.P., Diehl, V.A., and Norman, K.L. (1988) Development of an instrument measuring user satisfaction of the human–computer interface. *Proceedings of the ACM Conference on Human Factors in Computing Systems*, 213–218.

Couper, M. (2000) Web-based surveys: a review of issues and approaches. *Public Opinion Quarterly*, **64**: 464–494.

Couper, M. (2005) Technology trends in survey data collection. *Social Science Computer Review*, **23**(4):486–501.

Dillman, D. (2000) *Mail and Internet Surveys: The tailored design method*. New York: John Wiley & Sons.

Feng, J., Lazar, J., Kumin, L., and Ozok, A. (2008) Computer usage and computer-related behavior of young individuals with Down Syndrome. *Proceedings of the ACM Conference on Assistive Technology (ASSETS)*, 35–42.

Fogg, B., Marshall, J., Laraki, O., Osipovich, A., Varma, C., Fang, N., Paul, J., Rangnekar, A., Shon, J., Swani, P., and Treinen, M. (2001) What makes web sites credible? A report on a large quantitative study. *Proceedings of the ACM Conference on Human Factors in Computing Systems*, 61–68.

Hanks, K., Odom, W., Roedl, D., and Blevis, E. (2008) Sustainable millennials: Attitudes towards sustainability and the material effects of interactive technologies. *Proceedings of the ACM Conference on Human Factors in Computing Systems*, 333–342.

Kirijian, A., Myers, M., and Charland, S. (2007) Web fun central: Online learning tools for individuals with Down Syndrome. In J. Lazar (ed.), *Universal Usability: Designing computer interfaces for diverse user populations*, 195–230. Chichester, UK: John Wiley & Sons

Lazar, J. (2006) *Web Usability: A user-centered design approach*. Boston: Addison-Wesley.

Lazar, J. and Preece, J. (2001) Using electronic surveys to evaluate networked resources: From idea to implementation. In C. McClure and J. Bertot (eds), *Evaluating Networked Information Services: Techniques, Policy, and Issues*, 137–154. Medford, NJ: Information Today.

Lazar, J., Tsao, R., and Preece, J. (1999) One foot in cyberspace and the other on the ground: A case study of analysis and design issues in a hybrid virtual and physical community. *WebNet Journal: Internet technologies, applications, and issues*, **1**(3):49–57.

Lewis, J.R. (1995) IBM Computer usability satisfaction questionnaires: Psychometric evaluation and instructions for use. *International Journal of Human–Computer Interaction*, **7**(1):57–78.

Lin, H.X., Choong, Y.-Y., and Salvendy, G. (1997) A proposed index of usability: A method for comparing the relative usability of different software systems. *Behaviour & Information Technology*, **16**(4/5):267–278.

McKenna, K. and Bargh, J. (2000) Plan 9 from cyberspace: The implications of the Internet for personality and social psychology. *Personality and Social Psychology*, **4**(1):57–75.

Nov, O., Naaman, M., and Ye, C. (2008) What drives content tagging: The case of photos on Flickr. *Proceedings of the ACM Conference on Human Factors in Computing Systems*, 1097–1100.

Ozok, A. (2007) Survey design and implementation in HCI. In A. Sears and J. Jacko (eds), *The Human Computer Interaction Handbook*, 2nd edition, 1151–1169. New York: Lawrence Erlbaum Associates.

Ozok, A. and Salvendy, G. (2001) How consistent is your web design? *Behaviour & Information Technology*, **20**(6):433–447.

Pitkow, J. and Kehoe, C. (1996) Emerging trends in the WWW population. *Communications of the ACM*, **39**(6):106–110.

Schmidt, W. (1997) World wide web survey research: Benefits, potential problems, and solutions. *Behavior Research Methods, Instruments, & Computers*, **29**(2):274–279.

Schonlau, M., Asch, B., and Du, C. (2003) Web surveys as part of a mixed-mode strategy for populations that cannot be contacted by e-mail. *Social Science Computer Review*, **21**(2):218–222.

Shklovski, I., Kraut, R., and Cummings, J. (2008) Keeping in touch by technology: Maintaining friendships after a residential move. *Proceedings of the ACM Conference on Human Factors in Computing Systems*, 807–816.

Slaughter, L., Harper, B., and Norman, K. (1994) Assessing the equivalence of paper and on-line versions of the QUIS 5.5. *Proceedings of the 2nd Annual Mid-Atlantic Human Factors Conference*, 87–91.

Spears, R. and Lea, M. (1994) Panacea or panopticon? The hidden power in computer-mediated communication. *Communication Research*, **21**(4):427–459.

Sue, V. and Ritter, L. (2007) *Conducting Online Surveys*. Los Angeles: Sage Publications.

Sussman, S. and Sproull, L. (1999) Straight talk: Delivering bad news through electronic communication. *Information Systems Research*, **10**(2):150–166.

Diaries

6.1   Introduction

A diary is a document created by an individual who maintains regular recordings about events in their life, at the time that those events occur (Alaszewski, 2006). These recordings can be anything from a simple record of activities (such as a schedule) to an explanation of those activities to personal reflections on the meaning of those activities. When you are asking people to record information that is fluid and changes over time, such as their mood, or about multiple events that occur within the day, diaries are generally more accurate than other research methods (Alaszewski, 2006). Many people keep a diary and don't even realize it. Informal diaries are kept online and are known as blogs. Many people now send out tweets using "Twitter" or status updates using "Facebook" and both of these, where individuals record what they are doing, as they are doing it, are in fact a form of diary (although probably not used for any research purposes).

The diary method used in human–computer interaction (HCI) has been adopted from other fields, primarily sociology and history (Hyldegard, 2006). For instance, diaries in history have been used to understand the feelings, experiences, and stories of both famous and unknown figures. Personal diaries of world leaders give insight to historians, while personal diaries of unknown individuals allow a documentation of the lives of those who are often left out of the official record of history (Alaszewski, 2006). In sociology, diaries are used to understand what individuals experience but otherwise seems ordinary and unremarkable to those individuals, and might be hard to understand by outsiders (Alaszewski, 2006). Other fields, such as medicine, also frequently use the diary method for research. While the focus of much experimental research in medicine is on measuring objective data that can be observed, other data which is not objective, such as the individual's feelings of pain or fatigue, can best be understood through the use of a diary (Alaszewski, 2006).

One form of diary is a time diary. A time diary focuses on how individuals utilize their time in different activities. The major difference between a general diary and a time diary is that general diary entries may be on an infrequent or non-temporal basis, whereas time diaries have a time focus. Individuals are asked to record entries on a regular basis, record entries when events occur and note time information, or a combination thereof. Because much of the research in HCI focuses on how long we spend in some software application, how much time we spend on a website, or how much time we lose due to frustrations or task switching, time diaries are often the prevailing type of diary used in HCI research.

Research In Practice

Time Diaries to Study User Frustration

Time diaries have been used in researching the presence of frustration among users interacting with computers. A series of research studies have examined what frustrates users on the computer, how they respond to those frustrations, and how it impacts on the users' time. One study focused on 111 university students and their friends; one study focused on 50 workplace users; and a third on 100 blind users on the web (Ceaparu *et al.*, 2004; Lazar, Jones and Shneiderman, 2006; Lazar *et al.*, 2007).

The methodology was essentially the same for all three studies: users were asked to fill out a time diary of their computer usage over a given amount of time (such as a few hours). At the beginning and end of their usage session on the computer, the users were asked to record their mood by answering a series of questions. The users were requested to fill out a "frustration experience form" (see Appendix A) each time during the session that they felt frustrated, with no minimum or maximum number of forms. Throughout the process, the time of day was recorded by users, which helped both to validate the quality of the data and to ascertain how much time was lost due to these frustration experiences.

There are a number of different findings from these studies relating to causes of frustration and how users responded to the frustrations. One of the most interesting findings was how much time was lost due to frustrating situations. In the study of the student users, 38–43% of the time spent on the computer was lost due to frustrating experiences. In the study of workplace users, 42.7% of time on the computer was lost due to frustrating experiences. In the study of blind users, 30.4% of time on the computer was lost due to frustrating experiences.

6.2 Why do we use diaries in HCI research?

Diaries fill the gaps in HCI research methods between observation in naturalistic settings, observation in a fixed lab, and surveys (Hyldegard, 2006). Many say that controlled studies in controlled settings (such as usability labs) are ideal and others say that observing users in their natural settings (such as homes or workplaces) is ideal. However, in many cases, it is not feasible to either bring users into a fixed setting or visit the users in their natural setting. In addition, having observers present in either setting can sometimes change the actions of the users (Carter and Mankoff, 2005). It might seem that surveys are an appropriate solution, as they allow users to record data in their own settings and time and reach a geographically distributed set of users. However, surveys can lead to biased data in behavioral research and diaries offer some advantages over surveys in certain research situations. In many cases, diaries are used in conjunction with other methods; when this is possible, it is ideal, as adding one research method often ameliorates the shortcomings of another method.

All research methods have strengths and weaknesses, and by using two or three different research methods, you can often get a much better understanding of phenomena than you would with only one research method. For instance, Kientz *et al.* developed a technical solution (called FETCH) to help blind people track everyday items, such as keys, iPod, remote controls, and sunglasses. A small Bluetooth tag was added to these items to help in tracking. While a laboratory study was conducted first, a controlled laboratory study clearly wouldn't be sufficient to determine how this approach to finding items could be used in someone's daily life. After the laboratory study discovered some needed improvements in the interface, a diary study was used in which participants would track when they lost items that they needed and how long it took them to find the item. In the first two-week phase of the diary study, the participants didn't use FETCH. During the second two-week phase, the participants used the FETCH system and recorded when they lost items and how long it took to find them (Kientz *et al.*, 2006). The diary study was then followed up with interviews with the participants. The use of the diary in conjunction with other methods strengthened the findings of this research project. However, while ideal, it is often not possible to use two or three different research methods (due to time, cost, or participant availability).

With a good understanding of what you want to learn, if you must choose only one method, you can choose the one that best meets your needs. For instance, diaries allow for collecting of more detailed research than surveys, which often use pre-defined questions and allow little flexibility for respondents. Alaszewski said it best, "While survey research is good at describing what people do, it is rather less effective at explaining or understanding why they do it." (Alaszewski, 2006, p. 36). Surveys ask users to recall information. This may be appropriate if you are asking users to recall information that does not change over time, such as their date of birth, their income, or other demographic data. Any data that is fluid, occurs only at a specific time, and changes, such as mood, feeling, perception, time, or response, needs a very short time period between the occurrence of the event and the recording of the event. Surveys can skew this type of data because, when users are asked to recall their mood, their feeling, their response, or the time that an event took, their response to a survey can be biased or incorrect. In some cases, users might simply forget the details of what occurred. In other cases, an individual user's personality might bias the response. If you ask different people to recall a similar challenging event in their life, some will recall it with optimism and remember the event as being not so bad. Others, who are pessimistic, may look back and remember the event as being worse than it actually was. Differences in personality can skew the recollection. For instance, an 80-year-old friend of one of the authors recalled that when he owned a food store in the 1950s, he once had a robbery where a man held the employees up with a gun and forced them to go into a meat locker for hours. The next comment from the man was "You know, it was a hot day in July, so actually, a few hours in the cooler wasn't too bad!" His personality made him look back on what was most likely a traumatic event and remember a joke. A diary allows for a very small gap between the occurrence of the event and the recording of the event. Ideally, this gap is as close to zero as possible.

Diaries are a very good method for recording measurements that cannot be accurately collected by experimental or observational means, or may result in increased overall validity

Strengths	Weaknesses
Good for understanding how individuals utilize technology in non-workplace, non-controlled, or on-the-go settings	Participants are sometimes not introspective and not aware of the specifics of what they are doing; they may therefore have trouble recording it in a diary entry
Good for understanding the "why" of user interaction with a technology or any technology phenomenon	Participants may not follow through and record a sufficient number of entries
More accurate time recording than in a survey	Time recording may be less accurate than in a controlled laboratory setting or automated data collection
Good for collecting data that is fluid, and changes over time (such as time, mood, perception, or response)	Generally harder to recruit participants for a diary study than for a less intrusive study, such as a survey
The limited gap between an event happening and it being recorded can help limit the impact of individual personality on interpretation of what occurred	Since data is both qualitative and quantitative, data analysis may take a long time
Good for collecting user-defined data (for instance, when a user intended to perform an action but did not do so)	Hard to strike a balance between a frequent-enough series of diary entries, and infringement on daily activities (user participation may then trail off)

Table 6.1 Strengths and weaknesses of diaries.

when used in conjunction with these other methods. While research methods such as experimental design focus on objectively measuring human performance and automated data collection methods focus on studying data that computers can collect unobtrusively, surveys and time diaries ask users about themselves. How did they perceive a certain experience with the computer or device? How did they feel? How did they respond? How much time did it take them? How did it impact on their mood? When did they use it? How did it impact on their feelings of self-efficacy? The time diary elicits this information in a way that neither outside observation nor automated data collection can. For instance, how do you determine when a user intended to perform an action, but did not do so? (Carter and Mankoff, 2005) Neither observation nor automated data collection would be able to record that. A summary of the strengths and weaknesses of diaries appears in Table 6.1.

Diaries can investigate the use of technology that exists at multiple stages:

- technology that doesn't exist yet but could (where researchers investigate communication or information usage patterns, separate from the technology);
- technology that exists but needs to be improved (how people use existing technology);
- prototypes of new technology that need to be evaluated.

Diaries are excellent for recording the existence and quantity of incidents that are user-defined, and where there is little previous data documented on the topic. For instance, one study examined how often users feel that they have learned something while using a computer. The moment when the user realizes that they have learned something new about the computer interface, dubbed a "eureka moment", was recorded using a diary. Over a period of five days, 10 individuals recorded 69 eureka moments, but two of the individuals reported more than 50% of the moments (Rieman, 1993). In another study, "rendezvousing" (face-to-face meetings with friends and family) was studied using a diary method. It was determined that the 34 participants reported a total of 415 rendezvous incidents over a two-week period (an average of six per day) (Colbert, 2001). Documenting in a diary the time involved, both for a specific incident and throughout the day, can help strengthen the validity of the data.

Diaries are very good at examining situations where users don't stay in one place during the time period of interest (i.e. users are on the go). Diaries are also good for studying the use of a technological device in a real-world setting, where a controlled setting would not be able to provide ecological validity. For instance, you could not examine the use of a global positioning system (GPS) device by studying how people use it within a laboratory setting. In the rendezvous study, diaries were used to examine how people meet up, with the goal of understanding how technology could help support them in their meetings (Colbert, 2001). Clearly, this is a phenomenon that could not be studied in the laboratory and interviewing people or surveying them after-the-fact could lead to biased or incorrect data. Diaries are also good at examining situations that involve both computer usage and non-computer usage. For instance, a time diary study was used to examine work-related reading, where the goal was to use an understanding of how people read at work, to inform the design of digital readers or electronic books. For the 15 participants in that diary study, an average of 82% of their work time was spent reading or writing documents (Adler et al., 1998).

Diaries are a research method used heavily in sociology. For instance, long-running studies of how people use their time have used a time diary, which requires users to account for all their time within specific guidelines (such as all time during the work day, all time while awake, or all time within a 24-hour period). While humans generally have problems remembering details of events that have occurred in the recent past, they are especially prone to inaccurately remembering details about time. For instance, in a number of national surveys, people have indicated that they did activities for more than the 168 hours within that week, which is impossible (Robinson and Godbey, 1997).

6.3   Participants for a diary study

To develop a diary for appropriate use within a research study, there are a number of steps involved. Like any other type of research method, prior planning and testing are a requirement to ensure a valid outcome. When deciding to do a diary study, one of the first questions is who will take part in the diary study? While survey methods sometimes call for strict random sampling, this is not realistic for a diary study and it is generally not feasible to get 500 or 1000 users to record diaries. However, strict representation is not as important for diaries as it is for large-scale surveys or experimental design. Many research projects start out with a hypothesis that needs to be tested with statistics. However, diaries should be used when the goal is not to test a hypothesis, but rather, to learn more about situations or behaviors that are not well-understood (Alaszewski, 2006).

In survey research and experimental research, the goal generally is to recruit large numbers of individuals. However, with diary research, it is generally more important to connect with individuals who can provide useful insight (Alaszewski, 2006). Often, an initial set of users can provide access to other users that they know who are also willing to take part in the diary study, a technique called snowball sampling. An introduction from a trusted source (such as a well-known organization or individual) to potential diarists, can help in recruiting potential diarists. It is important to make sure that potential diarists are representative of the user population of interest. Not only must the potential diarists meet certain demographic rules (for example, women over 70 years old) but they must also have a general level of computer experience and a willingness to take part. In the past, computer users, who were often primarily technically oriented people, might not have been as open about their lives. However, as technology has spread throughout the entire population, and as social networking sites (e.g. Facebook and MySpace) and blogging have become popular, many individuals are likely to feel comfortable with the process of keeping a diary. The challenge may not be in recruiting people who are comfortable with and capable of keeping a diary, but rather making sure that you can recruit users that meet the demographic qualifications necessary. Potential diarists must not only meet demographic requirements but also possess three qualities (modified from (Alaszewski, 2006)):

- an understanding of the purposes of maintaining the diary;
- the motivation to keep a regular and accurate record;
- competence in using the technology that is the subject of the diary and the method used to record the diary.

The diary study must be structured in a way that yields useful data without imposing an unreasonable burden on the lives of the diarists. For instance, keeping the diary should not in any way negatively impact on the diarists' employment, health, or relationships with others. A payment of some form (either money or a product) should be offered to the diarists for their participation. Sometimes, when diaries are used to understand new technology, the diarist is allowed to keep, free of charge, the technology about which they have been recording diary entries. Of course, as in any type of research, the participants need to be informed of their rights and their participation in the research should remain anonymous (See Chapter 14 for more information on human subject protection.)

6.4 What type of diary?

There are a number of different methodological decisions to make when using diaries in HCI research: What type of diary? How will the diary be recorded (paper or electronic)? For what period will the users be asked to keep the diary? Diaries are typically kept for a period of one or two weeks (Rieman, 1993). Any longer than that and participation tends to drop off.

At a high level, diaries can be split into two types of purpose: feedback and elicitation (Carter and Mankoff, 2005). A feedback diary is one in which the data from the diary itself provides the feedback to the researchers. The feedback diary is the data collection method; the diary is not meant as a springboard to anything else. In an elicitation diary, the data recorded in the diary is used for prompting, when interviews take place at a later point, and the users are encouraged to expand upon each data point (see Chapter 8 for more information on interviews). Feedback diaries usually focus on the events that interest the researcher, whereas elicitation diaries usually focus on events that interest the user. Feedback diaries tend to have instructions for users that they should make a diary entry when a certain event or threshold occurs. Elicitation diaries tend to encourage users to make diary entries based more on events that have meaning to the user. Feedback diaries can be more accurate (since users record events on a regular basis as they occur) and more objective but elicitation diaries can provide a view that is more representative of what the user is feeling (Carter and Mankoff, 2005). In a similar fashion to a survey, with an elicitation diary users must recall in a later interview what has occurred and this can lead to bias. However, the data points recorded by the user in the elicitation diary can provide some level of validation, which does not exist in the survey.

6.4.1 Feedback Diary

Feedback diaries come in many different formats. But probably the most important research question in a feedback diary is how often a diary entry is made. For instance, what event, time, or threshold triggers the need for the user to make a diary entry? Users could be asked to make a diary recording when an event occurs, such as when they feel frustrated with an interface, or when they complete a certain task. Users could be asked to make a diary recording at a set time every day (say, 9 p.m.), or during a specified time period (say, from noon to 6 p.m.). Users could be interrupted throughout the day at random times, to get a random sample of the user's daily life (Carter and Mankoff, 2005). Typically, an individual in this type of time diary study wears a beeper and must record what they are doing whenever the beeper goes off (at random times) (Robinson and Godbey, 1997).

Just as surveys can be very structured or very unstructured, diaries can have different levels of structure. For instance, diaries can be set up like a structured survey, with Likert scales (e.g. "on a scale of 1–7, with 1 being strongly disagree and 7 being strongly agree"), multiple-choice questions, and closed-ended questions. If the diary has a time focus, it can be set up where individuals must record all events within their day in 15-minute increments. Very structured diaries could include pre-defined categories, checkboxes, counts of how often things occurred such as events, and time stamps. On the other hand, a time diary could be set up in such a manner that it encourages general reflection ("how are you feeling right now about your computer?") (Hyldegard, 2006). Other common questions in an unstructured diary could include "how do you think an activity could be improved?" or "what is notable?" (Palen and Salzman, 2002). The most unstructured diaries would be similar to blogs, where users aren't actually being solicited to take part in a study, but they are just recording their general thoughts on a topic. While blogs are not solicited or structured by researchers and may have issues with validity, there are many blogs on the web where users record their feelings about new technologies. It might be useful for you to examine any blogs that document user experience with the technology that is of interest to you.

6.4.2   Elicitation diary

The goal of an elicitation diary is to have users record only basic information about the important events occurring in their day. These data points are used as prompts to encourage users to expand the explanation during an interview at a later time. Typically, the data points recorded in elicitation diaries are very quick and simple. In many cases, for elicitation diaries, users simply record pictures, short audio clips, short snippets of text, or a combination (Brandt, Weiss and Klemmer, 2007; Carter and Mankoff, 2005). By using digital cameras and cell phones, the number of diary entries might be higher. The trade-off is that a user taking many different photos and being asked to recall why they took all of those photos may not be able to remember why they made those diary entries (Carter and Mankoff, 2005). After the recordings are made, users are later asked to expand upon these recordings. For instance, in one study related to the development of a new handheld document scanner, 22 users were asked to record their diaries over seven days by taking photos using a digital camera. Half of the users were asked to take a digital photo any time they felt that there was a paper document that they wanted to capture electronically and half of them were asked to take a digital photo any time there was any information that they wanted to capture electronically (e.g. audio or video). The pictures were then used during a series of semi-structured interviews to prompt users to expand upon the photos that they took. Over the seven days, the 22 users made 381 diary entries (Brown, Sellen and O'Hara, 2000). In another diary study, related to the information-seeking needs of mobile device users, the participants were asked to send in a short text message, identifying when they had an information need. These short text messages weren't the main diary entry but they were used to remind the participants of what had occurred and, at the end of each day, the participants were requested to go to the project website and answer a series of questions (including "where were you?", "what were you doing?" and "what was your information need?") about that specific occurrence (Sohn et al., 2008). This is a great example of the elicitation approach to diaries.

6.4.3   Hybrid feedback and elicitation diary

Like any other type of research method, the approaches used are modified to meet the needs of a specific research study. For instance, in one study, examining how students use transportation, aspects of both feedback and elicitation diaries were used (Carter and Mankoff, 2005). For a two-week period, the users were asked to use their cell phones to call a specific phone number every time they made a transit decision. At that phone number, they were asked a series of questions about their choice. These aspects were similar to a feedback diary. At the same time, the location of the user at the time of each diary recording was noted, using the built-in GPS features of the phone. At a later time, during an interview, the users were presented with the recordings that they made via cell phone and the GPS information of their location and were prompted to expand their thoughts on that specific decision. These aspects were clearly similar to an elicitation diary.

6.5   Data collection for the diary study

It is important for researchers to decide how the diaries will be recorded. Will the diaries be recorded on paper, in electronic format, text, voice, video, or pictures? Traditionally, diaries have been recorded on paper and, if that is the case, enough paper must be provided and appropriate columns and fields should be designated in a structured format. Within the field of HCI, it seems natural to use technology as a tool to record diary entries. Diaries can be recorded using websites or word processing (Ceaparu *et al.*, 2004), and appropriate structure and guidance should be provided on those forms. However, this is not the prevalent form of diary study at this time.

Increasingly, portable electronic devices are being used for diary entries. This makes diary recording easy and natural, especially for younger users who may be very comfortable using cell phones, music players, and PDAs throughout the day. In addition, when a cell phone, PDA, or MP3 player is used, it does not appear that a user is taking part in a study but, rather, that they are just doing a daily activity. This removes any potential stigma of taking part in a research study. This is similar to how many applications for people with cognitive impairment are implemented using PDAs, because when a user with a cognitive impairment uses a PDA, they look like any other individual using a PDA, they don't look "odd" or out of place in any way (Lazar, 2007). When you are using a PDA, you look just like any other user – no one knows that you are using an assistive device because you have an impairment.

The crucial factor in choosing the media should be the type of media that will be most natural for the diarists in their everyday life. For instance, if participants will be performing the tasks of interest while sitting at their computer, it might make sense to use word processing documents or web-based forms (diary study of task switching sidebar). However, if participants will be recording diary entries about the use of mobile devices, you would expect these entries to occur while the participants are on-the-go (See the Recording Entries on the Go sidebar).

Diary Study of Task Switching

Czerwinski, Horvitz, and Wilhite (2004) did a diary study of task switching between different projects (and related interruptions) during a week. They were trying to examine how interruptions impact on task switching, with the end goal of improving how user interfaces support users recovering from interruptions. They used a diary study, which they felt was most appropriate since there were no existing empirical studies of tools for dealing with task switching and recovery. In addition, diary studies, because they take place in the users' natural settings and tasks, have high ecological validity.

Eleven users took part; all were professionals who multitasked among at least three major projects or tasks. Before the diaries started, users filled out a baseline survey with demographic information and perceptions about computers. The diaries were recorded using an Excel spreadsheet, where the researchers had labeled columns for each parameter that they wanted to track (see Appendix B). For instance, the researchers were interested in learning how users defined tasks, at what level of granularity. The diaries also tracked the difficulty of switching tasks and the amount of time spent on the tasks.

Due to the qualitative nature of the data, two researchers tested and validated the rich coding scheme. Using the coding scheme, first frequency counts and descriptive statistics were carried out on the diary data, followed by regression analysis. Among the significant findings were that users reported an average of 50 task shifts over the week, and that long-term projects, which involved multiple documents, and involved more re-visits, were very hard to return to, once interrupted.

Recording Diary Entries on the Go

Palen and Salzman (2002) carried out two studies which used diaries to learn about the usage of new mobile phone users. They wanted to know how the mobile phones were used in various situations on a daily basis. If you want users to make diary entries in real time, it does not make sense to ask the diarists to record entries about mobile phone use on paper or PCs, since the diarists would then be likely to make entries at a later time (which would subject the diary entries to recall bias).

It was decided that voicemail entries would be used to record the diary entries. However, another challenge is that there could be complications stemming from the fact that the subject of the diary (the cell phone) might also be the method of making the diary entries. So participants were given the option to record voicemail messages using any type of phone that they wanted – a landline, their current mobile phone, or a different mobile phone. A phone number with voicemail was dedicated to the project, so that participants wouldn't have to use any features on their mobile phone to record, just make a standard outgoing call. This aspect limited the complications of using the mobile phone to record data about the mobile phone.

The goal of the first study was to learn more about the usability of the features in the phone handset. In this portion of the research, 19 users participated and they were paid $1 per day for calling in. The goal wasn't to collect rigorous, qualitative data, but rather to get a better understanding of when they used their phones in a new environment, used new features, or contacted the phone service provider. Participants at first started phoning in their diary entries from landlines and then gradually switched to using their mobile phones. The second study had 18 participants, and the researchers used a much more structured approach, where they asked specific questions. In the second study, participants reported things such as confusion about services and signal coverage, and even the ergonomics of the phone (some asked if rubber grippers could be added so that the phone would not slip).

6.6   Letting participants know when to record a diary entry

Regardless of whether the diary format is paper or electronic, participants should be given information about the goal of the study, the types of activities that are of interest, when to make diary recordings (at a given time every day or when a certain type of incident occurs), and definitions of terminology. Definitions of terminology are especially important, as many individuals may use different terms for the same events or similar terms for different events. For instance, if someone using a personal computer records a "crash," what does that mean? Does it mean that the application crashed but the operating system was OK? Did the operating system crash? Or was it a hard drive crash? It is necessary to provide participants with a list of terms and how they should be used, along with specific details of what should be recorded.

It is also very important to define for participants when they should make a diary recording. Just saying, "when you feel like it" is not sufficient as, many times, this will not provide enough motivation or clarity. Often, diarists do not immediately sense the importance of their entries and, especially with diaries that are relatively unstructured, one of the big challenges is convincing participants that what they are doing is important. They may feel that there is nothing to report, that what's going on is mundane. At the same time, the number of diary entries should not be linked directly to payment for participation. For instance, if participants are paid, $2 for each diary entry, there is a good chance that they will attempt to make many diary entries. In the Time Diaries to Study User Frustration sidebar, if the method had been modified so that users were paid $5 every time that they filled out a frustration experience report, the chances are good that users would get frustrated very often and fill out many reports, regardless of how they were feeling; this could bias the data so that it is unrepresentative. Any payment should be for regular participation but should not be linked directly to the number of entries. Participants should get paid for taking part in the study, regardless of the number of entries. Each diary entry should be triggered by an event, a time, or a sense of importance, not by financial compensation.

Throughout the period of the study (and two weeks is often an appropriate length of time), it might be necessary to encourage participants to keep making diary entries. If diary reports are turned in during the study period (not only at the end), you may be able to monitor the diary reports, and give feedback to users who aren't providing useful data. For instance, in a recent diary study of the information-seeking needs of mobile device users (Sohn *et al.*, 2008), the participants were sent five text messages a day, reminding them to send in text messages which served as basic diary entries (and which were then followed up later in the day). It is always a good idea to give feedback to diary participants, not on their specific entries (which might bias the data) but on the existence of their diary entries, on a regular basis.

6.7 Analysis of diaries

Once the diaries are collected, the next step is to analyze the diary entries or reports. Depending on the media used to collect the diary entries (such as paper), it may be necessary first to transfer the diary entries to an electronic format. Hopefully, if any handwriting was done in paper diaries, the handwriting is legible and not open to potential debate!

Some data collected in the diary will be relatively easy to analyze, if it is in quantitative format. Those types of data points can be entered in a spreadsheet and traditional statistical tests and measurements can be used (see Chapter 4 for more information on statistics). However, it is expected that much of the data in a diary will be of a qualitative nature. Since diaries are often used for more exploratory research, where little is known, it is expected that much of the diary data will be in qualitative format, in text described by the diarist. This descriptive text can then be subjected to some form of content analysis (see Chapter 11), in which researchers develop coding categories and code text according to the meaning of the descriptive text (Alaszewski, 2006). Content analysis can help to understand the meaning of the text, allowing for a comparison between diary entries.

Assuming that the diary is somewhat structured in nature, coding and analysis should not be overwhelmingly challenging, although researchers analyzing unsolicited unstructured diaries (such as blogs) may find it very challenging to code diary entries. An example of a diary report that collects both qualitative and quantitative data is in Appendix A. Follow-up interviews with participants who keep an elicitation diary may involve the participants themselves interpreting the data recorded. In many cases, even if the diary is not an elicitation diary, the researchers can contact the participants to ask for clarification of diary entries.

Finally, after data analysis is performed, it is always a good idea to note how, in the future, your approach to data collection through diaries might be modified and improved.

Summary

Diaries have a long history as a research tool in sociology and history, but have only recently been adopted as a research tool in HCI. Diaries are very useful in a number of different research situations. For instance, diaries are appropriate where little is known about the usage patterns of a new technology, and there is not enough background research for an experimental study. Diaries are useful where technology is being used on the go and observation or experimental design would not be appropriate. Diaries are also useful where the research questions lead to data points that cannot easily be observed or measured (such as feelings of frustration). Finally, diaries are useful in triangulation: using multiple research methods to explore the same phenomenon from different points of view. Diaries can help with the understanding of why something happened, not only in documenting that it did happen.

Discussion Questions

1. What is the major difference between diaries in general and time diaries?
2. What bias often present in survey responses do diaries sometimes eliminate?
3. Why are diaries good for collecting data on user-defined events?
4. What aspects of hand-held or mobile devices make them appropriate for diary studies?
5. Why is strict random sampling not necessary in diary studies?
6. What is the main difference between feedback diaries and elicitation diaries?
7. Why is it important to clearly define appropriate definitions of terminology for diary participants?
8. Why do you not want to pay participants for each diary entry?
9. What is generally considered to be the longest appropriate time period for a diary study?

Research Design Exercise

Imagine designing a research study to learn more about the use of genealogy (the study of family history) websites, applications, and databases. Not much is previously known about the user habits for this type of work. What types of participants might be appropriate for a research study? What characteristics might they have? Why might a diary study be superior to a survey or observation study? Specifically, provide information on how a feedback diary and an elicitation diary might be implemented for this study. If the diary was relatively structured, what types of questions should be asked? Would time be an important consideration in this type of diary? Would random sampling of time be appropriate?

References

Adler, A., Gujar, A., Harrison, B., O'Hara, K., and Sellen, A. (1998) A diary study of work-related reading: Design implications for digital reading devices. *Proceedings of the ACM Conference on Human Factors in Computing Systems*, 241–248.

Alaszewski, A. (2006) *Using Diaries for Social Research*. London: Sage Publications.

Brandt, J., Weiss, N., and Klemmer, S. (2007) txt 4 l8r: Lowering the burden for diary studies under mobile conditions. *Proceedings of the 2007 ACM Conference on Human Factors in Computing Systems*, 2303–2308.

Brown, B., Sellen, A., and O'Hara, K. (2000) A diary study of information capture in working life. *Proceedings of the 2000 ACM Conference on Human Factors in Computing Systems*, 438–445.

Carter, S. and Mankoff, J. (2005) When participants do the capturing: The role of media in diary studies. *Proceedings of the 2005 ACM Conference on Human Factors in Computing Systems*, 899–908.

Ceaparu, I., Lazar, J., Bessiere, K., Robinson, J., and Shneiderman, B. (2004) Determining causes and severity of end-user frustration. *International Journal of Human–Computer Interaction*, **17**(3):333–356.

Colbert, M. (2001) A diary study of rendezvousing: Implications for position-aware computing and communications for the general public. *Proceedings of the 2001 ACM Conference on Groupware*, 15–23.

Czerwinski, M., Horvitz, E., and Wilhite, S. (2004) A diary study of task switching and interruptions. *Proceedings of the ACM Conference on Human Factors in Computing Systems*, 175–182.

Hyldegard, J. (2006) Using diaries in group based information behavior research: A methodological study. *Proceedings of the Information Interaction in Context*, 153–161.

Kientz, J., Patel, S., Tyebkhan, A., Gane, B., Wiley, J., and Abowd, G. (2006) Where's my stuff? Design and evaluation of a mobile system for locating lost items for the visually impaired. *Proceedings of the ACM Conference on Assistive Technology (ASSETS)*, 103–110.

Lazar, J. (ed.) (2007) *Universal Usability: Designing computer interfaces for diverse user populations*. Chichester, UK: John Wiley & Sons.

Lazar, J., Allen, A., Kleinman, J., and Malarkey, C. (2007) What frustrates screen reader users on the web: A study of 100 blind users. *International Journal of Human–Computer Interaction*, **22**(3):247–269.

Lazar, J., Jones, A., and Shneiderman, B. (2006) Workplace user frustration with computers: An exploratory investigation of the causes and severity. *Behaviour & Information Technology*, **25**(3):239–251.

Palen, L. and Salzman, M. (2002) Voice mail diary studies for naturalistic data capture under mobile conditions. *Proceedings of the ACM Conference on Computer-supported Cooperative Work*, 87–95.

Rieman, J. (1993) The diary study: A workplace-oriented research tool to guide laboratory efforts. *Proceedings of the ACM Conference on Human Factors in Computing Systems*, 321–326.

Robinson, J. and Godbey. (1997) *Time for Life: The surprising ways Americans use their time*, 2nd edition. Pennsylvania, USA: Pennsylvania State University Press.

Sohn, T., Li, K., Griswold, W., and Hollan, J. (2008) A diary study of mobile information needs. *Proceedings of the ACM Conference on Human Factors in Computing Systems*, 433–442.

Appendix A Frustration Experience Form (Time Diary)

Source: Ceaparu, I., Lazar, J., Bessiere, K., *et al.* (2004) Determining causes and severity of end-user frustration. *International Journal of Human–Computer Interaction,* **17**(3):333–356. Reproduced by permission.

FRUSTRATING EXPERIENCE

Please fill out this form for each frustrating experience that you encounter while using your computer during the reporting session. This should include both major problems such as computer or application crashes, and minor issues such as a program not responding the way that you need it to. Anything which frustrates you should be recorded.

1.   What were you trying to do?

2.   On a scale of 1 (not very important) to 9 (very important), how important was this task to you?

Not very important 1   2   3   4   5   6   7   8   9   Very Important

3.   What software or program did the problem occur in? If the problem was the computer system, please check the program that you were using when it occurred (check all that apply).

___ email   ___ spreadsheet programs (e.g. Excel)
___ chat and instant messaging   ___ graphic design
___ web browsing   ___ programming tools
___ other internet use   ___ database programs
___ word processing   ___ presentation software (e.g. PowerPoint)
___ file browsers   ___ other: _____

4.   Please write a brief description of the experience:

5.   How did you solve this problem?
___ I knew how to solve it because it has happened before
___ I figured out a way to fix it myself without help
___ I asked someone for help. Number of people asked ___
___ I consulted online help or the system/application tutorial
___ I consulted a manual or book
___ I rebooted
___ I ignored the problem or found an alternative solution
___ I was unable to solve it
___ I tried again
___ I restarted the program

6.   Please provide a short step by step description of the process you used to resolve this incident.

7.   How often does this problem happen? ___ more than once a day ___ one time a day ___ several times a week ___ once a week ___ several times a month ___ once a month ___ several times a year ___ first time it happened

8.   On a scale of 1 (not very frustrating) to 9 (very frustrating), how frustrating was this problem for you?

Not very frustrating 1   2   3   4   5   6   7   8   9   Very frustrating

9.   Of the following, did you feel: ___ Angry at the computer ___ angry at yourself ___ helpless/resigned ___ determined to fix it ___ other

10.   How many minutes did it take you to solve this problem?   _____

11.   Other than the amount of time it took you to solve the problem, how many minutes did you lose because of this problem? (if this has happened before, please account only for the current time lost)._____

Please explain:

Appendix B Excel Time Diary Form

Source: Czerwinski, M., Horvitz, E., and Wilhite, S. (2004) A diary study of task switching and interruptions. *Proceedings of the ACM Conference on Human Factors in Computing Systems*, 175–182. Reproduced by permission.

Please enter your daily activities in the columns below (you might need to scroll to the right to see all columns). For each activity, please enter:

   a) the time you started it
   b) a brief description of the task
   c) the application or the device you used to perform the task
   d) the priority of the task (hi, med or low)
   e) what caused you to switch to the task
   f) level of difficulty getting started (hi, med, or low)
   g) what other documents or data you needed to find to start the task
   h) whether or not it was on your to do list
   i) whether you forgot anything related to the task, or any other comments you might have

Remember to use the worksheet at the bottom of the spreadsheet corresponding to the day of the week.
At the end of each day, please go to row 50 and fill out the 3 questions listed there. Thanks again!
Please email your diary as it stands at the end of each day to marycz@microsoft.com.

(a) Time (HH:MM)	(b) Project/task description	(c) Application or device	(d) Priority (hi, med, low?	(e) What caused the switch?	(f) Difficulty initiating task (hi, med, low)? Why?	(g) What docs/data needed to be found?	(h) On ToDo List (if keep one)?	# of Interruptions?	Time completed (if done)?	(i) Forget anything? Comments?

Case studies

7.1   Introduction

Research into human–computer interaction (HCI), like most other research, is often a numbers game: the more, the merrier. Whether you are collecting data to help you understand the requirements for a new system, evaluating the usability of a new system, or conducting an empirical study aimed at validating a new theory, more participants is better. It takes more time and effort to run 20 subjects than 10 and it may be harder to find 100 people than 30 for focus groups, but the advantages are significant. When you involve large numbers of people, you get a broader, more representative sample. With a small number of people, your chances of getting outliers – those who are significantly faster or slower, inexperienced or expert – are vastly increased. For empirical studies, results that may be statistically clear with a large sample may be ambiguous with a smaller group.

Unfortunately, large samples aren't always possible. For some research projects, getting a large sample is extremely difficult, if not completely impossible. Fortunately, this is not a cause for despair. *Case studies*, in which researchers study a small number of participants (possibly as few as one) in depth, can be a useful tool for gathering requirements and evaluating interfaces.

A case study is an in-depth study of a specific instance (or a small number of instances) within a specific real-life context. Case studies generally use a theoretical framework to guide both the collection of data from multiple sources and the analysis of the data (Yin, 2003b). Close examination of individual cases can be used to build understanding, generate theories and hypotheses, present evidence for the existence of certain behavior, or to provide insight that would otherwise be difficult to gather. Because a case study does not necessarily aim to provide a broadly replicable representation of the class from which the instance is drawn, case-study subjects are often carefully chosen with an eye towards generating interesting and novel insights.

Case studies present a different set of challenges from studies involving larger numbers of participants. The first question you might face is determining whether or not a case study is appropriate. Given the small sample size, identifying the appropriate participants may be even more important than it is for larger studies. The duration, content, and format of the study will depend upon your goals and resources. Finally, data analysis and interpretation are particularly important: you may want to be careful about making broad, sweeping claims on the basis of your study of one case.

In a truly reflective style, we look closely at an example of case-study research in HCI to understand what is involved. Specifically, we examine a particular case study to understand when case studies are appropriate, how case studies might be designed, how cases are chosen, how data might be collected, and how the data can be interpreted. Examination of the specific details of the case provide us with a clearer understanding of the general issues and concerns regarding case-study research.

7.2 Observing Sara: a case study of a case study

Concerns over the limits of narrowly constructed usability studies led Shinohara and Tenenberg to conduct an in-depth examination of a blind person's use of assistive technologies (Shinohara and Tenenberg, 2007). By examining the use of a range of technologies in the user's home, they were able to address several questions that would have been difficult to consider in a lab-based usability study. Specifically, they looked at types of task that were common across multiple technologies, including both digital and physical objects, in order to identify general strategies and understand the trade-offs involved in hardware and software design.

Shinohara and Tenenberg used a series of semi-structured interviews (see Chapter 8) to collect the observations that form the basis of the case study. In a series of six, two-hour sessions in her home, Sara (not her real name) demonstrated how she used technologies such as tactile wristwatches and screen readers; discussed early memories of using various objects and her reactions to them; and imagined improved designs for various objects or tasks. Notes, audio-recordings, interviewer reactions, and photographs from these sessions provided the raw data for subsequent analysis. Insights and theories based on early observations were shared with the subject for validation and clarification.

Analysis and presentation of the case study data took multiple forms. Twelve tasks were recorded in terms of their intentions/goals, limitations, workarounds, and desires for future improvements (see excerpt in Table 7.1). This table can be used to compare and group seemingly unrelated tasks in search of common themes. Detailed descriptions – complete with representative quotations – of Sara's use of a tactile watch and screen-reader software complement this table with illustrative details. For example, discussion of the tactile watch led to a deeper understanding of the importance that Sara placed on aesthetics and her desire to be unobtrusive, as she preferred the comfortable, silent tactile watch to a talking watch, which was both noisier and larger. Examination of Sara's use of a screen reader led to the observation that she would examine all possible options, possibly even re-starting from scratch, in order to achieve a goal (Shinohara and Tenenberg, 2007).

Building upon the insights from the individual tasks, Shinohara and Tenenberg identified several general insights that could guide the design of improved tools. Examples included the importance of designs that would not make users feel self-conscious when interacting with sighted friends or colleagues; the importance of control, efficiency, and portability; the need for tools that ease the process of distinguishing between similar items (such as CDs); and the need for flexibility and interoperability.

Although Sara does not provide a comprehensive picture of the needs and concerns of blind people, the investigations of her needs and goals led to valuable insights that might apply to many other blind people.

The remainder of this chapter uses this specific case study to develop a broader understanding of case studies in general.

Object/task	Description	Intentions/ goals	Limitation (What exactly is going on?)	Explanation (Why does the limitation happen?)	Workaround (How is the limitation overcome?)	Usability of workaround (Efficiency, memorability, satisfaction)	Wish (Desires for the future)
Navigating with JAWS	Incorrect key strokes may cause her to lose her bearings	Execute an action through specific hotkeys	JAWS is doing something other than the intended action	Other keys may have been hit by mistake	Keeps trying different key combinations to execute intended action	Satisfactory but not efficient	JAWS could help gather her bearings before executing commands
Searching for a CD to play	Linearly searches all CDs	To select a specific CD to listen to	She cannot quickly read CD covers	CD jewel cases not easily identifiable Labels do not fit on case spines	Labeled CDs, mentally organized by preference, read one at a time	Slow but satisfactory	
Organizing CD collection	CD collection is placed on two shelves, in almost no particular order	To distinguish CDs in player, preferred ones from least favorites	Discs are not organized in conventional means	She does not have much time; she has a lot of CDs	3 discs currently in CD player have a special spot on CD shelf	Efficient, quick and straight-forward	

Table 7.1 Analysis of Sara's tasks (excerpted from (Shinohara and Tenenberg, 2007)).

7.3   What is a case study?

A case study is a detailed examination of one or more specific situations. The Shinohara and Tenenberg (2007) case study helped the researchers to understand how Sara used a variety of technologies to accomplish multiple tasks. They were specifically interested in understanding "what technologies were most valued and used, when they were used and for what purpose." Conducting the research in Sara's home helped the investigators gain insights into how she actually addressed real challenges, as opposed to the more contrived results that might have been seen in the lab.

Four key aspects of this design can be used to describe case studies:

* in-depth investigation of a small number of cases;
* examination in context;
* multiple data sources;
* emphasis on qualitative data and analysis.

7.3.1   In-depth investigation of a small number of cases

The substantial effort needed to conduct a thorough investigation of each case leads directly to a practical limit on the number of cases that can be included in any given study. The entire Shinohara and Tenenberg (2007) study was focused on a single individual: data was collected in her house for approximately twelve hours and post-meeting debriefings, transcriptions of audio tapes, and photos were also compiled for analysis. The substantial effort required to collect and collate this body of data is difficult – if not impossible – to replicate for dozens of participants.

In this regard, case studies are quite different from experiments that ask large numbers of participants to perform specific, well-defined tasks, leading to results that can be interpreted as applying to a broad range of users. Case studies use in-depth, broad examinations of a small number of cases in order to address a broad range of concerns.

A case study need not be limited to only one individual. Involving two or more cases is a highly-recommended technique for increasing the credibility of both analyses and results (Yin, 2003b). As we will see, the precise definition of a case is not clear (Section 7.5.2). Was Sara's study an example of a case study with one case – the individual – or with twelve cases – the tasks? These questions are not necessarily clear cut.

7.3.2   Examination in context

Lab-based usability studies have a huge role to play in HCI research. The controlled environments of usability labs are wonderful for removing undesired external influences, but they don't provide a very realistic picture of how people really work. Computer use generally takes place in homes or offices that have distractions, competing concerns demanding attention, and the stress of multi-tasking in the hopes of meeting competing deadlines. As these factors do not arise in controlled usability labs, observations made in the lab might not generalize to "real-world" behavior.

Unlike lab-based experiments, case studies focus on observation of phenomena in a meaningful context that is beyond the control of the investigator. Case studies focus on activities as they occur in the real world, outside the sterile confines of the usability lab. By observing and closely examining these activities "in the wild", free from the pre-determined goals and narrowly-defined questions that often accompany usability studies and controlled experiments, researchers can develop detailed understandings of interaction techniques and coping strategies – understandings that might be hard (if not impossible) to develop through usability studies.

7.3.3 Multiple data sources

Case studies often rely upon multiple data collection techniques to act as sources of corroborating evidence. In Shinohara and Tenenberg (2007), three types of technology biography (Blythe, Monk and Park, 2002) were used: demonstrations of devices (*technology tours*), reflections on memories of early use of and reactions to devices (*personal histories*), and wishful thinking about possible technological innovations (*guided speculation*). More generally, these data sources are examples of three commonly used types of case study data: artifacts, observation, and interviews. The case study of Sara also involved the impressions and subjective responses of the researchers.

These three approaches to technology biography provide opportunities for gathering insights that might be difficult to acquire using only one method. By asking Sara to talk about both past experiences and future aspirations, the research design allowed for the possibility of understanding changes in her relationship to technology. Sara's demonstrations of the tools provided an example of the use of artifacts. The examination of tools (such as the tactile watch and screen-reading software) can be an important source of data for case studies, particularly when you are interested in understanding how users complete tasks.

Multiple data sources can also provide corroborating evidence to increase your confidence in observations. In a case study of workplace information management, you might start your data collection with interviews with employees. These discussions provide useful data but they are limited: participants may have different understandings of practices and habits, they may be unwilling to comment on the details of their work, or they may simply forget important details (Chapter 8). Investigation of the artifacts of their work – computer files, paper records, archives, and e-mail messages – can provide concrete understanding of actual practices, free from the limitations of interviews. This analysis may confirm statements made in interviews, thus increasing your confidence in their validity. The use of multiple sources to provide corroborating evidence is known as *data triangulation* – a reference to the practice of taking measurements relative to multiple known reference points in order to precisely measure location.

Multiple data sources can also help deal with any concerns about the quality of the data provided by any single source. Due to the relatively small number of cases involved, the use of any single data collection technique with a particular case may not give you the data that you really need. For example, if Sara had had some residual vision that allowed her to make use of some visual display components on a computer screen, she might not be an appropriate participant in the case study. We have more to say about selecting cases in Section 7.7 but, for now, we mention that simply asking Sara about her use of technology might not have revealed her use of visual displays. A combination of interviews along with direct observation of her work might provide more appropriate measurements; logs of computer activity – taken when she wasn't being directly observed – might be even more realistic.

Of course, the use of multiple data sources does not guarantee nice, clean corroboration of results – if only it were that easy. Two scenarios may arise that make life more interesting. Your data sources might diverge, with each source of data covering different observations. This is not necessarily a problem, as all of the observations may have some validity. When this happens, your use of multiple data sources has not increased the validity of your analyses – you've simply got many observations that fail to support each other. You may need to be cautious about your interpretation, refraining from strong claims until you can find some corroboration.

The possibility of contradiction is a more troubling concern. Suppose one source says that something is true, while another says that it's not? You may need to look carefully at the specific details of the claims and the specific sources, in order to determine which is plausible. Contradictions may also motivate you to dig deeper, asking additional questions of existing sources or consulting new data sources in order to develop explanations that resolve the inconsistencies.

Case studies often draw upon many types of data source. Documents, data archives, direct observation, and participant observation (similar to ethnography – see Chapter 9) are just a few of the possibilities (Yin, 2003b).

7.3.4 Emphasis on qualitative data and analysis

The researchers were not specifically interested in measuring how quickly Sara completed various tasks, how many errors she made, or how quickly she learned how to use an interface. Case studies always contain a substantial qualitative component, focusing on questions that help describe or explain behavior (Yin, 2003b). In Sara's case, questions might have included "How did she use technology to achieve various goals?" or "which tools did she use in a given circumstance?" The data needed to answer questions such as those tends to be more qualitative than quantitative.

Case studies can certainly include quantitative components measuring traditional metrics, such as task completion time, but these measures are not usually the sole focus of the investigation. In Sara's case, the investigators might have measured the time it took her to complete certain tasks or how frequently she used the tactile watch. As interesting as these measurements might have been, they would not have been sufficient to meet the goal of the study: a deeper understanding of her use of assistive technology. The qualitative interviews, which provided room for in-depth discussion, elaboration of concerns, and discussion of contextual issues, were crucial for achieving this goal.

Quantitative data might be used as a triangulation tool for corroborating results. In this case, Sara's frequency of use of the tactile watch might be used to provide supporting evidence for interview comments describing her perceptions of how she uses the watch. If you choose to use quantitative data in a case study, you should be acutely aware of its limitations: as your case or cases are unlikely to be representative of a larger class, statistical comparison may be difficult if not impossible. Having collected data on the frequency of Sara's use of the tactile watch over a period of weeks, investigators might have sufficient data to investigate how Sara's use of the watch changed over time, but they would not have been able to make any comparison between Sara and other tactile-watch wearers, or blind people in general.

7.4   Goals of HCI case studies

Broadly speaking, HCI case studies have four goals:

- *exploration*: understanding novel problems or situations, often with the hopes of informing new designs;
- *explanation*: developing models that can be used to understand a context of technology use;
- *description*: documenting a system, a context of technology use, or the process that led to a proposed design;
- *demonstration*: showing how a new tool was successfully used.

7.4.1   Exploration

New research projects – whether in a lab or a product development environment – often begin with an incomplete or preliminary understanding of a problem and its context. Case studies can provide invaluable feedback when a project team is in the early stages of understanding both the problem and the merits of possible solutions. Such studies would have members of the project team examining the goals and constraints facing likely users. Using processes similar to those used in ethnographic work (see Chapter 9), researchers might observe how potential users currently accomplish tasks, use available tools, and respond to problematic situations. The insights that result from this inquiry can inform both system design and further investigation.

7.4.2 Explanation

Technologies in general, and computer systems in particular, are often used in ways that were not considered in the initial design, often with impacts that are completely unexpected. Case studies of tools in use can provide understanding of these uses and outcomes. An examination of the use of a tool for browsing photo collections on mobile devices provides an example of an explanatory study: in-depth interviews with nine users provided substantial insight into how the tool was used and how specific designs might engage users (Naaman, Nair and Kaplun, 2008).

The Extreme Cases sidebar describes a case study of the use of GPS location devices for tracking parolees. In addition to explaining how these systems affect – often in surprising ways – the behavior of the individuals required to wear them, this case study provided the basis for reconsideration of broader issues regarding mobility and privacy.

Extreme Cases

Cases are not always selected because they are representative or typical. *Edge cases* – extreme or unusual examples – often present combinations of characteristics that make them particularly worthy of further study. This strategy is used extensively in medical education, where profiles of individuals with puzzling and unusual symptoms are presented as compelling challenges for budding diagnosticians.

As HCI researchers often use a case study as a tool for understanding the technology usage and needs of populations of potential users, HCI case studies often largely draw upon representative users and use cases, omitting extreme cases. As understandable as this strategy might be, a focus on general cases may miss out on some of the insights that might be gained from examining less familiar perspectives.

Geo-location services – tools that combine global-positioning system (GPS) facilities with data and communication tools – have spawned numerous computing tools and services. Possibilities include facilities for finding nearby friends or restaurants; games; educational systems based on the location of items of interest in natural environments; and location-based data collection covering entire cities.

A case study based on extremes was used to explore some of the questions regarding perceptions of location and privacy (Troshynski, Lee and Dourish, 2008). It examined the habits and perceptions of a group of sex offenders who were required to have their locations tracked via GPS as part of their parole agreements. Building from theories that argue that marginalized groups may possess instructive insights into society, these researchers hoped to use this extreme population to reconsider HCI questions about location-based systems. Data collection involved semi-structured focus group sessions with 10 parolees who were already participating in a pilot study on the use of GPS for parole supervision for sex offenders. Although several individuals participated, comments were analyzed as an undifferentiated whole, making this a single case study of the group of parolees.

Analysis of the focus group data led to the identification of three main themes describing the impact of the system on the participants. The GPS systems structured their perception of space, making them acutely aware of how far they were from home and how close they may have come to forbidden locations such as schools and parks. The systems also constrained their time: the need to regularly charge batteries limited their ability to spend long periods of time away from convenient sources of electricity. The parolees' sense of their bodies was also changed, as the ankle-mounted GPS units both made certain clothing choices (such as short pants) impractical and effectively prohibited swimming, bathing, or other activities that might have exposed the unit to the possibility of water damage. The researchers use these insights to fuel a more general consideration of location-based interfaces in specific social and cultural contexts (Troshynski, Lee and Dourish, 2008).

The value of these extreme cases lay in the distance between their perspectives and motivations and those of "typical" users of GPS-based computing systems. Generalization was not the goal of this study – it's hard to see how the concerns of a group of parolees who were required to use these systems might be applied to voluntary users of location-based systems for game playing or locating friends. Instead, the comments of this atypical user group provided a richer understanding that might not have emerged through investigation of the expected case.

7.4.3 Description

A description of a system and its impact can be of interest. In some cases, particularly those involving new design methodologies, the process behind the design may be the focus of a case study. In general, a single-case study describes a problem, the steps that were taken to understand it, the details of the eventual design, and the lessons learned that might be of more general interest. Case studies that describe design processes and results have been written for a wide variety of topics, including interfaces for people with Alzheimer's disease (Cohene *et al.*, 2007) (see sidebar), fire alert services in South Africa (Davies *et al.*, 2008), browsers for a collection of music written by a composer (Hochheiser, 2000), and mobile interfaces for sharing navigation information in cities (Bilandzic, Foth and De Luca, 2008).

Research In Practice

Interfaces for People with Alzheimer's Disease

The process of developing a novel interface or interaction technique is often as interesting, if not more interesting, than the resulting product. This is particularly true for design efforts that tackle novel problems involving challenging contexts of use.

A University of Toronto project involving the design of an assistive technology tool for people affected by Alzheimer's disease provided the basis for an intriguing case study (Cohene *et al.*, 2007). This project was based in a body of prior work that firmly established the importance of reminiscences for people with Alzheimer's disease. Specifically, the researchers were interested in developing multimedia "life histories" that people with Alzheimer's disease could use to recall and relive old memories. The case described the process of developing a system to be used by a 91-year old woman named Laura.[1] The participation of Laura and her two daughters formed a crucial part of the study.

The initial phases in the study included exploratory efforts aimed at developing an understanding of the challenges faced by people with Alzheimer's disease and their families. Although the study was focused on developing a tool specifically for Laura, the researchers conducted a variety of inquiries aimed at providing greater understanding of the needs and abilities of individuals with Alzheimer's disease. The researchers conducted a modified ethnographic inquiry (see Chapter 9), interacting with groups of individuals engaged in recreational therapy activities. These observations provided a detailed understanding of the range of abilities and impairments of the participants, leading to a set of design principles. Discussions with caretakers and other experts formed the basis of a set of categories and themes that would assist with reminiscing.

Interviews with Laura's family members informed both the content of the life histories and an understanding of important needs and outcomes. Family members also completed a "family workbook" that contained storyboards describing stories that would be recounted with the tool to be developed. Photographs, home videos, and music were collected to form the basis for the multimedia components of the tool. This data provided the basis for several generations of prototype, culminating in designs including multimedia DVDs to be controlled by a customized input device and an interactive photo album, with pages that could be displayed on a TV monitor. These descriptive elements in the case study give a detailed picture of how the research was conducted and how it informed the system design.

Elements of explanation and demonstration can be found in the discussion of how the prototypes were evaluated and refined. As with many HCI projects that examine new tools, this effort involved having the participant make frequent use of the tool over an extended period of time – in this case, eight times in four weeks.

---

[1] All names of participants in this study were changed to protect their privacy.

This led to ideas for refining some designs, including modifying the design of the one-button remote control, while abandoning others, such as the interactive photo album, which was perceived to be too cognitively demanding. Follow-up interviews with family members confirmed initial hypotheses that the system would have multiple benefits for the participants, including providing perspective, sharing experiences, and communicating.

This project as whole is an exploratory case study. As relatively little work has been done on user interfaces for people with Alzheimer's disease, the description of a successful process is valuable in and of itself. The design ideas presented raise interesting possibilities, but in many ways they raise more questions than they answer. The broad range of cognitive impairments experienced by people with Alzheimer's disease and the varying impacts that their condition have on family members makes generalization very hard: what works well for one individual and their family might not work well for others. Extending the applicability of this work – particularly by scaling the design process – was clearly a goal of the research team, as they describe further efforts involving additional participants and improving the process of designing life histories.

The intensive nature of the research – requiring substantial time commitments both from the individual with Alzheimer's disease and from family members who are dealing with the emotional strain of the decline of a family member – made the work extremely resource intensive. The elaboration of the design process and the completion of one specific design are important contributions, even if the resulting design does not generalize to other users.

The most broadly applicable results from this story lie in the lessons learned. The authors concluded that new design methods and principles were needed for working with individuals with Alzheimer's disease, that active participation was more stimulating than passive, and that working with both the patients and their family members throughout the entire design process was necessary. Practical concerns included the resource-intensive nature of the research, the emotional commitment required of the family members, the need to make the approach practical for larger numbers of families, and the need for standards for evaluation (Cohene *et al.*, 2007). Although drawn from this particular project, these insights might be extremely valuable to others interested in conducting related research.

7.4.4 Demonstration

Usually shorter and less in-depth than descriptive case studies, demonstrations are often found in papers describing new designs. Short anecdotes describing how one or more individuals successfully used a new tool to complete one or more appropriate tasks often complement usability studies, controlled experiments, and other data documenting the success of the design.

Demonstration case studies can play an important role in describing the success of a new design or tool, particularly when a controlled user study is inappropriate or impractical. This is often the case with a complete tool, which may have many elements and multiple metrics for evaluation. Demonstration case studies can also be appropriate in cases where the broad scope of the interface may preclude the use of a controlled study.

Demonstration case studies tend to follow a common pattern. The report generally starts with an introduction of the participants and their context of use. Other elements often found in the report include descriptions of how the participants used the system, problems they faced, strengths of the system design, and discussions of subjective responses. See the Interfaces for Quadriplegic People sidebar for a discussion of such a case study.

Research In Practice

Interfaces for Quadriplegic People

Building interfaces for quadriplegic people is a significant challenge: without the use of their hands, fingers, or feet, these individuals may be restricted to using input devices that consist of a single action, such as blowing on a straw or pressing a single switch. Interfaces for such users are generally based on some form of scanning: a graphical window on the computer screen contains a grid of buttons that are scanned – highlighted in some predictable order – with each button being active for a given amount of time. When the desired button is highlighted, the user activates the switch to make a selection.

Steriadis and Constantinou (2003) include a demonstration case study as a partial validation of the proposed design of a new interface architecture. This paper presented widgets for single-switch input devices ("wifsids") that support a model of button selection appropriate for both discrete text input from the keyboard and continuous mouse movement. These widgets were used to build a set of applications that would run in Windows, supporting cursor movement, keyboard entry, selection of applications, macros for common functionality, and other features.

The case study described how the system was used by a 35-year-old man with amyotrophic lateral sclerosis (ALS), which left him bedridden and unable to speak. The paper describes how the participant decided to use a button between his knees to make selections, after having rejected the inputs as being difficult to use, cumbersome, or unattractive. The description of the participant's success in learning how to use the system, and in using it for communicating with family and the Internet, forms an important part of the description. Details of his use of the various components, along with initial difficulties and their resolutions, are also described (Steriadis and Constantinou, 2003).

This individual's success may not be generalizable: the system might not work so well for others. However, this is not the only evaluation found in the paper. An empirical study of how the typing rates of two additional quadriplegic users varied with word-prediction schemes formed the basis for a discussion of factors that might influence typing rate. Even though this study only involved two users, it provides some insight into the factors that influence success in using the tool to type text. The case study and the empirical study work together in a complementary fashion to demonstrate the strengths and limitations of the proposed system.

The four classes of case study are not mutually exclusive. Sara's case study has elements of both exploration and explanation. The Interfaces for People with Alzheimer's Disease sidebar describes a study involving elements of exploration, description, and demonstration.

7.5   Types of case study

7.5.1   Intrinsic or instrumental

Case studies are often conducted to shed light on a specific situation. You may be working with a client to design a new organizational website. A case study of the client's work processes, corporate organization, and information-sharing practices and procedures would inform your design process, but the results would be likely to apply only to that client. These *intrinsic* studies (Stake, 1995) describe cases that are of inherent interest.

Case studies can also take a broader approach, trying to develop a broader understanding. These *instrumental* case studies ask questions in the hope of generating insights that go beyond the case at hand. They become tools that lead to a broader understanding. Sara's case study involved the instrumental goal of searching for "common kinds of task failure and workaround" (Shinohara and Tenenberg, 2007).

Case studies can be both intrinsic and instrumental: it might be argued that Sara's case is both interesting in its own right (intrinsic) and aimed at broader understanding (instrumental).

7.5.2   Single case or multiple cases

Although Sara's case study focused on one person's use of technology, case studies are certainly not limited to single cases. The use of multiple cases may initially seem to be a bit of a contradiction in terms, but there's nothing strange about doing case-study research with two or more cases.

To understand why you might use multiple cases when one might seem to do just as well, we must consider one of the important goals of many case studies: generalization. An in-depth discussion of one individual (such as Sara) is interesting, but the real value in a study of this sort lies in generating insights that can be applied to a broader class of design challenges. We might be pleased if Sara's case study led to some suggestions for the design of assistive devices that would help Sara with her daily challenges, but we'd often like to go further. If the case study led to insights that apply to many blind people, any resulting designs might be useful to a much broader range of blind users.

If our goal is to generalize, we would ideally argue that our cases are somehow representative. They must be similar to the members of the broader group that is the focus of our generalization, at least in ways that are relevant to the study at hand. A single case may or may not be representative, and we may not have any way of evaluating whether or not any single case provides a basis for generalization. From the description of her tasks and challenges, we might infer that Sara is a reasonably representative blind college student, but we really can't say for sure. She may be more (or less) experienced with computers than other blind college students, more (or less) willing to try new technologies, and so on. Casting a broader net, we might wonder if insights gained from interviewing Sara can apply to blind people of different ages or education levels, such as working professionals or elementary school students.

Just as scientific experiments of all sorts rely upon replication to provide increased confidence in observed results, case studies can use multiple cases to provide critical support for confidence in the generality of any results. Suppose another college student had been interviewed, following the same protocol that was used with Sara. If the observations and insights gained from the two studies were similar, we might be more inclined to believe that these results were applicable to blind college students in general. This use of closely comparable cases to demonstrate consistency of results is known as *literal replication* (Yin, 2003b).

The analogy between case studies and other scientific experiments can lead us to another useful form of multiple case studies. Experimentation relies upon contrasts between situations that are similar but differ in specific, controlled ways. When these situations are created correctly, observed differences in experimental outcome can be attributed to the differences between the groups. Multiple case studies might use cases with specific differences in much the same manner. Imagine an extension of Sara's study that involved a blind executive instead of another student. Differences between Sara and the executive in terms of how they use technology might be due to differences in their occupations.[2] The use of comparable cases to generate results that differ in ways that can be explained by differences between the cases is known as *theoretical replication* (Yin, 2003b). The International Children's Digital Library sidebar describes a multiple-case study involving theoretical replication.

---

[2]Differences in age and economic resources might also play a role. Strictly controlling for differences is difficult with cases involving human participants.

The International Children's Digital Library

The International Children's Digital Library (ICDL, www.childrenslibrary.org) is an online repository of thousands of books from around the world. Built "to help young people understand the value of tolerance and respect for diverse cultures, languages and ideas" (Druin *et al.*, 2007), the ICDL provides interfaces specifically designed to support children in searching for and reading books. Search tools support strategies that children might use for finding books (such as the color of the cover, the types of character, or the length of the book) and several reader tools support a variety of reading strategies (Druin *et al.*, 2007).

The ICDL's ambitious goals of serving a diverse group of children from all over the world presented a challenge and an opportunity. By studying how children in different countries with different economic and social backgrounds, used the ICDL, the research team hoped to gain a better understanding of how children in varied settings would interact with the ICDL. As both the interface and content are multi-lingual, they could examine the use of this single tool in diverse contexts, in order to understand how usage patterns differ across cultural boundaries.

The resulting multiple-case study involved students in four distinct geographical locations: Munich, Germany; Le Ceiba, Honduras; Wellington, New Zealand; and Chicago, USA. Three eight-year-old children participated in each location, along with parents, teachers, and administrators. Data collected over the course of four years included open-ended interviews with both children and adult participants, drawings that children made to illustrate their ideas about libraries, and book reviews that the children wrote. Grounded theory and content analysis approaches (see Chapter 11) were used to analyze the 152 interviews, 236 drawings, and 301 book reviews that were collected over the course of the study.

Although there were multiple participants at each site, data analysis focused on understanding how use patterns and responses differ across these varied circumstances. As the individual children were not the units of analysis, this case study can be seen as a holistic case, multiple-case study. The four groups can be seen as theoretical replications, with their varied backgrounds providing opportunities to examine how observed phenomena differ across cultures.

As differences between the groups were largely attributable to pre-existing cultural differences, the results of this study demonstrate the likely outcome of theoretical replication. All children seemed to appreciate the digital library and the range of books that they read over time increased. Children in all four locations found books in languages that they did not know to be difficult or frustrating and they all liked the search tools but preferred to read physical books. They all valued libraries and children in all groups became more interested in learning about different cultures. Differences in responses may have been due to specific differences in circumstances. Compared to children in the other countries, German children showed less increase in confidence in their ability to use technology effectively. However, the German children may have started out with higher levels of exposure to technology. Similarly, children in the US – who live in a relatively homogenous environment – showed greater increase in interest in diverse cultures than children from the other, more diverse cultures (Druin *et al.*, 2007).

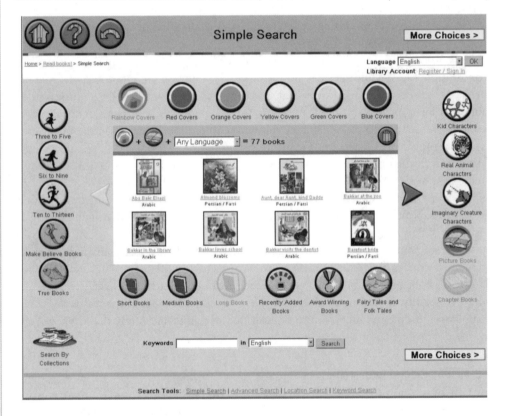

Figure 7.1 The search interface for the International Children's Digital Library (www.childrenslibrary.org) provides young readers with search tools designed to meet their interests.

Increased confidence in the results may be a compelling argument for involving multiple cases in your studies. Multiple cases help to combat criticisms that you have chosen a single case that is unrepresentative. Any single case can be idiosyncratic, but multiple cases are much less likely to be unrepresentative in the same ways. "Cherry-picking" a single case to support hypotheses or justify a pre-existing model might be possible, but this sort of bias – whether intentional or not – is less likely with multiple-case studies.

Despite the advantages of multiple-case studies, there may be some times when a single case design is the more – or only – appropriate option. If you are studying the use of a custom piece of software in a single workplace, you may be unable to find additional cases. Single-case designs are the only option in such cases (Yin, 2003b). Cost – both in terms of financial and human resources – can also play a role in the decision to use a single-case design. Case studies can often be labor-intensive, requiring extensive effort for preparation, data collection, and analysis. You may be unable to find the time needed for additional cases, as much as you might want to include them.

The goals of your study may play a role in determining whether you should use a single case or multiple cases. Multiple cases are most useful when you are interested in generalizing your results, but this may not be your goal. Some case studies may describe a unique case that cannot easily be compared to others, making a multiple-case study difficult, if not impossible. Other studies – such as Sara's – may be exploratory in nature, focusing on the generation of ideas and formulation of questions for future research (see Section 7.10).

Although this section began with a discussion of generalization as the goal of many case studies, extrapolating from a small set of cases to a larger population is not something that should be done lightly. Even if you do choose to use multiple cases, you should always be very cautious about any claims of generality. Some researchers feel that generalizing from case studies is always inappropriate – without a broad-based sample that can be shown to adequately represent a population, how can you conclude that any of your findings apply to all members of the larger group? Multiple cases can help you identify phenomena that might apply across larger groups, but you would need to conduct further research to truly justify claims of generality. By all means, look for these trends, and use multiple cases to show that they apply in multiple instances, but steer clear of any claims that imply that they will always apply.

7.5.3 Embedded or holistic

Even with only one participant, Sara's case study may be more complex than you might initially think. Although only one individual is involved, this case study discusses 12 separate tasks. Each of these tasks is discussed and investigated separately, as its own *unit of analysis*. The inclusion of multiple units of analysis within a single case is referred to as an *embedded* case study, in contrast to *holistic* studies that address only one unit in each case (Yin, 2003b).

This distinction arises at least in part from the nature of the questions being asked: as Sara uses multiple tools in different ways to address daily activities, any investigation of her use of technology should discuss these differences. A case study that did not address these differences might miss many interesting insights. Other examples of embedded designs might include academic departments in a university or designers on a product team.

Integration of the multiple units of analysis is an important aspect of embedded case study design. If the various pieces are not tied together, the individual units might as well be separate cases in a multiple-case study (Yin, 2003b). In Sara's case, insights from the various tasks were combined in a classification of challenges that she faced, including control, efficiency, portability, and interoperability. Just as these categories provide additional understanding of the individual tasks, individual units of analysis in an embedded design might be grouped or viewed from common perspectives.

The inclusion of multiple participants in a case does not necessarily imply an embedded case study. If participants are not discussed individually, with analyses identifying similarities and differences between them, they are not distinct units of analysis. In this case, the group is the unit of analysis in a holistic study. A study of virtual collaboration in a school in Finland provides an illustration (Lakkala, Ilomäki and Palonen, 2007). Although the class involved 14 students and seven teachers, the case study does not discuss students and teachers in any detail. Specific comments from both teachers and students are cited in the paper, but there is no attempt to discuss any of the participants as individuals, making this a single-case, holistic study.

A paper discussing strategies for sustaining a "community computing infrastructure" provides an interesting example of an embedded case study (Farooq *et al.*, 2007b). This single-case study examined an online community aimed at supporting professional development for teachers. Four "design interventions" – contact and bug forms, "needed features" group, task list, and help desk – were chosen as the units of analysis, due to their differences in terms of goals, primary mode of communication, participants, and implications for use. Separate discussions of each of these interventions complemented a general examination of how they worked together to support the continuing success of the community.

Although the distinction between holistic and embedded analysis might ideally be made before the study is conducted, the need for multiple units of analysis may not be clear until after data collection has started. A study of the use of a groupware tool in a corporate setting might start out as a holistic study of the tool's use in a given group, only to evolve in time to include embedded analyses of the differing tasks for which the tool would be used, the roles of the various members in the group, or the types of project for which it might be used.

7.6 Research questions and hypotheses

As with almost any other form of research, a good case study is built on the foundations of a theoretical model. Although these theories might not be cleanly testable hypotheses that can be easily disproved, they can be used to describe what you are looking for, what you think you might find, and how you will use your data to support your theories.

Roughly speaking, there are four components of a case study design:[3]

- questions;
- hypotheses or propositions;
- units of analysis;
- data analysis plan.

---

[3] This list is based on Robert K. Yin's list of five components. His list divides the "data analysis plan" into two components: the logic linking the data to the propositions and the criteria for interpreting the findings (Yin, 2003b).

Research *questions* describe the goals of your study – what you are interested in understanding. *Hypotheses or propositions* are statements of what you expect to find. The *unit of analysis* defines the granularity of your study – what exactly you are focusing on. Are you studying an organization, a group of people, an individual, or individual activities? These questions will guide your data collection. The final component – a *data analysis plan* – is described in Section 7.8.

Just as in other forms of research, your research questions and hypotheses guide your efforts. You may be interested in understanding how users accomplish certain goals or tools, how the introduction of a new tool changes the work flows and patterns in an organization, or what a team needs from a new collaboration tool. Even if your case study is exploratory or descriptive, you should try to make your research questions and propositions explicit.

Taken together, your research questions and hypotheses form a preliminary model that will guide your development of the case study. By mapping out your interests and the range of concerns that you are trying to address, you will gain greater understanding of the criteria that you will use to choose your cases, the data sources that you might need to include, and how you will conduct your analysis. The approach of ignoring theory in favor of simply collecting data indiscriminately can be a recipe for failure (Yin, 2003a).

In Sara's case study, the researchers were interested in understanding how a blind person might use a variety of assistive technologies to accomplish tasks and to recover from task failures using workarounds. These questions led to several propositions. The investigators expected to see common types of failure and workaround strategy. They also expected that the choice of implementing features in hardware or software might influence user interaction, including failures and response to those failures.

A different set of research questions might have led the researchers to a very different case study. If, for example, a preliminary study had led them to believe that education or socio-economic status might play an important role in determining how blind people use technology, they might have chosen a multiple-case design, including participants with backgrounds that differed in these relevant respects. They might also have asked a broader range of questions about background and included consideration about other aspects of their participants' lives.

A study of sociability in massive, multiplayer, online games provides another example of the important role of theory in case-study design. In (Ducheneaut, Moore and Nickell, 2007), the researchers were interested in asking whether social spaces in these games acted as "third spaces," where players would socialize, just as coffee shops and other spaces support socializing in the real world. This question led them to choose a particular online game that provided strong support for social spaces, a data collection strategy involving active participation in these spaces in the game, and an analysis strategy that combined analysis of observations from their participation with quantitative analysis of activity in the game.

Once you have defined your questions and hypotheses, you can move on to consider other questions of case-study design, including the type of case study, selection of cases, data collection, and data analysis.

7.7   Choosing cases

Single-case studies may present little, if any, difficulty in case selection. Case studies often involve cases that are somehow unique or incomparable to others. Intrinsic case studies limit you to consideration of the specific instance of interest. Convenience can also be a factor – you may choose a specific case "because it's there". This is often the case when you're not particularly concerned about generalizing: when conducting an exploratory case study aimed at building initial understandings of a situation, any case might work (see Section 7.11). In all of these instances, selection is straightforward: you work with what you have available. Otherwise, you will want to put careful consideration into your criteria for selecting cases.

There are a few general guidelines that apply to almost any sort of case study. Like ethnographic investigations (Chapter 9), case studies require a great deal of time, careful preparation, and often close cooperation with one or more individuals or organizations. Given these challenges, the individuals, groups, organizations, or systems that you choose should be chosen carefully. You will want to try to identify case-study participants who have an interest in committing some of their own resources to work with you to make the research successful. You should also try to maximize convenience, working with geographically convenient participants whenever possible.

Further considerations in your choice of cases will be driven by the details of your research design. If you are conducting an instrumental case study aimed at developing generalizable models of classes of users or contexts, you should aim for cases that are representative in the appropriate aspects. Although the analysis tools may be different, this is the same problem faced by quantitative user studies (see Chapter 2): if the participants in your study are sufficiently different from the group to which you are generalizing, your findings may not hold up, no matter how strong the analysis. Thus, if you are doing a case study to understand how technically unsophisticated users interact with anti-spyware and anti-virus tools, you probably don't want to ask computer science undergraduates, who are likely to be more technically savvy than most users. The additional credibility that comes from having appropriate participants is referred to as *external validity* (Yin, 2003b).

Multiple-case studies reduce concerns about external validity somewhat, as consistent findings across your cases can be used to counter the argument that you are describing some idiosyncrasy of your specific participants. However, these problems re-appear if you are attempting theoretical replication – members of each group must both represent that group appropriately while differing from other groups in the appropriate dimensions.

Sara's case study provides an instructive example of case selection. When reading the paper, all we are told about Sara is that she is a blind college student. We are not given any other details about her age, background, or socioeconomic status. However, we can infer from the list of tasks – which includes activities such as organizing CDs, cooking, and receiving text messages by cell phone – that she is fairly active and self-reliant. In other words, as far as we know, she may be an appropriate participant for a study of the workaround strategies used by people who are blind. We might not be able to make generalizations that apply her results to other people, but that would be true of any single participant. Furthermore, as the study was described as descriptive and explanatory (Yin, 2003b), the authors do not make any claims of generality.

Some case studies specifically seek out unusual, distinctive, or "edge" cases. When studying anti-spyware or anti-virus tools, you might argue that computer science undergraduates are worth studying because you would look for an understanding of how their domain expertise helped them approach challenges that would stop less knowledgeable users. The Finnish study of virtual collaboration in a school setting was conducted in a school that was chosen specifically because "the pedagogical setting had several features that may be described as innovative" (Lakkala, Ilomäki and Palonen, 2007). See the Extreme Cases sidebar for a description of a case study that specifically sought out an atypical set of participants in order to get a fresh perspective on an established problem.

Some studies use *critical cases* – cases that are somehow particularly distinctive or notable with respect to the problem that is being considered (Flyvbjerg, 2006). For example, a case study examining the use of anti-virus software by employees of a large company might focus on a firm that required all staff members to complete extensive training in the use of the tools in question. This required training makes the firm a strong candidate for success: if anti-virus software isn't used there, it might not be used anywhere. Thus, the company becomes a critical case.

Still other strategies for identifying cases are possible. You might search for cases that are most or least likely to exhibit behavior that you are interested in investigating (Flyvbjerg, 2006).

If you find yourself trying to choose from a large pool of potential cases, consider expanding your research agenda to include a screening survey (Yin, 2003a). A carefully-constructed survey of potential participants can provide data that informs your selection process. Such surveys might assess both the fit between the participants and your criteria and the willingness of the participants to commit their time and energy to the success of the study. Ideally, screening surveys stand on their own as research results, providing insights into the larger group of respondents not selected for closer examination in your case study (Yin, 2003a). See Chapter 5 for advice on conducting surveys.

7.8   Data collection

Having defined your research questions, chosen the number of cases and the units of analysis, and determined whether your study is embedded or holistic, you are ready to plan your data collection. Specifically, you need to define the types of data you will collect and the specific procedures you will follow for collecting those data.

7.8.1   Data sources and questions

As described in Section 7.2, case studies often, if not always, rely on multiple data sources. Data sources for case studies in other fields include documentation, archival records, interviews, direct observation, participant observation (similar to ethnography), and physical artifacts (Yin, 2003b). For HCI research, you may find yourself adapting and adding to this list as appropriate. If you're trying to understand someone's use of existing computer tools, e-mail messages, web history logs, and related data sources may be considered archival. Logs of specific activities with applications of interest might be available or you might be able to use a variety of technical approaches for collecting such data (see Chapter 12).

Your research questions and hypotheses will play a significant role in determining which of the available data sources you will use. Documentation and archival records are likely to be most interesting if you want to understand past and current practices and use of existing software tools. Interviews are helpful for understanding perceptions, concerns, needs, and other user reactions. Direct observation can help you understand what people do in circumstances of interest, while participant observation can be a powerful tool for understanding complex organizational dynamics. For HCI researchers, artifacts can be used to provide valuable examples of how people bridge the gap between computer work and the rest of their lives. Classic examples include paper notes stuck to the edge of computer monitors.

Your choice of the types of data that you will collect should be guided by the goal of using multiple sources that address your questions from different perspectives. For example, if you are interested in improving a data visualization tool, you might start by interviewing the user about impressions of the shortcomings and strengths of the current tool. This would provide some insight into subjective perceptions of the tool and its fitness for the user's work. A subsequent session of direct observation might find you looking over the user's shoulder as she analyzes some data. Think-aloud protocols can be particularly useful here. These sessions might help you observe techniques that she uses to accomplish her tasks, identify techniques that she uses to fix problems and recover from mistakes, and to hear other comments that might prove useful (such as "I wish I could ..." or "I wish there was a feature for ..."). Archival interaction logs (if available) might provide useful data regarding the frequency of use and subsequent interviews might invite your participant to describe her vision for the ideal tool for the task. Sara's case study took this approach, combining interviews about early technology use, demonstrations of various physical and software artifacts, and speculation about desired designs.

By using your research goals to guide a careful selection of data sources and specific questions, you will increase your chance of generating the multiple sources of evidence that form the backbone of data triangulation. A design that makes clear and explicit links between each of the data sources and your research questions will help you understand which questions are addressed by multiple data sources, and which are not. If you find that you have questions that are only represented in one of the data sources, you might want to rethink your design, adding additional data sources or questions.

7.8.2 Collecting data

Once you have identified your data sources, you need to develop protocols for how you will use each of them to collect data. For interviews, this will include the type of interview, questions, and an interview guide (see Chapter 8). Similar approaches can be used for examination of artifacts. Observations require you to specify the structure of the tasks that will be performed and the questions that will be asked. Each data source, in effect, becomes a mini-experiment within the larger case study, all tied to the common goals of the study as a whole.

You should also develop a protocol for the case study as a whole. In addition to the specific data sources and the procedures that you will use in examining each of these sources, the protocol includes important details that are needed to conduct the case study from start to finish. The case study protocol should start with an introduction, including the questions and hypotheses. It should continue with details of data collection procedures, including criteria for choosing cases, contact information for relevant individuals; and logistical plans for each case, including time requirements, materials, and other necessary preparations. Specific questions and methods for each of the data sources should be included in the protocol. Finally, the protocol should include an outline of the report that will be one of the products of the case study (Yin, 2003b).

Although this may seem like an excessive amount of overhead, effort spent on careful development of a protocol is rarely wasted. The process of developing a clear and explicit explanation of your research plan will help clarify your thinking, leading to a better understanding of possible shortcomings and challenges that may arise during the study. Any problems that you identify can stimulate reconsideration and redesign, leading to a stronger research plan.

A draft outline of your report serves a similar purpose. Constructing a report before you collect any data may seem strange, but it's actually quite constructive. Many of the sections of your report are easy to enumerate: your report will always contain an introduction to the problem, a description of your questions and hypotheses; an explanation of your design and how it addresses those questions; informative presentations of data and analysis; and discussions of results. Within each of these components there is substantial room for adaptation to meet the needs of each project. An outline that is as specific as possible – even down to the level of describing charts, tables, and figures to be used for presentation of data and analysis – will help guide your design of the questions and methods that you will use to generate the necessary data.

A case-study protocol can be a powerful tool for establishing reliability (Yin, 2003b). If your protocol is sufficiently detailed, you should be able to use it to conduct directly comparable investigations of multiple cases – the protocol guarantees that differences in procedures are not the cause of differences in your observations or results. Ideally, a research protocol will be clear enough that it can be used by other researchers to replicate your results.

Consider running a pilot case study. Pilot tests will help you debug your research protocols, identifying questions that you may have initially omitted while potentially exposing flaws in your analysis plans. For some studies, a pilot may not be possible or desirable. If you have a unique case, this may not be possible. If your study is exploratory, you may find that a single case will provide you with sufficient data to generate an informative analysis.

7.9   Analysis and interpretation

As qualitative data is a key component of case-study research, your analysis will use many of the techniques and strategies discussed in Chapter 11. You should start planning your data analysis early in the process, before you collect any data. Grounded theory, content analysis, and other techniques from Chapter 11 are commonly used to analyze case-study data.

Perhaps the largest challenge in the analysis of case-study data involves the limited range of data samples. Unlike controlled quantitative experiments, which use large numbers of participants to generate statistically significant results, case studies rely on a few samples, which may be idiosyncratic. This may present challenges if you are interested in building general models: how can you be confident that conclusions drawn from experience with your cases generalize to others?

To some extent, these validity concerns are inherent in case-study research. No matter how carefully you choose your cases, collect your data, or conduct your analysis, your case study may lead to interpretations that are not valid or do not generalize to other cases. You should always keep in mind that case study results may not generalize. Even if yours seems to point to trends that hold in all cases, you should avoid assuming that those trends are truly general.

Careful attention to the strategies described in Chapter 11 can help increase the rigor of your analysis and confidence in your conclusion. Triangulation, documentation of chains of evidence, and consideration of rival theories are all appropriate tools for case-study analysis.

Case-study analysis generally proceeds in a bottom-up fashion, using techniques from grounded theory to code and categorize data (see Chapter 11). In Sara's case, the analysis might have involved examining all of her descriptions of previous interactions with technology, her current approaches and speculative desires for solving a specific task. Any conclusions that were supported by all three of these approaches might be seen as being reasonably valid. These analyses could then be used to form an integrated description of the unit of analysis – the specific task.

After analyzing individual units of interest, you are likely to want to push your analysis to help you understand larger trends that describe your case as a whole and (for multiple-case studies) can be used to support comparison of similar cases. The goal here is not necessarily to make everything agree: there may be fundamental differences between individual units of analysis or cases. That's fine. The point is to facilitate understanding of the differences and similarities between the individual elements.

The multiplicity of data sources used in case-study research can support data source triangulation (Chapter 11). If you can use artifact, interview, and observation data together to provide a consistent interpretation of certain aspects of the case under examination, you will have a strong argument in favor of the validity of your interpretation.

Appropriate data displays can prove invaluable in this process. If you have multiple units of analysis that can be described in many ways, you may create a matrix display (Miles and Huberman, 1994) that lays out the data in a tabular format. With one unit of analysis per row and a specific aspect of the analysis in each column, these displays can easily be used to understand an individual unit (reading along a row) or to compare some aspect of each unit (reading down a column) see Table 7.1.

The relationship between the theory behind the case-study design and the analysis of Sara's individual tasks provides an opportunity for the use of an important case-study analysis technique – pattern matching. In this approach, case-study observations can be matched to predictions from the theory behind the design. Matches between the observations and the theory provide support for the theory (Yin, 2003b). The specific pattern that is being matched in Sara's study can be found in the researchers' discussion of their study: they initially believed that Sara would use a wide range of technological approaches and creative workarounds to solving problems, and that these practices would help provide a greater understanding of factors influencing the success or failure of tool designs. The description of each task in terms of the situation that led to the difficulty and the characteristics of the individual workarounds allowed each task to be matched directly to the theoretically proposed model.

A final level of analysis takes the comparisons between the units or cases and combines them to develop a model or framework that communicates the results of your case study and the over-arching themes that emerged from your analysis. As you analyze the individual pieces and their relationships, you may identify higher-level patterns, common concerns, or recurring ideas that may help explain, categorize, or organize your results. These explanations might cut across individual units of analysis or multiple cases, forming the basis of a case description (Yin, 2003b), which might organize your case study into specific areas of interest. In Sara's case study, the researchers identified several criteria that technologies must meet to satisfy her needs, including efficiency, portability, distinguishability of similar items, and suitability for socially appropriate use in a sighted community (Shinohara and Tenenberg, 2007). As always, you should be very careful to consider rival explanations (see Chapter 11).

Although case studies may rely heavily on qualitative data, quantitative data is often vitally important. A study of massive, multiplayer, online games (Ducheneaut, Moore and Nickell, 2007) used quantitative analysis to address questions left unresolved in the qualitative analysis. By defining measures of activity such as the number, frequency, and length of visits to social places, the researchers were able to conduct a quantitative analysis that provided a much richer description of the interaction dynamic than would have been possible with the qualitative data on its own.

7.10   Writing up the study

Documenting a case study can be a challenge. More so than many other presentations of research results, case studies often read like descriptive discussions. Instead of presenting quantitative data or statistical results, you may find yourself trying to construct a narrative argument that uses the strength of the organization and writing to construct a convincing argument. In other words, your case study may live or die on the strength of your writing.

As discussed in Section 7.8.2, starting your write-up early helps. Documenting your theory and your design in detail as soon as possible helps to clarify your thinking – you have these artifacts to go back to. You don't want to be in the position of having to reconstruct these important details from memory or incomplete notes long after the fact.

You should make your theories, data, methodologies, analytic steps, and models as explicit as possible. Clear presentation of these important components help readers to understand where you have come from and how you got to any particular conclusions that you may have derived.

Presentation of data and analysis may take many forms. You might present summaries of your data followed by detailed analysis or you might intersperse data with interpretation. Case study reports often use analyses of individual observations or incidents to draw attention to noteworthy details. These analyses set the stage for discussions of broader themes that arise from the analysis. Case study data are usually presented in one of two forms – either thematically (Shinohara and Tenenberg, 2007) or chronologically (Farooq *et al.*, 2007a). Chronological presentation is particularly useful for case studies that describe a project or process.

Story-telling is often an important component of a case-study report. Carefully chosen anecdotes bring concrete details to your discussion, supporting your analytic results. These stories are particularly useful – and often required – in cases of direct interpretation (Stake, 1995). If you have chosen a specific incident as warranting detailed interpretation, you should relate all of the relevant details. Stories can also be used to introduce discussions of various components of your analysis. Short *vignettes* (Stake, 1995; Yin, 2003a) that illustrate factors that you discuss in your analysis can make your subsequent analysis more concrete. These stories need not be narrative descriptions of specific incidents: direct quotes from interviews describing behaviors (Shinohara and Tenenberg, 2007) or individual perceptions (Troshynski, Lee and Dourish, 2008) work very well in this regard.

A case study of the use of participatory design in support of a community organization developing a website (Farooq *et al.*, 2007a) provides an example of a compelling and readable case study report. After introducing the problem and reviewing the literature, this report introduces the methodological approach of combining traditional participatory design methods with measures aimed at encouraging the learning that would need to happen for the project to continue to succeed after the research team ceased to be actively involved. The report continues by providing detailed background of the organization, including its context, goals, and staff resources. The data collection methods and analytic methods were then discussed. The case-study data were discussed chronologically, with analysis interspersed, leading to a discussion of implications of the results. The resulting report has details that might be of interest to a wide range of users, including HCI researchers, technology experts, and community organizers.

When appropriate, your case study report should also discuss rival explanations. Having taken the time to consider alternative explanations for any of your analytic results, you should document the results of this effort. Introducing the rival theories and explaining why the available evidence better supports your conclusions can bolster the credibility of your report. If you don't find any evidence in favor of the alternatives, say so (Yin, 2003a, 2003b).

Your write-up of your case study should reflect the limitations of case study research. Any discussions of observations that may apply to the community as a whole should be phrased so as to avoid claims of generality. If you make the same observation for several cases, you might say that your observation appears to apply to a broader population, but you should not claim that your conclusion is definitively general. You might also say that these recurring trends merit further investigation, implying the need for a more rigorously sampled study that would determine whether the findings were generally applicable. Proper attention to the validity of the claims that you are making will help defend you from critics who may feel that you are being overly broad in your interpretation.

Once you have written a draft of your report, you might consider letting your participants read it. This can be a valuable reality check – if your participants believe that you have the facts wrong, you may have a problem that needs to be revisited. If this happens, you may need to collect some more evidence to clarify the situation (Yin, 2003b). Participants may also provide alternative viewpoints on the data, possibly including explanations or theories that might (or might not) complement yours. You may not agree with all of the comments that your participants make, particularly with regards to interpretation of the data, but you should do your best to be receptive to constructive criticisms from your participants. Having taken the time to work with you, they are likely to have some interest in helping make your work and your report as accurate as possible.

Case study write-ups often face the troubling question of anonymity. When you're dealing with an individual or a specific group, concerns about privacy are very real: particularly for unique cases, your write-up may be too revealing for comfort. In some cases, protocols for the protection of human research subjects (see Chapter 14) might require that you do not identify the participants in a research study. A good rule of thumb might be to be conservative – when in doubt, protect your participants.

7.11 Informal case studies

Although careful planning and design are never completely inappropriate in HCI research, there may be times when the construction of a fully fledged case study is overkill. You may be starting a completely new project, without any understanding of the application domain or the needs of the users. Or, you might be interested in getting some initial response to a proposed design for a new feature that you've designed for a software tool. Yet another possibility involves validation: can you collect some data to document the success of your completed design?

In situations like these, your goal is not to develop a general model or to construct a rigorous argument. Rather, you're more interested in feedback that will help you understand a new situation or a "sanity check" that will indicate whether a new idea is worth pursuing. Informal case studies with a small number (as few as one) of carefully chosen participants can be very valuable sources of feedback. Informal case studies are frequently used by HCI researchers to describe the successful use of a tool – see the Interfaces for Quadriplegic People sidebar for an example.

These case studies are "informal" in the sense that some of the guidelines and procedures might be relaxed in favor of expediency. As you're not looking to make broad, generally applicable claims, you do not need the rigorous planning and record-keeping that is necessary to establish chains of evidence. You might forego a theoretical background or defined analytic framework in favor of simple note-taking and observation.

Imagine a foray into designing a tool for an unfamiliar domain. You might consider running a fully fledged case study, asking several experts in the domain what they do, how they do it, and what they might want in a tool. The potential utility of this study might be significant, but you might need some initial background to plan the details. An informal case study with one potential user might help you gather the initial understanding that is necessary for designing the complete case study. Sometimes, you may find that limits on available resources (time and personnel) make it impossible for you to conduct a complete study. If this happens, informal case studies may be your best option for understanding the problem.

If you're looking for feedback on a proposed design or constructed interface, an informal case study can be an attractive alternative to user studies or observation sessions. Particularly if you can work with a participant who will use your tool on a problem that interests her, you can use an informal session to document an instance of the successful use of your tool in the intended domain. A negative result can be informative here as well: if it turns out that your design is fundamentally flawed, your single case can help you identify the error early, before you go to the trouble of designing a more thorough summative evaluation.

Even if your case study is informal, your criteria for selecting participants should not be. Although the lesser time commitments of these shorter studies may make them more appealing to many participants, the relatively loose and informal nature may be troublesome to some. You probably don't want to do an informal, preliminary study of a proposed interface with a critical participant who won't be able to handle a few glitches along the way. People who are invested in the success of your project and willing to try out new ideas often make the best participants in informal case studies. It's not uncommon to rely upon such individuals for repeated sessions at different stages in a project: in such cases, these individuals become informants (see Chapters 8 and 9), providing a detailed understanding of the problem and regular feedback that (ideally) helps keep your project on track.

Although informal case studies may appear to be somewhat simpler than fully realized studies, you should still strive to be as rigorous as possible. An informal study conducted during an hour-long session can still involve multiple methods of data collection, a theoretical basis, and careful definition of the units of analysis. Although your data collection procedures might be relatively simple, you still want to keep careful notes and document your analysis appropriately.

Informal case studies trade scientific rigor for ease of data collection. By foregoing the use of multiple data sources, triangulation, and analytic techniques that give full-blown case studies scientific rigor, informal studies provide for the possibility of "quick-and-dirty" study and insights. Effective use of this approach and appropriate communication of results requires a clear understanding of the limits of this approach.

The example of Sara's use of technology provides a clear picture of the difference between formal and informal case studies. In studying Sara, the research team made multiple visits to Sara's home, using several techniques to examine technologies from differing perspectives. Building from a theoretical grounding in theories of interaction with devices in the home and the importance of failures and workarounds, the analysis of observations from these sessions led to a number of insights that point to potentially generalizable insights that might be addressed by designers of technologies for blind people (Shinohara and Tenenberg, 2007).

Imagine, instead, an informal case study of the same situation, involving a single, hour-long visit, using only observational techniques, and lacking a theoretical basis. This study might yield some interesting observations, but you'd be hard-pressed to gather the data that would inform the insights identified in the full case study. The abbreviated nature of the data collection session might limit your use of multiple sources, leaving you with less confidence in any particular result. As trends and themes that might arise during a longer session might not be apparent in the single visit, generalization of insights would be difficult, if not impossible. You might be able to use the session to generate some discussion that would be part of a longer report, but this informal case study would not stand very well on its own.

Reports of informal case studies should take these limitations into account. If your investigation is truly informal, you may wish to avoid the term "case study" altogether. This will help you avoid the possibility of creating a false impression of a rigorous study. Instead, you might talk about the lessons learned from observations of one or more individuals. Appropriately cautious statements about the significance of your observations and candid admission that more study is needed can help you avoid criticisms that the informality of your procedures does not justify the claims that you are making.

Informal case studies are often most effective as intermediate steps in larger research processes. This can be true of studies that are used as a pilot investigation of user needs prior to a more formal study with multiple cases or as initial investigations of a tool in use before conducting larger summative evaluations. Descriptions of these case studies and how they influenced the subsequent investigations can be valuable pieces of your eventual write-up.

Summary

As every individual who uses computing tools does so in a unique context, with specific goals, back-grounds, and abilities, every use of a computer interface is, in some sense, an HCI case study. Close examination of these contextual factors can give researchers a rich, detailed understanding of the factors that influence system requirements and determine the success or failure of proposed designs. Unlike controlled experiments, which attempt to find general answers to fairly narrow questions, case studies are deep and narrow, focusing on thorough exploration of a small set of cases.

If your research leads you to a situation that seems to be in some sense notable or perhaps unique, you might find yourself considering a case study. Possibilities include studying a domain expert's information management techniques in order to inform the design of a new system; comparing two installations of a new collaborative tool in different contexts; or describing your use of a new participatory design technique in the development of a new tool. Regardless of the context, you should be clear about your goals, as they impact how you design and conduct your study. If you are interested in generalizing from your cases to make broader claims, you should be particularly careful about your research design and analysis, making sure that the data favor your arguments over alternative explanations. Open-ended explorations aimed at generating ideas and descriptions of a unique or unusual situation may not make any broader claims, but they will still benefit from a clearly thought-out design and analysis plan.

Case-study research is harder than it may look. Although the small number of participants and the lack of quantitative analysis may be appealing, the studies present substantial analytical and logistical challenges. Selecting cases is often difficult, whether you are identifying the most promising participants from a large pool or worrying about the representativeness of the sole case that you have been able to find. Collecting multiple, corroborating pieces of data may be difficult and teasing interesting insights out of potentially messy and inconsistent data can be tricky, scheduling the appropriate meetings and working around the needs of your participants.

The case study's focus on deep, narrow investigation leads to inevitable concerns about validity. How can we learn anything general from the study of a small set – sometimes only having one member – of instances of a given phenomenon? With rigorous evaluation involving multiple participants and (very often) statistically-analyzed quantitative results playing such a pivotal role in recent HCI research, it may be hard to convince some critical readers that case-study research is worthwhile. "This study only includes one participant", they might say, "so how can we apply it to others?"

Case studies that make broad claims of generality are particularly likely to infuriate these critics, who may feel that any generalization from case studies is inappropriate. When conducting and describing case study research, always take care to remember the limits of this approach, and try to avoid making claims that cannot be sustained by a small number of cases.

Although concerns about validity and reliability are certainly appropriate, critics of case studies risk the loss of a valuable research tool. In digging deep into concrete situations, they can help researchers identify design particulars that are likely to go unnoticed by research in usability labs. In focusing on specific situations, they provide concrete illustrations of needs, motivations, and successes or failures. As explanatory tools, they take requirements from the abstract to the specific. Particularly when presented alongside complementary user studies that provide broader-based data, case studies can paint rich pictures that deepen our understanding of complex phenomena.

Case studies succeed when they build upon the fundamental human activity of learning through story-telling. If your case study can use the details of a specific situation to tell the story behind some HCI research question, it will succeed in its ultimate goal of increasing understanding and communicating that understanding to a broader audience.

Discussion Questions

1. Case studies can be useful tools for exploring user requirements for software tools, but they present challenges: given a small number of cases, your results may not be generally applicable. Some user requirements from a case study might be easy to implement with minimal impact on a design – these might be included even if they are not of broad interest. Other requirements might require fundamental changes to system design. How can you be confident that you have gained a thorough, general understanding that is suitable for designing an application of broader interest? If additional cases are not available, how might you use other HCI research techniques to bolster your confidence in the results of your case study?

2. Case studies involve working closely with individuals who may have a substantial interest in the results of your work. This might lead some participants to put "spin" on their interactions with you, framing their activities and responses to questions to increase the likelihood of achieving their desired outcomes. How might you design your study and choose your data sources to account for this concern?

3. Although the case study of Sara's use of technology is a good example of case-study research, our discussion of it represents a different type of case study: case study for educational purposes. Based on the discussion and analysis found in this chapter, how does an educational case study differ from a research case study? Consider questions such as the type of study, the number of cases, the data sources, and the analysis.

Research Design Exercises

1. Sara's case study is an embedded, single-case study, with the individual tasks as units of analysis. Suppose you wanted to conduct a literal replication of this study with another blind person. Keeping in mind the potential differences in living arrangements, lifestyles, and personal habits that might distinguish Sara from other blind college students, describe the challenges that you might face in conducting this replication. If you could ask the authors of the paper about Sara for access to their notes and records, which items would be of particular interest? How would these challenges differ if you were to do a theoretical replication with another blind individual who was different from Sara in some potentially important regard, such as a retired person?

2. Case studies often focus on groups or organizations as their units of analysis. As specific details of group dynamics can influence the success or failure of software tools, these studies can be very helpful for understanding the use of tools for collaboration or other organizational goals. Design a case study aimed at understanding the information sharing and management processes of your research groups. What would your underlying questions be? What hypotheses would you wish to explore? Describe your units of analyses, data sources, and analytic approach.

References

Bilandzic, M., Foth, M., and De Luca, A. (2008) CityFlocks: Designing social navigation for urban mobile information systems. *Proceedings of the ACM Conference on Designing Interactive Systems,* 174–183.

Blythe, M., Monk, A., and Park, J. (2002) Technology biographies: Field study techniques for home use product development. *Extended Abstracts of the ACM Conference on Human Factors in Computer Systems,* 658–659.

Cohene, T., Baecker, R., Marziali, E., and Mindy, S. (2007) Memories of a life: A design case study for Alzheimer's Disease. In J. Lazar (ed.), *Universal Usability: Designing Computer Interfaces for Diverse User Populations.* London: John Wiley & Sons.

Davies, D.K., Vosloo, H.F., Vannan, S.S., and Frost, P.E. (2008) Near real-time fire alert system in South Africa: From desktop to mobile service. *Proceedings of the ACM Conference on Designing Interactive Systems,* 315–322.

Druin, A., Weeks, A., Massey, S., and Bederson, B.B. (2007) Children's interests and concerns when using the International Children's Digital Library: A four-country case study. *Proceedings of the ACM/IEE-CS Joint Conference on Digital Libraries,* 167–176.

Ducheneaut, N., Moore, R., and Nickell, E. (2007) Virtual "Third Places": A Case Study of Sociability in Massively Multiplayer Games. *Computer Supported Cooperative Work,* **16**(1):129–166.

Farooq, U., Ganoe, C.H., Xiao, L., *et al.* (2007a) Supporting community-based learning: Case study of a geographical community organization designing its website. *Behaviour & Information Technology,* **26**(1): 5–21.

Farooq, U., Schank, P., Harris, A., *et al.* (2007b) Sustaining a community computing infrastructure for online teacher professional development: A case study of designing tapped in. *Computer Supported Cooperative Work,* **16**(4):397–429.

Flyvbjerg, B. (2006) Five misunderstandings about case-study research. *Qualitative Inquiry,* **12**(2):219–245.

Hochheiser, H. (2000) Browsers with changing parts: A catalog explorer for Philip Glass' website. *Proceedings of the ACM Conference on Designing Interactive Systems,* 105–115.

Lakkala, M., Ilomäki, L., and Palonen, T. (2007) Implementing virtual collaborative inquiry practises in a middle-school context. *Behaviour & Information Technology,* **26**(1):37–53.

Miles, M.B. and Huberman, A.M. (1994) *Qualitative Data Analysis.* Thousand Oaks, CA: Sage Publications.

Naaman, M., Nair, R., and Kaplun, V. (2008) Photos on the go: A mobile application case study. *Proceedings of the ACM Conference on Human Factors in Computing Systems,* 1739–1748.

Shinohara, K. and Tenenberg, J. (2007) Observing Sara: A case study of a blind person's interactions with technology. *Proceedings of the ACM Conference on Assistive Technology (ASSETS),* 171–178.

Stake, R.E. (1995) *The Art of Case Study Research.* Thousand Oaks, CA: Sage Publications.

Steriadis, C.E. and Constantinou, P. (2003) Designing human–computer interfaces for quadriplegic people. *ACM Transactions on Computer–Human Interaction*, **10**(2):87–118.

Troshynski, E., **Lee, C.**, **and Dourish, P.** (2008) Accountabilities of presence: Reframing location-based systems. *Proceedings of the ACM Conference on Human Factors in Computing Systems*, 487–496.

Yin, R.K. (2003a) *Applications of Case Study Research*. Thousand Oaks, CA: Sage Publications.

Yin, R.K. (2003b) *Case Study Research: Design and methods*, 3rd edition. Thousand Oaks, CA: Sage Publications.

Interviews and focus groups

Direct feedback from interested individuals is fundamental to human–computer interaction (HCI) research. What should a new tool do? Ask the users. Does a proposed design do what it should do? If not, what should be changed or revised? Ask the users. As discussed in Chapter 5, surveys can be very useful in this regard, particularly for reaching large numbers of people easily. Unfortunately, surveys are somewhat limiting: respondents only answer questions that are asked and open-ended questions that invite long, written responses are likely to go largely unanswered. As a result, surveys often end up being broad but not deep.

An alternative approach is to go deep but not broad. Direct conversations with fewer participants can provide perspectives and useful data that surveys might miss. Conversation and interaction with the right people can be both a hugely important source of insight and a significant challenge. What you ask, how you ask it, and who you ask can determine the difference between novel insight and wasted time. As with so many other topics in computing, garbage in leads to garbage out.

Direct discussions with concerned participants usually takes one of two forms: *interviews* with individuals and *focus groups* involving multiple users at one time. Interviews and focus groups have different strengths and challenges: which approach you should use is perhaps the first key question to be answered. Other questions address structure and timing. How formal do you want to be? Conversations can range from free-form unstructured interviews to semi-structured and fully structured interviews. When should you conduct your interviews or focus groups? As with other data collection approaches, interviews and focus groups can be used for both formative and summative purposes.

Having answered these questions, you're ready to face the big challenge – actually conducting interviews or convening focus groups. Successful use of these approaches is an art in itself, requiring significant conversational and observational skills. Moving conversation along, eliciting meaningful responses, revising questions based on interview responses, interpreting subtle cues, and interpreting detailed responses all require practice and experience.

This chapter discusses these issues, with an eye towards preparing you for designing and conducting interviews and focus groups. The challenges are real, but the value is there. If you don't listen to your users, you might miss some of the most important feedback that you can get.

8.1 Pros and cons of interviews

The ability to "go deep" is perhaps the strongest argument in favor of interviewing. By asking questions that explore a wide range of concerns about a problem and giving interviewees the freedom to provide detailed responses, researchers can use interviews to gather data that would otherwise be very hard to capture. Given a chance to talk, and questions that encourage reflection and consideration, interviewees may go on at great length, generating ideas and sharing insights that would have been lost to surveys.

Like ethnography (Chapter 9) and other observational techniques, interviews can be open-ended and exploratory. Although almost all interviews have specific questions that must be asked, interviews can be extremely flexible. Based on interviewee responses, interviewers can choose to re-order questions or invent completely new lines of inquiry on the fly. Opportunistic interviewing – taking an interesting idea and running with it – can be particularly useful for increasing understanding.

The flip side of this compelling flexibility lies in the challenges of managing potentially unbounded discussions. Interviews are much more difficult to conduct than surveys. Interviewing is a skill that can take significant practice to develop. Furthermore, it's hard work. Sitting with one interviewee (or a dozen focus group participants) for an hour, listening carefully, taking notes, trying to decide which comments to pursue with further questions, and trying to understand non-verbal reactions all take substantial effort.

Higher effort requirements also limit interview-based studies to relatively small numbers of participants. Surveys can easily be sent to dozens, if not hundreds, of potential respondents who can complete them at their leisure. Interviews, however, are much more limiting. If each interview is one hour long, someone on your research staff team has to spend that hour with an interviewee. You're likely to find that your personnel resources are the limiting factor: don't be surprised if you find that you simply don't have the time to conduct all of the interviews that you were hoping for.

Analysis is also a major challenge. Transforming raw notes and recordings of open-ended responses to broad questions can take a great deal of time – as much as 10 hours for a single hour of audio recording (Robson, 2002). Deciding what is important and what is not – separating the good from the bad – can be a challenge.

Interviews share some inherent shortcomings with surveys. As both involve data collection that is separated from the task and context under consideration, they suffer from problems of recall. As participants report on their perceptions of needs or experiences, they are telling you what they remember. While this may provide some very useful data, it is, by definition, one step removed from reality. If you ask a software user which features they might need, the answers you get during an interview may be very different from the answers that same person might provide while sitting in front of a computer and actually using the tool in question.

To avoid these potential disconnects, you might consider combining your interviews with other techniques, such as observation – possibly during the interview session. These observations will help you understand the relationship between what interviewees say and what they do. As some researchers have suggested, "look at behavior, listen to perceptions" (Miller and Crabtree, 1999).

One study of the habits of users of in-car navigation systems used both road trips and interviews. During the rides, researchers observed drivers as they used the navigation systems to find their way. Detailed questions were asked after the drive in separate interviews, as responding in-depth while driving may have been too distracting. Observations from the ride, audio recordings, and the interviews were studied to understand how drivers used the navigation system (Leshed *et al.*, 2008).

8.2   Applications of interviews in HCI research

HCI researchers use interviews and focus groups to help build an understanding of the needs, practices, concerns, preferences, and attitudes of the people who might interact with a current or future computer system. In their focus and breadth, interviews share strengths with several other research techniques. Like usability studies and surveys, interviews can involve a moderately large group of participants, often including quantitative results. At the same time, interviews are subjective and more open-ended, often providing deeper insights similar to those associated with ethnographies and case studies.

HCI researchers can use interviews in almost any phase of a project, from initial exploration to requirements gathering, evaluation of prototypes, and summative evaluation of completed products.

8.2.1   Initial exploration

Imagine that you've just been asked to investigate new possibilities for helping people to manage digital artifacts of their lives (pictures and videos). You've got a strong feeling that the current tools are insufficient but you'd like to develop a better understanding of what people are doing and what they'd like to do. Ideally, this understanding would help you generate some ideas for developing a tool that will be the next great sensation.

In situations like this, where you're starting out from an almost clean slate, interviews and focus groups can be vital tools. You might sit down with various potential users to understand their goals and needs. What would they like to do with their pictures and videos? How do these artifacts play into their daily lives? Where and when are they most likely to reach for a picture or video? How do they use these records to tell stories about their lives? You might ask about existing technology practices, but your primary goal is to understand user needs and goals, so you might want to focus on asking high-level questions about types of functionality that are and aren't available, as opposed to specific details of design that may be troublesome.

Asking these broader questions in an interview or focus group can help you generate a deeper and more nuanced understanding of the problem. You might ask the following exploratory questions to understand how people use these media:

- What sort of recordings do you make of personal events? Pictures? Videos? Audio Recordings?
- How do you view these recordings? On a computer? On a TV?
- Where do you view them? Any particular rooms in the house? Outside the house?
- Who do you show them to? On what sort of occasions?
- How do you organize recordings?
- Do you ever make multiple records of a single event? How do you keep them together?
- Do you share these artifacts with friends or family? If so, how?
- Have you ever lost track of any particularly valuable photo or video?

- Do you edit photos or video?
- Do you distinguish between recordings that you've made and those that were made by family members or others?
- Have you found yourself interested in doing something with your recordings that your tools did not support? If so, what?

Note that interviews at this stage are not focused on specific questions of functionality and design. The goal is to understand the needs and challenges presented by a particular situation. Once those needs are well-understood, you can move on to specific details that would lead to a concrete design.

Exploratory interviews share much in common with case studies (Chapter 7) and ethnography (Chapter 9), as they are all intended to provide understanding of a complex and multifaceted situation. Interviews and focus groups have the advantage of being relatively easy and inexpensive to conduct: a series of four or five focus groups in different neighborhoods, each containing 5–10 individuals, could be used to collect a broad range of data in a matter of weeks, where case studies and ethnography might take months.

A recent study used this approach to understand why and when people replace cell phones, in the hopes of finding possibilities for designing phones and practices that would be more sustainable (Huang and Truong, 2008). Researchers combined web surveys with follow-on telephone interviews with a small number of participants. Analysis of over 700 items from the surveys and the interviews led to an understanding of why people replace phones (for example, incentives to renew contracts or phone malfunctions) and what they do with old phones (give them to friends, donate to charities, hold on to them, or throw them out). These and other insights led to design suggestions, including the possibility of using contact lists to automatically identify friends who might need a new phone, modular designs that might allow for easy upgrading of appearance and features, and repurposing phones for other purposes, such as museum guides.

The Finding and Reminding and Green Living Interviews sidebars provide in-depth descriptions of two examples of the use of exploratory interviews for improving understanding of user needs, in the interest of building tools to meet those needs.

Research In Practice

Finding and Reminding

In the early 1980s, desktop information systems were relatively new and understanding of how people should organize information was incomplete at best. The desktop model (with files, folders, and other items that might be found on an office desk) was gaining popularity at this time. Thomas Malone, a researcher at Xerox's Palo Alto Research Center, noticed that although desktop interfaces claimed to mimic how people worked at their desks, this argument was not supported by research. None of the proposed desktop systems had any basis in research into how people actually organized information (Malone, 1983).

To address this shortcoming, Malone interviewed 10 workers in their offices. At the start of each interview, the interviewee would describe the layout of their office, indicating where information was stored and why. The interviewer did not ask any structured questions during this tour, but he did ask for clarification. At the end of the interviews, some interviewees were asked to find documents (suggested by co-workers who believed that those documents would be in that office). All participants were asked the following set of questions about their practices:

1. How well organized would you say your office is on a scale from 1 to 5? [1 = not very well organized, 3 = about average, and 5 = very well organized]
2. What would you say are the biggest problems you have with the way your office is organized?
3. Do you keep lists of things to do?
4. Do you keep a calendar of appointments?
5. How often are you unable to find something you are looking for in your office? [Number of times per week or month]
6. How often do you forget to do something you were supposed to do? [Number of times per week or month]

The analysis of the data took several forms. Two participants – one with a "neat" office and another with a "messy" office – were described in detail to illustrate very different approaches. Malone divided participants into these categories based on his observations and used the answer to the question 1 as validation: the people he rated as "messy" all had low scores, while the "neat" people had high scores. Photographs were used to verify that the messy people had more piles.

Malone used his observation of the workers and their offices to note that people used structured named *files* alongside unnamed, unorganized *piles*. This led him to suggest that information systems should support the creation of unnamed collections of information. Piles appeared to play the special role of *reminders* of work that had to be done: fully two-thirds of the piles were piles of things to do. Malone also noted that respondents often left information unclassified because they weren't quite sure how to organize it.

These observations led several suggestions for information environments. According to Malone, information systems should support the creation of hierarchies that would allow multiple classifications for any artifact. However, information systems should also allow for deferred classification – essentially giving the user the ability to create an electronic pile that might not be named until much later (if ever). Automatic classification – perhaps based on when information was accessed – might help as well. Powerful search facilities would be helpful, as would graphical aids for indicating the priority of various items on the to-do list.

More than 25 years later, Malone's investigation of information management practices is still relevant and more than a few of his suggestions remain absent from desktop operating environments. His methods, questions, and analysis illustrate how well-conducted interviews can inform and guide HCI research.

Research
In
Practice

Green Living Interviews

Environmental concerns have led to an interest in applying HCI techniques and practices to the development of tools and systems that encourage people to make environmentally responsible choices. To understand more concretely what this would mean, a group of researchers conducted a qualitative study with people in the United States who had made substantial commitment to the use of environmentally responsible systems or construction in their homes (Woodruff, Hasbrouck and Augustin, 2008). These criteria were used because people who were willing to take the time and money to install solar panels or use salvaged materials to renovate their home were presumed to be deeply concerned about environmental matters. The researchers used green movements, green-home tours, and email lists to find appropriate participants, which led to a diverse group of 56 participants living in 35 homes in several locations in California, New Mexico, and Oregon.

Home visits were used to conduct the bulk of the data collection. Each of the visits included a semi-structured interview, a tour of the house, and other activities aimed at understanding user needs and perspectives, typically over the course of two to three hours. The visits were video-taped and photographed. These visits generated a substantial amount of data. Verbatim transcripts of all visits totaling around 3000 pages were analyzed by affinity clustering (Beyer and Holtzblatt, 1998). The roughly 5000 photos taken during the visit were analyzed as well.

This analysis led to a detailed understanding of participants' motivation, practices, and choices. Motivations ranged from concerns about stewardship of the earth to self-reliant tendencies and a desire to be sustainability trend-setters. Participants tended to be very thoughtful about their choices, which frequently involved an ongoing and gradual process. Many spoke of the continuing effort required to maintain the systems and tools that they used, comparing the effort to living on a ship. Participants were generally highly independent, valuing uniqueness, but they also saw a value in teaching and providing an example to others.

The research team used these perspectives to identify a number of implications for design in support of sustainable behavior. Detailed, "in-depth" learning opportunities, mentoring, and interactive tools that aid in the exploration of the impact of various alternatives might help people make decisions regarding the adoption of green tools. Social networking tools might also be used to help people establish appealing green identities. Noting that broader adoption of sustainable practices might require making these choices more approachable to a broader population, the authors suggest the development of tools that would support broader social change. Interactive technologies in support of digital democracy aimed at changing environmental policy, sharing and distribution of environmental data, and even construction of opportunities for social protest might prove constructive in this effort (Woodruff, Hasbrouck and Augustin, 2008).

8.2.2   Requirements gathering

During the process of gathering requirements for the design of a new tool, interviews can be invaluable for understanding user needs and concerns. Interviews conducted at this early stage in the process are likely to be fairly broad. What are the user's goals? How are they being met by current tools (if any are available)? What do users want to do that they are currently unable to do? What are the frustrations? Are the tasks associated with a given problem flexible enough to communicate with tools that solve different, but related problems?

Interviewing in search of requirements requires an appropriately broad and open-ended view of the possibilities. A focus on narrow questions or existing tools might be too limiting. Instead, you want to ask broader questions about current – possibly non-computer – practices, future goals, frustrations and concerns. You might even ask your participants to try to describe things that they'd like to do, regardless of the ideas' feasibility with current software: "If you could describe the perfect system for solving your problem, what would it look like?"

Returning to the example of managing digital artifacts (Section 8.2.1), suppose your initial interviews led to the idea of building a tool that would allow users to create digital scrapbooks combining photos, audio, video, text, and other multimedia. You would like your tool to support "one-stop shopping" – letting users do all of the necessary steps in one application without having to move data between multiple tools. To make this work effectively, you would need to understand the sorts of thing people currently do to construct these scrapbooks, so that you might understand how to build a tool that would meet user needs.

Asking users how they lay out photos in a page-layout or web-page-creation system may be at too low a level of detail. In response to this question, an interviewee might talk about very specific tools for managing page content. As interesting and relevant as this may be – and it could be very interesting indeed – this line of inquiry might fail to uncover some insights that could be much more intriguing. If you instead were to ask the interviewee what he wanted to communicate with the scrapbooks and who the audience would be, you might get the inspiration for a new product or set of features aimed at completing similar tasks – insights that you would never have had with the simpler interview questions. The following list of questions might be asked to gather requirements for this scrapbook creation activity:

- What sort of scrapbook are you creating? Will it cover one event or many? Is it for family, friends, coworkers, or all of the above?
- How do you create traditional scrapbooks? What do you put into them? What do they look like? Can you show me a scrapbook that you've made?
- What sort of things do you want to put in the scrapbook? Pictures, music, movies, artwork? Anything else?
- How do you want to arrange things? Do you want to have individual pages like a traditional scrapbook, or should the layout be more open-ended, as if you were working on a large canvas?
- How would people read your scrapbook? Do you want them to have a set start-to-finish order or should readers be free to explore in any way that they like?
- How many items would you want to put in a scrapbook?
- How and where would people read the scrapbook? Do you want to project it on a wall? Send it via email? View it on TV or on a phone? Post it on a web page?
- Do you want to give users tools to make comments and notes on your scrapbook?
- How would your scrapbook relate to others? Would you create links between scrapbooks posted on your own web pages or on social networking sites?

Note how little these questions have to do with the specific tools being used.

Although this approach to interviewing may help you get started, you may find that you need more information to truly understand user needs. Ethnographic techniques (see Chapter 9) and interviewing strategies such as contextual inquiry (see Section 8.4.2) are among the strategies that HCI researchers have used to gain a deeper and more nuanced perspective on work processes and related user needs.

Low-level questions about how tasks are completed may be more appropriate if you are trying to improve interaction and process details for specific tools. You might ask how users accomplish various goals, which approaches they use (for example, menu selections or keyboard shortcuts), what problems they face, which facilities work well, and which don't, and what sorts of functionality they'd like to add to their current software.

To really understand how someone uses current tools, you might ask them to demonstrate how they complete typical tasks. As they go about their tasks, you might ask questions aimed at helping you understand what they are doing and why. This approach may blur the line between interviewing and observation. Effectively, the tool acts as a "probe" – an external aid that encourages interviewees to provide more detail and explanation. The following list gives examples of questions relating to the use of available tools for the scrapbook example:

- Which tools do you use for scrapbook creation? What do you use each of them for?
- What types of data do you use in your current tools for scrapbook creation?
- Do you have to make frequent use of multiple tools? Do you often move data between tools?
- How do you enter or organize the data values?
- Which calculations do you make? How do you make them?
- Can you preview your output?
- Do you print your scrapbooks on paper?
- What do your tools *not* do that you would like to be able to do?
- If you could change or improve this process, what would you do?
- Please show me how you create a scrapbook. Please explain which steps you take and why.

8.2.3   Evaluation and subjective reactions

Interviews can also be very useful during the development process. As prototypes are developed, interviews can capture the reactions of various users. Early user feedback on information flow, location of controls, use of language, and other aspects can help designers validate their approach and identify areas in need of revision. Interviews at these stages focus on specific questions aimed at eliciting reactions to various design elements. Similarly, interviews can provide useful input for summative evaluations of completed products. A broader focus in such interviews may be productive, as the summative reactions to a completed tool can inform the process of designing the next revision. Interview questions for evaluating the design of proposed interfaces for the scrapbook tool may include:

- Do you find this interface easy to use?
- Do you understand the menus, icons, and language?
- Are you able to complete the comparisons that you want to do? If not, where do you have trouble?
- Are any parts of the interface particularly useful or helpful?
- How does this interface compare to your current tool?
- What (if anything) would you like to change about this tool?

Additional questions for understanding user reactions to interface designs might be based on existing usability surveys, such as the Questionnaire for User Interface Satisfaction (QUIS) (Chin, Diehl and Norman, 1988).

The strengths and weaknesses of interviewing make it a strong complement to several other techniques. For understanding a problem during requirements gathering, a broad-based survey might be combined with a small number of in-depth interviews. Complementary questions in the two formats would allow researchers to combine a deep understanding of user needs and challenges (from the interviews) with an appreciation of how well those concerns generalize to a larger set of potential users.

For evaluation of an existing interface, you might combine usability tests or empirical studies aimed at understanding specific details of interface usability with interviews that ask about general reactions. These interviews can help you understand user perceptions, likes, and dislikes. This combination of results from different approaches can be informative and perplexing: don't be surprised if the usability or empirical studies are completely at odds with your interviews. This seemingly inconsistent state of affairs may arise if you're comparing two alternative designs: interviewees may prefer design A over design B, even though your studies indicated that design B was somehow superior (perhaps faster or less error prone) to A. These results present an opportunity for you to dig deeper in search of insights that might help you reconcile the contradiction. If you can find out why they preferred A, despite B's superior performance, you might use that information to develop a design C that combines the best elements of A and B.

8.3   Who to interview

Who should you interview? When you are running usability studies, empirical tests, or observations, the question of participant selection starts from an obvious point: current or potential users of your proposed system or alternatives. If your interviews are aimed at trying to understand the pros and cons of specific features of a proposed interface, users might be appropriate interviewees. In either case, you might find that there are different categories of users who have differing views. Including representatives of each type of user will help ensure that you are not missing important perspectives. For investigations of broader concerns, such as system requirements or overall evaluation of system operation, a broader pool of interviewees drawn from all categories of *stakeholder* might be more informative.

A stakeholder is anyone who is affected by the use of a system. Relatively simple applications, such as games or Internet chat clients, might have only one type of user that you would want to interview. Then again, simplicity might be illusory – novice game-players may have different perspectives from experts. Enterprise information systems, such as university course registration and management tools may have multiple types of users (or stakeholders), ranging from administrators who approve purchases of the tool and rely upon it for high-level reports, faculty who use it to manage course enrollment and grades, and students who must register for courses and pay tuition. In some cases, stakeholders may not be users at all: patients and their families may have valuable insights regarding hospital information systems, even if they never use them directly. For any reasonably complex system, you can expect that different groups of stakeholders will have very different perspectives on requirements, necessary functionality, and usability. Interviews with representatives of all of the stakeholder groups – or, at least, as many as possible – will provide a more complete picture of the situation.

Particularly when you are involved in an ongoing, long-term project with an organization or a group of users, you may find that there are certain individuals who are particularly good sources of information. These people may be particularly knowledgeable about how relevant work is done, they may play pivotal roles in the organization in question, or they may simply be unusually forthcoming. These individuals may play the role of *key informants*: individuals who are repeatedly called upon to provide important insights, usually over an extended period of time. Key informants can provide invaluable perspectives, if your interactions and relationship are well-managed. Key informants must be selected carefully and their insights must be validated by external confirmation from other sources. A disgruntled employee with an axe to grind would not make a good key informant. Particularly in a workplace situation, you should take care not to abuse any information that might be used against the informant (Gilchrist and Williams, 1999). Working with key informants is closely related to – and, indeed, can be the first step in – ethnographic research, a topic discussed in detail in Chapter 9.

As with any other research, interviews should be conducted in a manner that respects the participants (see Chapter 14). For studies that involve populations of participants facing special needs or challenges, this may require extra care in planning and execution. Le Dantec and Edwards' study of the information practices of homeless people illustrates some of these challenges. Noting that simply looking for homeless people on the street could be problematic, they worked with outreach groups who provided feedback and acted as mediators between the researchers and the homeless interviewees. In consultation with caseworkers, they offered participants a choice of store gift cards or public transportation cards as incentives. Staff at the centers worked with the researchers to identify appropriate participants. Subjects were given disposable cameras and asked to take pictures of daily activities, places where they needed help, and things that they use. Subsequent interviews used the photos that the participants took to guide discussions about their use of phones, Internet, transportation, and other technology. The researchers found that their respondents made substantial use of voicemail and mobile phones, while relatively few used computers or the Internet. These observations formed the basis for a detailed discussion of the challenges of both meeting the needs of, and continuing to work with, this challenging population (Le Dantec and Edwards, 2008).

8.4 Interview strategies

8.4.1 How much structure?

Fully structured interviews use a rigid script to present questions in a well-defined order. Although some questions may be skipped, based on answers to previous questions, there is no room for asking questions out of order or for adding questions not found in the pre-defined interview script. You might think of a fully structured interview as a survey administered by a researcher, with some important differences. It's easier to answer an interview question than it is to write an answer to the same question in a survey. An interview question might yield an extensive answer to a question that would generate only a few words in a survey response.

Fully structured interviews also have the advantage of being relatively easy to analyze. If each subject is asked the same questions in the same order, and related topics are grouped together in the ordering, interviewees are likely to comment on similar topics at similar points. Analyzing these responses may be as easy as collecting all answers to each question in a single place.

The framework provided by a fully structured interview can be a curse as well as a blessing. In a fully structured interview, you must follow the script. If the interviewee makes some comments that you'd like to follow up or if you think of some unanticipated question that you'd like to ask, you're out of luck. Requests for clarification or additional questions are inappropriate, as they interfere with the primary motivation for using a fully structured interview: ensuring that each interviewee is asked the same questions.

If you want some room to ask for clarification, add questions, or follow interviewee comments wherever they may take you, a *semi-structured* interview may be more appropriate. These discussions generally start with a set of questions, which may be similar (if not identical) to questions that might be used in a fully structured interview. However, in a semi-structured interview, you can feel free to let the conversation go where it may. If your interviewee mentions something of interest, you can say "tell me more about that . . . ." After she clarifies, you might inquire "how does this relate to . . ." or perhaps ask a question from further down on your list. Your goal should be to dig through the interviewee's comments, opportunistically looking for opportunities to gain additional insight and understanding.

Unstructured interviews take this idea to its logical extreme. An unstructured interview may simply be based on a list of topics or questions known as an interview guide (Robson, 2002). To conduct an unstructured interview, you would start off with an initial question for your interviewee, and then you would listen, letting the interviewee respond as she sees fit, discussing topics of her choosing. If conversation slows or stalls, you might introduce another topic or question from your interview guide. As the main benefit of using unstructured interviews lies in letting your interviewees focus on the topics and concerns that they find important, you should avoid imposing too much structure.

Semi-structured and unstructured interviews open up the possibility of exploring topics in a depth and breadth that may be harder to achieve with fully structured interviews. As interviewee comments lead you to ask questions that you hadn't thought of and as they discuss issues that you had overlooked, your understanding of their concerns and perspectives will broaden in directions that you might have missed with a fully structured interview.

Of course, there is no such thing as a free lunch: interviews with less structure require more skill to conduct. When do you dig deeper in response to a comment? When do you back off and move on to something else? How do you keep interviewees on track or deal with those who answer in monosyllables? Effectively managing these challenges requires a fair amount of skill, which may come only with experience.

Less structure also means more challenges in interpretation. Semi-structured or unstructured interviews may go all over the map, with related topics discussed in multiple places throughout the interview. You may need to collect comments made at very different points, searching through your notes, recordings, or transcripts, to find closely related topics.

These different types of interview can also be distinguished by considering who's in charge. As they are controlled largely by the interviewer, fully structured and semi-structured interviews are often described as *respondent* interviews. In unstructured interviews, the interviewee's comments direct the course of the interview, with the interviewer following along and responding as necessary. As the interviewee is in control, these interviews are also described as *informant* or *non-directive* interviews. These names help remind us that the comments of the interviewee may be very structured, even if the interviewer does not impose any structure on the conversation: the perceived presence or absence of structure depends upon the viewpoint that is being considered (Robson, 2002).

How should you choose between these different styles? Fully structured interviews are most appropriate when you hope to compare responses across individuals. All interviewees are asked the same questions, so comparison should be straightforward. These comparisons are often most useful for evaluations aimed at understanding user responses to designs or systems.

Unstructured and semi-structured interviews can be most appropriate when you are looking to dig deeper, in search of critical comments, design requirements, and other insights. These approaches can be particularly helpful when you are unfamiliar with a problem domain or set of users – when you don't even know which questions to ask. In these cases, semi-structured or unstructured interviews give participants the chance to educate you. The understanding that you gain from their comments can help you understand their needs and, potentially, generate appropriate questions for subsequent structured interviews. Follow-up structured interviews can be particularly helpful for validating the results of your initial semi-structured or unstructured attempts: if a second round of interviews elicits comments that are generally consistent with feedback from the first group, you might comfortably conclude that those comments apply generally to a broad range of users. The Green Living Interviews sidebar describes a research project that made extensive use of semi-structured interviews and other complementary techniques to understand the practices of a very specific group of people, in the hopes of identifying possibilities for the design of new tools.

Greater ease of both conducting the interviews and analyzing the results makes fully structured interviews appropriate for your first effort. When all of your questions are explicitly spelled out, conducting an interview can be relatively straightforward. You simply ask a question, note the answer, and move on to the next question. Semi-structured and unstructured interviews can require significantly more effort, as you will find yourself trying to decide when and how much to manage the interview process. When do you let the interviewee digress to seemingly unrelated topics? When should you let the interviewee talk and when should you direct the conversation? If you are working with someone who is not at all talkative, how can you get them to open up? Given these and other challenges, you might want to stay away from less-structured techniques until you've had some experience in interviewing.

8.4.2   Focused and contextual interviews

Interviews in HCI research often revolve around the specific context of a problem of technology. We might be interested in how people use an existing system or how they solve a problem that might be addressed by software that has not yet been built. In circumstances such as these, an interview might go beyond simply asking questions; it might ask for demonstrations and more in-depth explorations. By asking interviewees to *demonstrate* how they solve a problem, instead of *explaining* how they do it, these interviews have the potential to illustrate aspects of the problem that might have been forgotten in a strictly verbal interview.

Thomas Malone's classic work on office organization (see the Finding and Reminding sidebar) provides an example of this approach. To understand how people organize information, Malone asked people to show him around their offices, indicating where they store things (Malone, 1983). Interviews aimed at understanding how technologies are currently used might include technology tours, which ask participants to show researchers how they use technology in a home (Petersen and Baillie, 2001) or other familiar space. Technology biographies build upon this approach, asking participants to discuss past uses of technology and to speculate about desirable future scenarios (Blythe, Monk and Park, 2002).

A separate set of interview strategies relies upon artifacts and context provided by the researcher, not by the subject. External aids aimed at eliciting feedback or reactions relevant to the subject at hand are known as "probes" (Gaver, Dunne and Pacenti, 1999). As the goal of a probe is to promote engagement, it need not be technological: an interviewer interested in understanding user needs for organizing photos might ask interviewees to organize a small set of pictures on a table top. Observations of this process may prove significantly informative than a strictly verbal interview.

Software prototypes can also be used to focus interviews. Technology probes are simple prototypes that demonstrate new ideas (Hutchinson *et al.*, 2003). Although they may be interesting as tools, technology probes are primarily designed to explore possibilities and understand needs and practices regarding technology use. A study of everyday technologies in family life used two forms of technology probe – a zoomable space for digital notes on a writable LCD tablet and a tool for capturing short, shareable videos – to understand how unfamiliar technologies might be used by family members (Hutchinson *et al.*, 2003).

Interviews aimed at evaluating proposed designs for software tools often go one step further, asking users to comment on proposed interface designs, either on paper or as more-or-less functional prototypes. As prototypes become more fully functional, these interviews might even ask users to complete sample tasks. Although this feedback can be very useful – particularly early in the design process – such interviews must be conducted carefully. If participants are aware that they are evaluating a tool that you have designed, they may be overly favorable in their responses. When conducting an interview like this, you might want to discount favorable responses and give more credence to critical remarks.

8.5   Interviews vs focus groups

As a data collection technique, interviewing is powerful, but labor-intensive. To gather input from 20 individuals, an interviewer must meet with each person individually, perhaps for an hour or more. An attractive alternative might be to meet with several participants in *focus groups*. These group discussions provide a reasonably effective and inexpensive tool for easily gathering a broad range of opinions. Although opinions differ on optimal sizes, focus groups are generally not large. Some suggest between eight and 12 people (Robson, 2002), while others argue that smaller groups of five to seven participants might be more appropriate for in-depth conversation (Krueger, 1994). A series of as many as five focus groups (Brown, 1999) could be used to engage up to 60 people in a few hours. Relying on a single focus group session is discouraged, as any single group could be unresponsive or unrepresentative. Two or more groups will increase your chances of success (Krueger, 1994).

The participation of several individuals in a focus group provides the possibility of a broad range of viewpoints and insights. Discussions can reveal the similarities and differences between opinions. Limited doses of disagreement and debate can be very informative, as varying viewpoints can lead to a broader understanding than you would gain from a number of people who were in complete agreement. These conflicting perspectives might also lead you to new areas for further study (Brown, 1999). Perhaps you can develop a model or system that will handle all perspectives well.

The conversations that can arise in a focus group can help overcome many of the shortcomings of interviews. In a one-on-one setting the interviewer and interviewee are left to fend for themselves. If the interviewee is not talkative, or if an awkward dynamic stifles the discussion, the interview may fail. Group discussions support interactivity, with participants ideally balancing each other. Participants can encourage each other to speak up, either in support of or opposition to earlier statements. This highly dynamic situation can stimulate participants to raise issues that they might not have identified in one-to-one interviews.

As the rigidity of a fully structured interview is ill-suited for group settings, focus groups are generally semi-structured or unstructured. A fully structured focus group would require asking each question of each individual in order, without any room for interaction between participants. A fully structured focus group would essentially be equivalent to multiple individual interviews conducted simultaneously.

Interactive focus groups present researchers with several logistical and management challenges. As conversation takes time, focus groups might be limited to a relatively small number of questions – fewer than you would cover in comparable interviews.

Conflicts may arise, particularly in focus groups involving controversial topics. Participants may be unwilling to discuss topics involving potentially sensitive information – perhaps relating to health care or finances – in a group setting. Individual interviews might be more appropriate for discussion of these topics.

Particularly talkative and opinionated participants can monopolize conversations, crowding out other viewpoints. If this happens, you will need to find a diplomatic way to ask chatterboxes to yield the floor. Simply cutting them off brusquely may give offense and discourage further participation. Disrespectful conduct can cause similar problems. When conducting a focus group, you must be careful to avoid power struggles or other confrontations with participants, as such battles can sabotage the whole process (Brown, 1999).

Group dynamics can impose other limits on the extent to which you can generalize from focus group results. Although you'll know when people disagree strongly enough to speak up, you may not know how to interpret silence. Participants who sit quietly may agree with expressed opinions or they may simply be opting out of the conversation.

Extracting useful data from a focus group requires skillful facilitation. You need to manage personality conflicts, encourage participation from all participants, keep the conversation going, monitor the clock, and work through your list of questions, all the while collecting the data that is at the heart of your effort. With a roomful of participants to manage, this can be quite a challenge. Fortunately, this need not fall on only one person's shoulders. A focus group might have two moderators: someone who is skilled in running such groups can work alongside an HCI researcher who is familiar with the problem at hand (Brown, 1999). Together, these collaborators can work together to ensure successful data collection.

The selection of focus group participants can be an art in itself. Should your participants represent multiple backgrounds and perspectives, or would a more homogenous group be appropriate? What about familiarity – do you want participants who are unknown to each other or groups consisting of friends or colleagues? Participants in homogenous groups have common backgrounds and experiences that may help promote discussion and exchange, giving you viewpoints that represent that shared context. In some cases, you may not be able to find a broadly diverse group of participants. If you are developing a system for use by a narrowly defined group of experts – such as brain surgeons or HCI researchers – your groups are likely to be largely homogenous, at least in the relevant respects.[1] Homogenous groups have the disadvantage of narrowing the range of perspectives. For projects that aim to support a broad range of users – for example, systems aimed at meeting the needs of all patrons in a large metropolitan library – broadly based focus groups representing multiple viewpoints may be more helpful. Groups that are too diverse may pose a different set of problems, as a lack of any common ground or shared perspectives may make conversation difficult (Krueger, 1994). In any case, participants in focus groups should have an interest in the topic at hand and they should be willing to participate constructively (Brown, 1999).

Focus groups are probably inappropriate for topics that may involve sensitive or controversial topics. Many participants may be reluctant to discuss deeply personal issues in a group setting. Controversial topics may lead to arguments and bitterness that could destroy the group's effectiveness (Krueger, 1994). Although such concerns may seem unrelated to much HCI work, group discussions can take on a life of their own, possibly bringing you unanticipated difficulties. If you have any concerns at all about difficult issues, you may want to use one-on-one interviews instead.

8.6   Types of question

As seemingly small differences in the phrasing and form of interview questions can lead to big differences in responses, you should pay careful attention to what you ask your interviewees and how you ask it. Although writing these questions is more of an art than a science, there are some guidelines that should help you get started in the right direction.

One of the first considerations in the construction of any interview question involves the degree of structure. Structured, closed questions limit users to a small number of pre-defined choices. Examples include yes–no questions, multiple choice, true–false, and Likert-scale questions, asking for ratings on a scale of 3, 5, 7, or more possibilities (Robson, 2002). These questions have the advantage of being easy to analyze, as responses can be tabulated across all participants, and statistical methods can be used to describe the distribution of responses. However, giving your interviewees a small set of pre-defined responses might discourage elaboration and further comments. If you ask someone "Did you like the design of the home page?", they might just say "yes" or "no". However, if you ask "what do you think about this home page?", interviewees may be more inclined to elaborate, describing their reactions in more detail.

This second example – asking "what do you think about...?" – is an *open-ended* question. These questions ask for responses, opinions, or other feedback, without imposing any external constraints on the responses. This freedom invites the respondent to answer in depth, exploring any aspect of the issue that may be of interest. Such answers can often

---

[1] There may be significant racial, ethnic, gender, and age diversity in any group of brain surgeons or HCI researchers. However, from the perspective of tools designed to support their professional activities, their shared training and experiences are likely to be much more important than any demographic diversity.

stimulate conversation and generate insights that closed questions might not reveal. Increased difficulty in analysis is the price that you pay for this insight. Instead of simply counting answers in different categories, you'll have to analyze the content of responses to open-ended questions, using techniques described in Section 8.9.

Knowing how you will analyze answers may help you determine which kind of question to ask. If you want to divide participants into groups, a closed question asking them which group they belong to is ideal. If you want to understand the relationship between education level and reactions to a proposed community information system, you might ask people to state their highest level of education completed. This would clearly establish your categories of interest. In other circumstances, you might find it useful to divide interviewees into those that have unfavorable, favorable, or neutral reactions to an existing system. In this case, a closed question with three choices would be more helpful than an open-ended question that might lead to a more ambiguous response.

If you're not quite sure how you're going to use the data, you might be better off starting with the least restrictive approach. If you're not sure how you intend to use interviewee age, you might prefer to ask for exact ages rather than ranges (such as 20–29, 30–39, etc.). This will preserve the option of reporting age statistics and aggregating them into ranges for a histogram. If you start by asking for the ranges, you can't switch to statistics later.

Other forms of interview "questions" are tasks or exercises that ask participants to provide useful information, without presenting a question as such. You might ask users to complete a sentence: "The most frustrating problem that I have with my word processor is….." (Krueger, 1994). This may not be all that different from asking a direct question, but it does add some variety to the interview process. Another possibility involves *conceptual mapping*: asking participants to draw pictures or graphical layouts that describe their understanding of a situation. (Krueger, 1994) For a study of perceptions of websites, you might provide a list of 20 sites, asking interviewees to organize the list into groups of similar sites. In one study of user perceptions of web security, interviewees were asked to draw diagrams depicting their understanding of how secure web connections work. These pictures provided concise and informative illustrations of how users understood – and misunderstood – web security (see Figure 8.1) (Friedman *et al.*, 2002),

Interview questions should be as simple as possible, without any technical terms or jargon. You don't want your questions to be puzzles that confuse your interviewees. Compound questions with multiple parts may cause problems for some participants (Robson, 2002). If you find yourself writing such a question, break it up into multiple simpler questions. Complex comparative questions may be particularly challenging in this respect. Instead of asking "What were the strengths and weaknesses of the menu layout and the toolbar?", ask separate questions: "What did you think of the menu layout? What did you think of the toolbar? Which did you prefer?"

Your questions should be as unbiased and unjudgmental as possible. In particular, you should watch out for phrasing that might encourage your interviewee to give you the answer

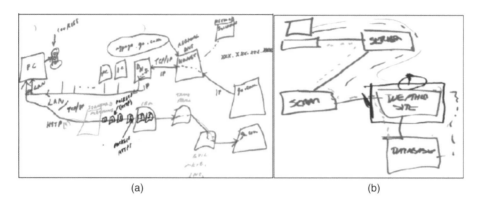

(a)   (b)

Figure 8.1 Interview participants were asked to draw a secure web connection: a secure web connection is (a) correctly depicted as protecting information transmitted from the PC to the web server and (b) incorrectly depicted as secure data storage (Friedman *et al.*, 2002).

that they think you want to hear. This is another reason to prefer questions that ask "what do you think of...?" rather than "did you like...?" Particularly if you're talking about something that interviewees know you (or your team) have designed, asking if they like (or dislike) something or find it easy (or hard) to use, might influence responses. Questions that ask people "Why do you like this design?" (Robson, 2002) or "Don't you think this is hard to use?" are particularly bad in this regard. Some suggest avoiding questions with negative answers – simply ask "What did you think?" instead (Angrosino, 2005). You may find it hard to completely eliminate questions that have subtle potential for bias, but avoiding the worst pitfalls should not be too difficult.

You should construct questions to be appropriate for your audience. If your audience consists of well-educated professional adults – similar to many HCI researchers – language that you are comfortable with may work well for your participants. Interviews or focus groups with participants with substantively different backgrounds from those of the researcher pose additional challenges – you have to learn to "speak their language". For example, interviews or focus groups involving young children may fare better if appropriately designed questions and options for answers are used. Instead of using a Likert scale for a closed question regarding subjective reaction to a system, you might consider using the "funometer" or "smileyometer", continuous and discrete rating scales based on a range from a deep frown to a broad smile (Read, MacFarlane and Casey, 2002). In more complex cases, this may require spending some time to understand the context before you design an interview – see Chapter 9 for background on ethnographic observations.

When your interview is less than fully structured, you may be generating questions on the spot, in response to specific interviewee comments. On-the-fly phrasing of questions that are clear, simple, and free from jargon and bias is an art requiring practice and experience.

This may be another reason to stick with more structure until you gain some experience, but all is not lost: the informal give-and-take of semi-structured and unstructured interviews gives you some room for rephrasing and revisiting questions as needed.

Human nature being what it is, interviewee responses may be inconsistent. This is to be expected. Including questions that are slightly redundant may help you assess the degree of consistency in responses, but you should probably decide in advance how you will handle any inconsistency. Possibilities include reporting inconsistencies and discounting responses from interviewees who appear to be particularly inconsistent.

The Finding and Reminding sidebar in Section 8.2.1 discusses Thomas Malone's study of how people organize information in their offices – an example of a semi-structured interview that generated some influential results.

8.7 Conducting an interview

8.7.1 Preparation

With all of the details that must be addressed, appropriate planning and preparation is obviously important. Pilot-testing your interview – both with research colleagues and partici-pants – is always a good idea. In addition to helping you find questions that are hard to understand, pilot testing can give you some idea of the potential length of an interview. If your pilot test runs past the two-hour mark, you may want to ask yourself if there's anything that you might trim. Although pilot testing may be harder for a focus group, it's not impossible. One approach might be to use your colleagues as pilot focus group participants. Other possibilities include asking experts familiar with focus groups to review your questions and other materials. You might also consider your first group to be the pilot: if it goes well, great. If not, you can revise it and remove the results from further consideration in your analysis (Krueger, 1994).

Practice can be very helpful. If you have run through your interview process and script a few times on your own, you will feel more comfortable when you sit down with interviewees. Ask a colleague to play the role of interviewee and provide some constructive comments regarding your handling of the interview.

If your interview is complex, a clear and concise guide can help you remember which steps to take and when. Guides are particularly helpful for focus groups (Brown, 1999) and for any situation where more than one researcher is acting as an interviewer or moderator.

Proper preparation includes appropriate backups. Assume that your computer will crash, your recorder won't work, and the power will fail. Can you conduct your interview in the dark on paper? That might be a bit extreme, but extra batteries, paper, and perhaps even a backup recording device will prepare you for almost any contingency.

8.7.2   Recording the responses

Having chosen the format of your interview, identified your participants, and written your questions, you are ready to plan the details of conducting the interview. Written notes and audio or video recordings all have advantages and disadvantages. You'll probably always want to have a notebook on hand. If you have an interviewing partner, she might take notes with the computer while you write your thoughts on paper, but it's probably too distracting for the primary interviewer to be typing on the computer during the course of the interview session. In any case, you should have a paper notebook available as a backup.

Written notes can be useful for recording interviewee responses and interviewer comments. Even if you are using audio or video recording devices for your main records of participant comments, you should use written notes to document non-verbal cues or concerns (Brown, 1999). Do your interviewees seem bored, anxious, or tired? This can be particularly important for focus groups: you'll want to note if you see body language cues indicating disagreement with the current speaker, general frustration, or lack of interest.

Simply writing down interviewee responses is likely to be most effective for simple, closed questions. Answers to open-ended questions and comments made in free-flowing unstructured interviews may be hard to capture adequately in writing. Transcribing spoken text in real time is a cognitive challenge. If you are busy trying to write down what your interviewee said a few seconds ago, you might miss an interesting comment. Participants may find it distracting as well, particularly if you are so focused on writing that you appear not to be paying attention to them.

Due to the pressures of writing notes during the course of an interview, the notes taken can be somewhat cryptic. To maximize the value of such records, you should strongly consider summarizing and possibly rewriting your notes as soon as possible after each interview. This will give you a chance to clarify any comments, add details that will help you remember the context, and clarify in other ways that increase the likelihood of extracting useful data from the record, even after a gap of months or years.

Audio and video recordings record every word of an interview, at the potential cost of difficulty of transcription and interpretation. Turning a single hour of recorded discussion into text may take several hours (Robson, 2002) and substantially sized projects can generate massive amounts of content (see the Green Living Interviews sidebar in Section 8.2.1). Digital recorders make recording inexpensive and easy enough that you might decide to record interviews before committing to transcribing them, but such recordings may go unheard.

If you are going to record, the choice between audio and video can be important. Video recording is logistically harder, usually requiring a tripod and some maneuvering that might be challenging if you are in a tight space. Some interviewees may initially be uncomfortable with the video camera, but most forget about it within a few minutes. In many cases, the additional details captured by a video recording can be quite informative. Interviews with professionals aimed at understanding work in context would benefit from video recordings of workspaces and offices. You might even use a video camera to capture the use of a current software tool, but you should not count on using an inexpensive video camera to record screen output from a computer: such recordings generally don't work well. Screen-capture software operating directly on the computer would be a better bet. Audio recording is, of course, simpler and more straightforward. You might consider using audio recording along with still pictures from a digital camera. This will give you much of the benefit of video without the overhead.

Whatever approach you take to recording, you should be careful to respect the privacy and anonymity of your subjects. Written notes and recordings should be treated as identifying information which should be kept securely and treated as confidential.

You should have a consistent policy for dealing with comments made after you close your notebook or turn off the recording device. As you are wrapping up or even walking out the door, some participants may make comments that are of interest. You can certainly pull your notebook back out or restart your audio recorder or camera, but you should deal with these comments consistently (Robson, 2002).

Paper notes, photos, and electronic recordings need not be the only records of your interview. If you ask users to complete a task on the computer, you might collect (with their permission) screen shots illustrating their tasks in progress. Any conceptual maps, drawings, or other outputs from tasks associated with your interview questions should be considered as part of the interview record and analyzed accordingly.

8.7.3 During the interview
8.7.3.1 *Rapport*
From the start of the interview, you should strive to help your interviewee feel comfortable and at ease. If you can convey the impression of being a professional, friendly, and likable person, your interviewees will be more inclined to trust you with honest and useful feedback. You may find that interviewees who are more at ease will be more candid with responses, providing useful input instead of telling you what they think you want to hear.

Steps that you take to make your interviewees feel more comfortable may have the added benefit of making the experience more enjoyable for you as well. This can be particularly important for projects involving a large number of interviews: if you dread the thought of conducting the next interview, it may not lead to much in the way of useful data.

Creating an environment that encourages open conversation is easier said than done. The first few minutes of an interview are crucial (Kvale, 2007): if you establish good rapport quickly, the rest might flow easily. Conversely, it's hard to get off to a good start. To make the all-important good first impression, you should be friendly and supportive. Listen carefully, sincerely, and respectfully (Kvale, 2007): after all, you've invited the interviewee to participate – if you can't be bothered to be interested, why should they? Be respectful, straightforward, clear, and non-threatening (Robson, 2002). Judgmental responses are inappropriate. Cringing or frowning when you hear a response that you don't like won't encourage interviewees to share more with you. This is one area where some practice might help: you'll want to develop a poker face.

When you are conducting an interview or focus group, you are, to some extent, acting as a host. When appropriate, you might consider providing simple refreshments. A glass of water will help an interviewee or focus group participant feel comfortable enough to keep talking. Snacks may be nice, but should be chosen carefully to respect participants' cultural and dietary sensitivities. Loud, crunchy food is inadvisable, as it may distract participants and interfere with audio recordings (Barbour, 2007).

Finding some common ground of shared experience or perspective is a tried-and-true technique for building good relationships. Although this may be related to the topic of the interview, it need not be. If an interviewee comments on travel delays due to traffic or the need to leave early due to family obligations, you might respond with a short personal comment indicating your understanding of those challenges. Alternatively, you might include an initial interview question aimed at establishing some common ground. If it's at all relevant, you might consider asking interviewees to describe a notable technology failure: almost everyone will have a story to tell and you can commiserate with a story of your own. If you can focus this question on a specific technology relevant to your interview, so much the better.

As you work to establish rapport with your interviewees, be careful to avoid anything that gets too personal. As the interview is about you learning from the interviewee, you should be listening most of the time. Talking too much about your own experiences is inappropriate and may make some people uncomfortable. You might make brief comments about your own experiences or opinions as appropriate and then steer the conversation back to focusing on the interviewee.

8.7.3.2   The introduction

Most interviews or focus groups follow the same general outline. You should start with an introduction, telling the interviewees about the research and your goals. If appropriate, this would also be a good time to complete any paperwork, including the informed consent form. You should also tell participants if you are recording the session and how. For focus groups, you might use the introduction as an opportunity to encourage differing viewpoints (Krueger, 1994).

You might want to keep the introduction to your research brief. You should not go into too much detail regarding your goals and aims (Kvale, 2007), as a detailed description of your aims and goals might encourage your participants to provide answers that they think you want to hear. This is particularly a concern if you're asking about reactions to a system that you have built. You can provide more context after the session is over (see Section 8.7.3.4).

8.7.3.3 *Getting down to business*

The interview proper will start with relatively easy questions, useful for building trust and preparing the interviewee for harder questions. Risky questions come towards the end, perhaps followed by some simpler questions aimed at defusing any tension or anxiety. After your questions are complete, be sure to thank interviewees for their time (Robson, 2002).

During the interview, you must be on your best behavior. The first and most important rule is to remember that as the interviewer, your job is to *listen*. You are meeting with your interviewees to learn from them and you can't do that if you're doing all of the talking. After you introduce the interview and go over any administrative details, you should let the interviewee do most of the talking. You can certainly ask the questions, provide clarification if needed, and encourage further details, but that's about it – the interviewee should do the bulk of the talking. You'll have to give them time to speak – don't rush – and provide multiple opportunities to continue: "is there anything else you wanted to tell me?" or "take your time" are good ways to give your participants room to gather their thoughts without feeling pressured. Don't rush to move on to a new question until you are absolutely sure that the interviewee has finished answering the current question. Careful listening also involves paying attention to non-verbal cues: if your interlocutor seems anxious or agitated, you may have interrupted her. If this happens, back up and give her a chance to continue.

Being adaptable and flexible is particularly important for semi-structured or unstructured interviews. If you want to get the full benefits of ceding some control to your participants, you will have to be willing to go where they will lead you. This may mean re-ordering or eliminating certain questions and letting the conversation take some unexpected twists and turns. In some cases, you may be able to come back to those questions later, while other interviews may leave their original script and never return. As long as your interviewees don't go completely off-topic, you should try to follow them. If they digress into totally unrelated areas, you might want to gently nudge them back on track. Careful and early attention to conversational style can help you avoid irrelevant digressions. If you notice early on that you are talking with someone who is prone to wander off into unrelated topics, you can prepare yourself to repeatedly – but politely – interrupt and guide the conversation back on track.

Interviewees and focus group participants have their own need for clarity and continuity. You should take care to explain why you are asking each question, and how it relates both to the overall topic of the interview and to questions that you have previously asked. If participants aren't sure why you are asking a question, they might misunderstand it and provide an answer to what is, in effect, a different question.

Terminology, particularly also introduces possibilities for misunderstanding. Provide definitions of any terms that might involve technical jargon or otherwise be unclear or ambiguous. If a participant introduces a term that may be problematic, ask for a clarification:

"What exactly do you mean when you say . . . ?" If the definition is not the one that you would tend to use, it's probably best to make a note of this difference and then to stick with it.

As the interview or focus group session progresses, you should try to distinguish between answers that the participants give because they are trying to please you and answers that genuinely reflect the respondent's opinions. The tendency of research participants to try to please researchers, particularly by providing information that would be perceived as confirming a hypothesis, is well-known (Orne, 1962). If you hear participants saying uniformly positive things about a system that you developed or a model that you suggested, you might be a bit cautious about over-interpreting those responses.

As with all research involving human subjects, interviews must be conducted in a manner that respects the rights and concerns of the participants (see Chapter 14). Be sure to clearly explain to your interviewees that they can decline to answer any question. This is particularly important if you are discussing potentially sensitive topics. When they do decline to answer, simply move on to the next question and note their lack of response. Participants should have the chance to take breaks, particularly if the interview is long. Interviews and focus groups should be kept to a reasonable length – probably less than two hours (Brown, 1999).

Focus groups present additional challenges. Listening is still paramount, but you may want to jump in to keep conversation on track. Focus groups can go badly wrong in many different ways: discussions can digress; participants might talk at length to the exclusion of others; disagreements might arise; or you might simply have a group that doesn't get along well. If you see any signs of trouble, you can jump in, gently urging participants to stay on topic, let others speak, be polite, and so on. You might try to be particularly sensitive to participants who seem to be quietly observing without saying much. Although some quiet folks might not have anything to say, others might be intimidated. Particularly if your quieter participants appear to be agitated or uncomfortable, you might address them directly, offering an opportunity to speak: "Joan, is there anything you'd care to say about . . . ?" Having asked this question, you must be ready to accept "no, thanks" as an answer.

8.7.3.4 *Promoting discussion*

What if you hold an interview (or focus group) and nobody talks? Spending an hour in a room with someone who responds in monosyllables is both unproductive and unenjoyable. You certainly can't force anyone to talk in any detail, but you might be able to encourage them. If your interview is fully structured you may not have much wiggle room, but you can add questions to semi-structured and unstructured interviews, in the hopes of eliciting comments. If you are asking about user reaction to a given tool, you might rephrase the question in various different ways – do they use the tool at home or at work? Have they had problems at home or at work? Is the spreadsheet tool good for personal finances and for taxes? In some cases, overly general questions might discourage responses: if you dig deeper into specifics, you might remind your interviewee of some specific incident or need that is relevant.

Physical props, note cards, and other probes can also stimulate feedback. In Section 8.2.2, our sample exploratory questions included asking participants how they currently arrange items in scrapbooks. Instead of simply asking this question, you might give your interviewee a small pile of photos and ask him to arrange them as if he were constructing a scrapbook, explaining the process as he goes along. This use of probes can be particularly helpful for revealing attitudes and practices that your participants may not have fully articulated: even though your interviewee knows what he's doing and why, he may not have thought about it enough to put it into words. Probes also provide a potentially entertaining alternative to a steady stream of questions.

Some techniques for eliciting responses are specific to focus groups. If a participant's comment is followed by silence, you might specifically ask others to react: "does anyone have a different opinion?" A short pause can also provide an opening for someone who has been waiting for a chance to make a comment (Krueger, 1994).

8.7.3.5   *Debriefing*
Set aside some time at the end of the interview or focus group for wrapping up and debriefing. When you have finished covering the questions or topics on your list, you might ask participants if they have anything else to add and for their reactions to participating in the interview or focus group (Kvale, 2007). This will provide an opportunity for the sharing of thoughts that did not seem to fit earlier in the conversation.

Once your participants have finished answering questions, you might want to provide detail about your research goals and the purpose of the interview, without the risk of biasing their responses. This additional detail can help interviewees feel that their time has been well-spent and satisfying. Your debriefing might also include a brief summary of what you have learned during the session. This summary gives participants an opportunity to correct any misunderstandings.

Consider turning off any recording devices before you begin the debriefing: if participants are aware that you are no longer recording, they may share some comments that they would not have made earlier (Kvale, 2007).

After you have thanked your interviewee or focus group participants, try to take a few minutes to gather your thoughts, summarize the results, and otherwise reflect upon the session (Kvale, 2007). Even if you have recorded the session and taken detailed notes, your initial reactions may include insights that will be difficult, if not impossible, to reconstruct even a few hours later.

8.8   Electronically mediated interviews and focus groups
Modern communication technologies present the attractive option of conducting interviews and focus groups electronically. Online chat, conference calls, and one-to-one phone calls can all be used to communicate directly with participants from the comfort of your own office. You can even conduct interviews by email, sending questions and answers back and

forth in an ongoing dialog. In some cases, electronically mediated interviews may be your only possibility. If you are working with domain experts who are geographically distant, face-to-face conversations may simply be too expensive to arrange. Even when face-to-face meetings are possible, cost considerations may lead you to choose the convenience of telephone or online interviews.

8.8.1 Telephone

Telephone interviewing seems straightforward enough: simply pick up the phone, call, and talk. Focus groups require conference call support, but numerous commercial and freely available services can provide these services easily. However, it would be a mistake to assume that the ease of initiating communication means that the rest is smooth sailing. Before conducting phone interviews, you may want to consider a few concerns that make these interviews qualitatively different from face-to-face discussion.

Your first practical decision may involve recording. Inexpensive tools for recording telephone calls are readily available, but they should only be used as appropriate. There may be local or national laws that dictate appropriate behavior for recording phone calls: for example, you might need to inform participants and get their explicit consent.

The dynamics of a telephone interview are likely to be somewhat different than they would be if you were talking to the same person face-to-face. Phone conversations lack the non-verbal cues that inform in-person conversations: you may not be able to tell if someone is bored, tired, or distracted. In fact, you probably won't have any information about what the other person is doing: you might be conducting a phone interview with someone who is cooking dinner, doing dishes, or attending to other distractions instead of paying attention to what you are saying.

That said, the lack of direct face-to-face contact may, in some situations, prove advantageous. Particularly if the conversation involves sensitive topics, interviewees may be willing to make some comments over the phone that they would not make in person.

Conference calls for focus groups pose different problems. When you have multiple unfamiliar people on a call, it's hard to keep track of who is speaking. Asking participants to state their name before each comment may work, but it quickly gets tedious. As anyone who's participated in a conference call knows, simply getting a chance to speak can often be a big challenge.

8.8.2 Online

Computer-mediated interviews are generally conducted via email, instant-messaging or chat tools. An email interview might involve an extended exchange of messages, as interviewers send questions and interviewees respond. Instant-message interviews and focus groups are closer in spirit to traditional face-to-face interviews, with questions and respondents coming in near real time.

Recruiting challenges in online interviewing include the usual problems associated with online research: you may or may not know who you are talking with (see Chapter 14). Identifying suitable participants for non-face-to-face interviews may require some extra effort in building relationships with potential interviewees and externally validating their identities and suitability for your work. However, respondents can also be anonymous, which may be useful if you are discussing illegal or otherwise undesirable activities.

Online interviews and focus groups are usually trivially easy to record. Email programs save both sent and received messages, and instant-messaging programs generally record transcripts of all comments. These running logs can be quite helpful for reviewing and interpreting the conversation, even while it is still in progress. For example, the interviewer can review the conversation to verify that all appropriate topics have been covered. Another possibility would be to use the respondents' previous comments to ask for further clarification: "Earlier, you said . . . ." Reviewing these comments can also help the interviewer ask repetitive questions. At the close of a discussion, you might ask the interviewee to review the logs to see if there are any final comments that she would like to add to the conversation (Voida *et al.*, 2004).

Contextual feedback in online interviews may be even more impoverished than with telephone interviews. Email and text-only instant messaging lack both the visual feedback of face-to-face meetings and the audio information generally available on telephone calls. Many participants may be multi-tasking and perhaps carrying on other instant-messaging conversations during the course of an online interview (Voida *et al.*, 2004). Text-based interviews via chat or email may lead to very different types of responses, as some respondents will be more formal than they might be in person. This is particularly the case for email, as some might take time to carefully organize thoughts. Different expectations of pacing may also influence the content and quality of responses. In a face-to-face conversation, we rarely pause for 30 seconds or one minute before responding to a question. Online chats, by contrast, frequently have delays of several minutes, and who among us hasn't let several days go by without responding to an email? This delay can be constructive in allowing consideration of the question, but it might also contribute to distraction and half-hearted answers. Delays might indicate other potentially interesting behavior, including revision of initial responses. Many chat programs provide visual indicators of activity, such as a series of dots indicating that the person is typing. If a participant in an instant-messaging conversation provides a short answer after having been typing for quite some time, you might consider asking them to clarify their thinking (Voida *et al.*, 2004).

Pacing in online interviews is also a challenge. Going too slowly might cause participants to lose focus and interest, but moving too quickly might prove unnerving. Expecting participants to respond to emailed interview questions within a matter of minutes is probably unrealistic. On the flip side, online messaging need not always be instant. Given the breaks that seem to occur naturally in instant-messaging conversations, taking some time to rephrase a question or consider a response may be quite appropriate. On the other hand, cutting and pasting a question from an interview script into a messaging client may seem a bit too quick. (Voida *et al.*, 2004).

Online focus groups also lessen the presence of moderators – instead of being a powerful presence at the front of the room, the moderator is reduced to simply being another voice or line on the chat screen. This may reduce participant fear that the moderator may somehow disapprove of them or their comments (Walston and Lissitz, 2000).

In some studies, respondents using computer-based systems have reported a higher frequency of socially undesirable behavior, as compared to those participating in traditional surveys, possibly because responding directly to a computer (without the presence of a human) encourages more openness in responses (Walston and Lissitz, 2000). In comparison, in one study of behavior relating to HIV/AIDS in sub-Saharan Africa, interviews were administered using both paper and computers. In both cases, interviewers asked the questions of the interviewees and recorded the answers on the paper or computer. Analysis of the results indicated that participants who were interviewed with the computers were more likely to provide socially desirable answers regarding risky behaviors. Although more study would be needed to understand these responses, the researchers conjectured that interviewers who used computers may have appeared to have been either affluent or outsiders. Participants may simply have been trying to impress the interviewers (Cheng, Ernesto and Truong, 2008).

8.9   Analyzing interview data

Having conducted a series of interviews or focus groups, you'll find yourself faced with the daunting task of interpreting your data. Countless pages of written notes and hours of video or audio recordings pose a significant challenge – how do you make sense of it all? Your goal in analyzing interview data is to generate an accurate representation of interviewee responses. Usually, your analysis works towards a general, holistic understanding: the analysis of answers to individual questions are combined to form general models of user needs for a particular task, reactions to a proposed design, or other focus of the interview. This may not be possible – you may find that there are no consistent patterns. This is interesting as well.

Whichever techniques you choose to use, you should try to analyze your data as soon as possible. When the interview is fresh in your mind, you will be well-positioned to remember details and nuances that you may not have captured in your notes. As time passes, you will find it increasingly difficult to remember potentially important non-verbal cues or comments. Your notes will also become less useful over time, as hastily scribbled cryptic comments will be hard to interpret weeks or months later.

Effective analysis works to avoid bias and reliance on pre-conceived notions. The absence of "hard", numeric data makes interview responses and similar qualitative data sources particularly susceptible to biased manipulation. An emphasis on data points that confirm your favorite hypothesis, at the expense of comments that argue against it – a practice known as "cherry picking" – is just one of the possible biases in the analysis of results. Biased consideration of responses from specific participants, or classes of participants, can be a problem for focus group data. If your analysis pays disproportionate attention to female participants relative to male participants (or vice versa), any resulting interpretation will be somewhat distorted. Your analysis activities should always strive to be inclusive and data driven.

Additional information about the use of qualitative data analysis methods can be found in Chapter 11.

8.9.1   What to analyze

Fully structured interviews consisting only of closed questions are the easiest to analyze. As all interviewees are asked the same questions and all answers are taken from a small set of possibilities, analysis is essentially a tabulation problem. You can tabulate the frequency of each answer and use straightforward statistical tests to determine when differences in response rates are meaningful (see Chapter 4). Quantitative results can also be used to group characteristics (see the Finding and Reminding sidebar in Section 8.2.1 for an example).

Analysis gets harder as your questions become more open-ended and the interview becomes less structured. Open-ended questions can be answered in a different way by each interviewee. Two participants might answer any given question in entirely different ways, creating the challenge of identifying the common ground. Unstructured or semi-structured interviews introduce the additional complication of questions and topics arising at very different stages in different interviews. Analysis of these interviews may require tying together comments made at very different times in very different contexts.

Should your analysis be based on written notes or on audio or video recordings? Unlike written notes, recordings provide complete and unfiltered access to everything that an interviewee said or did, even months after the fact. This record can be used to reconstruct details, focus in on specific comments, and share user feedback with colleagues. The disadvantage, of course, is the expense and challenge of wading through hours of video or audio data. You can analyze recordings by listening to comments piece by piece, repeatedly replaying pieces of interest until you gain an understanding, but this can be a slow, often tedious process. Verbatim transcriptions translate these hours of discussion into pages of written text that might be more amenable to analysis and editing via software, but transcribing can also be an expensive, unappealing process. Although it may be possible to use automated speech recognition techniques to generate a transcript, these tools are subject to recognition errors that might limit the quality of the output.

Notes written during the interview have the advantage of being relatively compact and easy to work with. Your written notes may omit some interesting details, but it's likely that the comments you managed to get down on paper were among the most important made during the session. Even if you have to transcribe your handwritten notes into an electronic format, the amount of transcription required will be substantially less than that needed for a transcript of an audio recording of the same discussion.

These practical considerations play an important role in determining how you analyze the data. If time and money are particularly tight, you might be best served by an analysis of written records. Detailed examination of recordings is most appropriate for situations where you are interested in digging into the details as deep as possible and you are willing to commit the resources (time and money) to do this work.

8.9.2　How to analyze

After you decide whether to work from a recording (either directly or via a transcript) or interview notes, the next step is to decide upon a technique that might be used. The choice of analysis technique should be made early on, and the interview should be designed accordingly. Don't bother with open questions in an unstructured interview unless you'll have time to go through all of the responses. Choose something simpler instead.

Interviews and focus groups are usually analyzed via one or more *qualitative data analysis methods* which attempt to find common structures and themes from qualitative data. In the case of interviews, your goal is to identify the important ideas that repeatedly arise during an interview.

One technique that is commonly used for analyzing interview data involves examination of the text of the interview for patterns of usage, including frequency of terms, co-occurrences, and other structural markers that may provide indications of the importance of various concepts and the relationships between them. This approach – known as *content analysis* – builds on the assumption that the structure of an interviewee's comments provides meaningful hints as to what he finds important and why (Robson, 2002). Discourse analysis goes beyond looking at discussions of words and contents to examine the structure of the conversation, in search of cues that might provide additional understanding (Sharp, Rogers and Preece, 2007). For example, do users say "we log out of the system when we are done" or do they say "the proper procedure is to log out when we are done"? The answer to this question might help you understand differences between what users actually do (the first option) and what IT managers might want them to do (the second option).

Other approaches to the analysis of interview data involve the organization of comments and responses into various categories, which may be defined prior to analysis or based on interpretation of the contents of the text. Approaches that start from pre-defined categories may be somewhat more systematic and replicable, whereas those that define their own categories may be somewhat more interpretive (Robson, 2002). Affinity diagrams – see the Contextual Inquiry sidebar – are an example of the interpretive approach. If these techniques sound too abstract and theoretical for your taste, you might want to try something simpler – an introductory approach is given in the Interview Analysis for Novices sidebar.

Research In Practice

Contextual Inquiry

Many HCI researchers and practitioners have found that simply asking people about their practices is not sufficient for developing a complete understanding of user requirements. If you ask someone who regularly makes scrapbooks how they go about doing it, they may share certain interesting details that demonstrate their *explicit* understanding – those parts of the process that they can think of and easily describe to you. If you watch that same person complete the task, you might find many *implicit* practices that are crucial for success, even if they aren't stated directly.

A popular exercise used in HCI and other computing classes provides a nice demonstration of the notion of implicit knowledge. The challenge involves sandwich construction. Students are asked to describe how to make a peanut butter and jelly sandwich, assuming one is given a loaf of bread and new jars of peanut butter and jelly. Participants invariably find that seemingly simple tasks – such as getting a knife full of peanut butter to be spread on the sandwich – are complicated by challenges that may not be remembered explicitly – in this case, removing the foil seal that might be found under the lid of the unopened jar of peanut butter (Davis and Rebelsky, 2007). If you limit your investigations to direct interviews, you might never come across interviewees who remember this crucial step. If you instead choose to observe someone in action, your first participant's efforts to remove the foil points to the need to include it in your process.

Contextual inquiry techniques for conducting interviews (Beyer and Holtzblatt, 1998) are specifically designed to uncover implicit knowledge about work processes. Contextual inquiry starts from observation at workplaces, with a focus on specific details rather than generalizations.

The simplest form of contextual inquiry is the contextual interview, which consists primarily of a few hours of observation as the user completes his or her work. The goal is to form a partnership in search of a shared understanding of work. The preferred approach to this is to have the researcher and the interviewee work together in a manner similar to a master–apprentice relationship, with the participant describing what she is doing and why as she progresses through the various steps involved in completing her work. Researchers conducting contextual interviews are generally much more talkative than traditional apprentices, leading to a conversational partnership.

This collaboration extends into interpreting the data: the researcher begins to build a model of how the interviewee is working and asks if it reflects the user's understanding. If the interpretation is incorrect, the interviewee is likely to clarify: "No, that's not quite right." This discussion takes place in the context of a focus on the project as a whole, as opposed to any smaller components, such as the software that you might eventually design (Beyer and Holtzblatt, 1998).

Contextual interviews can be used to derive a variety of models that describe work. Flow models describe the sharing of information among individuals in a workplace; sequence models outline the steps in completing a task; artifact models collect the structure of information or other byproducts of work processes; cultural models describe the backgrounds and assumptions of the context in which the work is done; and physical models describe relevant physical and logistical constraints (Beyer and Holtzblatt, 1998). Explicit understanding of attitudes that users might have towards systems (cultural models) and of the environments in which a system is used (physical models) can be crucial for success.

In Beyer and Holtzblatt's model, individual interview sessions are analyzed in interpretation sessions, in which team members discuss each interview in detail. Notes from these sessions are organized into *affinity diagrams* – hierarchical groupings of structures and themes, built from the bottom up. Groupings are given names, and groups are collected into larger, collective groups. Affinity diagrams are often constructed with sticky notes, using different colors to represent layers in the hierarchy (Beyer and Holtzblatt, 1998). Collecting notes from a series of contextual interviews into a single diagram leads to a "map" of the problem "terrain", with hierarchies providing guidance for understanding the relationships of various concerns that fall under the topics and subtopics. In the course of analyzing a large set of notes (perhaps around 1500), members of a research team can build a shared understanding of a challenging work process (Beyer and Holtzblatt, 1998).

Interview Analysis for Novices

Research In Practice

Interview analysis can be somewhat intimidating. If you're feeling that you're in a bit over your head, don't panic. Although some analyses might best be done by an experienced collaborator, you don't need an advanced degree in the social sciences to get a basic understanding of interview data.

In school, many people have been taught to write notes on index cards – one idea per card – which can then be sorted and arranged as necessary. You can break responses to interview questions into individual thoughts or ideas, one per index card or one per line in a text document. Group lines with common ideas but don't restrict yourself to putting any idea into only one category. Feel free to place thoughts in multiple groups, as appropriate.

You might consider assigning categories to comments as they appear in the transcript. This can be done by annotating each line with a colored piece of text that names the category. Once you've done this, you can quickly search to find all of the instances of a particular category. As the categories begin to grow, you may see connections between them. You can then put these categories into broader categories, forming a hierarchy of ideas.

How do you categorize each comment or concept? One approach would be to group things by the content words – nouns or verbs. You can use these words to understand the objects with which people work and the actions that they use with those objects. Organizing comments along these lines can help you understand the outlines of the problem domain.

As you dig through the interviews, you may begin to find relationships, information flows, sequences, or other patterns that repeatedly arise out of the comments. Pictures, sketches, outlines, or other representations of these interactions can help clarify your understanding.

Focus groups introduce the additional challenge of differing viewpoints. You might consider grouping comments by individual or by the individual's role. This might help you understand potentially important differences in perspectives. In any case, if you are concerned about validity, enlist a colleague to work with you. You might each independently analyze the data and then compare your results, in the hopes of working towards a consensus analysis. Alternatively, you might work together, building agreement as you go along.

This informal analysis shares many characteristics with more rigorous established practices such as content analysis or discourse analysis. These approaches may differ in their level of attention to detail and their conformance to established practice but the goal is always the same: to help researchers move from an unordered and undifferentiated mess of interview data to a clear, structured understanding.

Informal techniques are often sufficient. If you are trying to build an initial understanding of a problem, gauge reaction to design proposals, or examine a problem without aspiring for generality and validity, this approach can be very productive. If you find that you need to add some rigor, you can always return to the data for a second, more rigorous analysis, perhaps with the help of a colleague with relevant experience.

Interviews and focus groups might also be examined for stories, responses, or comments that are particularly insightful, interesting, or otherwise important. Known as *critical-incident analysis*, this technique can be useful for identifying opportunities for digging deeper in search of useful information (Sharp, Rogers and Preece, 2007). In an interview, a critical incident might be a story that describes a notable failure of an existing system or a desired list of criteria for its replacement. As each critical incident becomes a case study – chosen not as a representative incident but rather as one that can provide useful information – techniques described in Chapter 7 can be applicable.

8.9.3   Validity

Analyses based on the interpretation of texts often face questions of validity. Due to the necessarily subjective nature of the process of reading texts, any single analysis may be influenced in subtle (or not-so-subtle) ways by the viewpoints and biases of the individual analyst. If validity is a particular concern – as it might be when your goal is to make a general claim that has some scientific validity – you might want to have multiple researchers conduct independent analyses of your interviews. Ideally, their comments will be largely in agreement with each other. High value measures of *inter-rater reliability* indicate a reasonably valid analysis.

Validity may not be a particular concern if your interviews are aimed at understanding user requirements. If you are working closely with users and customers, you will probably present your findings to them once your analysis is complete. If you have a good working relationship, they will let you know when your analysis has gone wrong. This feedback is very useful for refining your understanding.

8.9.4   Reporting results

After you have conducted countless interviews and spent untold hours analyzing responses, you must report the results. Expectations vary among contexts; descriptions of a given set of results in an academic publication might differ significantly from how the same results would be presented in a corporate memo or presentation for a client. Despite these differences, some common principles apply.

Your presentation of interview results should be as clear and specific as possible. Tabulations of frequencies of responses can be used to give specific reports. Instead of saying "many users complained about . . . ," say "seven out of 10 interviewees who responded complained about . . . ." Replacing terms such as "many", "most", "often", "frequently", "rarely", and other vague quantifiers with concrete counts help users to understand not only the specific points but their relative importance.

You can also use respondent's words to make your reporting more concrete. Instead of paraphrasing or summarizing, use direct quotes. A small number of direct quotes illustrating interviewee sentiment can make your arguments much more concrete. This strategy can be particularly effective when coupled with frequency counts indicating widespread agreement with the quoted views.

If you do decide to quote users directly, you should be careful to do so in accordance with best practice for respecting human participants in research. Don't use participant names.

If you have to repeatedly refer to an individual, use initials or a numeric code: S1, S2, etc. Don't use quotes that reveal any embarrassing or identifying details. You should always inform participants that their words may be used in research reports. This information should be explicitly included in the informed consent form (see Chapter 14). For questions that address particularly sensitive issues, you may wish to avoid quoting any interviewees directly.

Summary

Interviews and focus groups present substantial challenges for HCI researchers and practitioners. Writing questions, identifying appropriate respondents, conducting interviews, and analyzing data all require considerable skill and experience. For those of us who come to HCI from a technical background, the social science techniques and strategies that are involved may seem unfamiliar and somewhat daunting.

Despite these concerns, interviews and focus groups are invaluable tools for HCI researchers and practitioners, providing data into user and stakeholder needs and perceptions that would be difficult, if not impossible to get using other techniques. It's that simple – if you want to know what people want or what they think, you must ask them. For researchers, this might mean in-depth conversations aimed at building models to explain how systems are used and why. For designers and builders of interfaces, interviews can help build understanding of needs and reactions to interfaces. If you want to know why your last design failed, you can start by interviewing the users.

The choice of one-to-one interviews or focus groups involves trade-offs in time, expediency, depth, and difficulty. Focus groups let you hear from many people at once but with less depth from any given individual. You should consider the trade-off between this loss of depth and the potentially fuller understanding that may arise from a conversation between participants having multiple perspectives. Unfortunately, there are no guarantees: this intriguing dynamic conversation might not materialize. As the moderator of a focus group, you have a very important role to play: this is where the difficulty comes in. Skillful moderation can keep conversation focused and inclusive, increasing your chances of getting good data.

Interviews and focus groups might best be conducted as complements to other data collection approaches. Empirical studies, usability tests, ethnographic investigations, and case studies are among the methods that might be used alongside interviews. You can use multiple, complementary tactics to confirm findings or identify potential disconnects. Perhaps users prefer one interface design over another, even though it is slower. Why is that? Well-formed interview questions might help you understand the reasons.

If you feel intimidated by these challenges, start small. A simple, fully structured interview with closed questions will help you get started. As you become more comfortable with writing questions, talking to interviewees, and analyzing data, you might move on to interviews with less structure and greater challenges. Don't be ashamed to bring in some outside help. A colleague who is knowledgeable and experienced in interviewing can be an invaluable aide.

Discussion Questions

1. The trust required to successfully conduct an interview may be difficult to achieve under certain circumstances. If honest answers to difficult questions may have repercussions for your interviewees, they might be less than forthcoming. If you were interested in developing a tool that would encourage teens to pay for downloading music rather than illegally trading copyrighted songs, you might consider interviewing teens to understand their attitudes and practices. However, they may be reluctant to share information with you, for fear that their parents would learn of any inappropriate activity that they have been involved in. As parental consent is likely to be required for the participation of underage teens, these concerns are not necessarily invalid. How might you build trust with these teens? How might you evaluate their comments to determine whether they are being truthful?

2. The development of a tool to encourage teens to pay for downloaded music presents some challenges in data gathering. If teens are using home computers for potentially inappropriate activities, parents may feel that they have a legitimate interest and concern in what their children are doing. To better understand the problem, you might decide to interview parents as well as teens. Would you interview them separately or together? What sort of questions would you ask parents and how would they differ from questions that you might ask of teens? Would you use one-to-one interviews or focus groups? Why?

3. Interviews can become awkward if the interviewees start asking difficult questions about the research. Imagine you are interviewing hospital equipment repair technicians about their practices for recording their workflow, including repairs completed, time spent on each repair, and related tasks. What should you do if the workers' concern for their job security leads them to ask tough questions about why the data is being collected and what it will be used for? If you know that management is trying to collect data that might be used to raise expectations and workload or to reduce staff, what should you tell the technicians? How can you resolve your responsibility to the client (the management) who is paying the bills, while showing appropriate respect for the workers you are interviewing?

Research Design Exercises

1. Design and conduct an interview. Chances are pretty good that most of the people you know have or use cell phones. They are also likely to have strong opinions about their likes and dislikes regarding phone interface design and features. Design an interview that you might use to understand what cell phone users would like to see in a new generation of phone. What sort of questions would you ask and why? How much structure would you want to have? Would you use any props or observations?

Once you have this interview designed, try it on a friend, classmate, or colleague. What did this teach you about interviewing? Were there questions that you should have asked but didn't? What worked well, what didn't?

2. Revisit the cell phone usage interview from Exercise 1. What would be different if you were to collect this data via a focus group instead of interviews? Revise the questions to account for any differences between individuals, in terms of preferences, experiences and needs. How might you foster discussion and deliberation between focus group participants?

3. Revisit the cell phone usage interview from Exercise 1, but try it online this time. Sign up for an account on an instant-messaging service (if you don't have one already), and ask a friend or classmate to be your interviewee. Ask the same questions that you asked before. How do the responses differ? Did you get as much information or less? Did you notice any differences in the amount of feedback or the quality of the responses? Which did you find most useful? Which did you prefer?

References

Angrosino, M. (2005) *Projects in Ethnographic Research*. Long Grove, IL: Waveland Press.

Barbour, R. (2007) *Doing Focus Group*. Thousand Oaks, CA: Sage Publications.

Beyer, H. and Holtzblatt, K. (1998) *Contextual Design: Defining customer-centered systems*. San Francisco: Morgan Kaufmann.

Blythe, M., Monk, A., and Park, J. (2002) Technology biographies: Field study techniques for home use product development. *Extended Abstracts of the ACM Conference on Human Factors in Computing Systems*, 658–659.

Brown, J.B. (1999) The use of focus groups in clinical research. In B.F. Crabtree and W.L. Miller (eds), *Doing Qualitative Research*. Thousand Oaks, CA: Sage Publications.

Cheng, K.G., Ernesto, F., and Truong, K.N. (2008) Participant and interviewer attitudes toward handheld computers in the context of HIV/AIDS programs in sub-Saharan Africa. *Proceedings of the 26th Conference on Human Factors in Computing Systems*. USA: ACM.

Chin, J.P., Diehl, V.A., and Norman, K.L. (1988) Development of an instrument measuring user interface satisfaction. *Proceedings of the ACM Conference on Human Factors in Computing Systems*, 213–218.

Davis, J. and Rebelsky, S.A. (2007) Food-first computer science: Starting the first course right with PB & J. *Proceedings of the ACM Technical Symposium on Computer Science Education*, 372–376.

Friedman, B., Hurley, D., Howe, D.C., et al. (2002) Users' conceptions of web security: A comparative study. *Extended Abstracts of the ACM Conference on Human Factors in Computing Systems*, 746–747.

Gaver, B., Dunne, T., and Pacenti, E. (1999) Design: Cultural probes. *Interactions*, **6**(1):21–29.

Gilchrist, V.J. and Williams, R.L. (1999) Key informant interviews. In B.F. Crabtree and W.L. Miller (eds), *Doing Qualitative Research*. Thousand Oaks, CA: Sage Publications.

Huang, E.M. and Truong, K.N. (2008) Breaking the disposable technology paradigm: Opportunities for sustainable interaction design for mobile phones. *Proceedings of the ACM Conference on Human Factors in Computing Systems*, 323–332.

Hutchinson, H., Mackay, W., Westerlund, B., Bederson, B., Druin, A., Plaisant, C., Beaudoin-Lafon, M., Conversy, S., Evans, H., Rousel, N., and Eiderbäck, B. (2003) Technology probes: inspiring design for and with families. *Proceedings of the ACM Conference on Human Factors in Computing Systems*, 17–24.

Krueger, R.A. (1994) *Focus Groups: A practical guide for applied research*. Thousand Oaks, CA: Sage Publications.

Kvale, S. (2007) *Doing Interviews*. Thousand Oaks, CA: Sage Publications.

Le Dantec, C.A. and Edwards, W.K. (2008) Designs on dignity: Perceptions of technology among the homeless. *Proceedings of the ACM Conference on Human Factors in Computing Systems*, 627–636.

Leshed, G., Velden, T., Rieger, O., *et al.* (2008) In-car GPS navigation: Engagement with and disengagement from the environment. *Proceedings of the ACM Conference on Human Factors in Computing Systems*, 1675–1684.

Malone, T.W. (1983) How do people organize their desks? Implications for the design of office information systems. *ACM Transactions on Information Systems*, **1**(1):99–112.

Miller, W.L. and Crabtree, B.F. (1999) Clinical research: A multimethod typology and qualitative roadmap. In B.F. Crabtree and W.L. Miller (eds), *Doing Qualitative Research*. Thousand Oaks, CA: Sage Publications.

Orne, M.T. (1962) On the social psychology of the psychological experiment: With particular reference to demand characteristics and their implications. *American Psychologist*, **17**(11):776–783.

Petersen, M.G. and Baillie, L. (2001) Methodologies for designing future household technologies. Paper presented at Oikos2001. Aarhus: Aarhus University Press.

Read, J., MacFarlane, S., and Casey, C. (2002) Endurability, Engagement and Expectations: Measuring Children's Fun, Interaction Design and Children, Shaker Publishing.

Robson, C. (2002) *Real World Research*. Malden, MA: Blackwell Publishing.

Sharp, H., Rogers, Y., and Preece, J. (2007) *Interaction Design: Beyond human–computer interaction*, 2nd Edition. Chichester, UK: John Wiley & Sons.

Voida, A., Mynatt, E.D., Erickson, T., and Kellogg, W.A. (2004) Interviewing over instant messaging. *Extended Abstracts of the ACM Conference on Human Factors in Computing Systems*.

Walston, J.T. and Lissitz, R.W. (2000) Computer-mediated focus groups. *Evaluation Review*, **24**(5):457–483.

Woodruff, A., Hasbrouck, J., and Augustin, S. (2008) A bright green perspective on sustainable choices. *Proceedings of the ACM Conference on Human Factors in Computing Systems*, 313–322.

Ethnography

9.1   Introduction

You've just been offered a fantastic opportunity to become involved in the design of an innovative new health care information management system, to be used in hospital intensive care units in a country that you've always wanted to visit. Your job is to design an integrated set of user interfaces, based on a detailed understanding of system requirements, organizational concerns, work practices, and a multitude of other relevant factors.

As soon as you accept the job, you realize that you've got a big problem: where to start? How should you go about developing the understanding of the situation that you will need to design these interfaces? You've never worked in a hospital – let alone an intensive care unit – so you know almost nothing about how the people work, what information they need, how they want it displayed, and other factors that will be crucial elements of your designs.

This lack of background would be hard enough if the hospital was in your neighborhood, as you might be able to rely upon shared cultural background and perhaps even acquaintances to help you get started. However, you might find that the world of the hospital workers is very unfamiliar. If you haven't worked in that environment, the language, types of interactions, and values might effectively amount to a distinct subculture. Tackling these questions in a foreign country, with different social norms and work practices, seems that much harder.

Whether in your home country or in somewhere far from home, you should start by realizing that differences between cultures can be very important. An understanding of the ways that people work and interact is crucial for your success in designing the tool: assuming that your users are "just like you" might be a recipe for failure. How can you understand how people work and what they need from a computer system when you have almost no understanding of the context in which your designs will be used?

You might start by considering some of the other research techniques described in this book. Your first thought might be to consider surveying potential users. A survey containing questions about reactions to current information systems and hopes for future versions might help you build some initial understanding. Unfortunately, there are problems with this approach: not only do you not have much idea of which questions you should ask, you don't have much of an idea of how to ask them. You're also a bit concerned that your questions might fail to address certain key issues. Interviews might help, but they suffer from similar problems. Talking directly with potential users might be helpful, but is also prone to potential omission of important topics. Besides, you don't know if your questions would be culturally appropriate – you don't want to offend anyone.

Having reached this point, you might (perhaps not so reluctantly) conclude that you need to take a trip to observe workers in this environment in person. You decide to learn what you can about hospital workplace practices and general cultural background that will help you understand how things are done "over there". You talk to your clients to identify a hospital where you can observe potential future users working in the intensive-care unit. You ask them if they can introduce you to a trusted partner who can show you around. You talk to this person to get some basic understanding. You then observe the healthcare workers in action and talk with some of them in detail. You might spend several days "shadowing" some of them, following them around as they attend to various tasks and concerns.

As you go through these various steps, you begin to understand how these professionals work and what they need. You use this understanding to begin working towards lists of requirements and elements of proposed designs. As time goes on, you'll discuss these artifacts with your potential users, looking to them to either approve of your suggestions or to suggest revisions that might correct misperceptions. As your ideas become more fully developed, you travel to another hospital in a different city to determine whether or not your ideas are appropriate for this second group of users.

This combination of observation, interviews, and participation is known as *ethnography*. Ethnographic research projects use deep immersion and participation in a specific research context to develop an understanding that would not be achievable with other, more limited research approaches.

This added insight does not come without a substantial cost: ethnographic research can be very challenging. Participation in a specific context can help you understand how to build tools for that situation, but effective data collection requires well-developed skills in observation, conversation, and interpretation. Ethnographers must take significant care in deciding with whom they should be talking and how to reconcile contradictory data.

This chapter provides some background on ethnography and its use in human–computer interaction (HCI) research. We discuss the steps involved in an ethnographic research project: selecting groups to study, choosing a form of participation, making initial contact, building relationships within the group, iterative data collection and analysis, and reporting the results.

We discuss the use of ethnography in a variety of HCI projects, including examples from homes, workplaces, schools, and online, with a goal of understanding when it is appropriate for HCI research and how it might best be conducted. Although one chapter in a textbook is obviously no substitute for years of ethnographic research experience, we hope to provide an introduction that helps you make the most of this powerful technique.

9.2 What is ethnography?

One social scientist defined ethnography as "the art and science of describing a human group – its institutions, interpersonal behaviors, material productions, and beliefs" (Angrosino, 2007). At first reading, this definition may seem somewhat unsatisfactory. After all, many forms of research might be used to develop a description of a human group – we might do surveys, conduct interviews, observe activities, and use other approaches described in this book (and elsewhere). Later in this chapter, we see how these research methods are important parts of ethnographic studies. So, what's so special about ethnography?

Ethnography, as a research methodology, has its roots in anthropological studies of non-Western cultures. In attempting to develop deep understandings of unfamiliar civilizations, researchers found that limited interactions and observations were insufficient. Moving beyond these limits required stepping out of the role of dispassionate observer and engaging directly with people in their daily lives. Anthropologists spent years living and working in traditional villages and using this deeply embedded perspective to provide insights that would have been difficult, if not impossible, to get from other data collection methods. This form of participatory research evolved into what we currently call ethnography (Angrosino, 2007).

Ethnography is based in the notion that true understanding of complex human practices and contexts requires in-depth, engaged study. Individuals often describe what they do in a way that is not accurate. This may be due to a lack of awareness or understanding of what they are doing, or individuals may report more socially acceptable actions than their actual actions (Blomberg and Burrell, 2007). In Section 9.1, we saw how some research methods were inadequate for developing an understanding of a thoroughly unfamiliar environment. The proposed solution was to become immersed in the problem, spending significant amounts of time in the working environment, talking with the medical staff, watching how things are done, and learning from being in the world that is being studied. A core belief in ethnography is that "to gain an understanding of a world that you know little about, you must encounter it firsthand" (Blomberg and Burrell, 2007, p. 967).

Participation – in some form – is a critical practice in ethnography. Although researchers may not realistically be able to act exactly as if they belong to the group being studied, they try to be as involved as practically and ethically possible. Anthropologists conducting ethnographic studies of traditional societies live in these communities for several years, using participation in the activities of daily life as a means of understanding the dynamics of the group being studied. Section 9.4.2 has a more in-depth discussion of possible types of participation in an ethnographic study. Qualitative methods that involve no participation or observation, such as content analysis and document analysis, are presented in Chapter 11. The focus of this chapter is on traditional ethnography research, which involves some level of observation or participation.

As a descriptive technique, ethnography is usually *inductive,* moving from raw data to the identification of patterns that regularly occur in the data and, often, on to general theories that explain the patterns. This inductive focus stands in direct contrast to hypothesis-driven research, which defines a narrowly controlled experiment to test well-defined alternative explanations or designs (Angrosino, 2007). There are no controls in ethnography – every case is unique.

Although ethnographies are similar to case studies (Chapter 7), there are some important differences. Like case studies, ethnographies rely on multiple types of data to confirm observations, a process known as triangulation (Angrosino, 2007). Ethnographies and case studies are both time-intensive, personal, and largely based in the context being studied (Angrosino, 2007). The context often differentiates these research methods from methods such as surveys, experimental design, and other methods. In ethnography, context often is the main focus of understanding.

The primary difference between ethnography and case-study research lies in the use of theory. Case-study research is often based on hypotheses or propositions that guide the questions being asked. This theory-driven approach is subtly different from the inductive strategies used in ethnography.[1] Informally, you might think of an ethnographic study as being a very preliminary, exploratory case study.

Ethnographic research also differs from case studies and other qualitative research methods in the extent of the engagement with the group or situation being studied. The goal of ethnographic participation is to come as close as possible to achieving the rich perspective that comes from being part of the group being studied. Although this is rarely, if ever, possible (see Section 9.4.2), ethnographers tend to become deeply involved with the groups or situations that they are studying. Unlike case studies or other qualitative research projects that may use observations, interviews, and a similar range of data collection techniques in a relatively constrained manner over a short period of time, ethnographic research generally makes more fluid use of these techniques over a longer term, in close interaction with participants. In ethnographic research, the distinctions between "interaction", "interview", and "observation" are almost non-existent, with all of these activities potentially occurring in the space of a few minutes. Of course, these somewhat arbitrary distinctions exist along a continuum with no clear boundaries: a long-term, highly interactive case study may be hard to distinguish from an ethnographic study.

One final note in defining ethnography: traditionally, the term "ethnography" has been used to define both the practice and the written outcome. Thus, ethnography is both a process and the outcome of that process. Like case studies, ethnographies are often narrative, telling the story behind the context being studied (Angrosino, 2007). Often, these stories strive to convey perspectives of the people being studied: giving "accounts of an event like community members do" has been described as an important ethnographic goal (Agar, 1980).

9.3 Ethnography in HCI

The description of ethnography as the practice of using some form of participation in a group to develop an understanding of the group is straight from social science research. Social science ethnographers spend time living in traditional villages, hanging out on inner-city street corners, and otherwise immersing themselves in unfamiliar settings to understand the dynamics of groups of interest.

As fascinating as this might sound, it may also seem a bit far removed from research into human–computer interaction. After all, HCI researchers are usually trying to understand

---

[1] The role of theory has been the subject of much debate in ethnographic circles. There are numerous theoretical perspectives on ethnography (Angrosino, 2007). Some viewpoints reject the notion of ethnography as a tool for developing theories, claiming that it is (or should be) merely descriptive. This perspective has generated substantial discussion (Shapiro, 1994; Sharrock and Randall, 2004).

how to build systems or how users interact with computers. How does this relate to the in-depth study of groups and why is participation useful and helpful?

The connection becomes clearer once we consider the use of modern computer systems. Even when we are sitting in front of a traditional computer, conducting seemingly familiar tasks such as word processing, we're not really computing so much as we are communicating. Much of our computing work that does not directly involve communication or collaboration (email, instant messaging, online calendars, virtual worlds) – involves creating artifacts (documents, spreadsheets, presentations) that communicate ideas to others. Mobile and ubiquitous computing tools that make computing a more integrated part of daily life are even more focused on communication.

As soon as we start using computing technologies for communication and collaboration, we start forming groups. Whether these groups are "real" groups that have some physical existence outside the computing environment, such as schools (Wyeth, 2006), homes (Crabtree and Rodden, 2004; Taylor and Swan, 2005) and workplaces (Newman and Landay, 2000; Su and Mark, 2008), or are groups that would not exist without the technological intermediary, such as virtual worlds (Ducheneaut, Moore and Nickell, 2007), they have their own norms and dynamics that are legitimate and important subjects of study.

But what does the HCI researcher hope to learn about these groups? Often, the goal is just understanding: How is a technology used? How do the features of the design influence how people use the system? HCI researchers can use ethnographic techniques of participating in the group to gain a detailed and nuanced understanding that other methods cannot provide.

Lucy Suchman's study of the users of an electronic help system on a photocopier is perhaps the most famous example of ethnography in HCI. Starting from a framework that describes all action as being a product of the context in which it is taken – a model known as *situated action* – Suchman observed users attempting to complete a photocopying task with the help of an expert system designed to help them identify problems and complete tasks correctly. Through analysis of videos and a framework designed to demonstrate the relevant features of the interactions between the humans and the expert system, Suchman developed a rich and detailed understanding of how differences between the human model of the copier and the expert system's model led to communication breakdowns and task failures (Suchman, 1987). This study remains influential both as a fascinating discussion of how problems in human–machine communication can arise and as an example of the utility of ethnography in HCI.

Often, the human, social, and organizational aspects of information systems development are the ones most critical to ensuring the success of a project (Harvey and Myers, 2002). Ethnography can help in providing an understanding of the context in which specific interfaces or systems are developed and implemented. While research methods such as experimental design focus on reducing research to a small number of hypotheses with findings that are easily generalizable to other projects, ethnography focuses on the opposite: understanding the context of individuals in groups, their processes and norms, at a specific point in time, without generalization as a goal (Harvey and Myers, 2002). In addition, ethnographic approaches can be especially good for designing technology out of a workplace context: "Designing for pleasure demands a different approach from designing for utility" (Gaver *et al.*, 2004, p. 53).

In a study aimed at understanding the importance of communication to multitasking, researchers "shadowed" 19 workers at a large US corporation, noting all of the workers' activities at their desks and following them around wherever possible. The resulting 550 hours of data, including over 13 000 events, were analyzed and coded to understand how workers switch between tasks, interlocutors, and communication media. The finding that coordinating activities with multiple people was a stressful and difficult activity led the authors to suggest that communication systems might be designed to identify interruptions that might require significant coordination effort (Su and Mark, 2008). The detailed records of communication behavior collected in this study would have been difficult, if not impossible, to collect via other means: observing the workers' activities at their desks, analyzing email transcripts, or otherwise observing some subset of their activities would have given an incomplete picture of the activities and interactions between modes of communication.

The example of the hospital information system (see Section 9.1) illustrates the other primary goal of ethnography in HCI – to understand system requirements and user needs. Successful design of complex or novel interfaces for use in unfamiliar domains, requires researchers to build a detailed, multi-faceted understanding of how the work is done, how users interact, how tools are used, what users need, what policies are in place, and other related questions. It comes down to understanding the context surrounding where the information system will be used and who will be using it.

As in the case of the hospital information system, interviews, surveys, and other simpler data collection techniques may not be up to the task. Ethnographic research puts developers into the thick of the situation, letting them observe and study the situation firsthand. Extending the hospital example, most computer developers would not know how hospitals typically refer to patients. In a typical database design, data about individual humans is often referred to by an ID number or their last and first name. However, in hospitals, patients are often referred to by bed number. In typical database design, the ID does not represent anything physical or meaningful, but in a hospital situation there is a physical meaning (the bed number or location) behind the identifier. This is an important difference that might be uncovered using ethnographic techniques but otherwise would not be obvious to the average researcher or developer.

The use of ethnographic investigations for understanding the requirements for a computer system is closely related to a design philosophy known as *participatory design* (Schuler and Namioka, 1993). Starting from concerns about the impact of computer systems that are simply foisted on users without consideration of their needs and preferences, participatory design efforts involve users in every stage of design, from early discussions aimed at understanding problems, concerns, and needs, to brain-storming regarding design possi-bilities, evaluation of paper or other low-quality prototypes, and continued refinement of working systems. Although participatory design shares ethnography's interest in direct par-ticipation and engagement with the group being studied, the goal is generally different. Ethnography focuses on understanding people, their groups, their processes, their beliefs. Ethnography really focuses on understanding the problem. Participatory design is often the process of using ethnographic approaches with the end goal of designing a computer system. Participatory design can be seen as using ethnographic methods to understand the problem, and then intensely involving those same participants in building potential solutions to the problem. In ethnography, understanding the problem, the context, the culture, or the group interactions, is sufficient as a research study.

Participatory design as a development method is often used for systems development in three types of situations, where a deep understanding of the situation is required. The first situation is where the user tasks are not well understood, such as the many differ-ent and complex tasks that teachers carry out in an average day (Carroll *et al.*, 2000). The second situation is where the users themselves are not well-understood, such as people with cognitive impairment and memory loss (Wu, Baecker and Richards, 2007). The third situation is where even minor errors in task completion can lead to catas-trophic consequences, such as at a nuclear power plant or an aircraft carrier. While par-ticipatory design is ideal for developing all types of systems, it is very time and cost-intensive, and so participatory design is often used when the computer development projects are high-risk, have a high likelihood of failure, and a high payoff for success. Most design projects cannot afford the time or cost involved in intensive ethnographic approaches.

That said, the delineations between some of these forms of research are often blurred, at best. Some self-described HCI "ethnographies" may involve theoretical propositions that make them seem more like case studies. Studies that aren't driven by a theoretical basis may make some use of ethnographic tools to build an understanding of contextual issues, without going into the detail associated with a full-blown ethnography. Projects involving the design of tools for domain experts – such as the hospital scenario described above – may involve techniques from ethnography, such as the shadowing of experts, while other similar efforts may seem more like participatory design than ethnography. No matter: the interest here lies in identifying appropriate research techniques and understanding how they might be used.

9.4   Conducting ethnographic research

Ethnographic research can be extremely challenging. Ethnographic studies are usually con-ducted "in the wild," in homes, workplaces, educational settings, or other places where the "action" of interest takes place. As these studies often involve extended periods of in-teraction and observation, researchers may find themselves in unfamiliar environments for long periods of time. This time may be spent juggling two complex and inter-twined goals: understanding how to navigate the dynamics of these unfamiliar settings and conducting the observations that provide the data for subsequent analysis. This can be a challenge, to say the least.

Researchers are often advised to carefully consider how well suited they are for a given project before embarking on ethnographic projects (Agar, 1980; Angrosino, 2007), In some cases personal tastes and preferences may make participation in certain studies inadvisable: an otherwise highly capable HCI researcher who is uncomfortable with the sight of blood might not be a good choice for our hypothetical scenario of information systems in intensive-care units.

Other considerations involve differences in background. Researchers may be ethnically, culturally, or socio-economically different from members of the group being studied and these differences might prevent them from being complete participants. Subtler forms of bias are also a concern: as individuals with distinct perspectives, we pay more attention to some details than others, often in ways that we are unaware of. Ethnographers should strive to work past such biases to the greatest extent possible (Angrosino, 2007). Bias-awareness training, careful attention to methodology – including rigorous documentation of evidence – and the use of multiple researchers (Agar, 1980) are among the techniques that might be used to overcome the inevitable biases.

9.4.1 Selecting a site or group of interest

Selecting a target of ethnographic research is in many ways similar to selecting cases for a case study (Section 7.7). You will want to find groups that are interesting, logistically workable, and committed to supporting the goals of the study.

Selection may not be an issue. HCI ethnographies conducted in the interest of under-standing the requirements of a system for a specific customer may not have a great deal of latitude in the choice of site. If the intensive-care information system is to be used at a specific hospital, that is where the research should be conducted.

In some cases, you may be interested in finding groups that are representative of similar instances, while in others you may wish to study extreme cases. These goals will influence your choice of site: if you want to understand how technologies are used in schools, you might look for sites that have average funding levels and representative student bodies to get a representative understanding. On the other hand, comparison of extremes – for example, well-funded suburban schools with poorly funded urban schools – might provide interesting contrasts.

There may be barriers to your involvement and participation in specific types of ethno-graphic site. For instance, health-care systems in many countries protect the data of patients receiving health-care services. You can't just walk in and start examining data and going along with teams of doctors or nurses. A similar problem occurs in schools. You can't just walk into a school and spend time in a classroom. If there is sensitive financial information, you can't just walk in and start taking part in discussions at an investment bank. Similarly, governmental and military installations often have sensitive data and discussions, so your presence may pose a challenge. For these situations, you may need to go through multiple stages of approval, including not only traditional institutional review board approval for research (see Chapter 14), but also certification, security and background checks, fingerprinting, sexual harassment training, and similar hurdles. You may be required to sign confidentiality agreements or other legal agreements. None of these should stop you from selecting a potential research site, but they are important considerations to be aware of.

In some cases, the selection of sites may be based on convenience – organizations, places, and people that you know well increase familiarity and comfort, which may make the research less daunting. Familiarity is not without its own hazards, however, as you might find that foreknowledge limits your objectivity.

If you are faced with the good fortune of having several potentially viable candidate groups to choose from, you might want to do a bit of preliminary work to inform your choice. Your interactions with the individuals in a group may provide some indication as to whether that group is a good candidate for your research. You'll always need to work to build a relationship with the members of groups that you study, but you might be more inclined to work with a group that seems welcoming and encouraging, rather than a group that seems hostile or uninterested.

Some groups, or group members, may have very good reasons for being wary about participating in an ethnographic study. They may be legitimately concerned about your research agenda, as the questions you ask, the conclusions you draw, and the reports that you write might have a very real impact on them. Consider a study of the work habits of repair technicians. You might be interested in building an understanding of technicians' work habits, in the hopes of designing tools that will help them more effectively share information. If, however, a candidate group perceives this system as an attempt to "de-skill" their work, threatening their employment stability or autonomy, they may be reluctant to participate. You may have to work to build trust to convince group members that participation in your project will not be something that they will regret.

You should also consider the practical impact of your research on the group that you are studying. If you are going to be spending a great deal of time in someone's home, school, or workplace, you might be in the way. Questions that you might ask in order to help your understanding might distract from the goals of the people that you're working with. One rule of thumb might be to try to make sure that the benefits outweigh the costs for your participants: they should get something worthwhile out of the time that they commit to helping your research (Angrosino, 2007). If you're studying work practices in order to understand the requirements for a new system – as in our hospital example – the benefits to the participants might be clear: you'll be able to build a system that will support their work. If the benefits are less immediate, you might consider trying to find some way to compensate participants.

9.4.2 Participating: choosing a role

Participation is a critical part of ethnography. Realizing that there are limits in what can be learned by observing from the outside, ethnographers strive to be involved in the situations that they are studying. Participation removes the need for intermediaries. Instead of relying upon members of a group to describe situations of interest, a participant–researcher can experience it first-hand, relying upon their own powers of observation to understand the situation. Direct experiences of phenomena of interest can provide a richness of data that is almost impossible to get from any other research approach.

Having decided to participate, you must decide exactly what this means. You might be tempted to try to join the group – to become a member in order to study the group. This form of participation evokes images of anthropologists living in traditional villages. By sleeping, eating, and working with residents of the village, and becoming – as much as possible – part of their community, a researcher learns "from the inside." These *complete participants* (Gold, 1958) may learn a great deal, but at great expense, often involving years of fieldwork. Even if you are able to make this effort, you may run the risk of losing the ability to be a detached observer, as your identity as a member of the group may overwhelm your training as a researcher. Known as "going native" (Gold, 1958), this reaction may impair your ability to continue your research.

Some ethnographers have pushed complete participation to its logical limits, concealing their identity as researchers in order to make their membership in the group appear more authentic. This strategy has the advantage of easing access to the group: if you don't present yourself as a researcher, you don't have to explain your work or deal with concerns of group members. This strategy can be particularly appropriate in public or near-public settings where you generally would not be asked to justify your presence or behavior (Lofland *et al.*, 2006).

Private settings pose more of a challenge for such "covert" research, as concealing your identity may mean deceiving group members as to the reasons for your participation. Even when conducted in the interest of fidelity of research, it is often considered unethical for researchers to intentionally misrepresent the goals of their research. Deceptions about a researcher's identity are also considered unethical if they are conducted in order to get access to a group or context that they would not otherwise be able to join (Angrosino, 2007). Thus, creating an avatar for participation in a virtual world (Ducheneaut, Moore and Nickell, 2007) does not raise an ethical concern because membership in these worlds is not constrained and interactions are not intended to be private. However, falsely claiming to be a resident of a neighborhood in order to join a residents-only discussion group might be considered inappropriate. These concerns notwithstanding, some researchers have used covert participation in situations where they believed that it was the only way that they could gain access to the group (Lofland *et al.*, 2006).

Pragmatic considerations can also limit the practicality of complete participation. Let's return to the hospital information system that we described earlier. You might be able to spend a great deal of time watching intensive-care nurses and physicians up close, and you might learn a great deal about how medical care is given in the ICU, but you probably shouldn't be involved directly in patient care. Even if you are a trained and licensed medical professional, it's not at all clear that you could be working effectively both as an HCI researcher and as a caregiver at the same time.

The opposite extreme – minimal participation – addresses some of these concerns while raising different issues. The *complete observer* (Gold, 1958) observes without interacting directly, limiting participation to simply "being there" as events of interest transpire. Complete observers remain detached from the subjects of their observation – they rarely worry about "going native". However, they do so at the cost of losing out on a wealth of information. If a complete observer sees something of interest that she does not understand, she does not ask a group member for clarification: she simply does her best to interpret what she sees. As a result, complete observers may at times misinterpret the particular details or significance of events (Gold, 1958).

Usability testing (Chapter 10) is a research method that uses primarily observation, and not participation, in understanding what challenges users are having with an interface. However, usability testing is generally a short-term data collection method, only focusing on a few individuals (generally not working together) and generally not focused on groups, human dynamics, or context (Siegel and Dray, 2005). Furthermore, usability testing generally has the goal of simply finding and fixing flaws in an interface, not understanding any higher-level research questions. Usability testing tends to come into the picture after an interface feature (or multiple potential interface features) have already been developed. Like participatory design, usability testing is focused on the end product of design, although participatory design is an entire design lifecycle approach, whereas usability testing is one late-stage activity. Ethnography is an approach to understanding the problem, whereas usability testing is often a method for evaluating potential solutions (Siegel and Dray, 2005).

Most ethnographic projects in HCI avoid the extremes of complete participation and observation, opting for an intermediate approach. Some ethnographers become temporary members of the group that they are studying, with all participants fully informed as to the nature of their participation. Possibilities include combining some degree of participation with observation. These researchers might generally disclose their role as researchers and then get more or less involved in group activities, sometimes participating, other times observing. One common approach is to "shadow" group members – following them around as they go about their business, asking questions as needed for clarification and interpretation.

These roles form a continuum of possible research approaches (see Figure 9.1). Researchers may adopt multiple, evolving roles throughout the course of a single project. One common approach is to begin research as a complete observer, using initial findings to create questions and goals for more in-depth participation (Gold, 1958).

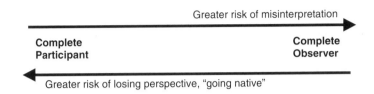

Figure 9.1 The spectrum of roles for ethnographic researchers (Gold, 1958).

Given both the difficulty of truly becoming a member of a group and the possibilities of misinterpretation associated with observation from outside the group, you might be tempted to observe a culture that you are already a member of. This approach has some appealing aspects. If you are part of a group, you already have access to group members, existing relationships, and trust. You also probably have some curiosity about how the group works and why it works this way (Lofland *et al.*, 2006). Together, these factors give you a real head start. You may have to do a good deal less preliminary work to build the groundwork for a study. You understand context and background that would be unclear to a newcomer, and group members might be less hesitant to respond to your questions. Even if you are open, and have disclosed that you are doing research, this may be seen with less skepticism.

If you find yourself intrigued by the ease of working with a group of which you are already a member, you would be well advised to reconsider this strategy as an automatic first choice. Your participation in a group may lead to bias and pre-informed opinions – even worse than the complete participant who has "gone native", you *are* native. You may have deeply ingrained habits, opinions, and preferences of which you are not aware. Furthermore, you lack the fresh perspective associated with learning about a new topic and problem domain.

These concerns aside, group membership may, on occasion, lead to the identification of interesting opportunities for research: see the Ethnographic Research of Your Own Community sidebar for one example.

Ethnographic Research of Your Own Community

In an ideal research world, you study groups or communities simply because they are interesting and in need of better understanding. In the reality of HCI research, you are often asked to study a specific group of people or work environment because:

- there are problems which need to be understood or improved upon, and you have relevant experience;

- there are problems or interesting research questions that you are aware of in a group of which you are already a member, and you could help to understand and address those problems.

Sometimes, you stumble across great ethnographic studies accidentally. In 1998, Jenny Preece, an HCI researcher, tore her anterior cruciate ligament (ACL) in her knee. She joined an online community called Bob's ACL Bulletin board to learn more about her injury, along with various treatments. She became a member of the group and later found the level of empathic support to be fascinating.

She decided to do ethnographically informed research to learn more about the people of the online community, what they communicated about, and how they communicated (Preece, 1998). She was not a strict observer, since she was already a member of the community. She could understand, more than a strict observer could, what it meant to have a torn ACL. The founder of the bulletin board, Bob Wilmot, was aware of her research and helped answer her questions.

In contrast, when her student Diane Maloney-Krichmar, continued to study the same community years later, she was a strict observer, not a participant in any form. As Maloney-Krichmar noted in her paper, to participate in the community fully would require faking the fact that she had the ACL knee injury, which she could not do, because doing so might also taint the findings of the research study, since she would be lying to community members and unable to take a full part in the discussions (Maloney-Krichmar and Preece, 2005).

Many of the previous examples focus on ethnography in physical locations, with face-to-face contact where researchers are physically present. Online research presents opportunities for ethnographic research that transcend these roles. The complete participant role in traditional ethnographic research is predicated on the notion that participation requires presence: to be a member of the group, you must be physically with the members of that group, interacting with them face-to-face. This proximity leads to many of the challenges of highly participative research, requiring researchers to be (at least passably) good actors and encouraging the connections that might cause some to "go native." More information about doing ethnographic research in online settings is in Section 9.5.5.

9.4.3   Building relationships

Ideally, every ethnographer would be warmly welcomed into the group that they are interested in studying. Members of the group would honestly and openly share secrets, discuss issues, and provide fair and unbiased assessments of how things work.

Unfortunately, this ideal may be realized only rarely. Even if there is nominal buy-in from someone associated from the group, that doesn't mean that all group members are interested or enthusiastic. Subjects of ethnographic research may be outwardly hostile or simply indifferent to the project. Workplace ethnographies may raise concerns among workers that the research may be used against them: "Maybe they're going to use this study to figure out how to eliminate my job."

Conducting ethnographic research would be very difficult indeed if you were working with people who didn't like, trust, or respect you. Careful attention to some fairly common-sense principles can help you define yourself as someone who folks in the group will want to work with. Trying to be helpful – being a participant instead of a burden – can help engender good will, if you follow through on your promises. If you're not acting as a complete participant, you should take time to explain to someone why you're there, what you hope to learn, and what you hope to do with that knowledge. You should also respect the needs and goals of the individuals you are speaking with: your need for research data should not trump their need for privacy, job security, or other things (Angrosino, 2007). Making people feel threatened is probably not the right way to get good research data.

It is important to try to understand the conventions and norms that are shared by members of the groups that you study (Agar, 1980). Even if you're working with groups of people who are culturally and socio-economically similar to you, they may have very different habits, expectations, values, or jargon. Understanding these cultural factors may not be easy to do, but it's worth the effort. You don't want to say something that offends someone in the group and you don't want to be misinterpreted. Slang and jargon are particularly challenging in this regard. You may think that you know the meaning of a slang term in your particular context, but you'd be well advised to make sure that your understanding is correct (Agar, 1980).

9.4.4 Making contact

Many ethnographic efforts start with discussions with a small number of individuals. Even if you are introduced to all members of the group from the outset, you can't start talking to them all at once – it's simply not possible. In some cases, particularly if the group of interest is not completely defined, your initial contacts may help you meet others.

Your initial contacts play a very important role. Well-chosen contacts can help you orient yourself to the ways and workings of the environment that you will be studying. Particularly if they are well-respected, they can help smooth the way, convincing others who trust them that you are "OK."

Because your first contacts will influence your perceptions of and interactions with other group members, you should carefully consider who you choose to work closely with at first. Experienced researchers have noted that the first people to talk to ethnographers often fall into one of two categories: *stranger-handlers* and *deviants* (Agar, 1980).

Stranger-handlers are people who make it their business to work with people who are new to the group. They introduce you to others, show you around, and appear to be very helpful. They might also show you a particularly slanted view, emphasizing details that they want you to know about while omitting others that they want to leave hidden. If there are factions within the group, a stranger-handler might encourage you to associate with his faction, possibly alienating members of other subgroups. As outcasts who may not be well-respected, a deviant might try to use you to gain attention, to validate their otherwise under-appreciated role in the group, or to denigrate their enemies. As your goal is to gain a broad understanding of the group, you should beware of such people.

Unfortunately, you may not know that you're dealing with a deviant or a stranger-handler until it is too late. You may want to rely upon your initial feel for each individual – do they seem trustworthy? Do you "click" with them? If so, they may be good bets. If, however, they seem to be providing you with selective information, bad-mouthing others, or trying to manipulate your efforts, you might want to watch out.

The people who you choose to work closely with should also be those who can provide good information. Someone who knows few people, doesn't get along with others, doesn't explain things well, or is unobservant is unlikely to be a good informant (Agar, 1980) and you probably want to avoid such people.

Even if you find an initial informant – or set of informants – who is trustworthy, seemingly unbiased, and well-respected by a broad spectrum of the group, you might be well-advised to avoid becoming too closely associated with any group members. You don't want the appearance of close ties with anyone to impair your ability to work with other group members (Agar, 1980; Angrosino, 2007). This may be easier said than done.

Whoever you choose to work with, you should remember that these informants are not necessarily telling you the truth. This is not to say that they're lying – they're simply giving you their viewpoint. The notion of truth in describing human interactions is more than a bit troublesome. Your job is to use your initial informants to help you derive questions, build theories, and plan further investigation. As we see below, you will use subsequent interactions with other group members to help provide a broader perspective.

Participating in a group can be difficult – you may find that you don't like the people that you are working with, that you don't have access to the information that you need, or that you are inappropriately identifying with the subjects of your research. You may also find that you have to work to maintain relationships. A variety of strategies, including presenting yourself as non-threatening and acting as if you are somewhat incompetent and need to be taught about the group that you are studying (Lofland et al., 2006), can help you convince participants that you are someone to be trusted.

9.4.5   Interview, observe, analyze, theorize, repeat

Ethnographic researchers have developed a variety of theoretical frameworks to inform their investigations (Angrosino, 2007). Many of these frameworks provide perspectives on how groups function and how meaning is constructed out of human relationships. As you go about your ethnographic research, you should always remember that your job is to create an interpretation of the potentially biased, incomplete, and somewhat contradictory data points that you collect from talking with and observing members of the group. The result may not be "the truth" about this group, but ideally it provides some understanding and explanation of how the group functions.

Like case studies (Chapter 7), ethnographic studies rely upon multiple data collection techniques to gain a broad perspective, with the hope of *triangulating* – using corroborating evidence from multiple perspectives to increase confidence in the validity of conclusions that are drawn. As with case-study research, ethnographic studies rely on interviews, case studies, and documents or other artifacts as their primary sources of data.

Interviews in ethnography serve many purposes. Unlike traditional interviews (see Chapter 8), in which a researcher has a single meeting with a study participant for a limited period of time, an ethnographic interview is often part of a longer, ongoing relationship. In the early stages of a study, interviews may be informal discussions aimed at building trust and understanding broad parameters. As you may not know what you're looking for at first, your early interviews are likely to be very open-ended and unstructured (Angrosino, 2007). In fact, these informal interviews may not even feel like interviews. You might be asking questions as people show you around, discussing issues of concern as you interact with group members, and otherwise participating in seemingly ordinary interactions. Although these conversations might not feel like interviews, they can be useful data collection techniques. A commonly used technique in ethnographic interviews involves presenting participants with items – known as "probes" – designed to provoke reaction and spark conversation (See Chapter 8 for a discussion of probes).

The goal of these informal interviews is generally to get people talking. As they say more about the environment that you're studying, your informants increase the breadth and depth of your understanding. Appropriately asked questions can be very useful in this regard. If they describe an interesting situation, you might ask how often it occurs. Leading questions present a viewpoint that invites either agreement or dissent: "Is this tool really that hard to use?" Other questions might invite comparisons, contrasts, or detailed explanation (Agar, 1980). The challenge of planning questions like these in the course of ongoing conversation may seem substantial, but you might find that your curiosity as a researcher takes you a long way. If a comment piques your interest, find a respectful way to ask for more detail.

Not all of your interviews will be completely informal. More structured techniques, such as life histories (Agar, 1980) (see the Design for Alzheimer's Disease sidebar in Chapter 7) and time diaries (Chapter 6), can be informative components of ethnographic studies. As your data collection and analysis leads you to build a deeper understanding of the group that you're studying, you may find it useful to conduct slightly more formal interviews with group members with whom you've not previously interacted. These discussions can help you validate models or conclusions derived from earlier interactions with other informants.

Observation is harder than it sounds. Just stand back and watch, right? If only it were that simple. Unfortunately, several factors work against us. As much as we might like to think that we're objective observers, we're not. By necessity, we filter what we see and hear, and interpret our observations through the lenses of our own history, experience, expertise, and bias. The goal of ethnographic observation is to shed this baggage, in the hopes of seeing things with "new" eyes, perhaps as a stranger would (Angrosino, 2007). Of course, this is easier said than done, particularly if you are in a situation that is somewhat familiar. A clear distinction between observation and interpretation might be helpful in this regard (Angrosino, 2007) . If you only record what you see ("the user opened the help facility and searched for several different terms"), you run less risk of misinterpreting or injecting bias than you do if you interpret what you see as it happens ("the user became frustrated when she was not able to find help with the feature"). You might try to regularly challenge yourself to broaden the scope of your observation: ask yourself, "is there anything I'm missing? Is there anything that I think doesn't look interesting?" If you force yourself to examine all aspects of a complex situation, you may get a broader, less biased picture of what is going on. That said, it's worth noting that observation is a skill that might require significant practice to develop.

Taking appropriate notes from ethnographic observations – and, to a lesser extent, informal interviews – is a daunting challenge. You might be advised to record relevant details such as time, place, identities of people present (perhaps anonymized to protect their privacy), and descriptions of the context, behaviors and interactions, and include word-for-word transcriptions of conversations (Angrosino, 2007). Although such information would undoubtedly convey a detailed picture of the situation that you have observed, there are significant practical problems involved with overly detailed notes. You will soon become overwhelmed, as the quantity of data will quickly become enormous. Furthermore, it's virtually impossible to record that much data and to observe at the same time: as you take notes, you simply miss out on what is happening (Agar, 1980). Audio or video recordings can help, but analysis of these records can be a tedious, time-consuming chore in itself.

Deciding what is interesting enough to include in your notes, and understanding how to describe it, may become somewhat easier once you have passed the initial stages of your work. When you first start out, you may not have much idea of what is interesting: you're in an unfamiliar context and everything is fair game. As you begin to build some understanding, you may work your way towards an understanding of what is interesting and what is not. Once you have this baseline, you might think of your field notes as recording observations that describe familiar events in terms of patterns that you've identified, while noting unfamiliar events that may be worthy of consideration. You might also make note of questions that arise: if you see something that you don't understand, it may be an appropriate subject for future investigation (Agar, 1980).

Timing is also a challenge in recording notes from observations and informal interviews. You might try to be prepared to record observations at all times, but you never really know when something interesting is going to happen. You might hear an interesting discussion or witness a relevant interaction just when you least expect it. In this case, the best that you can do might be to remember as much as possible and write notes as soon as possible. This is, of course, a highly fallible process, as you are likely to forget important details and misremember others (Agar, 1980). You would be well-advised to seek out additional validating evidence for any observations that are recorded long after the fact.

Documents, archives, and artifacts can also be useful sources of information. Records that describe past activities: pictures, letters, emails, deliverable documents, and even tools; can provide information about how a group works and what the dynamics are like. An ethnographic study of a software engineering group might investigate process documents, email exchanges over the course of one or more projects, papers, and presentations generated during the course of the work in order to understand how that group works. These archival data sources have the advantage of being relatively static and impersonal – you can take your time reading old emails and you don't risk asking an inappropriate question. At the same time, these materials may be incomplete, biased, or error-prone (Angrosino, 2007).

Having collected data from interviews, observations, and archives, your next step is to analyze it. Data analysis generally combines qualitative and quantitative analysis techniques. This chapter focuses on collecting data using ethnographic methods, but Chapter 11 helps you take your various observations and group them into categories and frameworks that help you understand and explain the situation. Quantitative techniques help you ask questions about the frequency or prevalence of certain behaviors. These analyses are very useful for moving your understanding from the general ("this happened frequently") to the specific ("this happened in 79% of cases").

Analysis in ethnographic research is often a pre-cursor to further data collection. As you examine your data points to identify patterns, you may find other questions arising. In some cases, you may be uncertain about the interpretation of an event or a comment – you may wish to ask someone for clarification or simply for confirmation that your interpretation is correct. Other data points may open up entirely new lines of questioning. Observations from a community event, such as a meeting or public gathering, may lead to multiple questions that you might ask at a subsequent interview – whether formal or informal – with someone who was present (Agar, 1980). This iterative process can continue for multiple rounds (Figure 9.2), until you run out of resources (time and money) or have learned all that you're going to learn.

Although many ethnographers strive to develop models and theories that place their observations in some sort of theoretical model or framework, this approach is not universally shared. Some researchers reject theories and models, claiming that ethnographers should simply describe what they see, without building models that may reflect researcher or procedural biases as much as (if not more than) they reflect the phenomena being studied. Others reject this viewpoint, arguing that researcher participation in deciding what should be observed and how it should be analyzed inevitably leads to bias (Shapiro, 1994; Sharrock and Randall, 2004). Of course, if the goal of your ethnographic research is to understand requirements for a system that will be built, you will probably find yourself building a model of some sort.

If you decide to use your ethnographic research to develop models, you should strive to develop robust explanations and descriptions that are based on all of your data. As you analyze

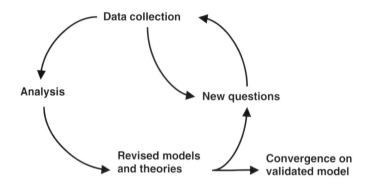

Figure 9.2 The iterative process of ethnographic research.

the data, you should try to make sure that you are not "cherry-picking" the data. If there are observations that are not consistent with your model, then you should consider revising your model or looking for other potential models. If you seek out, but do not find, data points that disagree with your model, you can be more confident of the correctness of the model.

Because all ethnography is inherently interpretive and qualitative, there are often legitimate questions as to why one model is better than the other. Comparison with alternative models can also help in understanding the strengths and weaknesses of your model, because you could potentially argue that your model fits the data better than other alternative interpretations.

Other measures that you might take to improve the validity of your findings include the use of multiple informants and multiple observers. Multiple informants help you avoid the distortions that might occur from talking to only one member of the group. Interacting with members who differ in background, perspective, experience, or demographic factors such as age, gender, and ethnicity, can help you understand the diversity of perspectives. Having another colleague (or two or three) study the group can minimize the impact of biases of any individual researcher. If your colleagues come to the same conclusions as you, despite having interviewed different people or observed different events, you can have increased confidence in those results. Just as with informants, diversity of observers can be a useful strategy. (Angrosino, 2007).

9.4.6   Reporting results

Ethnographic reports are similar to case study reports (Chapter 7). You want to describe your goals and methods, along with a justification of the specific groups – how were they chosen and why? You should describe your methods for data collection and analysis, along with presentation of raw data and analytical results. Matrices, charts, and figures can be very helpful, particularly for analyses involving quantitative data. Another important similarity with case study reports involves discussion of rival explanations: if you've considered and rejected alternative models because your preferred models were better-suited, say so.

Like case studies, ethnographic reports tell a story. You should consider interesting incidents and include direct quotes where appropriate.

A final similarity with case-study reports involves consultation with participants. When appropriate, you might consider sharing your report with group members before it is published. This gives them a chance to understand what you've done and why, thus increasing the chances that they have positive feelings about the experience. Your informants can also provide important reality checks – if they think you've misinterpreted important (or perhaps not-so-important) details, they'll let you know. This sharing of draft reports may not be appropriate in some circumstances, including (but not limited to) studies that involved complete participation (participants who weren't aware of the research might be somewhat upset at seeing the report) and situations in which participants might be interested in "slanting" the contents of the report to meet their (real or perceived) interests.

9.5 Some examples

Ethnographic methods have a rich history in the social sciences. However, they have only recently come to the forefront in the area of human–computer interaction. A number of studies have utilized ethnography methods to understand the context of technology usage. Most often, these ethnographic studies take place in homes, workplaces, educational settings, and virtual settings. While ethnographic research isn't limited to those four types of setting, they are the ones that seem to garner the most attention and examination in the human–computer interaction world. Studies of "on-the-go" mobile devices have also started to come to the forefront.

9.5.1 Home settings

One important context of technology usage is in people's homes. To separate out and examine the technology in a sterile lab would be to miss the rich context of home usage. One specific series of ethnographic studies of homes and technology use in different countries provides a baseline for understanding the challenges (Bell, Blythe and Sengers, 2005). The bottom line is that country, culture, and religion have a great impact on how technology is used in homes. While not specifically an article on ethnography, Chavan *et al.* (2009) report on examples of home technology products that failed because designers didn't understand the context of usage. For instance, in southern India, clothes washing machine sales were awful for Whirlpool, because traditional southern Indian clothes, using very thin fabrics, were often getting caught and shredded in the washing machines.

There are also, in many cases, gender issues to understand. In many countries, even though women work an equal amount in the workplace, women take on a majority of domestic household tasks (Bell, Blythe and Sengers, 2005; Blythe and Monk, 2002; Rode, Toye and Blackwell, 2004). In one ethnographic study, it was noted that while men may not do an equal share of the household work, they often feel guilty about this (Blythe and Monk, 2002). This ethnography study noted that many domestic technologies are aesthetically designed with a gender bent to them (often, towards women) and posed the question as to whether household technologies should be designed with more of a male focus (Blythe and Monk, 2002).

In another ethnographic study of domestic (home) use of technology, a "felt board" was used to help model daily home life (Rode, Toye and Blackwell, 2004). Felt icons were used to represent appliances typically found in homes. The board had different sections for the different rooms, such as bedroom, bathroom, and kitchen. In addition, participants were asked to identify if they programmed these devices in advance (although the term programming wasn't used). The fuzzy felt board was used to help understand patterns of usage, after participants provided a tour of where the devices were in the home (Rode, Toye and Blackwell, 2004).

Another ethnographic study examined the use of cleaning products by older individuals (Wyche, 2005). The goal was to better understand the challenges that older individuals face in trying to use cleaning products in their homes, to inspire some potentially useful designs for new cleaning technologies. The researcher observed 20 individuals, between the ages of 69 and 91, in their homes to learn what types of cleaning product and technology they use, where they store them, and which ones are very hard to use. The researcher then presented ideas for some potential technology solutions to these challenges (Wyche, 2005).

9.5.2   Work settings

Ethnographic methods are often used to examine the context of technology usage in the workplace. For instance, ethnographic methods were used to understand how insurance claims adjusters do their job in the workplace. Researchers observed the entire process of claims handling, with a special focus on fraudulent claims (Ormerod *et al.*, 2003). A number of process barriers were discovered, such as poor documentation and communication, and claims adjusters were discovered to use a number of heuristics and alternative explanations to discover fraud. This ethnographic research of how claims adjusters work was then used to help develop a new software tool for detecting insurance fraud.

Ethnographic methods were also used in studying a highways department from a state government. The goal was to understand the process of designing and building a bridge, so that an electronic-document management system could be built (Suchman, 1999; 2000). One of the challenges was in understanding how electronic documents and paper documents were used. It was discovered that it was important to design connections between the electronic and paper documents, and then determine who needed access to the electronic documents, since paper documents have limited access based on physical location but electronic documents don't have that limitation.

Healthcare settings are also of interest to ethnographers. Pedersen and Wolff (2008) documented ethnographic research in two physical therapy clinics in the USA, to understand how small health operations work. They had originally wanted to observe at general health care clinics (and they had done previous interviews with 10 small health care clinics), but had problems getting access to observe at these sites. Therefore, physical therapy, in which a lot of patient treatment occurs in a semi-public gym space, seemed like a good compromise (Pedersen and Wolff, 2008). Ethnographic observations helped in understanding work practices, and what challenges the physical therapy clinics might face as they moved towards full electronic medical records. Similarly, Balka, Bjorn, and Wagner (2008) documented ethnographic studies in Canada and Austria, where again, the goal was to better understand medical work practices, to assist in the development of a new health information system. The study looked at various departments within a hospital, such as emergency departments, oncology, and neurosurgery (Balka, Bjorn and Wagner, 2008).

While office settings are obviously the most common setting, ethnographic methods are even more useful in non-office-based work settings. For instance, one ethnographic study examined the potential use of technology in a vineyard setting. Specifically, the researchers wanted to understand the potential use of sensors across a vineyard (Brooke and Burrell, 2003). The researchers became participant-observers, working in vineyards, helping with harvesting, and assisting with grape crushing. The researchers were better able to understand how sensors could be used, to monitor microclimates (combination of sunlight, rain, temperature), which could then predict the chance of grape disease. This, in turn, could provide useful information on which areas of the vineyard needed more attention, labor, chemicals, and different harvesting times.

9.5.3   Educational settings

Ethnographic methods can be especially useful for understanding the complex context of school settings. For instance, ethnographic methods were used in understanding how children (typically between four and six years old) spend play times in a kindergarten (Wyeth, 2006). In the daily schedule of a kindergartener, there is both structured group time and "loosely structured, self-structured, free time activities." The free-play activities themselves could be divided into three categories: calm activities, play, and artistic interactions. This increased understanding of how young children play in classroom settings may hint at some potential possibilities for technology in early childhood settings. For instance, technology for young children may need to be more flexible, allowing for creativity and discovery, and not be separate from but, rather, work in tandem with the other activities going on in the classroom.

The importance of understanding the context increases when doing a cross-cultural study of educational settings. For instance, Druin *et al.* used a number of methods, including ethnographic observation in the classroom, to understand how children in different cultures used the International Children's Digital Library, how their reading patterns changed over time, and how their reading patterns influenced communication with others, interest in other cultures, and attitudes towards technology and libraries (Druin *et al.*, 2007).

Ethnographic methods for use in education are not limited to young children. Becvar and Hollan (2007) used ethnographic methods to better understand how dental hygiene students learn. The dental hygiene students were in post-secondary education and, after completing their academic program, had to pass both state and national certification exams. The researchers observed the tools and technologies used by students, the activities and circumstances that occurred, and how the students studied and practiced, both at the university and at their homes (Becvar and Hollan, 2007). The goal of this ethnographic research was to understand how dental hygiene students learn, with the eventual goal of designing instructional technology to assist students in their instructional program.

9.5.4   Ethnographies of mobile and ubiquitous systems

In taking computing beyond the desktop, mobile and ubiquitous systems create context-sensitive environments where computing is part of some other, larger opportunity, instead of a primary focus of its own. Understanding how people make use of these systems while traveling, meeting with friends, or going about their daily lives presents intriguing challenges for ethnographers.

A study of the use of in-car global positioning systems (GPS) used ethnographic techniques to understand how the tools changed perceptions of the larger environment and of the tasks of driving and navigating. To address these questions, a team of researchers went along for several rides – some planned and some conducted specifically for research purposes – with GPS users and, in some cases, additional passengers. Data from these rides – which lasted between one and three hours – included hundreds of pages of notes and transcriptions. Analysis of this data indicated that the GPS systems led users to be both less engaged (they didn't have to worry so much about seeing turns and landmarks) and more engaged (they were able to learn about parks and other attractions that were nearby but not visible from the road) with the surrounding environment (Leshed et al., 2008).

Ethnographic studies can be useful for understanding how technology use changes over time. A study of iPhone users used ethnographic techniques to understand how perceptions of the device changed over the course of several weeks. Six participants were recruited on the basis of their expressed interest in purchasing an iPhone. One week before purchasing the phone, each participant wrote a narrative describing their expectations and completed a survey indicating the importance of each expectation. After purchasing their phones, participants listed activities related to the phone, estimated the time spent, picked important experiences, and rated the product relative to each specific situation. Findings were used to build a model that described the use of the iPhone as a sequence from anticipation of using it, to orientation to features, incorporation of the device into everyday life, and then to identification with the phone as an important part of their lives (Karapano et al., 2009).

Ethnographic investigations of ubiquitous computing have required some HCI researchers to go into some unexpected places. One project examined the navigation needs of firefighters, in the hopes of identifying opportunities for developing ubiquitous systems that would help firefighters find their way out of hazardous, smoke-filled environments. The research team developed a series of simulations – conducting research in actual fires being, of course, too dangerous – aimed at exploring how a tool might work. Members of the research team then donned firefighting gear and joined in a simulation involving navigational activities commonly used by firefighters. Observations from their participation, and from observing firefighters in other simulations, helped the researchers understand how firefighters use improvisation and collaboration to navigate while fighting fires (Denef *et al.*, 2008).

9.5.5 Virtual ethnography

Most of the examples discussed thus far in this chapter involve "real-world" ethnographies – studies of groups and communities situated in familiar, physical settings. This is not an inherent limitation in the technique – ethnography does not always mean a researcher being present physically to observe the group or community. The growth of countless online communities supporting many different types of interaction presents the possibility of "virtual ethnography."

The term "virtual ethnography" has been used to describe different things, such as using web cams or videos (Blomberg and Burrell, 2007). However, this in no way involves participation and, furthermore, there is a high likelihood of missing a lot of contextual information as people may act differently for the camera, shut off the camera at times, or avoid the area with the camera. If the researcher is not in the context, this leads to a poorer quality of data collection and understanding. However, when ethnographic methods are used to research a community that is strictly virtual or online, there is less likelihood of missing anything, as the "there", the "place", is only online. If participation is the goal, if being in the context is the goal, researchers can "be" in a virtual community and experience it as everyone else is experiencing it.

The virtual nature of these communities presents some opportunities and challenges for ethnographic researchers. Online identity is much more fluid and controllable than it is in the real world. In many online groups, message boards, and virtual worlds, users can control exactly what others know about us and how they see us. This can be very convenient for ethnographic study, as researchers can easily define themselves as complete participants (with some limitations), without having to face the challenge of playing those roles in frequent face-to-face relationships. Furthermore, researchers might find that maintaining scientific objectivity is relatively easy when all interaction with the subjects of study are conducted through the mediation of a computer screen.

The tenuous nature of links between online identities presents some interesting possibilities for ethnographers. As many online communities require little, if any, direct link between a virtual identity and a real person, conducting an ethnographic study without revealing one's identity as a researcher is a very real possibility. Furthermore, the transient and artificial notion of participation in these virtual worlds makes complete participation a very real possibility. Before embarking on any study of this sort, you might want to consider what circumstances merit revealing your identity as a researcher. For example, you might decide to "out" yourself to an individual or a larger group if you feel that other participants are becoming suspicious of your motives.

The construction of multiple identities presents further intriguing opportunities. As many virtual communities allow users to create multiple online identities, virtual ethnographers might use multiple online manifestations to examine community responses to different types of behavior or even to create situations that might be the focus of studies. For example, a researcher conducting a virtual ethnography might start an argument between two online identities that she controls as a means of studying how other participants would react.

Of course, this multiplicity of identities cuts both ways as well. Virtual ethnographers may face greater challenges in evaluating the honesty of the people with whom they are interacting. Barring external confirmation – such as verifiable real-world interactions – it may be hard to confirm the claimed identities of online interlocutors.

As virtual environments run the gamut from simple text-based forums to social networks and online worlds, such as Second Life, the types of ethnography that may be conducted will also change. Fully graphical environments, such as Second Life, present opportunities for observing group interaction, physical positioning, and other visual cues that are not generally available in text-only environments. Although these cues may make ethnographies of graphical virtual worlds seem more "real" than other virtual ethnographies, it's important to note that the questions of identity don't ever disappear.

In Section 9.4.2, the Ethnographic Research of Your Own Community sidebar presented information about the ethnographic research done into online empathic support communities. The example given was of an online support community for people with a torn ACL (Maloney-Krichmar and Preece, 2005). Ethnographic methods have also been used to examine multiplayer virtual worlds. For instance, Ducheneaut and Moore used ethnographic methods to research the Star Wars Galaxies multi-person online role-playing game. The two researchers each created a character (one a combat-oriented character, the other an entertainer) and logged in for a minimum of four hours per week for three months. They later created two additional characters and tried to encourage other role-playing individuals in the Star Wars Galaxies to communicate with their characters (Ducheneaut and Moore, 2004). Specifically, they spent time in locations collecting data on the frequency and type of visitors, types of interaction, and related factors that could be used to characterize the social activity in these places (Ducheneaut, Moore and Nickell, 2007). As complete participants, they were able to participate in genuine interactions, without having to reveal themselves as researchers or to maintain the pretense of being "real" group members.

Of course, many online communities have face-to-face components and this is where the dividing line between virtual and physical can become very complex. The Researching Online Dating sidebar discusses the situation of research into online dating communities. In these communities, the interaction starts out virtual but has the stated goal of moving towards face-to-face meetings.

Researching Online Dating

Research In Practice

One of the more fascinating topics being addressed by HCI researchers in recent times is the topic of online dating. Individuals go online to various sites (such as www.match.com or www.eharmony.com), hoping to meet people for dates or relationships. These sites have millions of subscribers of various ages. At first this might seem like a research focus on individuals but online dating communities are groups with group norms, accepted practices, and shared group communication tools (such as chat rooms). These online groups differ primarily from work groups in terms of the goal of the interaction (dating, not work), the goal of the presentation (to look attractive and interesting, rather than to present information), and the transient population of members in the group (people join and leave the online dating community very rapidly). An example of a group norm and practice is that if you e-mail someone and they do not respond, it is considered totally inappropriate to e-mail them a second time.

Online dating is an example of one of those areas (mentioned in Chapter 1) that is new, interesting, and involves our social interactions and online communication. There are multiple, complex, human processes taking place, and a traditional experimental design would be inadequate to understand what is occurring. But there are so many important research questions that could be addressed within this topic area. Do people tend to lie in their online dating profiles? How can you tell if someone is being truthful? What approaches to messaging (e-mail, wink or flirt, and other features) are likely to lead to a response? What types of online interaction are likely to lead to a face-to-face meeting? It's a complex area, since it involves not only interface design but also identity and presentation, online communication, face-to-face meetings, and human attraction and sexuality (which probably is the most complex area). Since this seems like such an interesting research topic, the question at hand is "what research methods should be used?" A number of approaches have been used, as described in the next few paragraphs. These examples did not primarily use ethnography as a research method, however, the challenge is to determine if ethnography could, in fact, be used to study such questions. Can you use ethnography to study online dating? Should you?

Hancock, Toma, and Ellison (2007) took the approach of recruiting people who were already involved in online dating, to determine the accuracy of their online dating profiles. A self-selected group responded to their recruitment advertisement and the researchers met with these 80 participants, who presented copies of their online dating profiles (Hancock, Toma and Ellison, 2007). The researchers asked the participants to rate the accuracy of their profiles with regards to height, weight, and age. The researchers measured the height, weight, and age to better gauge the accuracy of the profiles against the perceived accuracy by participants. Only 18% of participants had inaccurate age information in their profile but 48% of participants had inaccurate height information and 59% of participants had inaccurate weight information in their online profile. The analysis of the participants' perception of profile accuracy showed that most participants were aware when their profile information was not accurate and were aware that this could be potentially deceptive.

Fiore and Donath (2005) examined how people in online dating communities tend to communicate with other people who have similar interests and preferences. The researchers were able to broker an agreement with a dating site to get access to profiles, statistics, and e-mails (Fiore and Donath, 2005). It is unclear in the paper if users were aware that their profile information was shared with researchers, although it is unlikely (since the researchers did analysis on over 236 000 messages sent from over 29 000 users to over 51 000 users). The researchers discovered that of 110 000 conversations (messages between a unique pair of users), 78% of these conversations were single messages that were not responded to by the recipient. More interestingly, users were more likely to contact other users who had similar characteristics (such as "wants children," smoking, educational level, religion, etc.) and responses to those initial contacts were even more highly correlated to the presence of similar characteristics. Note that "user" is a more appropriate term than "participant," since these users did not choose to participate in the research.

Lee and Bruckman (2007) examined the potential use of social networking sites (such as MySpace and Facebook) without a stated dating goal, for the use of dating. They interviewed 12 people who had used Friendster or MySpace for dating (Lee and Bruckman, 2007). These people were recruited through public postings (e.g. on Craigslist) and word of mouth. Although some of the interviews were in person and some were conducted by phone, all of the participants allowed the researchers to examine their social networking profiles. A general consensus emerged that participants like using the social networking sites for meeting potential dates, because the context of friends, many of whom post information about their friends, provides some level of credibility. The friends would be likely to challenge you or comment negatively if you were mis-representing yourself. Participants specifically found the set of "top friends" useful, as those were the ones that provided the most information and the most credibility. The number of friends, types of comment left by friends, and types of picture posted also provided clues on who the potential date really was. An interesting note was that participants commented that, when they began dating people that they had met on a social networking site, they could often get a better understanding of the status of their relationship by seeing where they were "ranked" on the top friends list.

Fiore et al. (2008) examined what features of online dating had the greatest influence on how users assessed the attractiveness of potential dates. Generally, online dating profiles include pictures, fixed-choice questions (such as age, drinking/smoking, and other questions with a closed set of well-defined responses), and a free-text section (where users write paragraphs that describe themselves). The researchers randomly selected 25 male and 25 female profiles from the Yahoo! Personals website, five each from different cities in the USA (Fiore *et al.*, 2008). The researchers then made four different versions of each profile: the picture, the free text, the fixed-choice answers, and the full profile which includes all three sections. A group primarily made up of university students evaluated the various profile components for attractiveness. The researchers found that the photo had the greatest impact on perceptions of attractiveness, but the free text also greatly influenced perceptions of attractiveness. Generally, the fixed-question responses did not impact on perceptions of attractiveness, except in cases where they were used to evaluate "deal-breakers", such as smoking.

Ethnography seems like it could be an appropriate research method for researching online dating. There are clearly complex phenomena at work, interesting group dynamics, and the exciting prospect of seeing how online and real-world perceptions and realities match up. But clearly, there would be a number of troubling ethical and logistical questions. If you were to research online dating communities, would you be a true participant? Would the emotion of meeting and dating these people cause you to lose your sense of objectivity? Furthermore, is it ethical to go on a date acting as if a long-term relationship was the main goal, when it is a research exercise? Would that be misleading? If you were to notify people that you are doing research, would that lead to loss of credibility or access into the community? If you were to not notify people about your research, wouldn't that be unethical? Would it even be possible to be a complete observer, watching from the sidelines? How would that work? Note that in two of the research studies above, profiles or data were taken from online dating sites and used in research studies, without the express permission of the owners (although the terms and conditions of site usage would allow it). These people weren't involved in the research, only their online profiles were involved. Clearly, if ethnographic methods were used and researchers went out on dates with unsuspecting research participants, this would be a far more serious ethical concern. This leads to an important question: how can you do ethnographic research and collect accurate data, while participants are aware of your research?

If a community has both a physical and a virtual component, both might be good candidates for ethnographic research. For instance, Ploderer, Howard, and Thomas (2008) were interested in researching the community of bodybuilders, people who are passionate about staying fit, building muscle, and taking part in bodybuilding competitions. The researchers used ethnographic methods in both the physical community and the online community. They went to seven bodybuilding gyms to observe and also attended two bodybuilding competitions. In addition, the BodySpace social networking website has over 160 000 people interested in bodybuilding. The researchers created a profile and, for four months, participated with and observed the members of the community and communicated with various community members (Ploderer, Howard and Thomas, 2008).

Summary

Ethnographic methods are very useful in understanding the context of technology usage. By examining the human, social, and organizational contexts of technology, a deeper understanding of who these users are can be developed. In ethnographic traditions, a better understanding of a group of people and their traditions and processes is itself a noble and worthwhile goal. However, in the human–computer interaction community, ethnography is often used as a first step, to understand a group of users, their problems, challenges, norms, and processes, with the eventual goal of building some type of technology for them or with them. Currently, ethnographic research methods are used most often in home settings, work settings, educational settings, and online. However, new approaches to ethnographic research are being developed to study, for example, how people use ubiquitous computing in real-world settings anywhere, such as the street, the subway, or a park, for activities including role-playing games, geocaching, and education (Crabtree *et al.*, 2006).

Discussion Questions

1. Ethnographic research has been described as inductive. What does that mean?
2. Is generalization a goal of ethnographic research?
3. How is participatory design similar to ethnographic research? How is it different?
4. What are three potential challenges in finding a group to study?
5. What are the four most common settings for doing ethnographic research in human–computer interaction?
6. Participating in a group implies changing it. In the most obvious sense, the group has one more member after the ethnographer joins it. More subtly, the addition of a new member might alter the dynamics of communication and interaction between group members. How does the role that the ethnographer plays influence the extent of the changes that his presence might bring? Can you suggest any approaches that ethnographers might use to minimize the impact of their presence upon groups being studied?
7. Some people might think that the ultimate form of participant research would be to conduct an ethnographic study of a group of which one was already a member. For researchers, this might mean studying research groups, academic departments, corporate teams, or professional societies. What concerns would you have about the appropriateness and validity of such research?
8. Go back and re-read the Researching Online Dating sidebar. How could ethnographic methods be used in researching online dating communities? How could you study the community in a way that was both ethical and did not greatly influence how people would act towards you?

9. Workplace ethnographies present specific challenges in navigating the often complicated interactions between employees at differing levels of authority and responsibility. If you are hired by management, workers may feel that they have nothing to gain by participating in your study, and potentially a great deal to lose, in terms of job security or responsibility. To make matters worse, you may not know all of the motivations behind the study: management might, in fact, be hoping to use the results of your work to build systems that change how work is done. Finally, you may be given an initial goal and problem description that is too narrow or inappropriately focused. Given all of these challenges, what strategies might you use to work with both employees and management to build the trust and participation necessary for conducting a methodologically sound study?

10. Working closely with research participants raises questions of trust regarding material that should or should not be included in a study. Particularly when working closely with an individual in a home or workplace setting, you may see or hear things that might be both very interesting and potentially sensitive. Examples include comments about a co-worker's (or manager's) incompetence or discussion of children hiding certain behavior from parents. Although these observations may be intriguing, fear of repercussions may lead you to be wary of reporting them. How might you deal with this conflict between research fidelity and the trust of your participants?

Research Design Exercises

1. Imagine an ethnographic study of how college students use technology to work on group projects. How would you go about designing such a study? You might say that you will pick a class that involves group work, but this is only the beginning – which courses would you consider? Which types of student? Which roles would be appropriate? What sort of data would you collect? How would your answer depend upon your status? In other words, would a college student conducting this study use the same approach as a professor?

2. Conduct a mini-ethnography. Working in a team of two or three, observe a group of people. You might observe students waiting outside a class on campus, families at a playground, friends at a coffee shop, meetings of a student group, or some other similar activity. (As this won't be a formal study, you probably shouldn't interview participants or use other data collection methods, but you can watch and listen in public places.) Write down your observations individually and try to describe what you have seen and learned. Once all group members have done this, meet and discuss your findings. Can you combine your observations and individual models to build a consensus model? Build a model that incorporates all of your conclusions and discusses differences in your findings.

References

Agar, M. (1980) *The Professional Stranger.* New York: Academic Press.

Angrosino, M. (2007) *Doing Ethnographic and Observational Research.* London, England: Sage.

Balka, E., Bjorn, P., and Wagner, I. (2008) Steps toward a typology for health informatics. *Proceedings of the ACM Conference on Computer-Supported Cooperative Work,* 311–320.

Becvar, L.A. and Hollan, J.D. (2007) Transparency and technology appropriation: Social impacts of a video blogging system in dental hygiene clinical instruction. *Proceedings of the GROUP'07: International Conference on Supporting Group Work,* 311–320.

Bell, G., Blythe, M., and Sengers, P. (2005) Making by making strange: Defamiliarization and the design of domestic technologies. *ACM Transactions on Computer–Human Interaction,* **12**(2):149–173.

Blomberg, J. and Burrell, M. (2007) An ethnographic approach to design. In A. Sears and J. Jacko (eds), *The Human–Computer Interaction Handbook,* 2nd edition, 965–988. New York: Lawrence Erlbaum Associates.

Blythe, M. and Monk, A. (2002) Notes towards an ethnography of domestic technology. *Proceedings of the ACM Conference on Designing Interactive Systems,* 277–281.

Brooke, T. and Burrell, J. (2003) From ethnography to design in a vineyard. *Proceedings of DUX'03: Designing for User Experiences,* 1–4.

Carroll, J., Chin, G., Rosson, M.B., and Neale, D. (2000) The development of cooperation: Five years of participatory design in the virtual school. *Proceedings of the ACM Conference on Designing Interactive Systems,* 239–251.

Chavan, A., Gorney, D., Prabhu, B., and Arora, S. (2009) The washing machine that ate my sari: Mistakes in cross-cultural design. *interactions,* **16**(1):26–31.

Crabtree, A. and Rodden, T. (2004) Domestic routines and design for the home. *Computer-Supported Cooperative Work,* **13**(2):191–220.

Crabtree, A., Benford, S., Greenhalgh, C., *et al.* (2006) Supporting ethnographic studies of ubiquitous computing in the wild. *Proceedings of the ACM Conference on Designing Interactive Systems,* 60–69.

Denef, S., Ramirez, L., Dyrks, T., and Stevens, G. (2008) Handy navigation in ever-changing spaces: An ethnographic study of firefighting practices. *Proceedings of the ACM Conference on Designing Interactive Systems,* 184–192.

Druin, A., Weeks, A., Massey, S., and Bederson, B.B. (2007) Children's interests and concerns when using the International Children's Digital Library: A four-country case study. *Proceedings of the ACM/IEEE-CS Joint Conference on Digital Libraries,* 167–176.

Ducheneaut, N. and Moore, R.J. (2004) The social side of gaming: A study of interaction patterns in a massively multiplayer online game. *Proceedings of the ACM Conference on Computer-Supported Cooperative Work,* 360–369.

Ducheneaut, N., Moore, R., and Nickell, E. (2007) Virtual "third places": A case study of sociability in massively multiplayer games. *Computer-Supported Cooperative Work*, **16**(1):129–166.

Fiore, A.T. and Donath, J.S. (2005) Homophily in online dating: When do you like someone like yourself? *Proceedings of the ACM Conference on Human Factors in Computing Systems*, 1371–1374.

Fiore, A.T., Taylor, L.S., Mendelsohn, G.A., and Hearst, M. (2008) Assessing attractiveness in online dating profiles. *Proceedings of the ACM Conference on Human Factors in Computing Systems*, 797–806.

Gaver, W.W., Boucher, A., Pennington, S., and Walker, B. (2004) Cultural probes and the value of uncertainty. *interactions*, **11**(5):53–56.

Gold, R. (1958) Roles in sociological field observations. *Social Forces*, **36**(3):217–223.

Hancock, J.T., Toma, C., and Ellison, N. (2007) The truth about lying in online dating profiles. *Proceedings of the ACM Conference on Human Factors in Computing Systems*, 449–452.

Harvey, L. and Myers, M. (2002) Scholarship and practice: The contribution of ethnographic research methods to bridging the gap. In M. Myers and D. Avison (eds), *Qualitative Research in Information Systems: A reader*, 169–180. London: Sage Publications.

Karapano, E., Zimmerman, J., Forlizzi, J., and Martens, J.-B. (2009) User experience over time: An initial framework. *Extended Abstracts of the ACM Conference on Human Factors in Computing Systems*, 729–738.

Lee, A.Y. and Bruckman, A.S. (2007) Judging you by the company you keep: Dating on social networking sites. *Proceedings of the GROUP'07: International Conference on Supporting Group Work*, 371–378.

Leshed, G., Velden, T., Rieger, O., et al. (2008) In-car GPS navigation: Engagement with and disengagement from the environment. *Proceedings of the ACM Conference on Human Factors in Computing Systems*, 1675–1684.

Lofland, J., Snow, D.A., Anderson, L., and Lofland, L.H. (2006) *Analyzing Social Situations: A guide to qualitative observation and analysis*. Belmont, CA: Wadsworth/Thomson Learning.

Maloney-Krichmar, D. and Preece, J. (2005) A multilevel analysis of sociability, usability, and community dynamics in an online health community. *ACM Transactions on Computer–Human Interaction*, **12**(2):201–232.

Newman, M.W. and Landay, J.A. (2000) Sitemaps, storyboards, and specifications: A sketch of Web site design practice. *Proceedings of the ACM Conference on Designing Interactive Systems*, 263–274.

Ormerod, T., Morley, N., Ball, L., Langley, C., and Spencer, C. (2003) Using ethnography to design a mass detection tool (MDT) for the early discovery of insurance fraud. *Proceedings of the ACM Conference on Human Factors in Computing Systems*, 650–651.

Pedersen, E. and Wolff, G. (2008) Paper interface to electronic medical records: A case of usage-driven technology appropriation. *Proceedings of the ACM Conference on Designing User Experiences*, 40–49.

Ploderer, B., Howard, S., and Thomas, P. (2008) Being online, living offline: The influence of social ties over the appropriation of social network sites. *Proceedings of the ACM Conference on Computer-Supported Cooperative Work*, 333–342.

Preece, J. (1998) Empathic communities: reaching out across the Web. *interactions*, **5**(2):32–43.

Rode, J., Toye, E., and Blackwell, A. (2004) The fuzzy felt ethnography: Understanding the programming patterns of domestic appliances. *Personal and Ubiquitous Computing*, **8**(3):161–176.

Schuler, D. and Namioka, A. (eds). (1993) *Participatory Design: Principles and practices.* Hillsdale, NJ: Lawrence Erlbaum Associates.

Shapiro, D. (1994) The limits of ethnography: combining social sciences for CSCW. *Proceedings of the 1994 ACM conference on Computer-Supported Cooperative Work*, 417–428.

Sharrock, W. and Randall, D. (2004) Ethnography, ethnomethodology and the problem of generalisation in design. *European Journal of Information Systems*, **13**(3):186–194.

Siegel, D. and Dray, S. (2005) Avoiding the next schism: Ethnography and usability. *interactions*, **12**(2):58–61.

Su, N.M. and Mark, G. (2008) Communication chains and multitasking. *Proceedings of the ACM Conference on Human Factors in Computing Systems*, 83–92.

Suchman, L.A. (1987) *Plans and Situated Action: The problem of human–machine communication.* Cambridge: Cambridge University Press.

Suchman, L. (1999) Embodied practices of engineering work. *Mind, Culture, and Activity*, **7**(1/2):4–18.

Suchman, L. (2000) Organizing alignment: A case of bridge-building. *Organization*, **7**(2):311–327.

Taylor, A.S. and Swan, L. (2005) Artful systems in the home. *Proceedings of the ACM Conference on Human Factors in Computing Systems*, 641–650.

Wu, M., Baecker, R., and Richards, B. (2007) Designing a cognitive aid for and with people who have anterograde amnesia. In J. Lazar (ed.), *Universal Usability: Designing computer interfaces for diverse user populations*, 317–356. Chichester, UK: John Wiley & Sons

Wyche, S.P. (2005) Designing speculative household cleaning products for older adults. *Proceedings of the DUX'05: Designing for user experiences*, 49.

Wyeth, P. (2006) Ethnography in the kindergarten: Examining children's play experiences. *Proceedings of the ACM Conference on Human Factors in Computing Systems*, 1225–1228.

Usability testing

10.1   What is usability testing?

Usability testing, in general, involves representative users attempting representative tasks in representative environments, on early prototypes of computer interfaces (Lewis, 2006). If that sounds like a very broad definition, it is meant to be that way. The world of usability testing includes:

- testing prototypes that have only been built on paper (known as paper prototypes);
- testing prototypes that look complete but have a human behind the scenes responding (known as the "Wizard of Oz" technique);
- testing working versions of software before it is officially released;
- testing software that has already been implemented in existing systems.

While the interfaces being usability tested are typically screen layouts for desktop or laptop computers, usability testing can also take place on any type of device and usability testing is increasingly being done on hand-held devices such as smart phones (Schusteritsch, Wei and LaRosa, 2007). Those devices frequently need usability testing, since the interaction approaches (such as multi-touch screens) are newer, more content is stuffed into a smaller screen size, and it can be easy to activate features by accident (e.g. holding the smartphone in your hand and hitting a button; or making a call, putting the phone up to your face, and accidentally selecting a feature).

All of these approaches to usability testing have one basic goal: to improve the quality of an interface by finding flaws in it. Usability testing should discover interface flaws that cause problems for users. At the same time, we want to discover what is working well with an interface design, so that we make sure to keep those features in place! Let's think of another phrase for usability testing; let's call it "user research." In reality, we're not researching the user, we're researching the interface. We're trying to figure out how to make the interface better. What's an interface flaw? It's some aspect, some component, some widget of the interface that is confusing, misleading, or generally sub-optimal. It's not about style or color preferences. Someone may prefer blue text or black text on a white background and that's fine. When it becomes a usability problem is when you have white, yellow, orange, or red text on a white background, all of which are hard for the eye to perceive. When we talk about usability testing, we are talking about discovering interface flaws that cause problems for a majority of people.

Figure 10.1 gives an example of an interface that has a major flaw. The screen shot shows the process of checking in online for an airline flight. Once you enter your information, the website asks if you would like to upgrade your seat to the class called "economy plus." Typically, most individuals would not want to upgrade. However, the user's eye naturally goes to the large yellow arrow on the right, which would seem to continue to the next screen. In reality, clicking the yellow arrow causes the user to upgrade their seat. To continue without an upgrade, the user needs to click on the textual link on the left, which is small (in comparison to the arrow) and not obvious. This is a confusing and potentially misleading

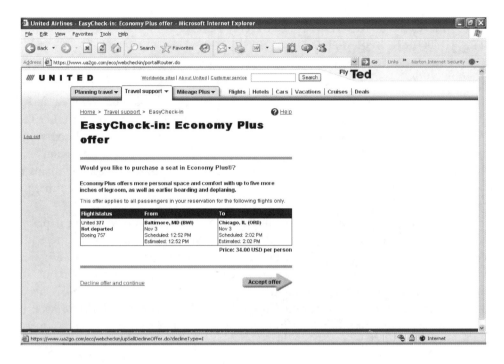

Figure 10.1 An airline check-in screen with at least one clear usability flaw. (*Source*: www.ua2go.com)

interface flaw. This is a very minor flaw to change, however, it will have a major improvement on user interaction and performance. Of course, maybe it was designed to be misleading!

The range of usability testing is quite broad. Usability testing can involve hundreds of users, have a number of controls, and use a true experimental design. Usability testing can also involve a software developer sitting down next to three users, watching them go through the interface, and then taking basic notes on where the problems are. While both of these exercises can be called usability testing, it is more likely that the former would be considered research and be published. Usability testing can involve hypothesis testing, tight controls, control groups, and a large enough number of participants to determine statistically significant differences. However, that's not the way that most usability testing happens (Rubin and Chisnell, 2008). Why? In industry, the extra time needed to plan controls and do random assignments, and the high number of participants needed, are often a barrier to entry (Rubin and Chisnell, 2008). If the choice is that you must do all of those or nothing at all, businesses often choose to do nothing. Therefore, more flexible, easier, and quicker methods are often used. Where does usability testing end and research begin? It's an unclear, fuzzy line and the distinction is not all that important.

10.2 How does usability testing relate to traditional research?

Usability testing can be considered a close cousin of research methods. In reality, the approaches utilized in usability testing are often the same as those used in classic research. Metrics utilized in usability testing include measurement of task performance and time performance, similar to experimental design. Methods utilized as part of usability testing include surveys to measure user satisfaction. Observation techniques, from ethnography, are often utilized in usability testing. Key logging (see Section 12.2.3) and click-stream analysis can be utilized in usability testing. In usability testing, the names of the participants must remain anonymous and participants have the right to leave the research at any time, just as in traditional research.

However, usability testing often has different end goals. Usability testing is primarily an industry approach to improving user interfaces. As an industrial approach, there is little concern for using only one research method or having strict controls. In fact, Wixon goes as far as to say that usability testing is a part of engineering, not research (Wixon, 2003). Wixon's assertion is that usability testing, like engineering, is involved in building a successful product, in the shortest amount of time, using the fewest resources, with the fewest risks, while optimizing trade-offs. Often in industry, schedule and resource issues, rather than theoretical discussions of methodology, drive the development process (Wixon, 2003). One practice that is somewhat accepted in usability testing is to modify the interface after every user test, when major flaws are discovered, to help immediately eliminate the flaws and improve the interface. Making immediate changes to the interface allows for those changes to be evaluated during the next user test, which can help ensure that no new interface problems have been introduced in making the changes (Wixon, 2003). While this may not happen due to time constraints, it's an acceptable practice. Clearly, this practice would be considered unacceptable in experimental design, where the goal would be to ensure that all users in a group have the same treatment. And since usability testing is an industrial, practical approach, it's also important to note that not all interface flaws discovered during usability testing are fixed. Very often, the list of interface flaws discovered is prioritized and only the most serious problems are fixed.

By now, it should be clear that the goal of usability testing is to be practical and have a major impact. Since the goal is often to improve interfaces and have an important impact on the financial bottom line of a company, many companies don't publish their usability test findings, as they consider it confidential and a part of their competitive advantage. There are, however, a number of documented cases of usability testing that we have included in this chapter.

In Chapter 9, we discussed some of the differences between ethnography and participatory design. Ethnography is more focused on understanding people, their groups, their processes, and their beliefs. Often, ethnographic methods are used as part of a systems

Classical research source	Classical research description	Usability testing description
Experimental design	Isolate and understand specific phenomena, with the goal of generalization to other problems	Find and fix flaws in a specific interface, no goal of generalization
Experimental design	A larger number of participants is required	A small number of participants can be utilized
Ethnography	Observe to understand the context of people, groups, and organizations	Observe to understand where in the interface users are having problems.
Ethnography	Researcher participation is encouraged	Researcher participation is not encouraged in any way
Ethnography	Longer-term research method	Short-term research method
Ethnography and experimental design	Used to understand problems or answer research questions	Used in systems and interface development
Ethnography and experimental design	Used in earlier stages, often separate from (or only partially related to) the interface development process	Typically takes place in later stages, after interfaces (or prototype versions of interfaces) have been developed
Ethnography and experimental design	Used for understanding problems	Used for evaluating solutions

Table 10.1 Differences between classical research and usability testing.

development method called *participatory design*. The end goal of ethnography is simply understanding a group, an organization, or a problem, whereas the end goal of participatory design is building a computer system. Usability testing follows a similar pattern. Usability testing has an end goal of improved interface design in a specific system. In fact, participatory design includes the stages of both ethnographic observation (in the user's situational context) and usability testing. Development methods or lifecycles, such as participatory design, the systems development lifecycle, the web development lifecycle, or community-centered design, can be thought of as recipes, with the individual activities, such as ethnographic observation and usability testing, as the ingredients in those recipes. The methods used in usability testing borrow most closely from experimental design and ethnography. Table 10.1 provides a comparison of classical research methods and usability testing.

To make things a bit more confusing, there is also research about usability testing! That is, research exists on evaluating which usability testing methods are most effective. For instance, in the debate on how many participants you need (see Section 10.4.3), the focus isn't on improving interfaces, but on understanding and improving the usability methods themselves.

But that isn't usability testing, that's research on how to do usability testing and that's a whole different topic!

10.3 Types of usability testing or usability inspections

There are many different types of usability testing. A more general term, usability engineering, has sometimes been used to describe any process or activity that aims to improve the ease of use of an interface. Under this heading, and sometimes under the heading of usability testing, there are three distinct categories: expert-based testing, automated testing, and user-based testing.

An expert-based test involves interface experts in using a number of different structured methods for finding interface flaws. An automated test is a software program that applies a series of guidelines (developed by the experts) to an interface and determines where the interface doesn't meet the guidelines. A user-based test involves representative users performing representative tasks (at various stages in the development process). While user-based tests are the majority focus of usability testing, expert-based tests and automated tests are sometimes used in human–computer interaction (HCI) research.

As multi-method research approaches gain strength, we expect to see a greater appearance of expert and automated usability testing. Note that expert and automated usability tests are sometimes known as *usability inspections,* and *usability testing* is reserved for user-based testing. Whole books have been written about each type of usability testing, so this chapter provides only a summary of each type. Since the primary interest in HCI research is users and collecting data from users, this chapter primarily focuses on user-based testing. First, we briefly discuss expert-based testing and automated testing.

10.3.1 Expert-based testing

Expert-based tests are essentially structured inspections by interface experts. The people who developed the prototype interface should not be involved with the expert review, as that may bias the results. People who are unfamiliar with the interface should carry out the expert reviews. Expert-based tests are often used in conjunction with user-based tests, but the expert-based tests always come first. Interface experts are experts in interfaces but they are typically not experts in the tasks to be performed within a certain interface. Conversely, representative users are typically experts in performing the tasks but are not experts in interface design. Often a certain portion of interface functionality can be understood and improved without a deep understanding of the tasks, but other portions of the interface can only be examined with a deep understanding of the tasks involved.

Expert users first use a structured inspection to attempt to uncover some of the more obvious interface flaws, such as confusing wording, inconsistent or misleading layouts, and color consistency. If possible, suggested improvements to the interface from the expert review should be made before user-based usability testing occurs. This timeline allows the experts to find the obvious interface flaws and get them fixed; the users can then find the deeper, more granular, and task-related interface flaws which may not be obvious to the interface

1. Strive for consistency
2. Cater to universal usability
3. Offer informative feedback
4. Design dialogs to yield closure
5. Prevent errors
6. Permit easy reversal of actions
7. Support internal locus of control
8. Reduce short-term memory load

(Shneiderman and Plaisant, 2009)

Table 10.2 Shneiderman's 8 Golden Rules of Interface Design.

experts (Lazar, 2006). If there are many interface flaws and no expert has reviewed the interface, the users may be distracted by the major interface flaws and may be unable to help the developers by identifying the more granular, task-based flaws.

There are a number of different types of expert review, also known as expert inspections or usability inspections. The most common expert reviews are the heuristic review, the consistency inspection, and the cognitive walkthrough. In a heuristic review, an expert takes a set of heuristics (rules of thumb) and compares the heuristics to the interface in question. Heuristics are short sets of usually no more than 10 interface rules. To be truly effective, the expert must be very familiar with the heuristics and have previous experience in interpreting them. Lazar provides a list of various sets of heuristics for different types of websites (Lazar, 2006) but the best-known set of interface heuristics is probably Shneiderman's golden rules of interface design (see Table 10.2).

In a consistency inspection, one or more experts review a series of screens or web pages for issues of consistency in layout, color, terminology, or language. Sometimes, an organization has a specific set of style guidelines (for colors and typefaces) and a consistency inspection can check for overall consistency with those style guidelines.

A cognitive walkthrough is an expert review method in which interface experts simulate users, "walking through" a series of tasks. The experts must have experience with general interface design and a good understanding of who the users are and what tasks they are expected to perform in the interface that is being evaluated. Because of the exploratory nature of a cognitive walkthrough, it can give an understanding of how users might interact with an interface the first time that they attempt to use it (Hollingsed and Novick, 2007). Both high-frequency tasks and rarely occurring but important tasks (such as error recovery) should be included in a cognitive walkthrough (Shneiderman and Plaisant, 2009). Because it is task-based, rather than rule-based, it is still somewhat controversial, as some people feel that it is not as productive as user-based testing.

Not as popular as the previous three methods, but still occurring often, is the guidelines review, in which an expert compares a set of interfaces to a previously written set of interface guidelines. While this sounds like a heuristic review, the main difference is that a guidelines review uses a large set of guidelines (usually 10–200). Heuristic reviews take place more often because they are easier and take less time. However, guideline reviews are more thorough. Probably one of the best-known sets of guidelines is the Web Content Accessibility Guidelines, created by the World Wide Web Consortium (http://www.w3.org/WAI). These guidelines documents provide guidance on making website content accessible for people with disabilities. Internationally, most laws that deal with accessible web content were written based on the Web Content Accessibility Guidelines. The Web Accessibility Initiative also has guidelines related to authoring tool accessibility, user agent accessibility, and rich Internet application accessibility. These guidelines, while commonly used, can be overwhelming in scope and so the Web Accessibility Initiative also offers shorter versions of the guidelines documents (such as checkpoints and quick tips) which can be considered as heuristics. Other commonly used guidelines include the operating systems interface guidelines documents from Apple and Microsoft, the research-based web design and usability guidelines from the US government (http://www.usability.gov/pdfs/guidelines.html) and the KDE or GNOME interface guidelines. In addition, firms such as the Nielsen Norman Group have large numbers of specialized guidelines sets that are available for a price (http://www.nngroup.com/reports/).

Other types of expert review, such as the formal usability inspection and the pluralistic walkthrough, are not as common (Hollingsed and Novick, 2007). If you are interested in different types of expert review, you should read the classic book on expert reviews (Nielsen and Mack, 1994) or recent HCI papers about expert review methods. However, since expert-based reviews really don't involve users, we won't go into any more details in this chapter.

10.3.2   Automated usability testing

An automated usability test is a software application that inspects a series of interfaces to assess the level of usability. Often, this works by using a set of interface guidelines (described in Section 10.3.1) and having the software compare the guidelines to the interfaces. A summary report is then provided by the automated usability testing application. Automated usability testing applications are often used when a large number of interfaces need to be examined and little time is available to do human-based reviews. The major strength is that these applications can read through code very quickly, looking for usability problems that can be picked up. These applications typically have features to either offer advice about how the code should be fixed or actually fix the code. The major weakness is that many aspects of usability cannot be discovered by automated means, such as appropriate wording, labels, and layout. And most automated tools are designed only to test web interfaces. For instance, an application can determine if a web page has alternative code for a graphic, by examining to determine the existence of an <alt> tag. However, an application can't determine if that alternative text is clear and useful (e.g. "picture here" would not be appropriate text but it would meet the requirements of the automated usability testing application). In situations like that, manual checks are required. A manual check is when one of these applications notes that because of the presence of certain interface features, a human inspection is required.

Automated usability testing applications are good at measuring certain statistics, such as the number of fonts used, the average font size, the average size of clickable buttons, the deepest level of menus, and the average loading time of graphics (Au *et al.*, 2008). These are useful metrics, but they do not ascertain how users interact with those interfaces, only how well those interfaces comply with guidelines. A large number of software applications, including RAMP, InFocus, and A-Prompt, exist to compare web pages to the Web Content Accessibility Guidelines from the Web Accessibility Initiative (http://www.w3.org/WAI). Other examples of automated usability testing include Dottie, which automates the web guidelines for older users from the US government, and WebSat, which automates general web usability guidelines. A classic article about automated usability testing can be found in the ACM Computing Surveys (Ivory and Hearst, 2001) and the sidebar lists some research that utilizes automated usability testing.

Accessibility Research with Automated Usability Tools

One of the most common research uses of automated usability testing is to quickly evaluate how accessible a certain category of websites is to people with disabilities. While human inspection of website accessibility is ideal, if the goal is to get an over-all sense of accessibility levels across multiple sites, then automated tools are often very appropriate. In this approach, an automated usability testing application, such as WebXACT, InFocus, RAMP, or A-Prompt, is used to quickly examine multiple web-sites and get an overall sense of how accessible sites are for people with disabilities. Often, manual checks are required to help clarify findings from the software testing tool. Using this methodological approach, recent research has examined the accessibility levels of:

- government, company, and university websites in the United Kingdom (Bailey and Burd, 2005);
- government websites in Taiwan (Chen, Chen and Shao, 2005);
- government websites in Brazil (Freire, Bittar and Fortes, 2008);
- government websites in Nepal (Shah and Shakya, 2007);
- government websites in Northern Ireland (Paris, 2006);
- non-governmental websites in the mid-Atlantic United States (Lazar *et al.*, 2003);
- state government websites in the United States (Goette, Collier and Whilte, 2006);
- 50 of the web's most popular sites (Sullivan and Matson, 2000);
- universities around the world (Kane *et al.*, 2007);
- large companies in the United States (Loiacono and McCoy, 2004).

10.4   User-based testing

User-based testing is what most people mean when they refer to usability testing. Mostly, it means a group of representative users attempting a set of representative tasks. This can take place very early in development or very late in development. It's better to start doing user-based testing earlier rather than later, when the results can influence the design more and when costs to make changes are much lower. Ideally, user-based testing would take place during all stages of development, but that is not always possible. Why do we do usability testing? As much as designers try to build interfaces that match the needs of the users, the designers are not users and even the users themselves sometimes cannot clearly identify their interface needs. So interface prototypes, at various stages, need to be tested by users. Note that users are testing interfaces, but users are not being tested. This is an important distinction. Furthermore, some authors even go so far as to say that the developers who create an interface design should not be the ones who moderate a usability test (Rubin and Chisnell, 2008). If you create an interface, you are likely to be supportive of that interface, feel that you have time invested in it, and may not be as open to user suggestions. From a strict experimental point of view, the interface developer shouldn't moderate a usability test or interact with the participants (although the developer can observe the testing). However, since perfect design isn't the goal of usability testing, there are situations where the interface developer serves double duty and moderates the usability test.

10.4.1   Types of usability testing

Usability testing that takes place early in development tends to be exploratory and to test early design concepts. Sometimes, this is known as *formative testing* and may include wireframes or paper prototypes, also known as low-fidelity prototypes (Dumas and Fox, 2007). This type of usability testing is often more informal, with more communication between test moderators and participants (Rubin and Chisnell, 2008). In early exploratory testing, there is more of a focus on how the user perceives an interface component rather than on how well the user completes a task (Rubin and Chisnell, 2008). Paper prototypes are especially useful, because they are low cost and multiple designs can be quickly presented and evaluated by participants. In addition, because paper prototypes involve little development time, designers and developers tend not to become committed to a specific design early on. And users may feel more comfortable giving feedback or criticizing the interface when they see that not much work has been done yet on the interface. With fully functional prototypes, users may be hesitant to criticize, since they feel that the system is already finished and their feedback won't matter that much. More information on paper prototyping can be found in Snyder, (2003).

Usability testing that takes place when there is a more formal prototype ready, when high-level design choices have been made, is known as a *summative test*. The goal is to evaluate the effectiveness of specific design choices. These mostly functional prototypes are also known as high-fidelity prototypes (Dumas and Fox, 2007).

Finally, a usability test sometimes takes place right before an interface is released to the general user population. In this type of test, known as a *validation test*, the new interface is compared to a set of benchmarks for other interfaces. The goal is to ensure that, for instance, 90% of users can complete each task within one minute (if that statistic is an important benchmark). Validation testing is far less common than formative or summative testing.

Different authors use different definitions for these terms. For instance, we have used the definitions from Rubin and Chisnell. West and Lehman, however, define formative tests as those that find specific interface problems to fix and summative tests as those that have a goal of benchmarking an interface's usability to other similar interfaces (West and Lehman, 2006). The one thing that most authors agree on is that earlier, formative usability tests tend to focus more on qualitative feedback, moderator observation, and problem discovery, whereas summative usability tests tend to focus more on task-level measurements, metrics and quantitative measurements (Lewis, 2006). The Kodak Website sidebar gives an example of formative and summative usability testing.

Research In Practice

Usability Testing of the Kodak Website

The Eastman Kodak Company is one of the world's largest manufacturers and marketers of imaging products. Both formative and summative usability testing took place on the Kodak website.

Formative testing took place on a paper prototype of the new home page design, specifically the links and groups. Twenty participants were given 30 tasks and were asked to identify the homepage link most likely to lead to the information that would complete that task. Participants were then asked to describe what type of content they expected to find behind each homepage link. Finally, participants were given descriptions of what actually was behind each home page link, and were asked to rate how well the label matched the actual content.

Later, summative testing with 33 participants took place on a working computer prototype of the new home page and all top-level pages on the site. A list of 22 tasks was developed, but each participant was given only 10 information-seeking tasks to complete. Some tasks were attempted by 33 participants, while other tasks were attempted by only 11 participants. All links were functional, although not all visual design elements on the pages were complete. Each participant was given a maximum of three minutes to complete each task. Task completion for individual tasks ranged from 100% to 9% in the allotted three minutes. Based on the results of the usability testing, changes were made to the pages, including removing images along the left side of the page, adding longer descriptors to more of the links, and labeling major chunks of information (Lazar, 2006).

Whether a usability test is formative, summative, or validation can influence how formal or informal the usability test is. At one end of the spectrum is a formal approach to usability testing, which parallels experimental design. This form of usability testing can involve specific research questions, research design (between-subject design or within-subject design), and multiple interfaces to test. If you are using inferential statistics, hypothesis, a control group, large numbers of subjects, and strict controls on user recruitment, usability testing may, in fact, become experimental design. The only difference would be that experimental design is looking for statistically significant differences between groups to learn some research truth, whereas usability testing is looking for ways to improve specific interfaces.

10.4.2   Stages of usability testing

Usability testing is not something that just happens. It requires a lot of advance planning. Different authors on the topic describe different steps, but the reality is that there are a lot of advance planning steps involved. See Figure 10.2 for examples of the stages of usability testing from two groups of authors.

There are a number of stages of usability testing that seem very similar to experimental design (see Chapter 3). Often, a usability expert, taking the role of the usability moderator, manages the process. For more detailed information about moderator roles, we suggest that you consult Dumas and Loring (2008). The moderator should determine which users would be appropriate, representative participants to take part in the usability testing. If the typical users of the new interface system are nurses at a hospital, it is inappropriate (and probably unethical) to use undergraduate students in business to perform the usability testing (although nursing students might be appropriate). If appropriate user-centered design methods have been utilized, there should be existing user personas and task scenarios that can help guide you in this process. Once you have figured out who the representative, appropriate users are, the next goal is to try and recruit them. Again, this is very similar to experimental design. For instance, users expect to be paid for their participation in usability testing, just as they expect to be paid for their participation in an experimental study. However, recruitment in usability testing is generally seen to be more flexible than in experimental design. While it's very

1. Develop the test plan	1. Select representative users
2. Set up the test environment	2. Select the setting
3. Find and select participants	3. Decide what tasks users should perform
4. Prepare test materials	4. Decide what type of data to collect
5. Conduct the test sessions	5. Before the test session (informed consent,
6. Debrief the participants	etc.)
7. Analyze data and observations	6. During the test session
8. Report findings and	7. Debriefing after the session
recommendations	
(Rubin and Chisnell, 2008)	(Lazar, 2006)

Figure 10.2 Stages of usability testing from different authors.

important that the recruited participants accurately represent the target user population, it's less relevant how you recruit those users. Unless you are dealing with multiple user populations across cultures, countries, or languages (in which case you may want to do usability testing at each site), it can be satisfactory, for instance, to recruit users from only one or two companies or in only one geographic area.

10.4.3 How many users are sufficient?

One of the most common questions when planning usability testing is "how many users do I need to have?" It's also a bit of a hotbed of discussion in the HCI community. If you were doing a strict experimental design, the types of research design and the statistical tests that you run would dictate the minimum number of participants required. However, usability testing has different goals and different requirements. Many people say that five users is the magic number and that five users will find approximately 80% of usability problems in an interface (Virzi, 1992). This has become a generally accepted number in HCI, but many other researchers disagree with the assertion. The major challenge in determining the right number of users, is that you don't know in advance how many interface flaws exist, so any estimate of how many users are needed to find a certain percentage of interface flaws is based on the assumption that you know how many flaws exist, which you probably don't.

Other research studies have found that five users are not sufficient to discover and identify a majority of usability flaws (Lindgaard and Chattratichart, 2007; Spool and Schroeder, 2001). In a classic paper, Nielsen and Landauer, who in earlier work had asserted the number five, expressed that the appropriate number depends on the size of the project, with seven users being optimal in a small project and 15 users being optimal in a medium-to-large project (Nielsen and Landauer, 1993). However, in that same paper, they indicated that the highest ratio of benefits to costs is when you have 3.2 users doing usability testing (Nielsen and Landauer, 1993). Lewis says that all authors could theoretically be right about the appropriate number of users, it depends on how accurate they need to be, what their problem discovery goals are, and how many participants are available (Lewis, 2006). Even if five users are enough, what happens when you have multiple user groups taking part in usability testing. Do you need five users from each group?

Lindgaard and Chattratichart take a different approach: they assert that the number of usability flaws found depends more on the design and scope of the tasks, rather than on the number of users (Lindgaard and Chattratichart, 2007). But by now, "five participants in usability evaluation" is part of the HCI lore, in the same way that "7 ± 2" is part of the HCI lore. We are told we should organize our menu items and menu bars into chunks of five to nine items, based on classic psychological research literature (Miller, 1956). However, this is misleading: the 7 ± 2 limitation in short-term memory applies to recall, not recognition, and most interface design is recognition, where we see or hear an icon or item and think, "oh yes, that's what I wanted" (Preece, Rogers and Sharp, 2002). However, "five participants" and "7 ± 2 menu items" remain part of the HCI folklore, even when there is real debate about their validity.

The reality is that most usability testing will never uncover all, or even most, of the usability flaws. And even if all of the flaws were uncovered, most of them will never be fixed. Instead, the goal should be to find the major flaws, the flaws that will cause most problems, and get them fixed. From an industry point of view, the exercise of finding flaws, without the consideration of whether they can be fixed, is not of value (Wixon, 2003). It simply would not make sense to expend all of the available "usability time" in a development lifecycle on finding flaws, rather than balancing time between finding flaws and fixing flaws. It may be useful to examine the effectiveness of various usability testing methods. But in industry, usability testing logistics are often driven not by what should or needs to be done, but instead, on how much time is left in the development process, how much money has been set aside by management for usability testing, and how many users are available and willing to participate. For instance, in usability testing on the website of the American Speech–Language–Hearing Association, the usability engineer identified 16 different user populations for the website. But after the prototype of the new website was built, the budget only allowed for usability testing with school-based, speech–language pathologists, the largest group of users for the website (Lazar, 2006). So instead of saying, "how many users must you have?", maybe the correct question is "how many users can we afford?", "how many users can we get?" or "how many users do we have time for?"

10.4.4 Locations for usability testing

Usability testing can take place anywhere. It can take place in a fixed laboratory, a workplace, a user's home, over the phone, or over the web. The location may be determined by what locations are available or where participants are, as well as what type of data you want to collect. None of the types of location are superior to any others. You should use whatever works for your specific usability testing project.

The most traditional setting for usability testing is a two-room setup. The user sits in one room and works on their tasks on a computer. Microphones and cameras record what the user is doing and output from the user's computer screen is also recorded. In the other room, the test moderators, and other stakeholders, sit and watch what the user is doing during the test. The moderators' room generally has a number of computer screens and monitors and the recording equipment, so all appropriate data can be recorded. In addition, the moderators' room often has a one-way mirror so that the moderators can directly observe what the user is doing, but the user cannot see into the moderators' room (see Figure 10.3). If a one-way mirror is not possible (either due to structural concerns or the moderators' room being located elsewhere in the building), a large image projected on to a wall is sufficient for the same purpose.

While a formal usability laboratory is typically used for desktop or laptop computer applications, with minor modifications to the camera angles and mounting, a formal

Figure 10.3 A formal usability laboratory with a one-way mirror. (Photo by Elizabeth Buie for UserWorks, Inc., a usability consulting firm located in Silver Spring, MD, www.userworks.com)

laboratory can also be utilized for usability testing of hand–held and mobile devices. For instance, one solution utilized for videotaping interactions on a mobile device is a document camera, which is often available in a classroom or presentation room. An article discusses different types of camera mountings and logistics for usability testing of hand–held devices (Schusteritsch *et al.*, 2007).

It's good to have a formal usability laboratory and the willingness to spend money and commit space may say something about the importance of usability to an organization (or it may not), but having a fixed usability laboratory is NOT necessary for usability testing. Figure 10.4 shows two examples of formal, fixed usability labs. One lab layout is located at a university, where there is only one participant room. The other lab layout is from the US Census Bureau, where three participant rooms are connected to one evaluation room.

Another possible location for usability testing is in the user's workplace or home. This may help in recruiting users, because it's less of a hassle for the users than having to go to a usability laboratory or central location. Visiting users in their workplace or home may also be easier if are working with users with impairments, for whom transportation is often a challenge (see Chapter 15). In many ways, the user's workplace or home setting is ideal for usability testing. The user is exposed to customary space, noise, and attention limitations while usability testing the interface. The user may feel most comfortable in their normal environment. In fact, testing in the user's natural setting goes along with the ideals of

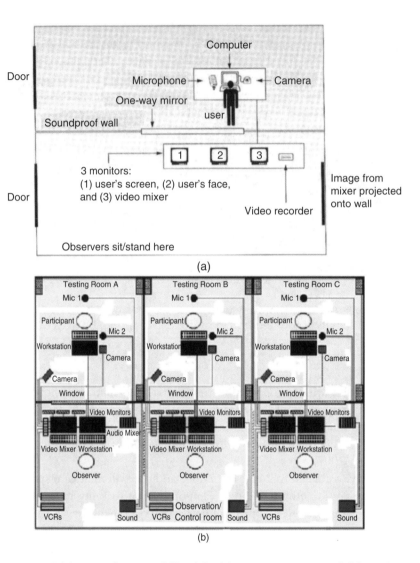

Figure 10.4 Potential layouts for a usability lab: (a) at a university and (b) at the US Census Bureau. (*Source*: Lazar, 2006, Murphy, Malakhoff, and Coon, 2007)

ethnography (see Chapter 9). For the user, it's the easiest and most natural form of usability testing. However, for the usability testing moderator, it can be the most challenging.

First of all, a lot of travel may be needed to visit each user. Secondly, a decision needs to be made: do you install the software or interface on the user's computer (which is more natural but may involve technical problems) or do you bring a laptop with the software or interface installed on it (which is technically easier but it's not the computer that the user is familiar with, so you may get some conflicting results). If you are usability testing a mobile device, you typically bring the device along. Thirdly, how are you going to record data? There are different approaches, all with benefits and drawbacks. If you observe the users by sitting near them, this may make them feel uncomfortable and they may act differently. You can use a number of technical approaches, but they take some time to set up before you begin the session. For instance, you could use data logging (where user keystrokes are recorded), record audio or send screen output to another local computer. If you have the equipment, or the budget to rent equipment, you could use a portable usability laboratory. A portable usability laboratory includes the same equipment (cameras, microphones, digital recording devices, etc.) as a fixed usability laboratory, but in a portable case, with very long wires (or a wireless signal). The idea is that, when you get to the user's home or workplace, you set up the equipment so that it essentially mirrors the setup in a fixed lab, so that a camera and a microphone are trained on the user and screen capture is in place (see Figure 10.5). You then find a location near the user (not next to the user, obvious to the user, or where you can physically see the user) but where the equipment wires are long enough to reach (or wireless signals can help with this). You can both record audio/video and watch a live feed and take notes. This may be ideal from a research point of view, since you get rich data capture and recording and the user is in their most comfortable and familiar setting, but the downside is that portable usability equipment is very expensive, takes a long time to set up, and there are often technical problems. If you are usability testing a mobile device,

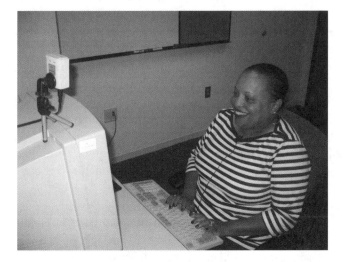

Figure 10.5 A camera and a microphone on a user in a portable usability lab. (Photo courtesy of Universal Usability Laboratory at Towson University)

how do you accurately observe or record user actions on a device that may be too small to watch, unless you are standing right behind the user? If they are continuously moving the device around their own environment (as most people do), how do you observe or record data, aside from data logging (Schusteritsch *et al.*, 2007)?

Sometimes, it is not feasible to do usability testing in a centralized location at a usability lab or in a user's workplace or home. It could be that the representative user population is not within easy traveling distance of the usability evaluators or moderators. Or there could be other logistical factors that limit the ability to do face-to-face usability testing. For instance, it could be appropriate to do remote usability testing with individuals with disabilities for whom transportation might be a problem (Petrie *et al.*, 2006). When an interface will be deployed in multiple countries, it is necessary to have users from all of the countries test the interface but it may not be possible for the evaluators to visit all the countries (Dray and Siegel, 2004). Remote usability testing is where users are separated from the evaluators by space, time, or both (Andreasen *et al.*, 2007). Video, audio, and network connections allow testing evaluators to monitor users, including streaming output from the user's screen (Hartson *et al.*, 1996). However, excellent quality connections are necessary, whether the testing uses videoconferencing on private networks or broadband connections to the Internet (Dray and Siegel, 2004).

One of the challenges with remote testing is the difficulty of picking up non-verbal and interpersonal cues. Remote usability testing, on the whole, works better for summative testing, when you are more interested in quantitative metrics, than for formative testing, where you tend to be more interested in the qualitative observations (Dray and Siegel, 2004). A recent research study has found that synchronous remote usability testing, where the evaluators are observing the users in different locations at the same time, may be more effective than asynchronous testing, where the evaluator observes at a later time (Andreasen *et al.*, 2007). Another approach recently presented for remote, asynchronous, usability testing is not to have a moderator but, instead, a control window or wizard that guides participants in the steps that they need to take. While this might be an interesting and potentially useful approach, even the authors of that paper acknowledge that, with no moderator or observer, several sources of data and information on the participants may be lost (West and Lehman, 2006). While remote usability testing can be technically very challenging and small problems can delay testing (since moderators aren't there to address any technical problems), it can be a very useful technique in the toolbox of the usability evaluator.

10.4.5 Task list

Creating the task list can be one of the most challenging parts of creating a usability test. Unless the usability testing is exploratory, formative, and takes place with very early stage prototypes (possibly on paper), it is likely that a task list will be needed. A task list is used so that when users go through an interface, they are goal-directed. Tasks need to be clear and unambiguous and not need further, additional explanation. While a background scenario may be presented at the beginning of the task list, just to set the participant in the context of the tasks, the task list should not require the participant to ask additional questions about the tasks. The tasks should typically have one clear answer or one clear method for task completion. The participants should clearly be aware when they have completed the task. Tasks should not be requests for information that the user could know regardless of whether they used the interface. For instance, it would not be appropriate to ask participants to use the interface to find out when Victoria was Queen of England or who won the US Super Bowl in 2002. Participants might already know the answers to these tasks and would not need to use the interface. The tasks should clearly require participants to utilize the interface.

Tasks are often chosen based on a number of factors (Dumas and Fox, 2007). For instance, it's important to have tasks that are performed often and are central to the goal that users want to accomplish. In addition, tasks that are critical, such as logging in or checking out, even if not frequent, should be included. If there are sections of an interface where there are existing questions about usability problems, they could be a focus of some of the tasks. In addition, sometimes, task lists try to be all-inclusive. For instance, if users can utilize menus, shortcuts, or a command line to reach material, some usability moderators design tasks that use all three approaches.

Typically, the task scenarios and the tasks themselves are representative, however they do not utilize any of the user's real data or personal information. Usability testing an interface does not involve any of the user's real financial, health, or contact information. Generally, while the moderators may need to have information about how old the users are, their level of education, and their home address (for example, to mail payment for participation), this information is not used as a part of the testing tasks themselves. Furthermore, if a task involves purchasing an item on an e-commerce site, participants should not be required to use their own credit or debit card. Rather, a separate credit card should be provided for their use, so that participants are not charged, and they do not need to provide any personal data. Zazelenchuk et al. (2008) describe how users' real personal data could potentially be used to get a more realistic usability test for financial interfaces, where users are familiar with their own data, emotionally engaged by their own data, and have no trouble understanding the meaning of it. While this may be more realistic from a testing point of view, there are many challenges and logistical concerns to using actual user data, regarding permission to use the data, disposal of the data, and permission from the users themselves. Zazelenchuk et al. even noted that when participants were asked to bring their own financial data to a usability testing session, a number of participants dropped out; to compensate and recruit more people, participants had to be paid a higher amount of money for the extra work and concern. Furthermore, if the usability testing needs to be approved by some sort of institutional review board (see Chapter 14), it is possible that this type of usability testing plan would be rejected. This would be especially likely if the usability testing involved user health care information, as many countries have specific laws relating to the privacy and security of health care information.

When creating the task list, it is important to provide direction on how to navigate the task list itself. Must participants go through tasks in the order listed? Can they skip tasks or start at the last task? Do certain tasks require that other tasks be completed first? How should participants respond if they get stuck and are unable to complete one task? Should they skip that task and move onto the next task? Is there a time limit per task? Is there an overall time limit for the usability testing session? While there might be research reasons for having a time limit per task or per session, there might also be practical reasons. For instance, the supervisor at the workplace may have said that participants can spend no more than 30 minutes on this outside activity or the moderators may only have use of the usability lab space (or another space) for a limited amount of time.

10.4.6   Measurement

There are many different types of data that can be collected during usability testing. The three most common quantitative measurements are task performance, time performance, and user satisfaction. Task performance or correctness means how many tasks were correctly completed. Time performance means how long each task took to complete (and the related measure of how long people spent on incorrect tasks before they gave up). User satisfaction is often measured by a standardized, validated survey tool. See Section 5.8 for a list of standard survey tools for measuring satisfaction.

While those are the three most common quantitative measurements in usability testing, there are many other metrics that could be useful. For instance, additional metrics might include average time to recover from an error, time spent using the help feature, and number of visits to the search feature or index. Depending on the purpose of the usability testing, additional specific metrics might be useful. For instance, if you have re-designed the search engine on a website and the usability testing tasks are focused on the search engine, then an important metric might be something like the average number of search engine responses clicked on, or the average search ranking of the choice that provided the solution. If you utilize key logging, there are many metrics that can be easily analyzed (such as the time spent on specific web pages, the number of web pages viewed, mouse movements, typing speed). Even complex interfaces, such as web-based AJAX applications, can use key logging to record data (Atterer and Schmidt, 2007). See Chapter 12 for information on key logging.

In usability testing, qualitative data is often just as important as quantitative data. For instance, users are often encouraged to "think aloud" as they are going through the interface (known as the "thinking aloud" protocol). This is more common in formative usability testing than in summative usability testing. When users state their feelings, their frustrations, and their progress out loud, there is often very useful feedback. For instance, a user may say things such as "Where is the menu choice? I would expect it to be right there" or "I certainly would not purchase anything from this website. It looks so unprofessional." Even younger users can make useful comments during a usability session (see the Leescircus sidebar). It is important to be aware that how comfortable someone may feel about speaking aloud during the tasks may be culturally influenced, so that people from some cultures may not feel comfortable expressing their concerns immediately (Shi and Clemmensen, 2008). Also, the more that users talk, the more their task or time performance data may be influenced (Dumas and Loring, 2008). The more they talk, the longer their task times will be (Dumas and Loring, 2008). If you want both true user comments and very accurate task and time performance data, it is possible to run a reflection session, also known as an interpretation session, after the tasks are performed. In an interpretation session, the users watch raw video of themselves immediately after attempting a series of tasks; working with the evaluators, they interpret the problems they encountered and where the major interface flaws are (Frokjaer and Hornbæk, 2005). In more traditional research with larger numbers of participants, the goal might be to categorize the qualitative comments using content analysis and look for patterns. With usability testing, we're trying to use those comments to help improve the interface. Certainly, there is an even more important message if you hear the same comment multiple times, but the strength of even one comment is important.

Research In Practice

Usability Testing of the Software Leescircus

Usability testing took place for an educational software package called *Leescircus*, designed for six- and seven-year-old children in the Netherlands. One example of a typical task is to match pictures that rhyme. A total of 70 Dutch children (32 girls and 38 boys), aged 6 or 7, took part in the usability testing. Most of the children had previous experience with computers and some had previous experience with the program. The children were asked to find problems with this version of the software. There were four sets of eight or nine tasks and each child performed only one set of tasks. Usability evaluators observed the children while they were performing the tasks. The children were encouraged to speak their comments aloud while using the software. The time period was limited to 30 minutes, as it was expected that the attention span of the children wouldn't last much longer. Although only 28 children did make comments out loud, the novice students (with less computer experience) tended to make more comments than the experts. Usability findings included the need to enlarge the clickable objects, clarify the meaning of icons, and improve consistency (so that it was clear whether an icon could or could not be clicked) (Donker and Reitsma, 2004).

10.4.7   The testing session

Before the testing session is scheduled, it is important to contact the participants, remind them about the upcoming session, and confirm the location, regardless of where the usability testing session will take place. Make sure to leave extra time in your schedule, since the participants may show up late, or take longer than expected. Immediately before the session starts, confirm that all computers, recording devices, and other technology is working properly. Just as in any type of research, participants must be given notice of their rights, agree to be video- or audio-taped, and be allowed to leave at any time. Let the participants know if there are any time constraints, either on the session as a whole, or on completing specific tasks. For more information about human subjects protections and IRB forms, see Chapter 14. In usability testing, when new interfaces are being tested, those interfaces might be confidential company information. So participants may also be asked to sign some type of confidentiality agreement, in which they agree not to release or discuss any details of this new interface product (Dumas and Loring, 2008). Finally, it should be clarified before the testing session begins whether participants will receive payment at the end of the session or if a check (or a gift card or something similar) will be mailed to their home. It should also be clear to the participants that even if they cannot complete the session or feel the need to end the session early, as is common practice, they will still be paid for their participation.

As noted previously, usability testing is about finding flaws that can be fixed, not about having a perfect methodology. One practice that is common in usability testing is to modify the interface after every user test, to help immediately improve the interface flaws discovered; those changes are then evaluated during the next user test (Wixon, 2003). If changes aren't made immediately after each user, changes may be made to the interface after a few users, and then a second round of usability testing is held, using the same tasks, to see if the performance improves and if the changes improved the interface. See the Fidelity Investments sidebar for an example of this practice.

Fidelity Investments

Usability testing took place at Fidelity Investments, evaluating the prototype of an interface to manage individual benefits, including company benefits, retirement savings, and pensions. A total of 27 participants tested the first prototype (this included both younger and older users, which would be expected for this type of interface). Each participant was given 15 tasks to complete, such as switching retirement money from one plan to another and determining what pension benefits would amount to if the individual retired at 65 years old. Task success rates were 64.2% for users under 55 years old and 44.8% for users 55 years or older.

Based on the usability testing of the first prototype, changes were made to the interface, including improved terminology, making links consistently obvious, adding more instruction for detailed table data, adding more titles, and removing false window bottoms and mouseover-based navigation tabs.

Usability testing then took place with the second interface prototype and a new set of 22 participants took part. The new participants had the same profile of age and computer experience as the participants in the first round of testing. The participants in the second round of usability testing were given the same 15 tasks as participants in the first round of testing, with a few minor wording changes due to the updated interface. With the new interface prototype, task success rates improved to 80.6% for users under age 55 and 58.2% for users 55 years and older (Chadwick-Dias, McNulty and Tullis, 2003).

It is common for the moderator to intervene, if the user gets totally stuck and indicates that they are unable to move on. This is not ideal but is a practical consideration. If the user gets stuck and cannot move any further or complete any more tasks, the moderator learns nothing new about the interface. If the moderator helps the user move onto the next step, it is possible to get useful feedback. This isn't ideal and, if it occurs, it should be clearly noted in any data results or write up (Dumas and Fox, 2007).

Unlike in other traditional research, in usability testing, it is considered standard practice to tell participants before they start that they are not being tested. Rather, the participants are testing the interface. Their feedback is important. They are the experts and have the right to criticize the interface. Users are not being tested. You may need to remind them of that fact multiple times.

Note that during the testing session, there are two "tracks" of data collection. One track is the quantitative metrics, such as task and time performance. Moderators may be timing the tasks, data logging may be keeping track, or video recording may be used for later review. The second track is the qualitative data. Sometimes, participants are very talkative and provide a verbal track of what they are doing. If the participants are not very talkative, moderators should try to encourage them to share more of how they are feeling. However, these reminders should not be often, since the more that the moderator interrupts the user, the more the user feels watched, the more the user's cognitive flow is interrupted, and the more that the user's behavior may deviate from normal. The thinking aloud protocol is more common in formative usability testing than in summative usability testing, since, if quantitative metrics are considered very important by the stakeholders of that interface, the more the participant stops to talk, the more that their task time is interrupted. So while it's acceptable for the user to stop every now and then to describe what they are doing, if the user talks continuously for 10 minutes, clearly, the task performance time is of questionable use.

Since usability testing is a practical approach to solving problems, hybrid approaches are often used. In a reflection or interpretation session, users, immediately after competing a series of tasks, review the raw video with the usability moderators, and help interpret the interface problems (Frokjaer and Hornbæk, 2005). Even without a formal interpretation session, users often make comments about the interface during the debriefing which follows the usability testing session. Without being prompted, users often make comments out loud during the usability testing session. All feedback from users is important data!

In addition, qualitative data, in terms of observation by moderators, is very important. Moderators can often tell a lot about how participants are managing with an interface even when the participant is not saying anything. Participants may sigh or grunt and their facial expressions may tell a story. It is possible to see frustration or anger in the facial expressions of participants. In fact, certain muscle movements in the face are clear signs of stress (Hazlett, 2003; 2006). Even without complex interpretation, it's very probable that, if a user keeps moving towards the screen or squinting, the icons or fonts on the screen may be a bit too small.

10.4.8   Making sense of the data

Analyzing data from usability testing is similar to analyzing data from any other type of research. However, the goal of the analysis is different. Since usability testing often uses fewer participants, inferential statistics often are not possible but simple descriptive statistics are possible. With traditional research, the goal is to write up the results in a paper, publish it in a journal, conference proceedings, or book, and help influence future research and design. With usability testing, the goal is to write up the results and help influence the design of the specific interface that was tested. Sometimes, a presentation about the results is made to a group of developers or managers who have the power to ensure that the interface is changed. The usability testing report (or presentation) should be oriented towards the goal of improving the specific interface and to those who will read it: interface designers, software engineers, project managers, and other managers involved in software development.

The usability test may have uncovered many different interface flaws which should be addressed. However, due to time concerns, not all of these flaws will be improved upon. So while the report should identify all flaws discovered during usability testing, the report should also prioritize which ones are most important to fix. For each flaw identified, the report should describe the problem, present the data from the usability test, identify the priority of the flaw, suggest a fix, and also estimate the time for the fix. Sometimes, data from usability testing can point to which flaws caused users to lose the most time or be unable to complete their tasks and which flaws were easily overcome by users. It's not always clear how to improve every single flaw. Sometimes, you may improve upon one flaw but introduce other problems. An experienced usability expert may use their expertise to determine which flaws should be prioritized, which flaws are not as problematic, and how to make improvements which do not introduce new problems.

Rubin and Chisnell (2008) suggest splitting the report into three sections:

- why you did usability testing and how you prepared;
- what happened during the testing;
- the implications and recommendations.

While typical research publications need to be thorough and detailed, if usability testing reports are going to management, they should be short and to the point. If certain aspects of the interface worked well, it might be useful to note that in the report as well. When interface flaws are fixed and changes are made, new flaws can be introduced into the interface. So it can be helpful to note the interface components that worked well and should not be changed.

It is important to note that you should never include names or identifying information for the participants who took part in the usability testing (Dumas and Loring, 2008). If all participants are from within a specific organization, even giving a combination of age, gender, and job title could be the equivalent of identifying someone. When in doubt, provide only the average age of participants, the number of each gender, and basic job titles. You never want to identify who took part in the usability testing, so it's a good idea to refer to the participants as Participant #1, Participant #2, and so on. You never know who and where your usability reporting results will be sent, so make sure you would be comfortable with that fact.

10.5   Other variations on usability testing

This chapter has presented traditional ways of doing usability testing. But, since usability testing is all about being practical and about changing methods to fit the needs that you have in a project, of course, there are new and different approaches to usability testing. If you read the proceedings of any well-established HCI conference, you can find new approaches, new hybrids, combining multiple methods, that could potentially be used in certain types of usability engineering activities. Two of the more well-known approaches are "technology probes" and "Wizard-of-Oz testing".

Technology probes wouldn't technically be considered usability testing, but they are certainly closer to usability testing than traditional research. A technology probe is similar to a cultural probe (described in Chapter 8). However, a cultural probe has the goal of generally learning more about people, their groups, and their lifestyles. Technology probes involve putting a technology into a real-world setting. Technology probes combine the social science goal of collecting information about people in a real-world setting, the engineering goal of evaluating a new technology, and the design goal of creating new ideas for potential technologies (Hutchinson *et al.*, 2003). A technology is installed in a real-world setting to see how it is used and then reflection on these experiences gives feedback on who the users are and what types of technology could be successfully used in these settings by these users. The technologies themselves are not the interfaces being tested for usability. Technology probes have been used to understand how family members communicate and share images (Hutchinson *et al.*, 2003) and how people in a relationship show public affection (O'Brian and Mueller, 2006). The focus in a technology probe isn't the probe itself but, rather, what can be learned about the people taking part and what technologies they could potentially use.

A Wizard-of-Oz[1] method is essentially a simulation of functionality that doesn't exist yet in an interface application. The user perceives that they are interacting with the actual interface and system. In reality, the user is interacting with another human being that is providing the responses to the user (Dahlback, Jonsson and Ahrenberg, 1993; Gould, Conti and Hovanyecz, 1983). Wizard-of-Oz methods can be used when the functionality has not been built due to cost concerns and when the technology doesn't exist, to test potential future interfaces (White and Lutters, 2003). In addition, due to the low time and cost involved, the method may also be helpful in determining feasibility and testing concepts prior to any real systems development (White and Lutters, 2003). Because there can sometimes be a time delay before the "wizard" responds, it can be helpful to have a set of pre-compiled responses that can quickly be accessed, which helps to improve the realism of the simulation (since participants typically don't know that the functionality isn't being provided by the computer system). The Wizard-of-Oz method has been used in evaluating motion-based computer games for children (Höysniemi, Hämäläinen and Turkki, 2004), spoken dialog systems in driving vehicle simulators (Hu *et al.*, 2007), and speech recognition systems (Sinha *et al.*, 2001).

Summary

While usability testing draws many approaches from established research methods, the overall goals and controls are very different. Usability engineering includes expert-based testing, automated usability testing, and user-based testing, but user-based testing still attracts the most attention and is considered the most effective. Business and development concerns help determine the type of usability testing, thoroughness of testing, and number and type of participants that take part. Usability testing is focused on practical usage in industry. Professional groups, such as the Usability Professionals Association (www.upassoc.org), provide useful information for practitioners and researchers.

Discussion Questions

1. Name two ways in which usability testing is similar to experimental design and two ways in which it is different from experimental design.
2. What business factors tend to drive the scope of usability testing?
3. Which should come first, a user-based test or an expert-based test and why?

---

[1] The name comes from the man behind the curtain in the movie *The Wizard of Oz*.

4. What is a manual check in an automated usability test?

5. What is the difference between a formative usability test and a summative usability test?

6. From a practical point of view, what business factors tend to determine how many participants take part in usability testing?

7. What are three qualities of a good task in a task list?

8. Why might it be challenging to utilize the user's personal data in a usability test?

9. What are the three most common quantitative measurements in a usability test?

10. What is the "thinking aloud" protocol and is it used more in formative or summative testing?

11. What is a reflection session?

12. What three things do you need to remind participants about before they begin a usability test?

13. Why should you not give any identification information about participants in the final usability testing report?

14. What are two good reasons for using a Wizard-of-Oz approach to testing?

15. How does a technology probe differ from a cultural probe?

Research Design Exercise

Imagine that you are planning a user-based usability test to evaluate a new interface that allows people to track online their medical information, such as blood tests, diagnostics, annual check-ups, and patient visits. Since many governments have set the goal to move to full electronic patient records in the next few years, this is an important project. Doctors will also use this application but, for this exercise, we're focused on patients. Where might you want to recruit potential participants? Would you utilize real patient data in the usability testing? What might five representative tasks be? Since privacy and security of medical data is important, how would you include tasks that assess how comfortable people are with the privacy and security of their data? Where should these usability tests take place? What type of setting would be most authentic and appropriate? How might you compare the usability of this interface with other interfaces for similar tasks? What specific steps might you take to make participants feel more at ease?

References

Andreasen, M., Nielsen, H., Schroder, S., and Stage, J. (2007) What happened to remote usability testing? An empirical study of three methods. *Proceedings of the ACM Conference on Human Factors in Computing Systems*, 1405–1414.

Atterer, R. and Schmidt, A. (2007) Tracking the interaction of users with AJAX applications for usability testing. *Proceedings of the ACM Conference on Human Factors in Computing Systems*, 1347–1350.

Au, F., Baker, S., Warren, I., and Dobbie, G. (2008) Automated usability testing framework. *Proceedings of the 9th Australasian User Interface Conference*, 55–64.

Bailey, J. and Burd, E. (2005) Web Accessibility Evolution in the United Kingdom. *Proceedings of the Seventh IEEE International Symposium on Web Site Evolution*, 79–86.

Chadwick-Dias, A., McNulty, M., and Tullis, T. (2003) Web usability and age: How design changes can improve performance. *Proceedings of the ACM Conference on Universal Usability*, 30–37.

Chen, Y., Chen, Y., and Shao, M. (2005) Accessibility diagnosis on the government web sites in Taiwan, ROC. *Proceedings of the 2006 international cross-disciplinary workshop on Web accessibility (W4A)*, 132–142.

Dahlback, N., Jonsson, A., and Ahrenberg, L. (1993) Wizard of Oz studies: Why and how. *Proceedings of the ACM International Conference on Intelligent User Interfaces (IUI)*, 193–200.

Donker, A. and Reitsma, P. (2004) Usability testing with young children. *Proceedings of the Interaction Design and Children Conference*, 43–48.

Dray, S. and Siegel, D. (2004) Remote possibilities?: International usability testing at a distance. *interactions*, **11**(2):10–17.

Dumas, J. and Fox, J. (2007) Usability testing: Current practice and future directions. In A. Sears and J. Jacko (eds), *The Human Computer Interaction Handbook*, 2nd edition, 1129–1149. New York: Lawrence Erlbaum Associates.

Dumas, J. and Loring, B. (2008) *Moderating Usability Tests: Principles and practices for interacting*. Amsterdam: Morgan Kaufmann Publishers.

Freire, A., Bittar, T., and Fortes, R. (2008) An approach based on metrics for monitoring web accessibility in Brazilian municipalities web sites. *Proceedings of the ACM Symposium on Applied Computing*, 2421–2425.

Frokjaer, E. and Hornbæk, K. (2005) Cooperative usability testing: Complementing usability tests with user-supported interpretation sessions. *Proceedings of the ACM Conference on Human Factors in Computing Systems*, 1383–1386.

Goette, T., Collier, C., and Whilte, J. (2006) An exploratory study of the accessibility of state government web sites. *Universal Access in the Information Society*, **5**(1):41–50.

Gould, J., Conti, J., and Hovanyecz, T. (1983) Composing letters with a simulated listening typewriter. *Communications of the ACM*, **26**(4):295–308.

Hartson, R., Castillo, J., Kelso, J., and Neale, W. (1996) Remote evaluation: The network as an extension of the usability laboratory. *Proceedings of the ACM Conference on Human Factors in Computing Systems*, 228–235.

Hazlett, R. (2003) Measurement of user frustration: A biologic approach. *Proceedings of the ACM Conference on Human Factors in Computing Systems*, 734–735.

Hazlett, R. (2006) Measuring emotional valence during interactive experiences: Boys at video game play. *Proceedings of the ACM Conference on Human Factors in Computing Systems*, 1023–1026.

Hollingsed, T. and Novick, D. (2007) Usability inspection methods after 15 years of research and practice. *Proceedings of the ACM Conference on Design of Communication*, 249–255.

Höysniemi, J., **Hämäläinen, P.**, **and Turkki, L.** (2004) Wizard of Oz prototyping of computer vision based action games for children. *Proceedings of the 2004 Conference on Interaction Design and Children*, 27–34.

Hu, J., **Winterboer, A.**, **Nass, C.**, *et al.* (2007) Context & usability testing: User-modeled information presentation in easy and difficult driving conditions. *Proceedings of the ACM Conference on Human Factors in Computing Systems*, 1343–1346.

Hutchinson, H., **Mackay, W.**, **Westerlund, B.**, *et al.* (2003) Technology probes: Inspiring design for and with families. *Proceedings of the ACM Conference on Human Factors in Computing Systems*, 17–24.

Ivory, M. and Hearst, M. (2001) The state of the art in automating usability evaluation of user interfaces. *ACM Computing Surveys*, **33**(4):470–516.

Kane, S., **Shulman, J.**, **Shockley, T.**, **and Ladner, R.** (2007) A web accessibility report card for top international university web sites. *Proceedings of the 2007 international cross-disciplinary conference on Web accessibility (W4A)*, 148–156.

Lazar, J. (2006) *Web Usability: A User-Centered Design Approach*. Boston: Addison-Wesley.

Lazar, J., **Beere, P.**, **Greenidge, K.**, **and Nagappa, Y.** (2003) Web Accessibility in the Mid-Atlantic United States: A Study of 50 Web Sites. *Universal Access in the Information Society*, **2**(4):331–341.

Lewis, J. (2006) Sample sizes for usability tests: Mostly math, not magic. *interactions*, **13**(6):29–33.

Lindgaard, G. and Chattratichart, J. (2007) Usability testing: What have we overlooked? *Proceedings of the ACM Conference on Human Factors in Computing Systems*, 1415–1424.

Loiacono, E. and McCoy, S. (2004) Web site accessibility: An online sector analysis. *Information Technology and People*, **17**(1):87–101.

Miller, G. (1956) The magical number seven, plus or minus two: Some limits on our capacity for processing information. *Psychological Review*, **63**(2):81–96.

Murphy, E., **Malakhoff, L.**, **and Coon, D.** (2007) Evaluating the usability and accessibility of an online form for Census Data Collection. In J. Lazar (ed.) *Universal Usability*. Chichester, UK: John Wiley & Sons Ltd, 517–558.

Nielsen, J. and Landauer, T. (1993) A mathematical model of the finding of usability problems. *Proceedings of the ACM Conference on Human Factors in Computing Systems*, 206–213.

Nielsen, **J. and Mack**, **R. (eds)** (1994) *Usability Inspection Methods*. New York: John Wiley & Sons.

O'Brian, S. and Mueller, F. (2006) Holding hands over a distance: Technology probes in an intimate, mobile context. *Proceedings of the 2006 OZCHI Conference*, 293–296.

Paris, M. (2006) Website accessibility: A survey of local e-government web sites and legislation in Northern Ireland. *Universal Access in the Information Society*, **4**(4):292–299.

Petrie, H., Hamilton, F., King, N., and Pavan, P. (2006) Remote usability evaluations with disabled people. *Proceedings of the ACM Conference on Human Factors in Computing Systems*, 1133–1141.

Preece, J., Rogers, Y., and Sharp, H. (2002) *Interaction Design: Beyond Human–Computer Interaction*. New York: John Wiley & Sons.

Rubin, J. and Chisnell, D. (2008) *Handbook of Usability Testing* (2nd. ed.). Indianapolis: Wiley Publishing.

Schusteritsch, R., Wei, C., and LaRosa, M. (2007) Towards the perfect infrastructure for usability testing on mobile devices. *Proceedings of the ACM Conference on Human Factors in Computing Systems*, 1839–1844.

Shah, B. and Shakya, S. (2007) Evaluating the web accessibility of websites of the central government of Nepal. *Proceedings of the 1st international conference on Theory and Practice of Electronic Governance*, 447–448.

Shi, Q. and Clemmensen, T. (2008) Communication patterns and usability problem finding in cross-cultural thinking aloud usability testing. *Proceedings of the ACM Conference on Human Factors in Computing Systems*, 2811–2816.

Shneiderman, B. and Plaisant, C. (2009) *Designing the User Interface: Strategies for effective human–computer interaction*, 5th edition. Boston, Massachusetts: Addison-Wesley.

Sinha, A., Klemmer, S., Chen, J., *et al.* (2001) SUEDE: Iterative, informal prototyping for speech interfaces. *Proceedings of the ACM Conference on Human Factors in Computing Systems*, 203–204.

Snyder, C. (2003) *Paper Prototyping: The fast and easy way to design and refine user interfaces.* San Francisco: Morgan Kaufmann Publishers.

Spool, J. and Schroeder, W. (2001) Testing web sites: Five users is nowhere enough. *Proceedings of the ACM Conference on Human Factors in Computing Systems*, 285–286.

Sullivan, T. and Matson, R. (2000) Barriers to use: Usability and Content Accessibility on the web's most popular sites. *Proceedings of the ACM Conference on Universal Usability*, 139–144.

Virzi, R. (1992) Refining the test phase of usability evaluation: How many subjects is enough? *Human Factors*, **34**(4):457–468.

West, R. and Lehman, K. (2006) Automated summative usability studies: An empirical evaluation. *Proceedings of the ACM Conference on Human Factors in Computing Systems*, 631–639.

White, K. and Lutters, W. (2003) Behind the curtain: Lessons learned from a Wizard of Oz field experiment. *SIGGROUP Bulletin*, **24**(3):129–135.

Wixon, D. (2003) Evaluating usability methods: Why the current literature fails the practitioner. *interactions*, **10**(4):28–34.

Zazelenchuk, T., Sortland, K., Genov, A., Sazegari, S., and Keavney, M. (2008) Using participants' real data in usability testing: lessons learned. *Proceedings of the ACM Conference on Human Factors in Computing Systems*, 2229–2236.

Analyzing qualitative data

11.1   Introduction

Both quantitative and qualitative data are frequently collected and studied in human–computer interaction (HCI) research projects. In Chapter 4, we discussed how to use significance tests to study quantitative data and measures such as speed, error rate, distance, adoption rate, and rankings. This chapter discusses strategies for analyzing qualitative data in the forms of observation or interview notes, survey responses, video and audio materials, and other data of a similar nature. We start with a general discussion of grounded theory (Glaser and Strauss, 1967), which serves as the basis for qualitative analysis. We also discuss techniques for ensuring high-quality analysis of qualitative data that is both *reliable* and *valid*. The use of context analysis to extract categories from diverse "texts" is described, along with a discussion of the analysis of two very important forms of qualitative data: text and multimedia.

The analysis of text and multimedia information is quite different from the analysis of quantitative data. Probably the most unique characteristic of content analysis is that it involves human coding. The absence of numeric data and direct measures makes qualitative data analysis more susceptible to biased interpretation or subjective manipulation. In order to control the impact of subjective interpretation, a commonly accepted coding procedure should be adopted and statistical methods are needed to evaluate the validity and reliability of the coding completed by human coders.

It should also be noted that the general strategy discussed in this chapter is just one of the many approaches available for analyzing text information. Substantially different strategies may be used for different disciplines, such as literature or art. The strategy discussed in this chapter was built on top of grounded theory. It originated from behavioral and social studies and is widely adopted in the field of HCI.

11.2   Stages of qualitative analysis

According to Corbin and Strauss (2008), qualitative data analysis generally consists of three stages. We usually start with a data set that contains information about a substance (i.e., a group of users, a specific technology, interaction behavior in a specific context, etc.). Via analysis, we hope to identify the major components of that substance. In the second stage, we drill down into each component and study the properties and dimensions of each component. In many cases, we need to understand not only the nature of each component, but also how they relate to each other. In the third stage, we use the knowledge we gained from studying each individual component to better understand the original substance and make inferences about that substance.

For example, if we are studying the online behavior of Internet users, we may find from the data that the users' online behavior is affected by their personality, education, and computer-related experience. We continue to study each of those three factors and how they relate to each other. We study the literature in psychology and sociology to understand the types of personality, how an individual forms and develops a specific personality, and how a specific type of personality affects an individual's social behavior. Once we have a thorough understanding of the three factors, we can tie the knowledge back to the original research substance "online behavior" and examine how each of the components affects a user's online behavior. It is important to note that existing experience and knowledge are critical for the appropriate interpretation of qualitative data and the entire knowledge discovery process.

11.3   Grounded theory

Grounded theory was first proposed by Glaser and Strauss (1967), who described a qualitative research method that seeks to develop theory that is "grounded in data systematically gathered and analyzed" (Myers, 2009). Grounded theory is an inductive research method that is fundamentally different from the traditional experimental research methods described in Chapters 2 and 3. As demonstrated in Figure 11.1, when conducting experimental research, we normally start from a pre-formed theory, typically in the form of one or more hypotheses, we then conduct experiments to collect data and use the data to prove the theory. In contrast, grounded theory starts from a set of empirical observations or data and we aim to develop a well-grounded theory from the data. During the process of theory development, multiple rounds of data collection and analysis may be conducted to allow the underlying theory to fully emerge from the data (Corbin and Strauss, 2008; Myers, 1997). Therefore, some researchers refer to the theory generated using this method as the "reverse-engineered" hypothesis.

Grounded theory can be applied to a variety of research methods discussed in this book such as ethnography (Chapter 9), observation (Chapter 9), case studies (Chapter 7), and interviews (Chapter 8). The major difference between qualitative research strategies

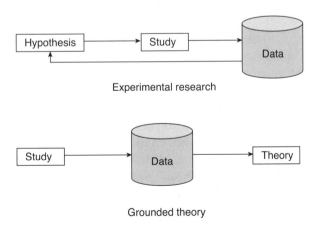

Figure 11.1 Experimental research compared with grounded theory.

that are mainly descriptive or exploratory and grounded theory is its emphasis on theory development from continuous interplay between data collection and data analysis.

Because grounded theory does not start from a pre-formed concept or hypothesis, but from a set of data, it is important for researchers to start the research process without any preconceived theoretical ideas so that the concepts and theory truly emerge from the data. The key to conducting successful grounded theory research is to be creative and have an open mind (Myers, 2009). Since grounded theory was first proposed in 1967, opinions on how to conduct research using grounded theory have diverged (Glaser, 1992; Strauss, 1987; Strauss and Corbin, 1990). The founders disagree on whether grounded theory can be formalized into a set of clear guidelines and procedures. Glaser believes that the procedures are far too restrictive and may contradict the very basis of this method: creativity and an open mind. Even with the public disagreement, the procedures and guidelines proposed by Strauss and Corbin have been widely used in the field of social science, probably partly due to the fact that the procedure makes grounded theory more tangible and easier to implement. We briefly introduce the procedures of grounded theory according to Strauss and Corbin (1990). For more details on grounded theory and Glaser's approach, please refer to the publications in the reference list.

The grounded theory method generally consists of four stages:

- open coding;
- development of concepts;
- grouping concepts into categories;
- formation of a theory.

In the open coding stage, we analyze the text and identify any interesting phenomena in the data. Normally each unique phenomenon is given a distinctive name or code. The procedure and methods for identifying coding items are discussed in section 11.5.2. In the second stage, collections of codes that describe similar contents are grouped together to form higher level "concepts." In the third stage, broader groups of similar concepts are identified to form "categories" and there is a detailed interpretation of each category. In this process, we are constantly searching for and refining the conceptual construct that may explain the relationship between the concepts and categories (Glaser, 1978). In the last stage, theory formulation, we aim at creating inferential and predictive statements about the phenomena recorded in the data. More specifically, we develop explicit causal connections or correlations between the concepts and categories identified in the previous stages.

While conducting research using grounded theory, it is important to fully understand the advantages and limitations of this research method. Grounded theory obviously has a number of advantages. First, it provides a systematic approach to analyzing qualitative, mostly text-based, data, which is impossible using the traditional experimental approach. Second, compared to the other qualitative research methods, grounded theory allows researchers to generate theory out of qualitative data that can be backed up by ample evidence as demonstrated in the thorough coding. This is one of the major attractions of the grounded theory and even novice users found the procedure intuitive to follow. Third, grounded theory encourages researchers to study the data early on and formulate and refine the theory through constant interplay between data collection and analysis (Myers, 2009).

On the other hand, the advantages of grounded theory can become disadvantages at times. It is not uncommon for novices to find themselves overwhelmed during the coding stage. The emphasis on detailed and thorough coding can cause researchers to be buried in details and feel lost in the data, making it difficult to identify the higher-level concepts and themes that are critical for theory formulation. In addition, theories developed using this method may be hard to evaluate. Unlike the traditional experimental approach in which the hypothesis is clearly supported or rejected by quantitative data collected through well-controlled, replicable experiments, grounded theory starts from textual information and undergoes multiple rounds of data collection and coding before the theory fully emerges from the data. The evaluation of the outcome depends on measures that are less direct, such as the chain of evidence between the finding and the data, the number of instances in the data that support the specific concept, and the familiarity of the researcher with the related topic. Lastly, the findings of the grounded theory approach may be influenced by the researchers' pre-conceived opinions and, therefore, may be subject to biases. In order to avoid these issues from happening, researchers should always keep in mind the key of this approach: being creative and open minded; listening to the data. When there is a gap between the concept and the data, additional data need to be collected to fill in the gap and tighten the linkage between the concept and the data. Due to these limitations, some researchers prefer to use grounded theory just as a coding technique, not as a theory generation method.

11.4   Content analysis

Content analysis is widely used in vastly different domains. There are various definitions of content analysis. Stemler (2001) summarized previous work and stated that content analysis is a systematic, replicable technique for compressing many words of text into fewer content categories based on explicit rules of coding (Berelson, 1952). This definition is specific and limits content analysis to the domain of textual information. A broader definition proposed by Holsti (1969) states that content analysis is "any technique for making inferences by objectively and systematically identifying specified characteristics of messages." According to this definition, content analysis not only applies to textual information, but also to multimedia materials, such as drawings, music, and videos.

Content analysis is normally in-depth analysis that searches for theoretical interpretations that may generate new knowledge. As described by Corbin and Strauss (2008), this type of analysis "presents description that embodies well-constructed themes/categories, development of context, and explanations of process or change over time." Although many people think content analysis is a qualitative research method, both quantitative and qualitative techniques are used in the process of content analysis (Neuendorf, 2002).

11.4.1   What is content?

The target of content analysis usually covers two categories: media content and audience content. Media content can be any material in printed publications (e.g., books, journals, magazines, newspapers, and brochures), broadcast programs (e.g., TV or radio programs), websites (e.g., news websites, web portals, personal websites, or blogs), or any other types of recording (e.g., photos, films, or music).

Audience content is feedback directly or indirectly collected from an audience group. Audience content can be collected through a variety of methods such as surveys, questionnaires, interviews, focus groups, diaries, and observations. Traditionally, information collected via those methods is text-based. Recently, multimedia content is collected in addition to text-based information thanks to convenient, low-cost audio- and video-recording devices. In the HCI field, researchers and practitioners frequently collect both text-based information and multimedia-based information from the participants.

11.4.2   Why do we need to collect text or multimedia information?

Text and multimedia information are great sources for researchers and practitioners to better understand their users or the interaction between their users and applications. Often, short interviews are conducted at the end of lab-based user studies to collect information on how the user feels about the application and suggestions for improvement. In surveys, it is common practice to offer a combination of closed-ended questions and open-ended questions. Some open-ended questions collect quantitative data such as age, years of computing experience, number of hours spent on the Internet per week, etc. Other open-ended questions collect text-based user input on a specific aspect of the application or the user.

Text-based data can provide information that can hardly be delivered through quantitative data. For example, in an empirical study that evaluates predictive typing software, you can recruit participants to enter some text using the software and record objective quantitative measures such as words generated per minute, number of words containing typos, etc. Those measures can be compared with performance measures collected under conditions without the word prediction software so that you know whether the use of the word prediction software improves efficiency and accuracy. However, those quantitative measures may not help much if you want to find out the underlying challenges that the users experienced when they used the software, the features that they like or dislike, or their suggestions for improving the software. So it is generally recommended to include questions in the post-session survey or interview to collect information on specific interaction obstacles and design recommendations.

Similarly, multimedia data serves as a critical information source for researchers and practitioners. During lots of user studies, the researchers record both audio and video information about the user and the computer screen. For some studies, the audio and video recording is necessary for basic data analysis. For example, when studying speech-based

Category	Sub-category	Examples
Media content	Publications	Books, journals, newspapers, brochures
	Broadcasting	TV programs, radio programs
	Websites	News, web portals, organizational websites, blogs
	Others	Films, music, photos
Audience content	Text	Notes from interviews, focus groups, or observations or diaries or surveys
	Multimedia	Video- or audio-recording of interviews, focus groups, observations, or user studies

Table 11.1 Major categories of content.

interaction, you need to evaluate the recognition error rate, which requires comparison between the audio record and the system output. Text or multimedia information used for content analysis can be collected through a variety of methods listed in Table 11.1. For more detailed information on each of those data collection methods, please refer to Chapters 5 to 9.

11.4.3 Questions to consider before content analysis

Before you start analyzing the data, you need to consider several questions that can help frame the scope of the content analysis as well as the specific techniques that should be used for the analysis (Krippendorff, 1980). First, you need to have a clear definition for the data set that is going to be analyzed. In some studies the definition of the data set is very straightforward. For example, if you interview 10 mobile device users on their daily usage of the device, the interview notes would be the data set that you are going to analyze. In other cases, the definition of the data set may not be that straightforward and special consideration is needed to select the appropriate content or messages that should be included in the data set. Suppose you want to study the development of interpersonal trust among members of an online community. The public messages that the community members leave on the bulletin board may contain valuable information. The messages that the community members exchange privately through applications such as Instant Messaging or email would also be useful. In this case, you need to consider the scope of your data set: Do you want to study the public messages only, the private messages only, or both? The answer to this question depends on both your research question and the practical issues of your study. If your research question is focused on the impact of the general community atmosphere and the sense of community on trust development, you may want to limit the data set to the public messages because they are the most relevant to your research question. In some cases, you may have to stick to the public messages because you have no access to the messages that are exchanged privately among the community members. You may also restrict the data set to messages posted during a specific time period. Overall, the scope of your data set may affect the key words or categories that you are going to use during the content analysis.

Once a clear definition of the data set is specified, you need to study the data closely and remove any data that do not meet the criteria of the definition. In the online community study example, if you decide to study the public messages posted in 2008, then all the private messages must be abandoned. Any public messages posted outside the time range also need to be filtered out. If those messages remain in the data set and are analyzed, the data set is polluted and the results may be biased or misleading.

You also need to clearly define the population from which the data set is drawn. This seems to be straightforward but many issues may be encountered in practice. In the online community study example, the term "community members" may raise some questions. How do you define community members? Do community members include all the people who have visited the online community website? If the answer to this question is "yes," it means you are interested in examining not only those visitors who have posted messages, but also the people who have visited the website but have never posted a message (lurkers). If your data set only consists of the public messages, then the data comes from a subset of your population (those who have contributed by posting messages) and, therefore, it is not representative of the overall population. In this case, it may be more appropriate to restrict the target population of your study to those people who have posted messages. And this may not be the end of the story either. You may find that the number of postings vary dramatically among those visitors who have posted messages. Some people might visit and post messages on a daily basis. Some people might only post one or two messages through the entire year. Do you count those extremely infrequent visitors as community members? If so, there may be concerns over whether those visitors' opinion or behavior is sufficiently reflected in the data set because the number of messages generated by them is very limited. Other factors that you need to consider when defining the population include, but are not limited to, age, gender, profession, education, and domain experience.

Thirdly, you need to know the specific context of the data. Data analysis out of context is meaningless and highly biased. Any words, terms, and claims need to be interpreted in the specific context from which they are extracted. There are different levels of context. Before the data analysis, you need to have a clear understanding of the higher-level context of your data set. For example, if you are studying the end-user's attitude toward security procedures in the organizational environment, you need to be aware that the type of business or profession may have a notable impact on the topic. An employee of a government agency who has access to classified information works in a very different environment from a person who works in an entertainment facility. The government worker may have to go through security training on a regular basis while the person working in the entertainment industry may have no security-related training. Therefore, the specific context of their work has great impact on the data that they provide. If you analyze their input without considering the context, it is like comparing apples with pears and the results are tainted. During the data analysis process, you need to consider lower-level context, such as the phrase, sentence, or paragraph. We discuss the interpretation of low-level context in Section 11.5.3.

11.5   Analyzing text content

The technical process and technique used to analyze text content is called "coding." A common misunderstanding is that coding is nothing more than paraphrasing the text and counting the number of key words in the text. Actually, coding is much more than paraphrasing and key word counts. As stated by Corbin and Strauss (2008; p. 66), coding "involves interacting with data, making comparisons between data, and so on, and in doing so, deriving concepts to stand for those data, then developing those concepts in terms of their properties and dimensions." A set of well-developed procedures for analyzing text content has been widely accepted in the social sciences and related fields. Because qualitative research is more vulnerable to bias than quantitative research, it is particularly important to follow the standard procedure to ensure the quality of the analysis and the robustness of the results.

11.5.1   Procedure

A typical procedure for content analysis starts with a set of text-based data. There are two different approaches to analyzing the data: a priori coding and emergent coding. If you take the a priori coding approach, the first stage of the analysis is to identify the potential coding categories or items based on established theories or frameworks in the related literature. After the major coding categories are identified, you can proceed to code the text data. To control subjective interpretation, normally more than one coder is needed to code the same data. Once the coding task is completed, a reliability check is needed to ensure that the coding is consistent. This approach works well in situations when you are investigating topics that have been studied before and the related literature is sufficient for the establishment of the coding categories.

If you are working on a new topic that has very limited literature to build on, you may not be able to find established theories that allow you to develop the coding categories in advance. In this case, the emergent coding approach is appropriate. Following this process, multiple researchers first examine a subset of the data independently and each develops a list of key coding categories based on their interpretation of the data. The researchers compare their category lists, discuss the differences, and reach a consolidated list that all agree upon. Then each of them applies coding independently using the consolidated list. In the next step, the codes of multiple coders are compared and reliability measures are computed. If a satisfactory reliability level is achieved, the coders can move on to code the entire data set. If the reliability evaluation is poor, the researchers need to repeat the process until a satisfactory reliability level is achieved. In the following sections, we discuss in detail how to identify coding categories, how to do the actual coding, and how to conduct a reliability check during and after the coding process.

11.5.2   Identifying coding categories

Solid qualitative analysis depends on accurately identified concepts that later serve as "categories for which data are sought and in which data are grouped" (Blumer, 1969). The concepts and categories are also a means of establishing relations (e.g., correlation, causal relationships, etc.) between different entities. Identifying the coding categories can be a very daunting task for inexperienced researchers. The coding categories may come from several sources: an existing theoretical framework, the researcher's interpretation (research-denoted concepts), and original terms provided by the participants (in-vivo codes).

11.5.2.1   Theoretical framework

Theoretical frameworks are commonly used in multiple stages of qualitative research (Corbin and Strauss, 2008). In the research design stage, theoretical frameworks can help you frame the research questions, decide on the specific research approach to adopt (i.e., survey, interview, focus group, etc.), and identify the concepts and questions to be included in each approach. When analyzing text information, theoretical frameworks can help you identify the major categories and items that need to be coded and explain the findings of your research. Therefore, at the beginning of a research project, it is important to study the research literature and find out whether there is any theoretical framework related to the research topic that you are investigating.

For example, suppose you interview a number of senior citizens to examine the major difficulties that they experience when using computers. One question you would like to answer is the underlying cause of those difficulties. You know a large proportion of the difficulties can be attributed to the gradual decline of human capabilities. According to well-established literature, human capabilities can be grouped into three major categories: cognitive, physical, and perceptual abilities. You can use those three types of capability as the high-level categories of your coding scheme and try to group the participants' responses in each of those three categories.

In the HCI field, theoretical frameworks are also called taxonomies and numerous taxonomies have been developed to help guide research and understand the data collected through various user studies. One example of the earlier taxonomies proposed is about the types of task that users conduct (Norman, 1991). By grouping tasks into categories, such as "structured and unstructured" or "regular and intermittent", and summarizing the different nature and requirements of each type of task, researchers and designers can study the interaction in a consistent way and make easier connections between different aspects of the result. For a comprehensive discussion on task analysis, see Courage, Redish and Wixon (2007). Another widely cited taxonomy in the HCI field groups human errors into mistakes and slips (Norman, 2002). Slips can be further categorized into capture errors, description errors, data-driven errors, associative-activation errors, loss-of-activation errors, and mode errors. Each type of slip has different causes, and different design techniques can be used to help prevent, detect, and recover from those errors. Well-studied and validated taxonomies can provide great insights for identifying the potential categories to be included for coding.

11.5.2.2 Researcher-denoted concepts

In many cases, especially when you are studying a new topic, you may find that there is no appropriate theory to apply and you have to establish the coding categories from scratch. Under this circumstance, you start from your data and try to identify the patterns, opinions, behaviors, or other issues that sound interesting. Since you are not constrained by pre-established theories, frameworks, or concepts, you are open to all possibilities that reside in the data. Corbin and Strauss (2008) refer to this process as *open coding*. During this process, you need to find terms to describe the interesting instances that emerge from the data. Those terms are called "researcher-denoted concepts." For example, if you read the following descriptions in the data, you may use the term "frustration" to describe the underlying theme of both responses:

> *My son just sits there and sobs when the computer does not do what he wants.*
> *He becomes irritated and keeps pushing the Enter button when the web page loads slowly.*

11.5.2.3 In-vivo codes

Sometimes the participants may provide a term that describes the instances so vividly or accurately that you can borrow the term directly and use it as a high-level or low-level category. Coding categories generated in this manner are called *in-vivo code*. In one survey that the authors conducted recently on computer usage by children with Down syndrome, we borrowed the term "curriculum integration" directly from one parent's response and used it as a low-level theme.

11.5.2.4 Building a code structure

After the key coding items are identified, they can be organized and presented in a code list (also called a "nomenclature"). A nomenclature is a list of numbered categories intended to represent the full array of possible responses to a specific question (Lyberg and Kasparzyk, 1997). When coding the content, the respondents may talk about the same idea or concept in various terms or presentations. The code list can help the analyst to group objects of responses that are similar or related. A code list is normally built into a hierarchical structure, containing multiple levels, each level representing concepts with increasing amounts of detail. Building a code structure is not an easy task. It requires both extensive knowledge of the existing theories and literature and a deep understanding of the data collected. Many times, the analyst needs to make compromises between the theoretical framework and the practical aspects of the study.

11.5.3   Coding the text

When the data set is not large, which is typically true for interviews, focus groups, or observations, it is recommended to read the text from beginning to end before starting to do any coding. During the first round of reading, you may find interesting issues and feel the urge to write among the text or in the margins. Those activities should wait until you start the coding. The purpose of this first round of reading is to immerse you into the life and experience of the participants and get a general, unbiased idea of the data set before focusing on any specific aspects.

Inexperienced coders may find it difficult to identify anything interesting (or anything that is worth being coded) in the data, especially when the coding category is not established and they are doing open coding to identify coding categories or themes. Other coders may experience the other end of the scale: they may feel that the data is so rich they need to code almost every word or phrase. Eventually they may be overwhelmed by the large number of coding items that they are trying to document. They may be distracted by the less important or even trivial coding items and fail to identify the most interesting or informative patterns in the data. In order to avoid both situations, we recommend the following steps for coding:

1. Look for specific items.
2. Ask questions constantly about the data.
3. Making comparisons constantly at various levels.

We'll discuss these steps in the following sections.

11.5.3.1   Look for key items

While coding the data, specific "statements" are more likely to carry valuable information. These statements are summarized in Table 11.2. Note that it is only a sample list of statements, not an exhaustive list. Data collected from specific fields may have unique groups of items that are particularly important.

Statement	Examples
Objectives	Use computers for educational purposes
Actions	Enter a password, chat online
Outcomes	Success or failure, whether the objective is achieved
Consequences	Files unintentionally deleted, a specific application abandoned
Causes	Limited memory, dated equipment
Contexts	User is computer savvy, user works with classified information
Strategies	Avoid specific tasks, multimodal interaction

Table 11.2 What to look for while coding.

Objectives deliver important information. A user's computer usage behavior and interaction style is largely affected by the objectives that they want to achieve. If a user uses a specific application just for entertainment, it may be unrealistic to expect the user to devote a substantial amount of time to learning how to use the application. It would be totally different if the application is a critical tool at work.

Words, phrases, and sentences that describe actions are also important. They tell you what the users do with the specific application or technique. They also tell you what functions are frequently used and what are less frequently used. Once you detect an action code in the data, you can follow up on that and examine whether the user described the outcome of the action. Was the action successfully completed? Did the action completely fail? Was the action partially completed? Whenever an action is not completely successful, you may want to pursue the consequences or costs of the unsuccessful action: Is the consequence highly detrimental? Does it cause the user to lose several days of work? Does it prevent the user from completing some tasks on time? Is it a minor nuisance or is it so frustrating that the user decides to abandon the action?

Causes are also associated with failed actions. Whenever an action completely or partially fails, it is worth pursuing the causes of the failure. Does the failure trace back to the user or the application? If it is caused by the user, what kinds of capability are involved? Is it due to cognitive overload? Is it due to lack of attention? Or is it due to physical or perceptual limitations? Statements about the context of the interaction or usage are also important. Different types of user may report different satisfaction levels for the same application with similar performance measures because the comparison context is drastically different (Sears *et al.*, 2001). Finally, descriptions of interaction styles and strategies are also valuable information that is hard to examine during empirical lab-based studies.

11.5.3.2   *Ask questions about the data*

A good way to help detect interesting patterns and connections in data is to constantly ask questions about the data. In Section 11.5.3.1, we listed a series of questions that you can ask once you identify an interesting action in the data. Those questions can be related to the specific action, its outcome, and its consequence, as well as the causes of failed actions. Most of those questions are practical questions that may help you identify interaction challenges and design flaws.

Corbin and Strauss (2008) discussed the art of asking questions in a larger context with the primary objective of theory development. They proposed four types of question and two of them are particularly important during the analysis phase: sensitizing questions and theoretical questions. Sensitizing questions help coders to better understand the meaning of the data: What is happening here? What did the user click? How did the user reach the specific web page? Theoretical questions help the researchers make connections between concepts and categories: What is the relationship between two factors? How does the interaction change over time?

11.5.3.3   Making comparisons of data

Both during the coding process and the stage afterwards to interpret the results, you are encouraged to make comparisons at multiple levels. First, you can compare instances under different coding categories. For example, if you are investigating the difficulties that older people experience when using computers, you can compare the frequency with which each capability (physical, cognitive, perceptual) is reported. You can also compare the degree of impact between different capabilities.

Secondly, you can compare the results between different participant groups. You may find that the capabilities and computer usage behaviors vary substantially among the users. You can further investigate this diversity via different dimensions: Is the diversity related to age, educational background, or community and family support? To answer these questions, you need to subdivide the data set and compare the results among subsets.

Thirdly, you can compare the findings in your data to previously reported literature. Do your findings align with the existing literature or is it contradictory? If your findings differ from existing literature, can you explain why? Is the existing literature incorrect? Or is the difference caused by a different context? Sometimes the need to compare your findings with a related population or tasks may facilitate you to conduct additional studies to collect more data. For example, if you observe some interesting computer usage behavior in children with autism, you may want to conduct the same study for neurotypical children to investigate whether there is a difference between the neurotypical children and autistic children.

11.5.3.4   Using computer software

A large number of computer software tools can be used to facilitate the coding process. Some software focuses on dictionary-based content analysis and offers basic functions such as keyword searching and counting, sorting, and simple statistics. Examples of this type of software include CATPAC, LIWC, SPSS TextSmart, and Concordance. The second group of software tools provides a more effective development environment for content analysis. They are designed to facilitate the construction of dictionaries, but do not automatically code the data themselves. Examples of this type of software include DIMAP and Visual Text. For more detailed information on content analysis software, please refer to Lowe (2003).

11.5.4   Ensuring high-quality analysis

Qualitative data analysis is not objective. During the data–coding process, a human researcher makes a series of decisions regarding the interpretation of individual observations: Which category does this item belong in? Are these items really members of the same group or should they be separated? No matter how expert the judgment of the individual making these decisions, the possibility of some conscious or unconscious bias exists. Given the inherent fallibility of human researchers, how can we increase our confidence in the results of qualitative analysis? More specifically, how can we make our qualitative analysis *valid* and *reliable*?

Before we can answer that question, we must be clear on what we mean by these terms. In terms of qualitative research, *validity* means that we use well-established and well-documented procedures to increase the accuracy of findings (Creswell, 2009). In other words, did we get it right? *Reliability* refers to the consistency of results (Creswell, 2009): if different researchers working on a common data set come to similar conclusions, those conclusions are said to be reliable.

11.5.4.1 Validity

Establishing validity implies constructing a multi-faceted argument in favor of your interpretation of the data. If you can show that your interpretation is firmly grounded in the data, you go a long way towards establishing validity. The first step in this process is often the construction of a database (Yin, 2003) that includes all the materials that you collect and create during the course of the study, including notes, documents, photos, and tables. Procedures and products of your analysis, including summaries, explanations, and tabular presentations of data can be included in the database as well.

If your raw data is well-organized in your database, you can trace the analytic results back to the raw data, verifying that relevant details behind the cases and the circumstances of data collection are similar enough to warrant comparisons between observations. This linkage forms a chain of evidence, indicating how the data supports your conclusions (Yin, 2003). Analytic results and descriptions of this chain of evidence can be included in your database, providing a roadmap for further analysis.

A database can also provide increased reliability. If you decide to repeat your experiment, clear documentation of the procedures is crucial and careful repetition of both the original protocol and the analytic steps can be a convincing approach for documenting the consistency of the approaches.

Well-documented data and procedures are necessary, but not sufficient for establishing validity. A very real validity concern involves the question of the confidence that you might have in any given interpretive result. If you can only find one piece of evidence for a given conclusion, you might be somewhat wary. However, if you begin to see multiple, independent pieces of data that all point in a common direction, your confidence in the resulting conclusion might increase. The use of multiple data sources to support an interpretation is known as *data source triangulation* (Stake, 1995). The data sources may be different instances of the same type of data (for example, multiple participants in interview research) or completely different sources of data (for example, observation and time diaries).

Interpretations that account for all – or as much as possible – of the observed data are easier to defend as being valid. It may be very tempting to stress observations that support your pet theory, while downplaying those that may be more consistent with alternative explanations. Although some amount of subjectivity in your analysis is unavoidable, you should try to minimize your bias as much as possible. Give every data point the attention and scrutiny it deserves, and keep an open mind for alternative explanations that may explain your observations as well as (or better than) your pet theories.

You might even develop some alternative explanations as you go along. These alternatives provide a useful reality check: if you are constantly re-evaluating both your theory and some possible alternatives to see which best match the data, you know when your theory starts to look less compelling (Yin, 2003). This may not be a bad thing – rival explanations that you might never find if you cherry-picked your data may actually be more interesting than your original theory. Whichever explanations best match your data, you can always present them alongside the less successful alternatives. A discussion that shows not only how a given model fits the data but how it is a better fit than plausible alternatives can be particularly compelling.

11.5.4.2   Reliability

The ambiguous data that is the focus of content analysis exemplifies many of the reliability challenges presented by qualitative data analysis. The same word may have different meanings in different contexts. Different terms or expressions may suggest the same meaning. The data may be even more ambiguous when it comes to the interpretation of body language, facial expression, gestures, or art work. The same people may interpret the same gesture differently after viewing it at different times. In many studies, the data set is very large and multiple coders may code different subsets of the data. Due to the nature of content analysis, it is more vulnerable to biases and inconsistencies than the traditional quantitative approach. Therefore, it is particularly important to follow specific procedures during the coding process and use various measures to evaluate the quality of the coding. The ultimate goal of reliability control is to ensure that different people code the same text in the same way (Weber, 1990).

Reliability checks span two dimensions: stability and reproducibility. Stability is also called *intra-coder reliability*. It examines whether the same coder rates the data in the same way throughout the coding process. In other words, if the coder is asked to code the same data multiple times is the coding consistent time after time? If the coder produces codes that shows 50% in category A, 30% in category B, and 20% in category C the first time; then 20% in category A, 20% in category B, and 60% in category C the second time, the coding is inconsistent and the intra-coder reliability is very low.

Reproducibility is also called *inter-coder reliability* or *investigator triangulation* (Stake, 1995). It examines whether different coders code the same data in a consistent way. In other words, if two or more coders are asked to code the same data, is their coding consistent? In this case, if one coder produces codes that shows 50% in category A, 30% in category B, and 20% in category C; while the other coder produces codes that show 20% in category A, 20% in category B, and 60% in category C, then the coding is inconsistent and the inter-coder reliability is very low.

A further step in demonstrating reliability might use multiple coders specifically chosen for differences in background or theoretical perspectives, leading to a theoretical triangulation (Stake, 1995). If individuals with substantially different intellectual frameworks arrive at similar conclusions, those results may be seen as being very reliable.

In order to achieve reliable coding both from the same coder and among multiple coders, it is critical to develop a set of explicit coding instructions at the beginning of the coding process. After that, all the coders need to be trained so that they fully understand the instructions and every single coding item. The coders then test code some data. The coded data is examined and reliability measures are calculated. If the desired reliability level is achieved, the coders can start the formal coding. If the desired reliability level is not achieved, the coders need to go through the training and text coding process again until the desired reliability level is met. After the formal coding process starts, it is important to conduct reliability checks frequently so that inconsistent coding can be detected as early as possible.

One of the commonly used reliability measures is the percentage of agreement among coders, calculated according to the following equation:

% agreement = the number of cases coded the same way by multiple coders/

the total number of cases

When analyzing a survey on software and technology for children with autism, Putnam and Chong (2008) coded the data independently and reported a 94% agreement between the two coders, which is quite a satisfactory level. However, the percentage agreement approach does have a limitation: it does not account for the fact that several coders would agree with each other for a certain percentage of cases even when they just code the data by chance. Depending on the specific feature of the coding, that percentage may be quite substantial.

To address this limitation, you can adopt other measures such as Cohen's Kappa. The value of Kappa ranges between 0 and 1, with 0 meaning that the cases that are coded the same are completely by chance and 1 meaning perfect reliability. Kappa is calculated by the following equation:

$$K = (P_a - P_c)/(1 - P_c)$$

where P_a represents the percentage of cases on which the coders agree and P_c represents the percentage of agreed cases when the data is coded by chance.

Suppose we conduct a survey of senior citizens and ask them to describe the primary causes of the difficulties that they encounter when using computers. We identify three major categories of causes: difficulties due to physical capabilities, difficulties due to cognitive capabilities, and difficulties due to perceptual capabilities. Two coders code the data independently. Their coding results are summarized in Table 11.3. The diagonal line from top left shows the percentages of cases on which the coders agreed. For example, the number of

		Coder 2			
		Physical	Cognitive	Perceptual	Marginal total
Coder 1	Physical	0.26 (0.14)	0.07 (0.08)	0.04 (0.15)	0.37
	Cognitive	0.04 (0.07)	0.12 (0.04)	0.01 (0.07)	0.17
	Perceptual	0.09 (0.18)	0.02 (0.10)	0.35 (0.18)	0.46
	Marginal total	0.39	0.21	0.40	1.00

Table 11.3 The distribution of coded items under each category by two coders (agreement matrix).

cases that both coders coded under the "physical difficulty" category accounts for 26% of the total number of cases. The other cells contain the cases on which the two coders disagreed (i.e., 7% of the cases were coded under "physical difficulties" by the first coder and under "cognitive difficulties" by the second coder). The "marginal totals" are calculated by adding up the values in each row or column. The "marginal total" values always add up to one. The value in parentheses in each cell represents the expected percentage agreement when the data is coded by chance, calculated by multiplying the marginal totals of the corresponding row and column (i.e., the expected percentage agreement for (physical, physical) is $0.37 * 0.39 = 0.14$).

Based on the data provided by Table 11.3, we can compute the value of P_a as:

$$P_a = 0.26 + 0.12 + 0.35 = 0.73$$

The value of P_c is computed by adding the expected percentage agreement (in parentheses on the diagonal):

$$P_c = 0.14 + 0.04 + 0.18 = 0.36$$

Therefore,

$$K = (0.73 - 0.36)/(1 - 0.36) = 0.58$$

A well-accepted interpretation of Cohen's Kappa is that a value above 0.60 indicates satisfactory reliability. Table 11.4 summarizes a more detailed interpretation of Cohen's Kappa (Altman, 1991; Landis and Koch, 1977). When the value of Kappa is below 0.60, the reliability of the analysis is questionable and the researchers need to re-evaluate and possibly modify the category definition and the coding instructions. The coders may need to go through another round of test coding to improve the consistency of their coding.

In addition to the percentage agreement and Cohen's Kappa, there are several other coefficients that measure coder agreement, such as Osgood's coefficient (also named CR) proposed by Osgood (1959) and the S coefficient proposed by Bennett, Alpert and Goldstein

Interpretation	Kappa range
Poor or slight agreement	$K \leq 0.20$
Fair agreement	$0.20 < K \leq 0.40$
Moderate agreement	$0.40 < K \leq 0.60$
Satisfactory agreement	$0.60 < K \leq 0.80$
Near-perfect agreement	$K > 0.80$

Table 11.4 Interpretation of Cohen's Kappa.

(1954). For detailed discussion of the differences among the agreement measures, please see Krippendorff (2004).

11.5.4.3 Subjective vs. objective coders

You should be aware of the advantages and disadvantages of using subjective or objective coders and their impact on coding reliability. When the coders are the same people who developed the coding scheme, and in many cases they also design the study and collect the data, they are called *subjective* or *inside* coders. When the coders are not involved in the design of the study, the data collection, or the development of the coding scheme, they are called *objective* or *outside* coders.

There are pros and cons to both approaches. Because subjective coders are usually the researchers themselves, they know the literature well and have substantial knowledge and expertise in the related topic. That knowledge and specialty can help them understand the terms and concepts provided by participants and detect the underlying themes in the text. They also require minimal training since they developed the coding scheme themselves. However, the fact that they have already worked so closely with the data becomes a disadvantage during the actual coding. The pre-acquired knowledge may constrain their abilities to think beyond the established concepts in their mind. Sometimes they may form hidden meanings of the coding without being aware of it. The consequence is that the reliability reported by subjective coders may be inflated (Krippendorff, 1980).

On the contrary, objective coders usually do not have pre-acquired knowledge of the subject and, therefore, may be more open to potential instances in the data. The reliability reported by objective coders is less likely to be inflated. However, their lack of domain knowledge and expertise may also hinder their ability to accurately understand the data and detect interesting instances. In addition, objective coders usually need a substantial amount of training and the entire process can be very costly.

In practice, it is very common for studies to use subjective coders for content analysis and this approach is usually considered acceptable as long as the appropriate procedure is followed and the reliability measure is reported.

11.6   Analyzing multimedia content

Multimedia data has become prevalent in our daily life thanks to the rapid advances in affordable portable electronic devices and storage technologies. Researchers can collect a large quantity of image, audio, and video data at fairly low cost. Multimedia information such as screen shots, cursor movement tracks, facial expressions, gestures, pictures, sound, and videos provide researchers with an amazingly rich pool of data to study how the users interact with computers or computer-related devices.

Multimedia information also presents substantial challenges for data analysis. In order to find interesting patterns in the interactions, the image, audio, and video data need to be coded for specific instances (i.e., a specific gesture, event, or sound). Without the support of automated tools, the researcher would have to manually go through hours of audio or video recordings to identify and code the instances of specific interest. This process can be extremely time-consuming, tedious, and in many cases, impractical.

The basic guidelines for analyzing text content also apply to multimedia content. Before you start analyzing the data, you need to study the literature and think about the scope, context, and objective of your study. You need to identify the key instances that you want to describe or annotate. After the analysis, you need to evaluate the reliability of the annotation. If a manual annotation approach is adopted, it may be a good idea to select a subset of the entire data set for analysis due to high labor cost. For example, Peltonen *et al.* (2008) picked eight days of data from a study that lasted for one month. They first automatically partitioned the video footage into small "sessions," then manually coded the information that they were interested in (the duration of interaction, the number of active users, and the number of passive bystanders).

Another application domain related to multimedia content analysis is the online search of media content. There is a huge amount of images, videos, and audios on the web. Users frequently go online to search for images, videos, or audio materials. Currently, most of the multimedia search is completed by text-based retrieval, which means that the multimedia materials have to be annotated or labeled with appropriate text. So far, annotation can be accomplished through three approaches: manual annotation, partially automated annotation, and completely automated annotation.

Considering the huge amount of information that needs to be annotated, the manual approach is extremely labor intensive. In addition, it can also be affected by the coder's subjective interpretation. The completely automated approach is less labor intensive. However, due to the substantial semantic gap between the low-level features that we can currently automatically extract and the high-level concepts that are of real interest to the user, existing automatic annotation applications are highly error prone (i.e., many images that have nothing to do with cats may be annotated with "cat" using this automatic annotation). A more recent development in this field is the partially automated approach. Human coders manually annotate a subset of the multimedia data. Then the manually coded data is used to train the application to establish the connection between the low-level features and the high-level concept. Once a concept detector is established, the detector can be used to automatically annotate the rest of the data (Rui and Qi, 2007). The same approach can be applied to images and video and audio clips.

The techniques for multimedia content analysis are built on top of multiple domains including image processing, computer vision, pattern recognition and graphics. One of the commonly adopted approaches used by all those fields is machine learning. The specific algorithms or techniques of multimedia content analysis are still seeing dramatic advances. For more detailed information on those topics, see publications in the related fields (Chang, Hanjalic and Sebe, 2006; Sebe *et al.*, 2007). The specific applications that are particularly interesting to the HCI field include action recognition and motion tracking (Zhu *et al.*, 2006), body tracking (Li *et al.*, 2006), face recognition, facial expression analysis (Wu, *et al.*, 2006), gesture recognition (Argyros and Lourakis, 2006), object classification and tracking (Dedeoğlu *et al.*, 2006), and voice activity detection (Xue *et al.*, 2006). A substantial number of studies have focused on automatic annotation and management of images. A number of applications, such as PodScope, EveryZing, and Plugged, allow the retrieval of speech information.

In addition to the automatic annotation applications, a number of other tools have been developed to facilitate the process of multimedia content analysis. Dragicevic *et al.* (2008) developed a direct manipulation video player that allows a video analyst to directly drag and move the object of interest in the video to specific locations along their visual trajectory. Wilhelm *et al.* (2004) developed a mobile media metadata framework that enables image annotation on a mobile phone as soon as a picture is taken. The unique feature of this system is that it guesses the content of the picture for the purpose of reducing the amount of text entry needed during the annotation. Kandel *et al.* (2008) proposed the PhotoSpread system, which allows users to organize and analyze photos and images via an easy-to-use spreadsheet with direct manipulation functions. Applications that support content visualization for easy data sharing and analysis have also been developed (Cristani *et al.* 2008).

The techniques for automatic annotation still need substantial advancements in order to achieve reliable coding. The applications to facilitate manual coding have shown promising results but improvements are also needed to improve the usability and reliability of the system.

Summary

Text, multimedia, and other qualitative data are important sources of information for HCI researchers and practitioners. The procedure and techniques commonly used to analyze qualitative data are quite different from those applied to the analysis of quantitative data. Probably the most unique characteristic of content analysis is that it involves human coding. The absence of numeric data and direct measures makes qualitative data analysis more susceptible to biased interpretation or subjective manipulation. Therefore, it is critical to adopt well established procedures and techniques to ensure high-quality analysis that is both valid and reliable. Although there is disagreement regarding its implementation process and guidelines, grounded theory is widely used for qualitative data analysis. The major difference between grounded theory and other qualitative research strategies is its emphasis on theory development in continuous interplay between data collection and data analysis.

When analyzing text content, we need to develop a set of coding categories that accurately summarizes the data or describes the underlying relationships or patterns buried in the data. Depending on the specific context of the research question, a priori coding or emergent coding may be used to generate the coding categories. In order to produce high-quality coding, multiple coders are needed to code the data. During the coding process, the coders should constantly look for statements likely to carry valuable information, ask questions about the data, and make comparisons at various levels. Reliability control measures such as Cohen's Kappa should be calculated and evaluated throughout the coding process. Cohen's Kappa at or above 0.60 indicates satisfactory inter-coder reliability.

The basic guidelines for analyzing text content also apply to multimedia content. Due to the special nature of multimedia data, the analysis can be much more labor-intensive than for text data if a completely manual annotation procedure is adopted. In order to address that challenge, a number of techniques have been developed to assist the annotation of multimedia data. To date, the completely automated annotation techniques are highly error prone. Applications to facilitate manual coding have shown promising results and may serve as a useful tool for analyzing multimedia data.

Discussion Questions

1. What is grounded theory?
2. How does grounded theory differ from the traditional empirical research approach?
3. What are the four stages of grounded theory?
4. What are the advantages and limitations of grounded theory?
5. What is content analysis?
6. What are the major types of content?
7. What do you need to consider before starting content analysis?
8. What is the procedure for analyzing text information?
9. What is in-vivo code?
10. How can you identify the major coding categories?
11. What is the difference between a priori coding and emergent coding?
12. What are the key items to look for while coding?
13. What can you do to improve the validity of qualitative analysis?
14. Why do you need to conduct reliability checking during and after the coding process?

15. What is "stability" in the context of a reliability check?
16. What is "reproducibility" in the context of a reliability check?
17. What is the formula for computing Cohen's Kappa?
18. How do you interpret a specific value of Cohen's Kappa?
19. What is the advantage and disadvantage of using a subjective coder?
20. What is the advantage and disadvantage of using an objective coder?
21. Why is analyzing multimedia content difficult?
22. How does the partially automated annotation method work?

Research Design Exercise

You interview 50 children between the ages of 8 and 15 to study their computer usage behavior. During the data analysis, you find that the objective of using computers can be grouped into three categories: educational, communication, and entertainment. Two coders independently code the data and the agreement of their coding regarding computer usage objective is summarized in the Table 11.5. Answer the following questions based on the agreement table:

1. Develop an agreement matrix. (Hint: You need to compute marginal totals for each row and column and the expected percentage agreement for each cell.)
2. Calculate Cohen's Kappa.
3. Discuss the result and determine whether the coding is reliable.

		Coder 2		
		Education	Communication	Entertainment
Coder 1	Education	0.49	0.05	0.02
	Communication	0.03	0.11	0.01
	Entertainment	0.04	0.02	0.23

Table 11.5 Children's computer usage objectives–coding agreement.

References

Altman, D.G. (1991) *Practical Statistics for Medical Research*. London England: Chapman and Hall.

Argyros, A. and Lourakis, M. (2006) Vision-based interpretation of hand gestures for remote control of a computer mouse. *Proceedings of ECCV 2006 Workshop on HCI*, 40–51. Graz, Austria.

Bennett, E.M., Alpert, R., and Goldstein, A.C. (1954) Communications through limited response questioning. *Public Opinion Quarterly*, **18**:303–308.

Berelson, B. (1952) *Content Analysis in Communication Research*. Glencoe, Ill: Free Press.

Blumer, H. (1969) *Symbolic Interactionism: Perspective and method*. Englewood Cliffs, NJ: Prentice-Hall.

Chang, E.Y., Hanalei, A., and Sebe, N. (2006) Multimedia Content Analysis, Management and Retrieval. *Proceedings of the International Society for Optical Engineering (SPIE)*, Vol. 6073.

Corbin, J. and Strauss, A. (2008) *Basics of Qualitative Research*, 3rd edition. Los Angeles, CA: Sage Publications.

Courage, C., Redish, J., and Wixon, D. (2007) Task analysis. In A. Sears and J. Jacko (eds), *The Human Computer Interaction Handbook: Fundamentals, evolving technologies, and emerging applications*. New York: Lawrence Erlbaum Associates.

Creswell, J.W. (2009) *Research Design: Qualitative, quantitative, and mixed methods approaches*. Thousand Oaks, CA: Sage Publications.

Cristani, M., Perina, A., Castellani, U., and V. Murino (2008) Content visualization and management of geo-located image databases. *Proceedings of the ACM Conference on Human Factors in Computing Systems*, 2823–2828.

Dedeoğlu, Y., Töreyin, B.U., Güdükbay, U., and Çetin, A.E. (2006) Silhouette-based method of object classification and human action recognition in video. *Proceedings of ECCV 2006 Workshop on HCI*, 64–77. Graz, Austria.

Dragicevic, P., Ramos, G., Bibliowicz, J., et al. (2008) Video browsing by direct manipulation. *Proceedings of CHI 2008*, 237–246.

Glaser, B.G. (1978) *Theoretical Sensitivity: Advances in the methodology of grounded theory*. Mill Valley, CA: Sociology Press.

Glaser, B.G. (1992) *Emergence vs. Forcing: Basics of grounded theory analysis*. Mill Valley, CA: Sociology Press.

Glaser, B.G. and Strauss, A.L. (1967) *The Discovery of Grounded Theory: Strategies for qualitative research*. Chicago: Aldine.

Holsti, R. (1969) *Content Analysis for the Social Sciences and Humanities*. Reading, MA: Addison-Wesley.

Kandel, S., Paepcke, A., Theobald, M., Garcia-Molina, H., and Abelson, E. (2008) PhotoSpread: a spreadsheet for managing photos. *Proceedings of the ACM Conference on Human Factors in Computing Systems*, 1749–1758.

Kirk, J. and Miller, M. (1986) *Reliability and Validity in Qualitative Research*, 12th edition. Sage Publications.

Krippendorff, K. (1980) *Content analysis: An introduction to its methodology*. Newbury Park, CA: Sage Publications.

Krippendorff, K. (2004) Reliability in content analysis: Some common misconceptions and recommendations. *Human Communication Research*, **80**(3):411–433.

Landis, J.R. and Koch, G.G. (1977) The measurement of observer agreement for categorical data. *Biometrics*, 33:159–174.

Li, Y., Ai, H., Huang, C., and Lao, S. (2006) Robust head tracking with particles based on multiple cues fusion. *Proceedings of ECCV 2006 Workshop on HCI*, 29–39. Graz, Austria.

Lowe, W. (2003) Content analysis software: A review. Technical Report for the Identity Project, Weatherhead Center for International Affairs, Harvard University.

Lyberg, L. and Kasprzyk, D (1997) Some aspects of post-survey processing. In L. Lyberg, P. Biemer, M. Collins, E. Leeuw, C. Dippo, N. Schwarz, and D. Trewin (eds), *Survey Measurement and Process Quality*. John Wiley & Sons

Myers, M. (1997) Qualitative research in information systems. *MIS Quarterly*, **21**(2):241–242.

Myers, M. (2009) *Qualitative research in business and management*. Los Angeles: Sage Publications.

Neuendorf, K.A. (2002) *The Content Analysis Guidebook*. Sage Publications.

Norman, D. (2002) *The Design of Everyday Things*. New York: Basic Books.

Norman, K. (1991) Models of the mind and machine: Information flow and control between humans and computers. *Advances in Computers*, **32**:119–172.

Osgood, E.E. (1959) The representational model and relevant research. In I. de Sola Pool (ed.), *Trends in Content Analysis*, 33–88. Urbana: University of Illinois Press.

Peltonen, P., Kurvinen, E., Salovaara, A. *et al.* (2008) It's Mine, Don't Touch!: Interactions at a large multi-touch display in a city centre. *Proceedings of the 26th annual SIGCHI Conference on Human Factors in Computing Systems (CHI 2008)*. 1285–1294.

Putnam, C. and Chong, L. (2008) Software and technology designed for children with autism: What do users want? *Proceedings of ACM ASSETS 2008*.

Rui, Y. and Qi, G. (2007) Learning concepts by modeling relationships. In N. Sebe, Y. Liu, Y. Zhuang, T.S. Huang (eds), *Multimedia Content Analysis and Mining International Workshop*, MCAM 2007, 5–13. Berlin: Springer-Verlag.

Sears, A., Karat, C-M., Oseitutu, K., Karimullah, A., and Feng, J. (2001) Productivity, Satisfaction, and Interaction Strategies of Individuals with Spinal Cord Injuries and Traditional Users Interacting with Speech Recognition Software. *Universal Access in the Information Society*, **1**(1):4–15.

Sebe, N., Liu, Y., Zhuang, Y., and Huang, T. (2007) Multimedia Content Analysis and Mining. *Proceedings of the Multimedia Content Analysis and Mining International Workshop*, MCAM 2007.

Stake, R.E. (1995) *The Art of Case Study Research*. Thousand Oaks, CA: Sage Publications.

Stemler, S.E. (2001) An overview of content analysis. *Practical Assessment, Research & Evaluation*, **7**(17).

Strauss, A. (1987) *Qualitative Analysis for Social Scientists.* Cambridge: Cambridge University Press.

Strauss, A. and Corbin, J. (1990) *Basics of Qualitative Research: Grounded theory procedures and techniques.* Newbury Park, CA: Sage Publications.

Weber, R.P. (1990) *Basic Content Analysis: Quantitative analysis in the social sciences*, 2nd edition. Newbury Park, CA: Sage Publications.

Wilhelm, A., Takhteyev, Y., Sarvas, R., Van House, N., and Davis, M. (2004) *Extended Abstracts of the ACM Conference on Human Factors in Computing Systems*, 1403–1406.

Wu, Q., Song, M., Bu, J., and Chen, C. (2006) EigenExpress approach in recognition of facial expression using GPU. *Proceedings of ECCV 2006 Workshop on HCI*, 12–20. Graz, Austria.

Xue, W., Du, S., Fang, C., and Ye, Y. (2006) Voice activity detection using wavelet-based multiresolution spectrum and support vector machines and audio mixing algorithm. *Proceedings of ECCV 2006 Workshop on HCI*, 78–88. Graz, Austria.

Yin, R.K. (2003) *Case Study Research: Design and methods*, 3rd edition. Thousand Oaks, CA: Sage Publications.

Zhu, G., Xu, C., Gao, W., and Huang, Q. (2006) Action recognition in broadcast tennis video using optical flow and support vector machine. *Proceedings of ECCV 2006 Workshop on HCI*, 89–98. Graz, Austria.

Automated data collection methods

Data are the building blocks of research. As the recorded output of research efforts, data are the raw materials that must be processed, analyzed, and interpreted to provide answers to research questions. Data collection is therefore a critical phase in any research effort.

Data collection is also often one of the most challenging aspects of research. Timing user task completion with a stopwatch, furiously writing notes describing user interactions with software systems, coding notes from ethnographic observations, and many other tasks are laborious, time-consuming, and often – as a result – error-prone.

Human–computer interaction (HCI) researchers have a formidable resource that can – and should – be exploited to overcome this obstacle. The very computers that are the subject of our research are also powerful data collection tools. Widely available and custom-built software tools can be used to collect vast amounts of user interaction data, often with little or no direct effort on the part of the researcher administering the study. In addition to simplifying the process, these automated approaches increase consistency and reduce error.

Approaches to automated data collection can generally be placed on a spectrum of ease of use and flexibility (Figure 12.1). Existing software tools such as website access log analyzers can often be easily used or adapted for research purposes, but capabilities might be limited. System observation and logging software may be somewhat more powerful, but installation and configuration issues can be challenging. Custom-built or modified software can be crafted to meet the precise research needs, but the development effort can be substantial.

All of the automated methods for computerized data collection are capable of producing voluminous data sets. This can pose a substantial problem for researchers: it is well known that while filling disks with data is easy, analysis and interpretation of that data is often much harder. Choosing the appropriate data granularity and proper data management are crucial components of any automated data collection system.

12.1   Exploiting existing tools

Many commonly used software tools collect and store data that can be used in HCI research. These tools have the obvious appeal of relative simplicity: although some effort may be

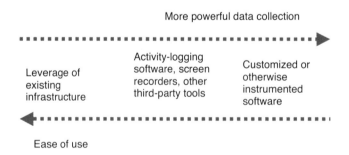

Figure 12.1 Computerized data collection systems present a trade-off between power and ease of use.

required for analysis, data collection tools may be available right on your desktop. For some widely analyzed data sources – such as web server logs – commercial and freely available tools can provide substantial assistance in interpretation.

These advantages do not come without a cost. Using unmodified, commodity software is likely to limit you to data that is collected by default. If your research questions require additional data, you may be out of luck. This is often not a real barrier – many successful research projects have been based on analysis of data from available software. A sound strategy might be to start with these tools, pushing them to see how far they can take your research efforts and moving towards more complex measures if needed.

12.1.1   Web logs

Like mail servers and database servers, web servers generate log files that store records of requests and activity. A sequential listing of all of the requests made to a server, a log file provides a record of how the server has been used and when. This detailed information can be useful for evaluating system performance, debugging problems, and recovering from crashes.

Web logs have also proven to be a potent tool in HCI research. Given a website and a log file, researchers can determine where users went and when. When combined with an understanding of the architecture of a site, this information can be used to assess the usability of a site. Timing data in web logs also presents opportunities for empirical studies.

12.1.1.1   Web log contents

Although web servers can be configured to store a variety of data fields along with each request, most log files store data that can identify a request and its source. Some log files also contain fields that are generally less useful. The useful data includes:

- *Host*: The Internet protocol address of the remote computer that made the request. As many people access the Internet via networks that use firewalls or proxy hosts that forward requests from internal machines, a host address may not correspond directly to a specific user's computer.
- *Timestamp*: When the request occurred, usually including a date and a time code. Times may be given relative to Greenwich Mean Time.
- *Request:* The HTTP request sent by the client to the server. The request has several fields that may be of interest:
  - *HTTP Method*: usually "GET or "POST"; the type of request being made (Fielding *et al.*, 1999);
  - *Resource*: the file, script, or other resource requested from the server;
  - *Protocol:* the version of the HTTP protocol used.
- *Status Code:* A numeric response from the server, indicating success (200–299), redirection (300–399), client error (400–499) or server error (500–599) (Fielding *et al.*, 1999).

```
10.55.10.14 - - [13/Jul/2007:13:42:10 -0400] "GET /homepage/classes/spring07/686/index.html HTTP/1.1" 200 8623

10.55.10.14 - - [13/Jul/2007:13:48:32 -0400] "GET /homepage/classes/spring07/686/schedule.html HTTP/1.1" 200 16095

10.55.10.14 - - [13/Jul/2007:13:48:33 -0400] "GET /homepage/classes/spring07/686/readings.html HTTP/1.1" 200 14652
```

Figure 12.2 Log file entries, containing host IP address, timestamp, request, status code, and number of bytes.

Several other potentially useful fields may be available:

- *Size*: The size – in number of bytes – of the item returned to the client.
- *Referrer*: The web page that "referred" the client to the requested resource. If a user on http://yourhost/index.html clicks on the "search.html" link, the request indicates that "http://yourhost/index" was the referrer. Some requests, such as those that come via an address typed in to a browser, do not arrive via a link and have a dash ("-") in the referrer field.
- *User-Agent:* The make and model of the web browser that made the request. As this is self-reported, it may or may not be accurate.

Figures 12.2 and 12.3 give some example log entries

Most web servers use the common log format (World Wide Web Consortium, 1995) as the basis for formatting log files. Customization facilities, allowing for the inclusion of specific fields, are usually provided. This can be very useful for adapting your logs to fit the needs of each project. If you are running a study involving users who are particularly sensitive to privacy concerns, you might configure your server to remove the client IP number from the log files. Similar changes can be made regarding the recording of the referrer, the user agent, or other fields. For many studies, it may be useful to create a special-purpose log in parallel with a traditional access log. The customized log file provides the information needed for your study, without interfering with access logs that might be used for ongoing website maintenance. Customized log file formats may require customization of the log analysis tools, but this is generally not hard to do.

Most web servers generate error logs in addition to access logs. The list of requests that generated server errors can be useful for identifying problems with a site design, such as links to non-existent pages or resources. Check your server documentation for details.

As web logs can become quite voluminous, proper care and handling is very important. Numerous software tools extract information from log files for static reports or interactive analysis: several approaches to this analysis are described in this chapter. Logs from publicly

```
10.55.10.14 %t "GET /homepage/classes/spring07/686/readings.html HTTP/1.1" 200 14652
"http://10.55.10.128/homepage/classes/spring07/686/schedule.html" "Mozilla/5.0 (X11; U; Linux i686; en-
US; rv:1.8) Gecko/20051202 Fedora/1.5-0.fc4 Firefox/1.5"
```

Figure 12.3 A detailed version of the last entry from Figure 12.2, including the referrer and the user agent.

accessible sites may include regular and repeated visits from web robots, tools used by search engines and other tools to retrieve web pages, follow links, and analyze web content. Before using the logs of your publicly accessible site for research purposes, you might consider using the robot exclusion protocol (Koster, 1994) to discourage these automated tools. Excluding robots reduces the proportion of your log entries that are generated by these crawlers, leaving you with more of the good stuff – visits from human users. As this step may have the (possibly undesirable) effect of reducing your site's visibility to search engines, you may wish to exclude robots for short periods of time while you collect data. Once your data collection is complete, you can disable your robot exclusion measures, thus allowing search engines to index your site and maintain your visibility.

12.1.1.2   Web usability/design research

By telling us which pages were accessed, and when, web access logs can provide valuable information for usability evaluations and understanding of usage patterns. Relatively simple page access counts tell us which pages are accessed frequently, and which aren't. When coupled with an understanding of page layout information, this can help identify opportunities for improving usability. Aggregate counts of timestamps, referrers, and user agents, can be used to understand when a site is being used, how people are getting to links within a site (external referrers are particularly interesting in this regard), and which browsers they are using – all potentially useful information in the context of evaluating a site design. Interactive visualizations of this data at multiple granularities – particularly when coordinated with views of the site – can provide guidance for improving site design (Hochheiser and Shneiderman, 2001). For example, if important areas of the site are infrequently accessed, links might be moved to more prominent locations or be made more visually distinctive. Post-modification analysis can be used to evaluate the success (or lack thereof) of such measures.

Web access logs also provide the intriguing possibility of extracting information about the actions of specific users as they navigate a website. This information can be very useful for understanding which path users take through a site and where they might run into problems.

As each entry in an access log can contain an Internet address, a timestamp, the requested URL, the referring URL, and a user agent, we might be tempted to combine this information with knowledge of a site's layout to infer the path of specific users through a site. If we see that an access to "index.html" is soon followed by a request for "help.html", with both requests originating from the same network address, we might think that these requests came from the same user. Matching user agents and an entry indicating that the referrer page for the "index.html" page was the "help.html" page might increase our confidence in this theory. Unfortunately, things are not necessarily that simple. Firewalls and other network address schemes may make requests that come from multiple users appear as if they all come from the same machine. Web browsers can easily be configured to provide misleading information for the user agent fields and referrer fields. Web cookies can provide additional useful information, but they may be disabled by some users. Despite the problems, these items can be used to generate useful models of user paths (Pirolli and Pitkow, 1999). Augmenting these models with additional information, including keywords extracted from visited web pages or URLs and page view time can provide increased accuracy in characterizing user sessions (Heer and Chi, 2002).

As a stand-alone tool, web log analysis is limited by a lack of contextual knowledge about user goals and actions. Even if we are able to extract individual user paths from log files, these paths do not tell us how the path taken relates to the user's goals. In some cases, we might be able to make educated guesses: a path consisting of repeated cycling between "help" and "search" pages is most likely an indication of a task not successfully completed. Other session paths may be more ambiguous: long intervals between page requests might indicate that the user was carefully reading web content, but they can also arise from distractions and other activity not related to the website under consideration. Additional information, such as direct observation through controlled studies or interviews, may be necessary to provide appropriate context (Hochheiser and Shneiderman, 2001).

Complex web applications can be designed to generate and store additional data that may be useful for understanding user activity. Database-driven websites can track views of various pages, along with other actions such as user comments, blog posts, or searches. Web applications that store this additional data are very similar to instrumented applications (Section 12.2.2).

The analysis of web log information presents some privacy challenges that must be handled appropriately. IP numbers that identify computers can be used to track web requests to a specific computer, which may be used by a single person. Analyses that track blog posts, comments, purchases, or other activity associated with a user login can also be used to collect a great deal of potentially sensitive information. Before collecting any such data, you should make sure that your websites have privacy policies and other information explaining the data that you are collecting and how you will use it. Additional steps that you might take to protect user privacy include taking careful control of the logs and other repositories of this data, reporting information only in aggregate form (instead of in a form that could identify individuals), and destroying the data when your analysis is complete. As these privacy questions may raise concerns regarding informed consent and appropriate treatment of research participants, some web log analyses might require approval from your institutional review board (see Chapter 14).

12.1.1.3 *Empirical studies*
Empirical studies of task performance times require some means of capturing timing data. Although hand-held stopwatches can do this job admirably, software that measures and records elapsed times between starting events and task completion is usually more reliable and easier to work with. As described later in this chapter, this approach has been used extensively in special-purpose software built specifically for HCI studies.

For experimental tasks involving selections that can be presented as links on web pages, web servers and their logs present an ideal platform for gathering empirical task performance data. In this model, a web server is run on the same machine that is used to perform the experimental tasks. This eliminates any delays associated with requesting materials over a network connection. The selection of a link from a starting page indicates the beginning of the task, with subsequent link selections indicating intermediate steps. Eventually, a link indicating successful task completion is selected. The elapsed interval between the selection of the start and completion links is the task completion time, with access records of intermediate requests indicating steps that were taken to complete the task and the elapsed time for each subtask.

This method is not without drawbacks. Extraction of the relevant information from logs may require manual interpretation or implementation of special-purpose log analysis software. Timestamps in server log files time events by the second, so this approach is not suitable for studies that require finer task-time resolution.

Web browser caches may cause additional problems. These caches store local copies of pages that have been recently accessed. If a user requests a page that is in the cache, the browser returns the copy that has been stored locally, instead of making a new request from the web server. This may cause problems if you are trying to track every user request, as requests for cached pages might not generate web server log entries.[1] You may want to turn off caching facilities before using a particular browser to run an experiment.

In practice, these drawbacks usually do not create serious problems. The Simultaneous vs Sequential Menus sidebar describes a study that used server logs to compare alternative web menu designs.

Simultaneous vs Sequential Menus

Computer interfaces may be designed to present choices in a hierarchical, sequential manner, even if the items in the menu are not necessarily hierarchical. A restaurant selection tool for a city might allow users to select a neighborhood, followed by a price range, and finally a type of cuisine, but this is not the only possibility order. A simultaneous menu scheme would allow selections to be made in each of these three criteria at any time.

A comparison of the strictly sequential menu approach vs. the simultaneous menu approach used a locally hosted web server to present alternative menu structures for the same underlying data set (Hochheiser and Shneiderman, 2000): US Census Bureau economic data for counties in the state of Maryland. A sequential menu allowed users

---

[1] Then again, they might. It all depends on the server configuration. However, it's best to be defensive about such matters: assume that they won't and take appropriate steps.

to select a county, followed by a business category, and then a year (Figure 12.4). Simultaneous menus allowed for selection in any one of these criteria at any time, with detail displays showing data based on values for the three attributes selected (Figure 12.5). Each task in each menu structure began with the selection of a "start" link, and ended with the selection of a link that led to the correct answer.

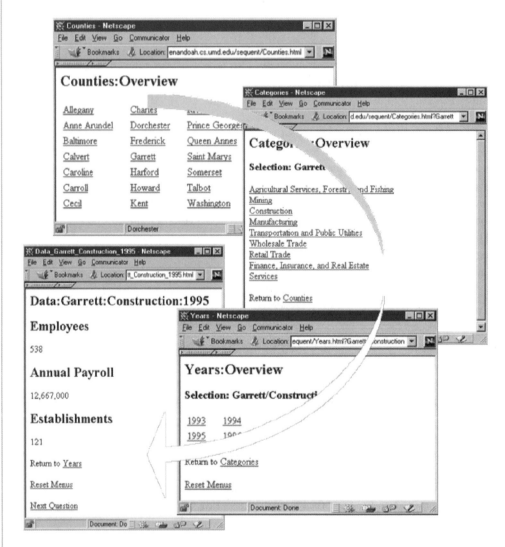

Figure 12.4 Sequential menus: users choose first from counties, then from categories, and finally from years, in order to get to a detail page.

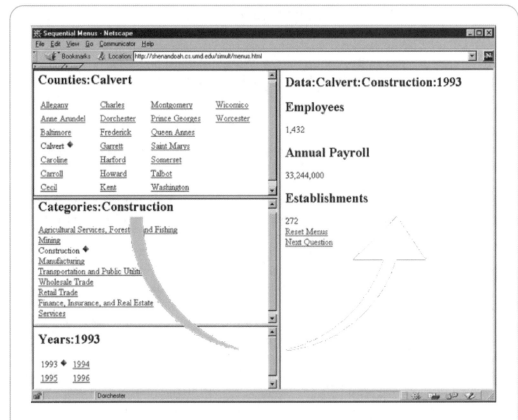

Figure 12.5 Simultaneous menus: once a user has selected a value for each of the three variables, details are shown on the right.

This study found that sequential menus fared well for simple tasks, but simultaneous menus were preferable for more complex tasks (Hochheiser and Shneiderman, 2000).

12.1.2 Stored application data

As we use computers, we leave traces that provide valuable information about how we interact with applications and store and manage information. The tools that we use collect substantial data trails that implicitly and explicitly describe user activities. Examples include (but are not limited to):

- File systems: The files and folders that we create and use present a model of how we organize information. Do we separate work activities from home? Do we have many folders, each containing a small number of files, or only a few folders, each with many files?

- GUI desktops: Some people have dozens of icons on their desktops, while others have only a few. Does this say anything about their organizational preferences?
- Email programs: Many people use an email "inbox" as a todo list, reminding them of tasks that must be completed. Some users make extensive use of filing and filtering capabilities, while others leave all messages in one folder.
- Web bookmarks can also be more or less organized.
- Social networking tools such as Facebook or LinkedIn provide detailed perspectives on how people connect to each other and why.

Each of these domains (and others) can be (and have been) studied to understand usage patterns and to potentially inform new designs. This research is a form of HCI archaeology – digging through artifacts to understand complex behavior patterns.

There are attractive aspects to using existing data that is stored by tools that users work with on a daily basis. Interference with the user's work or habits is minimal. Users do not have to participate in experimental sessions to be part of the study and no training is necessary.

The generality of this approach is limited by the tools involved and the data that they collect. The example tools given above (file explorers, email clients, web browser bookmark tools, GUI desktops, etc.) all provide tools that can be used to manipulate and maintain organizations of information. As a result, they can be used to identify which structures exist, which categories items might be placed in, etc. As more transient activities – such as selections of menu items – are generally not recorded, this approach is not well-suited for the study of specific implementations. Instead, this approach to data analysis is best suited for the study of long-term patterns of ongoing tasks such as those described above.

As the analyses may involve exploration of potentially sensitive matters such as email messages, file system content, and web bookmarks, investigators using these approaches should be sensitive to privacy concerns. In addition to properly informing participants of the privacy risk (see Chapter 14), researchers should exercise discretion when examining potentially sensitive data. Investigations should be limited to only the data that is strictly necessary. An exploration of email communication patterns might reduce privacy risks by examining message headers, instead of message bodies. If this is not sufficient, anonymizing the content to simply indicate that A had an email conversation with B can provide further privacy protection.

A final limitation of this approach involves the challenge of extracting data. Converting these computational artifacts from their native form to a representation suitable for analysis can be challenging. You may need to write special-purpose software to extract data from these tools. In some cases, this may require interpreting (or reverse engineering) non-standard file formats.

Although log files and implicitly stored data may prove useful for the analysis of many important tasks and activities, these approaches have some very real limitations. These tools are often limited in the granularity of the data that are collected. A web log that provides detailed information about the paths followed by various users in the course of completing some tasks does not contain any information about the users' activities while they were on a given site. Similarly, an email client may provide information regarding the structure of nested mailboxes, but information about intermediate states – such as the names of mailboxes that were created and later deleted – may not be captured.

12.2   Using software to observe and record

Special-purpose software that observes and records user actions provides one possible approach to the question of limited data granularity. These software tools – often known as proxies – intercept user actions and record appropriate data points before passing the actions on to the original software (Figure 12.6). Data returned from the application can also be intercepted and modified before being returned to the user. Both user interaction data and application response data can be stored in a log file. Proxies that record fine-grained detail regarding user interaction can substantially augment data available in web logs and similar repositories.

12.2.1   Web proxies

A particularly important example of this approach is the web proxy. Web proxies were initially designed as tools for optimizing web browsing: users in an organization would forward all of their web requests to a specified proxy server, which would store copies of requested sites in a local cache. If an outgoing request asked for a page that was in the cache, the proxy server

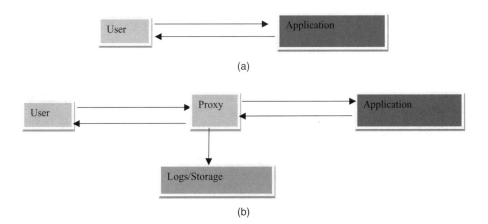

Figure 12.6 User actions: (a) passed directly to an application and (b) intercepted by a proxy.

would simply return the contents of the cache entry, thus saving the cost of making a new request to the remote server and processing the response.

Web proxies for HCI research involve a more general approach to this model. In essence, the proxy becomes an intermediary that receives all web requests from a group of users, retrieves the requested materials, and returns them to the users. As all requests from a group of users are handled by the proxy server, it can collect complete session data for all users. This provides a broader picture of user activities than standard server logs, which only contain records for requests from a single site.

Web proxies can intercept (and modify) user requests before sending them on to the server. Proxies can also modify the responses from the remote servers before the resulting web pages are displayed by the client software. Specifically, pages can be modified to include content necessary for the collection of additional interaction data (Figure 12.7) (Atterer, Wnuk and Schmidt, 2006).

The first step in using a web proxy – for any purpose, including HCI research – is selecting an appropriate computing environment. As the computational demands of handling web requests for a large group of users can be substantial, you probably want to dedicate resources (computers, disk space, and network bandwidth) specifically for this purpose. If your proxy server is not able to process web requests quickly and efficiently, users will notice delays in their web browsing. This may cause some users to change their browsing habits, while others may simply refuse to use the proxy server. Ideally, the proxy server should not impose any performance penalties on end users.

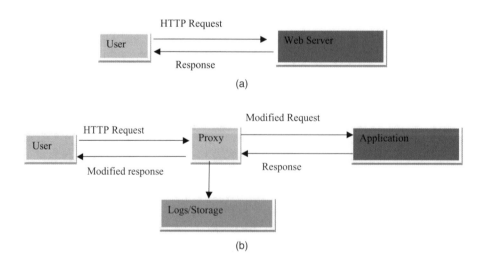

Figure 12.7 Web requests: (a) standard request–response and (b) intercepted by a proxy.

Many open-source, shareware, and commercial proxy servers are available for all major computing platforms. The Squid proxy server (www.squid-cache.org) is widely used on Linux and Unix systems. The popular Apache web server (http://httpd.apache.org) can also be configured to act as a proxy server. Microsoft Proxy Server can be used on Windows systems. The choice of platform and software is likely to be dictated by your specific computing needs.

Once installed, proxy software must be appropriately configured and secured. You need to consider who may use your proxy server – you can limit access to users only from certain Internet domains or numbers – which sites you will allow access to, and what sorts of information you might want to store in the logs. As configuration options differ widely from one proxy package to the next, you should carefully study your software documentation and related resources.

Web browsers must be configured to use general-purpose web proxies. The configuration process tells the browser to contact the appropriate proxy host for all web requests. The most straightforward approach is to specify the proxy server settings directly in a web browser configuration dialog (Figure 12.8), but this requires manual configuration of every browser. As various other approaches – both manual and automatic – can be used to

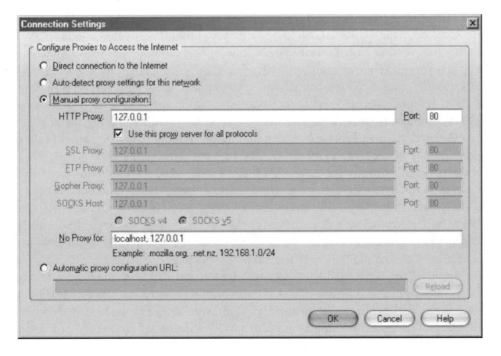

Figure 12.8 Firefox proxy configuration dialog for the web browser: the computer at address 127.0.0.1 will act as a proxy server on port 80.

```
- 127.0.0.1 - - [26/Sep/2007:10:22:19 -0400] "GET http://triton.towson.edu/~hhochhei/ HTTP/1.1" 304 -
- 127.0.0.1 - - [26/Sep/2007:10:22:19 -0400] "GET http://triton.towson.edu/~hhochhei/hhstyle.css
HTTP/1.1" 304 -
- 127.0.0.1 - - [26/Sep/2007:10:22:19 -0400] "GET http://triton.towson.edu/~hhochhei/hh.jpg HTTP/1.1"
304 -
- 127.0.0.1 - - [26/Sep/2007:10:22:19 -0400] "GET http://triton.towson.edu/~hhochhei/towson-header.gif
HTTP/1.1" 304 -
- 127.0.0.1 - - [26/Sep/2007:10:22:19 -0400] "GET http://triton.towson.edu/~hhochhei/arrow.gif HTTP/1.1"
304 -
```

Figure 12.9 Log entries from a proxy server.

configure browsers to forward requests to the web proxy, you may need to do some research to determine which approach is best for you.

Once the proxy server and web browser have been configured, users can continue to browse the web as before. Web requests are handled transparently by the proxy server and noted in the log files. In Figure 12.9, note that each request contains a full URL for a web resource, rather than a local path, as in Figure 12.2.

The resulting log files contain information on all sites visited by all users of the proxy. Although this information can be used to provide a rich picture of user browsing habits over time, care and discretion should be used when studying this data. As users may forget that they are using a proxy that logs their requests, they might visit sites that are potentially embarrassing or inappropriate. Records of this sort should be treated carefully. Possible approaches for avoiding embarrassment include anonymization of users or websites.

Logging of web requests is only the tip of the proxy iceberg. Several researchers have made extensive – and creative – use of web proxies to collect web usage data. WebQuilt (Hong *et al.*, 2001) is a proxy server specifically designed to aid in the collection of usability data. WebQuilt combines logging facilities with an engine for transforming log file entries into inferred user actions, a tool for aggregating log files into graph structures, and visualization components for the display of graphs displaying user paths through a site.

Unlike general-purpose web proxies, WebQuilt is designed to be used to collect data on a site-specific basis. To run a usability test for a given website, the experimenter asks users to visit a URL specifically designed to support proxy-based access to the site under investigation. The WebQuilt proxy handles all requests for the site, including the modification of page content to route subsequent requests for that site through the proxy. As a result, WebQuilt does not require any configuration of the browser software.

Proxies have also been used to collect web interaction data at a much finer resolution than individual web clicks. MouseTracks (Arroyo, Selker and Wei, 2006) and UsaProxy (Atterer, Wnuk and Schmidt, 2006) modify pages with JavaScript code that records low-level interaction data including mouse movements. This data is sent to the server for logging and visualization.

Proxy servers can be quite powerful, but they present numerous technical challenges. Installing, configuring, and managing a proxy server can be difficult. Your proxy server must have the processing power and network bandwidth for effective operation. If your study involves only a small set of users for a short time frame, a single machine might be sufficient. Large-scale studies involving multiple users for extended time periods might need a more robust solution, involving many machines and more bandwidth. Cutting corners on proxy capabilities might jeopardize your study: if users find that the proxy is too slow for effective web use, they might temporarily or permanently stop using the proxy, effectively removing their data from your study.

12.2.2   Instrumented software

Modern computing applications are complex: word processors, spreadsheets, email programs and web browsers may have dozens, if not hundreds of toolbar buttons and menu items. Which of these items are used and which are not? How would modifications to the interface change usage patterns for various functions? These questions are of interest both to researchers, who might be interested in understanding the efficacy of various strategies for grouping and re-arranging controls for complex operations, and for product developers interested in comparing the effectiveness of proposed interface changes.

There are several approaches to collecting detailed data on the usage of complex interfaces. User observations, interviews, videotape, and other strategies described elsewhere in this book can and have been used effectively for these purposes. However, these approaches are all laborious and expensive, requiring many hours spent observing users, asking questions, or coding events on videotape.

In many cases, a more attractive alternative is to have the software collect data on its own usage. A program designed for this sort of data collection would store every important user action – menu choices, toolbar button selections, key presses, and more, in a log file or database. Storage of these events in chronological order, including a timestamp, would provide a complete history of which options were selected and when. Analysis of this data might help developers understand which commands are used frequently, rarely, or usually in close combination with other commands (such as "cut" followed by "paste").

The practice of adding measurement and recording tools to software is known as *instrumenting*. Constructing instrumented software may require a fair amount of technical expertise, as code for handling user interactions must be substantially modified. For many commercial or "closed source" software products, this level of access to the source code may be available only to the vendor or the developer of the product. However, macro and extension facilities in some products have been successfully used to write instrumentation code for interface evaluation purposes. A third possibility involves open-source software. Researchers interested in studying the usage of the interfaces of open-source projects might produce their own, instrumented versions of popular programs for use in research data collection. Detailed versions of each of these approaches are described in the Instrumented Software for HCI Data Collection sidebar.

Instrumented Software for HCI Data Collection

Instrumented software has been used to collect usage data in support of widely used commercial products, research prototypes, and open-source tools. These examples are representative of some of the possibilities.

Microsoft office 2003

Microsoft's Customer Experience Improvement Program lets users opt in to having usage data collected anonymously. Data collected includes menu selections, keyboard shortcuts, and artifacts of user customization, including the number of mail folders and any modifications or customizations. This broad-ranging data collection was open-ended, rather than hypothesis-driven: "In short, we collect anything we think might be interesting and useful as long as it doesn't compromise a user's privacy" (Harris, 2005).

The large data set (over 13 billion user sessions) provided substantial insight that informed the redesign of the Office interface for the Office 2007 release (Harris, 2005). Even though the Paste command – the most popular, with more than 11% of all command usage in Word – was frequently accessed via shortcuts, the Paste button was the most frequently clicked button on the toolbar. This led Microsoft's UI team to place the Paste button prominently in the revised interface for Office (Harris, 2006).

This study also confirmed that Word users confirm previously observed patterns of frequently using a small subset of features while rarely using other features (McGrenere and Moore, 2000). The top five commands in Word accounted for more than 32% of all command usage, with frequencies declining quickly after the top 10 (Harris, 2006).

Personalized versions of application interfaces

Noting the potential difficulties associated with complex interfaces for desktop applications, Joanna McGrenere and her colleagues set out to investigate the possible utility of a simplified user interface containing only items selected by the user. Using the scripting tools in Microsoft Word 2000, they built an extension to Word that would allow users to work with this simplified interface. Tools for adding items to their personalized interface were included, along with a control that could be used to switch between the simplified interface and the full interface as desired. In a field study with 20 users, this software was installed along with a logging tool for capturing usage and a program that would upload usage logs to an Internet server. Usage data collected included histograms of function usage frequency. This data indicated that only a small number of commands were used very frequently and that the users added almost all of those commands to their personalized interfaces. A series of questionnaires indicated that users preferred the personalized interfaces in terms of navigation and ease of learning (McGrenere, Baecker and Booth, 2002).

Instrumenting open-source software

As few commercial products offer customization tools comparable to those found in Microsoft Office, instrumentation of open-source software has proven to be a fruitful alternative. One study of web navigation patterns used an instrumented version of the Firefox web browser to collect data on the use of browser features such as the "back" button, history views, and bookmarks. This relatively small study (25 users) combined instrumented software with web proxies in order to identify new patterns in web browser feature usage and browsing behavior, some of which may have been related to the rise in tabbed browsing and other relatively new browser features (Obendorf *et al.*, 2007).

Ingimp provides an example of broader use of instrumented open-source software for HCI data collection. Short for "instrumented GIMP", ingimp is an instrumented version of the Gnu Image Manipulation Program, a powerful open-source tool for photo editing and image processing. Created by a group from the University of Waterloo, ingimp is available from a website (www.ingimp.org), which has been widely publicized in the hope of motivating users to participate in the study.

Ingimp collects a variety of data, including usage timing, the number of windows and layers open at a time, command usage, and task-switching details. Instrumenting GIMP to collect this data required modifying the open-source program to record appropriate events and transmit them to a central server. Interaction data is transmitted at the end of each session. If the software crashes before a log is transmitted, the incomplete log is detected and sent to the server when the program is next used.

The Ingimp instrumentation approach involves several privacy protection measures. Although mouse events and key press events are recorded, specific details – which key was pressed or where the mouse was moved – are not recorded. A dialog box on startup provides users with the option of disabling event logging for the current session. As GIMP is an open-source project, the developers of ingimp have made all the source code available. Knowledgeable users can investigate "patches" – descriptions of the differences between the original GIMP and ingimp. These differences reveal where the logging code has been added and what details it logs. Although few (if any) users are likely to take the trouble to do this, this does represent a thorough attempt at full disclosure.

Ingimp's developers hope to use this information to improve the usability of GIMP and other free or open-source software tools (Terry, 2007; Terry *et al.*, 2008).

Whichever approach you select for implementing data collection instruments, you should think carefully about the data that you are collecting. Although you may be tempted to collect as much data as possible, doing so may not be beneficial. Instrumenting every possible interaction in a complex application may require a great deal of effort. The amount of data collected may increase with the extent of the instrumentation. Large data sets can be a blessing, as they may contain interesting details that are unrelated to the initial hypotheses. They may also be a curse, as finding interesting and meaningful tidbits might take on the feel of looking for needles in a haystack. In some cases, researchers may simply throw out much of the data. In studying the usage of Office 2003, Microsoft threw out 70% of the data collected from Outlook and Word (Harris, 2005). Careful attention to the relationship between your experimental hypotheses – what do you hope to learn? – and the data collected may help increase your chances of success. Pilot studies might be helpful in this regard.

12.2.3 Custom-built software

Another class of custom software tools for automatic data collection involves software that is explicitly created for the sole purpose of running an experiment. These tools generally present users with a series of tasks to be completed and record data regarding task completion time, errors, and whatever other data may be necessary. The Fitts' Law, Children, and Mouse Control sidebar discusses an example of a custom software package developed for a study of how well young children use computer mice. Researchers interested in studying how well young children use a mouse built a tool that tracked task completion time as well as the trajectory of mouse movements in tasks that involved moving between two targets. This study found that younger children were much less accurate mouse users than adults (Hourcade *et al.*, 2004).

Research In Practice

Fitts' Law, Children, and Mouse Control

Full-size computer keyboards, keypads on phone and small devices, mice, trackballs, jog wheels, and joysticks are familiar controls for computers and other electronic devices, but familiarity does not necessarily imply understanding. How do we use these tools? How efficient are we? What sort of mistakes do we make? What are the factors that determine task completion time, accuracy, and error rate? Although researchers – in cognitive psychology and more recently in HCI – have been asking these and similar questions for more than 50 years, detailed study of the human use of these devices can still lead us to valuable insights.

Target selection is an important task in this area. Given multiple targets that a user might want to select – keys on a keyboard or buttons on a graphical user interface – what determines how quickly and accurately a user can move from one to another? Studies of target selection performance guide the size and selection of graphical icons, placement of buttons on a cell-phone keypad, and many other aspects of interface design.

Paul M. Fitts conducted pioneering experiments in this area in the 1950s, leading to the development of Fitts' law, a frequently cited result in HCI research. Originally intended as investigations of the theoretical limits of human performance in performing tasks of differing amplitudes of movement, Fitts' experiments involved asking participants to move between two targets separated by a distance. Fitts found that the information content of the task was determined by the distance between the targets and the inverse of the width of the targets (Fitts, 1954). This result was later generalized to expressive movement time as being a function of the logarithm of the ratio of the movement amplitude to the target width (MacKenzie, 1992).

Fitts' law tells us that as the distance between targets increases, or the size of the targets decreases, the time required to move between them increases. This has a certain intuitive appeal: it's harder to reach small targets than it is to reach larger targets, just as we can cover short distances more quickly than we can cover long distances. As much of our interaction with computers involves target selection, Fitts' law can help us understand the impact of design decisions regarding the placement and sizing of icons on a screen or keys on a keyboard.

Fitts' law is important enough to have spawned follow-on works, with researchers examining a wide variety of variations on the original task (MacKenzie, 1992; MacKenzie and Buxton, 1992). More recent efforts have confirmed the relevance of Fitts' law to the use of mobile devices while walking (Lin *et al.*, 2007), have developed models for "two-thumb" text entry on small keyboards (Clarkson *et al.*, 2007), and proposed extensions for non-rectangular targets (Grossman, Kong and Balakrishnan, 2007).

Juan-Pablo Hourcade and his colleagues at the University of Maryland faced this problem in the course of their work with young children. Faced with five-year old children who had difficulty clicking on computer icons, they set out to understand how pre-school children differed from young adults in their ability to complete target-selection tasks. Although several researchers had conducted Fitts' law research with young children, none had specifically addressed the question of whether performance differences justified the effort required to build interfaces specifically for this class of young users.

Their study involved 13 four-year-old children, 13 five-year-old children, and 13 adults (between 19 and 22 years old). Participants were asked to move the mouse from a home area to a target to the right. Targets had three diameters – 16, 32, or 64 pixels – with three distances between start and target – 128, 256, or 512 pixels. Participants completed 45 tasks in roughly 15 minutes – about the limit of the attention span of 4–5-year-old children. Data collected measured accuracy (did they press the button inside the target), time, and measures of re-entry (leaving and re-entering the target). Software developed for conducting the experiments also collected mouse motion data sufficient for reconstructing mouse movement paths.

Comparison of the data from children and adults generated several important insights. Children were slower and less accurate than adults. Children also tended to hover over targets, re-entering much more frequently than adults. Hourcade and colleagues found that while Fitts' law does apply to children, the model is more accurate for adults.

Mouse motion paths (or "trails") provide striking illustrations of the differences between children and adults. While adults move accurately and quickly between targets, five-year-old children went far afield, often overshooting targets. Four-year-old children were even worse, moving all over the screen (Figure 12.10). Children were also much more likely to repeatedly enter, leave, and re-enter targets (Figure 12.11).

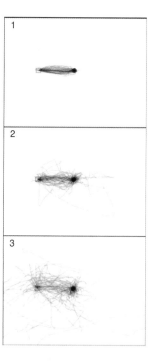

Figure 12.10 Aggregate mouse controls for all users show striking differences in the paths covered by different groups: (1) adults, (2) five-year-olds, and (3) four-year-olds (Hourcade *et al.*, 2004).

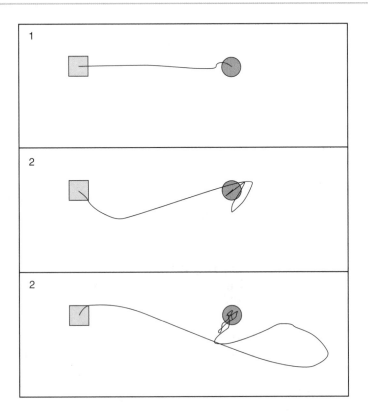

Figure 12.11 Typical paths illustrate greater re-entry rates for children: (1) adult, (2) five-year-old, and (3) four-year-old (Hourcade *et al.*, 2004).

Based on these differences in performance profiles, Hourcade *et al.* suggested several possible approaches to designing interfaces for young children. Possible solutions include larger icons, smaller mice, expanding targets, slower or accelerated mouse movement, and constrained motion between selections (using directional arrows and a selection button) (Hourcade *et al.*, 2004).

12.2.4 Handling stored data

Whenever you write or modify software to track user activities, you need to decide how to manage the data. Two approaches are commonly used: log files and databases. Log files are plain text files that indicate what happened, when it happened, and other details – such as the user ID – that might help when interpreting data. Log files are easy to write, but may require additional tools for interpretation. The comments from Section 12.1.1 are generally applicable to any application logs, with one important exception. As commonly available software tools that parse and interpret standard web log formats may not be immediately applicable to logs that you might develop for your own software, you may need to dig in and develop your own tools for parsing these log files.

Databases can be very useful for storing user activity information. Carefully designed relational databases can be used to store each action of interest in one or more database tables, along with all other relevant information. Powerful query languages, such as SQL, can then be used to develop flexible queries and reports for interpretation of the data. This approach may be most useful when working with an application that already connects to a relational database. When your tool uses a relational database to store application data, additional user activity information can often be added without much effort. This is often the case for database-driven web applications. If, however, your tool does not interact with a database, developing tools to parse log files might be easier than adding a database to the application.

12.2.5   Keystroke and activity loggers

Modern GUI windowing systems that support multi-tasking and concurrent use of multiple related tools present intriguing possibilities for HCI research. How often do users change applications? How many tasks do people work on at any given time? How long do users generally work within any given window before switching to another? What fraction of time is spent on overhead such as resizing windows, moving windows, or adjusting system controls? Answering these and other related questions requires data collected at the level of the operating environment.

Activity-logging software runs invisibly in the background, recording mouse movements, keyboard input, and windowing systems interactions including window movement, resizing, opening, and closing. Effectively, these tools act as proxies for user interaction events, recording events as they happen, and before they are passed along to applications or the operating environment. Keyloggers are a special subclass of activity-logging software, focusing only on keyboard input. Activity-logging software has achieved a fair amount of notoriety in recent years, as these tools have been used as "spyware", to surreptitiously record user interactions in the hopes of stealing passwords, finding evidence of criminal behavior, or collecting evidence of spousal infidelity.

Commercial activity-logging products are often marketed as being tools for employers and parents to track inappropriate computer use by employees and children (respectively). Although some of these tools might be appropriate for data collection for research purposes, some anti-spyware programs may defeat or remove activity loggers. You may want to test the logging software on relevant computers and disable anti-spyware measures before trying to use these tools to collect data.

The Disruption and Recovery Tracker (DART) (Iqbal and Horvitz, 2007) logs window positions and sizes, window actions, user activities, and alerts from various systems. DART's design presents an example of the responsible use of these tools for conducting legitimate research while remaining sensitive to privacy concerns. Keyboard logging was limited to a subset of possible choices, including menu shortcuts and some punctuation, and only a portion of each window title was collected. The resulting data therefore did not include file names, email addresses or subject lines, or web page titles. The analysis of more than 2200 hours of activity data collected from the main computers of 27 people over a two-week period generated numerous insights into time lost due to email or instant-messaging alerts, and how users respond to and recover from those interruptions (Iqbal and Horvitz, 2007).

12.2.6 Analyzing log files

Having collected some log files, you'll want to do something with them. Although log files for web servers, proxies, keystroke trackers, and custom-instrumented software might all have different formats and contents, the general approach towards instrumentation is roughly the same: in each case, you have one line in the file for each event of interest. Each line is likely to have some text indicating the time and date of the event (otherwise known as the timestamp), a description of what happened (such as the URL that was requested), and other related details.

How you proceed in your analysis is largely determined by your goals. If you are simply interested in trying to count certain events – for example, how many people pressed the Print button – you might be able to read through the file, classifying each event into one or more counters of various types. A single event in a log file might be classified according to the page that was requested, the day of the week, the time of day, and the type of web browser that made the request.

Reading through the file to extract the various pieces of information known about each event is an example of a common computing practice known as *parsing*. Often written in scripting languages, such as Perl and Python, log-file-parsing programs read one line at a time, breaking the entry for each event into constituent pieces and then updating data structures that keep counts and statistics of different types of event, as needed. Once the parser has read all of the relevant events and tallied up the numbers, results can be displayed graphically or in tabular form.

Countless programs for parsing and analyzing web log data have been developed since the web first came onto the scene in the 1990s. These tools range from freely available, open-source (but still highly functional) offerings to high-end commercial products. Tools such as Analog (www.analog.cx) and AWStats (http://awstats.sourceforge.net) provide a variety of ways to slice-and-dice data. Many of these tools work on data from proxy servers as well.

Data from non-web applications might prove a bit more challenging to analyze. Keystroke loggers and activity loggers may come with their own log-parsing and analysis packages, but you're likely to be on your own if you write your own software instrumentation to collect data. One approach in this case might be to design your log files to match the formats used by web servers. This mimicry would make your data amenable to analysis by web-log analysis tools. Another possibility is to create your own parsing and analysis software: if you can instrument your user interface to collect interaction information, you'll probably find this to be a reasonably manageable task.

More sophisticated questions might require fancier footwork in your analysis software. One common goal is to study the sequence of events. Do users click Print before Save more frequently than they click Save before Print? Answering questions like these may require moving beyond simple counts towards the application of data-mining techniques. Similar challenges are found when trying to infer the structure of interaction from web logs, leading to a variety of strategies that have been used to pick out user "sessions" (Heer and Chi, 2002).

Another approach might be to visualize log files. Highly interactive visualizations might show each event in a log file as a point on the screen, while providing tools for filtering and displaying data based on different criteria. As with other approaches for analyzing log files, visualization has been most widely used for web logs. WebQuilt (Hong et al., 2001) displays pages and links between them as nodes and links in a graph. Links are drawn as arrows, with thicker arrows indicating more heavily used links and shading indicating the amount of time spent on a page before selection of a link (Figure 12.12a). Users can zoom into a node to directly examine the page in question (Figure 12.12b).

Other approaches include the use of two-dimensional "starfield" displays for viewing individual requests by date, time, and other attributes (Hochheiser and Shneiderman, 2001) and finer-grained visualizations of mouse events on individual pages (Arroyo, Selker and Wei, 2006; Atterer, Wnuk and Schmidt, 2006).

12.3   Hybrid data collection methods

If one source of HCI data is good, then two must be better. Multiple channels of data collection can be combined to overcome the shortcomings of any one approach. Logging user interactions with a word processor may be a good start towards understanding how various controls are used, but log files provide little, if any, contextual information that might prove invaluable for interpretation and analysis. Video recordings or direct observation of users at work can help researchers understand users' goals, frustrations, and state of mind. Taken together, these data sources provide a much more detailed and complete picture of user activity than either would on its own.

Combining outputs from log files and video sessions may require specialized software support. Ideally, we might want to identify an event in a log file and jump right to the video recording that displays what the user was doing at that moment. HCI researchers have developed tools that provide this synchronized access (Crabtree et al., 2006; Hammontree, Hendrickson and Hensley, 1992). These features may also be available in professional tools for usability studies.

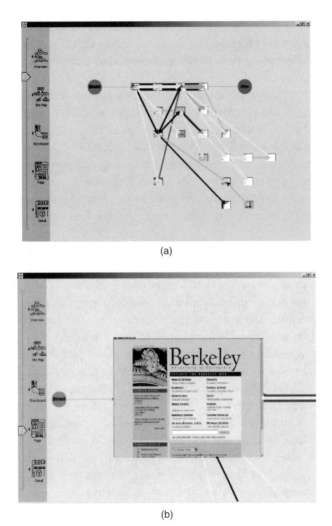

(a)

(b)

Figure 12.12 WebQuilt visualizations of log file data: (a) visualization of paths between two endpoints and (b) a page in context (Hong *et al.*, 2001). *Source*: Copyright ACM.

Similar approaches can be used for evaluation of web-based systems. Web log files and web proxies are limited in their ability to capture details of user interactions – and possibly in their ability to identify distinct users. However, they are relatively easy to configure and deploy. An instrumented web browser can provide vastly greater detail regarding specific user events, but it requires installation of unfamiliar software on end-user computers, potentially limiting the number of participants. One way to resolve this dilemma is to use both approaches in the same study. Specifically, data would be collected through both proxies and instrumented browsers (Obendorf et al., 2007). Although this approach might be more expensive and time-consuming than either approach used independently, the resulting data may be of higher quality.

Hybrid approaches have also proved useful in evaluations of ubiquitous computing environments. These environments involve multiple types of small, portable device, embedded sensors, and chat and voice interactions, all taking place "in the wild", free from the controls associated with laboratory assignments (Crabtree et al., 2006). Understanding how people engage in and interact with such embedded computing requires integration of chat transcripts, audio and/or video recordings, and system logs from a variety of devices. Although tools developed specifically for the integration and presentation of these disparate forms of data show significant promise, much work remains to be done in this area (Crabtree et al., 2006).

Another form of hybrid might combine automated data capture and analysis with observation or other qualitative approaches. As mentioned, log files from web activities or instrumented software are limited in their ability to describe the context of work. It is often difficult to go from the fine-grained detail of individual actions in a log file to a broader understanding of a user's goals and motivations. If we combine log data with active observation by a human researcher, we stand a better chance of understanding not just what the user was doing, but why she was doing it. The observer might sit behind the subject, watching her activities and making notes in real time, creating a log of observations that can be synchronized with the events in the server log. Alternatively, video recordings allow for annotation and observation at some later time. In either case, appropriate software can be used to view individual user events alongside observer annotations and content, thus providing a more detailed and informative picture than either source would give on its own. Combinations of multiple log approaches with observer annotations can provide even greater detail.

A recent study of movement throughout places in the home illustrates the potential for coordination of automated data collection with qualitative data – in this case, interviews (Aipperspach et al., 2006). To understand patterns of activity in homes, researchers placed location sensors at various points throughout several homes. These sensors captured where people were, when they were there, and for how long. Mathematical models were used to combine individual events in the log files into meaningful aggregates that identified "places" – locations of significant activity in the home. The models were evaluated by comparing the automatically identified places with the results of interviews with the participants. Interviews with the participants had the added advantage of providing context to explain some of the results of the models. In one case, models identified a "place" that included both a kitchen table and a living room couch. Interviews with the residents of this particular home indicated that this data was collected during the course of a birthday party, when they were continually moving between the kitchen and the living room, acting as if the two locations were part of one larger space(Aipperspach et al., 2006). Automated methods that focused only on the contents of the activity logs would not have had access to this more nuanced explanation of resident activity.

12.4   Automated interface evaluation

If using computers to collect data for HCI research is good, why not go further? Perhaps we can build software that automatically tests and evaluates user interfaces, generating data on usability issues or potential task performance times.

Automated inspection methods involve the analysis of aspects of user interfaces including layout, content, and language, in order to determine how well they conform to design guidelines (Ivory and Hearst, 2001). Generally, these tools provide reports indicating the extent to which an interface complies (or fails to comply) with guidelines. These reports can help designers understand where users might run into problems, and how an interface might be improved. The evaluations provided by these tools are generally based on empirical evidence, accepted design practices, and other accumulated experience. Automated inspection tools have been widely used in assessing the accessibility of websites. These tools examine web pages in search of images without explanatory text (<alt> tags), embedded scripts that might not be interpretable by screen readers, lack of navigation support, and other problems that may cause difficulties for users with disabilities. Dozens of web accessibility evaluation tools – ranging from free websites to expensive commercial software – have been developed, see Chapter 10 for more information.

Although these tools may provide some useful advice, the utility of any particular tool may be limited by the validity and scope of the underlying guidelines: analyses that are based on broad, well-supported guidelines are likely to be more appropriate than those that examine a narrower range of concerns. The use of multiple inspection methods to test interfaces from varying perspectives might be helpful. Ideally, these tools should be seen as companions to – not replacements for – traditional design reviews and user testing.

Other possibilities include the use of modeling or simulation to predict task performance times and other quantitative and qualitative characteristics of interface usage. These approaches are appealing, but they may be difficult to construct and limited in utility (Ivory and Hearst, 2001).

12.5   Challenges of computerized data collection

Automated software for HCI data collection has many advantages. The use of software to record user interaction events along with timestamps can ease data collection for structured experiments, simplifying work that previously would have been done with a stopwatch and paper records. Logs from web servers and other activity tracking tools document interaction events in unstructured, "natural" activities with far less difficulty than earlier techniques of observing or videotaping users.

However, effective use of these tools requires addressing several important challenges. As with any method for data collection, automated methods work best if their use is carefully considered in the context of the specific situation that is being studied and the research questions that are being asked. Before collecting data – or designing a system to collect data – you should ask yourself what you hope to learn from your research and how the data that you collect will help you answer those questions. Collecting too much data, too little data, or the wrong data, will not be particularly helpful.

Computer use can be considered over a wide range of time scales, with vastly different interpretations. At one end of the spectrum, individual keyboard and mouse interactions can take place as frequently as 10 times per second. At the other extreme, repeated uses of information resources and tools in the context of ongoing projects may occur over the course of years (Hilbert and Redmiles, 2000). Successful experiments must be designed to collect data that is appropriate for the questions being asked. If you want to understand usage patterns that occur over months and years, you probably do not want to collect every mouse event and key click; the volume of data will be simply overwhelming. Similarly, understanding dynamics of menu choices with specific applications requires more detailed information than simply which applications were used and when.

The amount of data collected is generally referred to as the granularity or resolution of the data. Fine-grained, high-resolution data involves every possible user interaction event; coarse-grained, low-resolution data contains fewer events, perhaps involving specific menu items, selection of specific buttons, or interaction with specific dialog boxes.

The specificity of the questions that you are asking may help determine the granularity of data that you need to collect. Many experiments involve structured questions regarding closed tasks on specific interfaces: which version of a web-based menu layout is better? To support these studies, automated data collection tools must collect data indicating which links are clicked, and when (see the Simultaneous vs. Sequential Menus sidebar for an example). Web server logs are very well-suited for such studies.

Open-ended studies aimed at understanding patterns of user interactions may pose greater challenges. To study how someone works with a word processor, we may need to determine which functions are used and when. Activity loggers that track individual mouse movements and key presses may help us understand some user actions, but they do not record structured, higher-order details that may be necessary to help understand how these individual actions come together to involve the completion of meaningful tasks. Put another way, if we want to understand sequences of important operations in word-processing tasks, we don't necessarily want a list of keystrokes and mouse clicks. Instead, we'd like to know that the user formatted text, inserted a table, and then viewed a print preview. Still higher-level concepts are even harder to track: how do we know when a user has completed a task?

Researchers have tried a variety of approaches for inferring higher-level tasks from low-level interaction events. Generally, these approaches involve combining domain knowledge of both the software being studied and user behavior to identify patterns that would be representative of defined tasks (Hammontree, Hendrickson and Hensley, 1992; Ivory and Hearst, 2001). These inferential efforts face many challenges. For example, applications that provide multiple methods for accessing given functionality (such as both a menu choice and a toolbar button for Print) may generate log files that contain all of these methods. However, log entry analysis approaches may not recognize these multiple paths as leading to a common goal. Establishing appropriate contextual information may also be difficult: log file entries that indicate a button was pressed are less informative than those that indicate which button was pressed (Hilbert and Redmiles, 2000).

Analysis challenges are particularly pronounced in the analysis of web server logs, which may contain interleaved requests from dozens of different users. Statistical analyses and visualization tools have been used to try to identify individual user sessions from log files (Heer and Chi, 2002; Hochheiser and Shneiderman, 2001; Pirolli and Pitkow, 1999), but these tools are imperfect at best. If a web browser coming from a given Internet address accesses a page on your site and then accesses a second page 10 minutes later, does that count as one session or two? Your log file cannot tell you if the user was reading the page between those two requests or if she was talking on the telephone. Those requests may not have come from the same person – for all you know, it's a shared computer in a library or classroom that is used by dozens of individuals on any given day.

Custom-built or instrumented software may alleviate some data-granularity problems by providing you with complete control over the data that is collected, at the expense of the time and effort required to develop the data collection tools. If you are willing and able to commit the resources necessary for software customization, you can configure the software to capture all of the data that you think might be interesting: nothing more, nothing less.

Unfortunately, matters are rarely so clean-cut. There may be a vast difference between what you think you need before you start large-scale data collection and what you may wish you had collected once you begin analyzing the data. The expense of running experiments – particularly those that involve substantial effort in participant recruitment – creates a tendency towards collecting as much data as possible. "It's easy to collect this information," the thinking goes, "so we may as well. After all, disk storage is inexpensive, and these details may prove useful later on."

Although there is a certain logic to the defensive approach of collecting as much data as possible, there are some limits to this approach. As anyone who's sifted through megabytes of event logs can tell you, collecting lots of data may simply leave you with lots of uninformative data junk to sift through. Even with software tools, the identification of meaningful patterns (as opposed to random coincidences) can be difficult. Lower-resolution data may be somewhat easier to analyze.

If your data collection tools can clearly distinguish between coarse-grained and fine-grained events, you might be able to have your cake and eat it too. Data collection tools might mark each event with an indication of the level of granularity that lets you fine-tune your analysis – looking only at high-level events, such as menu selections, only at low-level events, such as mouse movements, or perhaps some hybrid approach that examines low-level events that precede or follow interesting high-level events.

As with any HCI research, proper attention to pilot testing can be important. Pilot testing of both the data collection and data analysis pieces of the experiment can help you verify that the data you are collecting actually tells you what you want it to. Analyzing the pilot data may help you verify that you are collecting data of the appropriate granularity.

All of the approaches to automatic data collection raise potential security concerns. Logs of web browser activity can say a good deal about a person browsing the web. This information might be used to infer sensitive or embarrassing details about a person's habits, interests, or medical concerns. Although the potential harm from the logs of any single website may be relatively minimal, proxy servers can be configured to capture all of the interactions with every website visited by a given computer. Indirect (and sometimes non-existent) links between people and computers make matters even worse in this regard. Web logs track the identity (in terms of the IP number) of the computer that makes each request. A number in a web server log may correspond to the computer on your desk, but this does not mean that you were the person that was at the computer when the browser visited embarrassing websites.

Activity loggers and keystroke loggers make matters even worse. By tracking every input action, these tools collect enough data to reconstruct documents, emails, calendars, and other damaging evidence. These tools have been surreptitiously used in criminal investigations and divorce proceedings. Regardless of your views on the appropriateness of using secretive software to spy on family members, you should take care to ensure that your data collection tools don't gather data that others would find sensitive, damaging, or otherwise private. Some approaches include customizing your tools to avoid potentially problematic data, such as specific keys that are pressed (as opposed to simply noting that a key was pressed) and window titles (which may contain document titles).

Summary

Automated data collection systems give researchers the ability to easily collect detailed user interaction information. Appropriately configured software tools can be used to replace labor-intensive approaches such as manual observation or coding of events on videotape. The result is a qualitative, as well as quantitative difference: not only can more data be collected, but the increased ease of data collection allows researchers to conduct experiments that otherwise would be too difficult or expensive. These strengths make automated data collection a clear first choice for many HCI research efforts.

There are three broad categories of question that might benefit from automated methods of data collection:

- Retrospective analyses of information management behavior: These studies look at artifacts of computer use, including location of documents, email folders, and other structures created during the course of using and managing information, in order to understand how people use these tools.

- Controlled experiments: Web server logs and completely customized software can be used to collect timing and related data for experiments. As web logs contain entries for each link selection event, they are most useful for cases involving the study of selection of web links. With proper design, web links can be used to model menu layouts and related topics. Fully customized software may be needed if additional data (such as mouse movements) is required, but hybrids may be useful. For example, JavaScript embedded in a web page might be used to record mouse movements and translate those movements into events stored in a log file alongside the basic server logs.

- Usability studies and other explorations of how users work with tools: Web server logs, proxy server logs, keystroke loggers, and activity loggers record user interaction events with one or more websites, applications, or operating environments. The interactions can be used to examine which features of a tool a user used and when. With appropriate analysis, this data can be used to find interaction problems and identify opportunities for usability improvements.

Successful use of any of these approaches requires careful consideration of the appropriate granularity of data to be collected and the tools to be used for data analysis. As with other data collection approaches, the key is to precisely identify the data that is needed and collect only that data.

Tools that collect data on user activities have potential privacy implications. This is particularly important when the goal is to study how users work with tools to complete real tasks: providing artificial tasks in the hopes of reducing privacy concerns may decrease the realism of the data. Experiments involving this set of data should be carefully designed, in consultation with appropriate institutional review boards (see Chapter 14), to avoid violations of participant privacy and trust.

Discussion Questions

1. Online spreadsheets, word processors, and other office productivity tools blur the line between websites and traditional software. In doing so, they provide both opportunities and challenges for HCI researchers. As the software infrastructure for online tools resides completely on the hosting server, researchers can easily modify and redeploy interfaces without having to update individual computers. As with traditional web interfaces, requests for content from the server can be logged and resulting files can be analyzed. However, as client-side interactions (usually executed through JavaScript code) do not generate server requests, additional data recording measures may be necessary. Server-side storage of both activity data and user-created data such as documents or spreadsheets presents privacy challenges. What other challenges or opportunities can you see in such dynamic applications? Pick an online word processor, spreadsheet, or presentation tool: how would you design a system to study its usability?

2. A hybrid system for automated computer data collection might involve a combination of web server logs – ideally from a proxy that would track all of a participant's interactions – and one or more software packages instrumented to collect data of interest. What would be the pros and cons of such a system relative to a full-scale activity logger that would track all user interactions?

3. Legitimate concerns about user privacy have led some researchers to be very cautious about the data that they collect with keyboard or activity loggers. This appropriate concern for user privacy does not come without a cost: in throwing away details such as document titles, destination addresses for emails, and specifics of visited web pages, researchers lose information that might have been used to develop a more nuanced understanding of the underlying activity. For example, was the user sending email to colleagues at work, or at home? Can you think of ways to configure logging software to collect certain attributes of document titles, email headers, and related information in a manner that might prove useful for research purposes while still being respectful of user privacy? What effect might greater notification – perhaps telling participants that you might record sensitive information – have on your experiments?

4. The Fitts' Law, Children, and Mouse Control sidebar provides an example of experiments that used mouse motion data to study how children differed from adults in their use of mice. Although 3–5-year-old children don't make much of use keyboards, slightly older children might begin to type. How would you study differences between children and adults in terms of their use of keyboards? What sort of data would you collect and how would you interpret it? How would this differ if you were considering smaller keyboards such as those used on some cell phones?

Research Design Exercises

1. Experiment with web server logs and log analysis on your own desktop.
   (a) Start by getting or generating a web server log file. You might ask computing support people in your school or company for some web log data. Log files can be *very* large: you probably only want a small snapshot. If your school or department gets a good deal of web traffic, you should be able to get a few megabytes of log data. Be forewarned, some network administrators may not like the idea of handing out this information. You may have to convince them that you will use it responsibly. Alternatively, you can install your own web server and run it. If your computer does not have a web server installed, the Apache web server (http://httpd.apache.org) is available for most major platforms. Download the server, install it, and configure it. The server configuration file (httpd.conf) will have entries that indicate where log files can be found. On Windows systems, Apache usually installs into C:\Program Files\Apache Software Foundation\Apachex.y\, where x.y is the version number. The configuration file, httpd.conf, can be found in the conf subdirectory and log files in the logs directory. Once you get the server running, build a few web pages with links between them and access them.

(b) Examine the log files to see what they can tell you about pages that were accessed, when they were accessed, and other related details.

(c) Try using a tool to analyze the log files. Analog (www.analog.cx) is an open-source, freely available web log analyzer that can be used with ReportMagic (www.reportmagic.org) to create graphical displays of log analysis results.

(d) For a further challenge, try to configure and use a web proxy server, such as Squid (www.squid-cache.org).

2. Use implicitly collected information data from your computer to conduct an investigation of information management patterns. Start with folders and subfolders for documents: Do you have all of your documents in one folder or do you have many subfolders? How many documents in each folder? How many subfolders in each subfolder? What is the maximum "depth" of your subfolders? You can also look at the number of documents that you have on the desktop. Collect similar information for your email: How many items are in the inbox? How many folders? Repeat this analysis with a friend's data. Can you draw any conclusions about data management habits and practices?

3. Try to find and use an instrumented software program, such as ingimp (www.ingimp.org). You might be able to find a keyboard logger or general activity tracker. Install the program on your computer and use it to accomplish some tasks. Find and examine the log files: what do they tell you about how you used the program? Can you relate the contents of the log files to the tasks that you performed with the program?

4. Some simple excursions into collecting data on keyboard and mouse usage can be conducted without writing custom software.

(a) For keyboard usage, carefully remove the backspace and arrow keys from your keyboard. Disconnect your mouse as well. Ask someone to type a paragraph of text into a word processor and time their response. As your participant will be unable to delete any mistakes or use the arrow keys to move to a different part of the text, you'll get a record of exactly which keys were pressed. You can use this data to collect error rates.

(b) Mouse usage can be measured with a drawing program. Draw two circles on opposite sides of the screen. Select the "pencil" tool and ask the user to hold down the mouse while moving back and forth several times between the two targets. As long as the mouse is held down, this will lead to a set of trails similar to those found in Figures 12.10 and 12.11. Time the results. If you vary the distances between the targets and the size of the targets, you can run a Fitts' law study.

References

Aipperspach, R., Rattenbury, T., Woodruff, A., and Canny, J. (2006) A Quantitative Method for Revealing and Comparing Places in the Home. In Dourish, P., and Friday, A., (eds.), *UbiComp 2006: Ubiquitous Computing*, Lecture Notes in Computer Science 4206, Springer, 1–18.

Arroyo, E., Selker, T., and Wei, W. (2006) Usability tool for analysis of web designs using mouse tracks. *Extended Abstracts of the ACM Conference on Human Factors in Computing Systems*, 484–489.

Atterer, R., Wnuk, M., and Schmidt, A. (2006) Knowing the user's every move: User activity tracking for website usability evaluation and implicit interaction. *Proceedings of the 15th international conference on the World Wide Web*, 203–212.

Clarkson, E., Lyons, K., Clawson, J., and Starner, T. (2007) Revisiting and validating a model of two-thumb text entry. *Proceedings of the SIGCHI conference on Human Factors in Computing Systems*.

Crabtree, A., Benford, S., Greenhalgh, C., Tennent, P., Chalmers, M., and Brown, B. (2006) Supporting ethnographic studies of ubiquitous computing in the wild. *Proceedings of the ACM Conference on Designing Interactive Systems*, 60–69.

Fielding, R., Gettys, J., Mogul, J., Frystyk, H., Masinter, L., Leach, P., and Berners-Lee, T. (1999) Hypertext Transfer Protocol: HTTP/1.1, Retrieved October 14, 2009 from http://www.ietf.org/rfc/rfc2616.txt.

Fitts, P.M. (1954) The information capacity of the human motor system in controlling the amplitude of movement. *Journal of Experimental Psychology*, **47**(6):381–391.

Grossman, T., Kong, N., and Balakrishnan, R. (2007) Modeling pointing at targets of arbitrary shapes. *Proceedings of the ACM Conference on Human Factors in Computing Systems*, 463–472.

Hammontree, M.L., Hendrickson, J.J., and Hensley, B.W. (1992) Integrated data capture and analysis tools for research and testing on graphical user interfaces. *Proceedings of the ACM Conference on Human Factors in Computing Systems*, 431–432.

Harris, J. (2005) Inside Deep Thought. *An Office User Interface Blog: Why the UI*, Part 6. Retrieved October 8, 2007, from http://blogs.msdn.com/jensenh/archive/2005/10/31/487247.aspx.

Harris, J. (2006) No Distaste for Paste. *An Office User Interface Blog: Why the UI*, Part 7. Retrieved October 8, 2007, from http://blogs.msdn.com/jensenh/archive/2006/04/07/570798.aspx.

Heer, J. and Chi, E.H. (2002) Separating the swarm: Categorization methods for user sessions on the web. *Proceedings of the ACM Conference on Human Factors in Computing Systems*, 243–250.

Hilbert, D.M. and Redmiles, D.F. (2000) Extracting usability information from user interface events. *ACM Computing Surveys*, **32**(4):384–421.

Hochheiser, H. and Shneiderman, B. (2000) Performance benefits of simultaneous over sequential menus as task complexity increases. *International Journal of Human–Computer Interaction*, **12**(2):173–192.

Hochheiser, H. and Shneiderman, B. (2001) Using interactive visualizations of WWW log data to characterize access patterns and inform site design. *Journal of the American Society for Information Science and Technology*, **52**(4):331–343.

Hong, J.I., Heer, J., Waterson, S., and Landay, J.A. (2001) WebQuilt: A proxy-based approach to remote web usability testing. *ACM Transactions on Information Systems*, **19**(3):263–285.

Hourcade, J.P., Bederson, B.B., Druin, A., and Guimbretière, F. (2004) Differences in pointing task performance between preschool children and adults using mice. *ACM Transactions on Computer–Human Interaction*, **11**(4):357–386.

Iqbal, S.T. and Horvitz, E. (2007) Disruption and recovery of computing tasks: Field study, analysis, and directions. *Proceedings of the ACM Conference on Human Factors in Computing Systems*, 677–686.

Ivory, M.Y. and Hearst, M.A. (2001) The state of the art in automating usability evaluation of user interfaces. *ACM Computing Surveys*, **33**(4):470–516.

Koster, M. (1994) *A Standard for Robot Exclusion*. Retrieved August 1, 2007, from http://www. robot-stxt.org/wc/robots.html.

Lin, M., Goldman, R., Price, K.J., *et al*. (2007) How do people tap when walking? An empirical investigation of nomadic data entry. *International Journal of Human–Computer Studies*, **65**(9):759–769.

MacKenzie, I.S. (1992) Fitts' Law as a research and design tool in human–computer interaction. *Human–Computer Interaction*, **7**(1):91–139.

MacKenzie, I.S. and Buxton, W. (1992) Extending Fitts' law to two-dimensional tasks. *Proceedings of the ACM Conference on Human Factors in Computing Systems*, 219–226.

McGrenere, J. and Moore, G. (2000) Are we all in the same "bloat"? Paper presented at the Graphics Interface conference.

McGrenere, J., Baecker, R.M., and Booth, K.S. (2002) An evaluation of a multiple interface design solution for bloated software. *Proceedings of the ACM Conference on Human Factors in Computing Systems*, 164–170.

Obendorf, H., Weinreich, H., Herder, E., and Mayer, M. (2007) Web page revisitation revisited: Implications of a long-term click-stream study of browser usage. *Proceedings of the ACM Conference on Human Factors in Computing Systems*, 597–606.

Pirolli, P. and Pitkow, J. (1999) Distributions of surfers' paths through the World Wide Web: Empirical characterizations. *World Wide Web*, **2**(1):29–45.

Terry, M. (2007) Ingimp: Info. Retrieved October 8, 2007, from http://www.ingimp.org/info/.

Terry, M., Kay, M., Van Vugt, B., Slack, B., and Park, T., (2008) Ingimp: introducing instrumentation to an end-user open source application. *Proceedings of the ACM Conference on Human Factors in Computing Systems*, 607–616.

World Wide Web Consortium. (1995) Logging control in W3C httpd. Retrieved June 2, 2008, from http://www. w3.org/Daemon/User/Config/Logging.html.

Measuring the human

As understanding what people do, how they do it, and how they react can be critical for comparing and evaluating interfaces, participants in human–computer interaction (HCI) research form an important part of the systems that we study.

Seen in this light, participants in research studies can be important data sources: a wide variety of physical and emotional measurements can help us gain significant insight into the way that users work with our interfaces. Although we always, of course, strive to treat participants with the respect and dignity that they deserve (Chapter 14), they can also be treasure troves of detailed information that may otherwise be hard – if not impossible – to acquire. This makes familiarity with human data collection an important skill for any HCI researcher.

Automated human data collection techniques cover a range of complexity, cost, and invasiveness. Some of the simplest techniques involve data from familiar input devices, such as mice and keyboards. These familiar tools can help us understand how people navigate in graphical environments and provide textual input. More complicated approaches include eye-tracking tools for studying patterns in eye movements, galvanic skin response and blood volume and heart rate measurements for the study of physical and emotional responses. At the high end, functional MRI (fMRI) tools can be used to examine how different parts of the brain react and interact in various circumstances.

Although many of these techniques involve expensive equipment and may require training that is beyond the reach of many HCI researchers, they present intriguing possibilities for gaining understanding that would otherwise be elusive. Eye-tracking tools that tell us where people are looking on a screen can help us understand visual processes involved in navigating lists of options. Skin response or cardiovascular monitors can provide insight into a user's level of arousal or frustration. The rich, detailed information about user activities and responses provided by these tools can help extend our understanding of human use of computer interfaces.

This chapter discusses a variety of options, with an eye towards cost–benefit trade-offs: as some tools are clearly more difficult and expensive than others, we strive to use the simplest and least expensive tools suitable for a given job.

13.1   Eye tracking

Direct interaction data collection involves the measurement of mouse or keyboard interactions in an attempt to see how hand movements translate into interactions with computers. This approach can be very useful, but it paints a necessarily incomplete picture. Detailed information about interaction events with mice or keyboards does not help us understand what happens between events. Did the user's finger move between several different keys before choosing which one to press? What did the user look at on the screen before selecting a particular link on the web page?

Eye-tracking systems can help us begin to answer these questions. These systems use cameras or other sensors to continuously track the position or orientation of eyes or other parts of the body. Sophisticated software can be used to transform raw data from these sensors into detailed descriptions of where a user looked while examining a web page.

Our eyes are constantly in motion. Rapid motions (known as "saccades") help us re-orient, while larger motions indicate shifts in attention, leading to fixation on new targets (Jacob and Karn, 2003) – perhaps in anticipation of a new task or in response to some stimulus. This motion presents researchers with some intriguing possibilities. If we can understand how users move their eyes when completing various interface tasks, we might gain some insight into where attention is focused and how choices are made. This additional data can take us beyond the relatively uninformative traces of mouse and keyboard events, filling in the holes: just where did the user look before she moved her mouse from one menu to the next? Which portions of a web page initially attract user attention?

Technologies and applications have progressed significantly since the first use of eye tracking in the early 20th century (Jacob and Karn, 2003). Modern systems use sensors based on the desktop or on head-mounted devices to track the reflection of infrared light from the cornea or retina (Jacob and Karn, 2003; Kumar, 2006). Sophisticated software uses the geometry of the eye and the related optics to identify where the user is looking at any given point in time. Similar technology can be used for large-scale, motion-tracking systems that follow all or part of a human body as it moves through space. See the Motion Tracking for Large Displays and Virtual Environments sidebar for a discussion of an HCI research effort involving motion tracking.

Motion Tracking for Large Displays and Virtual Environments

Some forms of human–computer interaction inherently require users to move around in space. Users of wall-sized displays routinely move from one side to another, or up and down, just as teachers in a classroom move to different parts of a blackboard. Users of virtual environments turn their heads, walk around, and move their hands to grasp objects. Collecting data that will help understand patterns of motion – where do users move, how do they move, and when do they do it? – requires data collection tools and techniques beyond those used with desktop systems.

Motion-tracking tools using cameras and markers worn by study participants can track motion through a large space. As the participant moves through space, the cameras use the marker to create a record of where the participant went and when. One study used this approach to examine activity in the course of using a wall-sized display (24 monitors, arranged as eight columns of three monitors each, see Figure 13.1) to search and explore real-estate data. Researchers were interested to see whether users would move around more (physical navigation) or use zooming and panning mechanisms (virtual navigation).

Participants wore a hat with sensors for the motion-tracking system (Figure 13.2), which recorded their activity. Different display widths – ranging from one column to all eight columns – were used to study the effect of the width of the display. Participants generally used virtual navigation less and physical navigation more with wider displays. They also preferred physical navigation (Ball, North and Bowman, 2007).

Figure 13.1 A portion of the wall-sized display used in the navigation study (*Source*: Ball, North and Bowman, 2007, © ACM).

Researchers have used sensors that directly measure the position and orientation of various body parts to answer questions about movement and activity in immersive virtual environments. In one study, participants used a head-mounted display and a 3D mouse to interact with an immersive environment. Sensors monitored the position of the head, arms, legs, or other appropriate body parts. This approach provided insights into user activity in a variety of applications of virtual environments, including the diagnosis of attention deficit hyperactivity disorder (ADHD) and neurological rehabilitation of stroke patients (Shahabi *et al.*, 2007).

Figure 13.2 A hat mounted with head-tracking sensors for the study of navigation with wall-sized displays (*Source*: Ball, North and Bowman, 2007, © ACM).

Improvements in hardware and software notwithstanding, eye tracking presents significant challenges for HCI work. Commercially available eye-tracking systems are expensive, but USB cameras and other inexpensive hardware have inspired the design of low-cost alternatives (Kumar, 2006). Systems are often hard to use, requiring calibration for each user and inconvenience such as head-mounted devices or restrictions on the range of movement allowed to the user (Jacob and Karn, 2003).

Eye-tracking data can also be difficult to interpret. Eye trackers can tell where the user was looking at any given point in time, but they may or may not track what the user was looking at

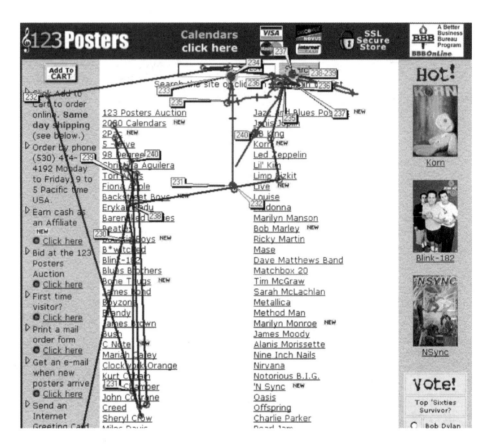

Figure 13.3 A web page annotated with eye-tracking data: lines indicating gaze paths link fixation points annotated with time stamps, providing a trail for a series of interactions (*Source:* Card *et al.*, 2001, © ACM).

when this data was collected. As where the user's eyes are looking and what they are looking at on the screen are both important (Jacob and Karn, 2003), appropriate use of eye-tracking data often requires integrating data from the eye-tracker with histories of interaction with the interface. Software tools that automatically synchronize these data streams can simplify the data interpretation process (Crowe and Narayanan, 2000). Systems that can overlay "trails" indicating the path of a user's gaze onto screen shots can be particularly useful (Figure 13.3).

Additional difficulties in interpretation are based in the inherent messiness of the data. Given the large number of constant small motions, determination of exactly when the user has focused (or "fixated") on a specific viewpoint can be hard to determine. Non-standard definitions of thresholds and terminology have made comparison of results from different experiments challenging, to say the least (Jacob and Karn, 2003).

Despite these challenges, eye tracking has been used both as a new form of computer input and as the basis for research projects aimed at using eye movements as a source of data for studying human–computer interactions (Jacob and Karn, 2003; Kumar, 2006). Eye tracking has been widely-used as an assistive technology for people with quadriplegia and others who are unable to use motor functions to operate a mouse, keyboard, or other adaptive input device (Barreto, Gao and Adjouadi, 2008; Hornof, Cavender and Hoselton, 2004). The use of gaze control for pointing and selecting objects – eye-gaze as complementing mice (Bieg, 2009; Zhai, Morimoto and Ihde, 1999) or replacing them (Jacob and Karn, 2003; Kumar, Paepcke and Winograd, 2007; Murata, 2006) – has been suggested by many researchers, leading to a variety of proposed designs.

Researchers have used eye tracking to study user behavior with a wide range of computer interfaces. Web browsing and navigation have been particularly well-studied in this regard. In a pair of studies, researchers at Microsoft used an eye-tracking system to examine the impact of factors such as the placement of a target link in a list of results and the length of the contextual text snippet that accompanies the results (Cutrell and Guan, 2007; Guan and Cutrell, 2007). In study of placement, users were observed to be more likely to look at links early in a list than later and to spend more time looking at the earlier links (Guan and Cutrell, 2007). Consideration of the length of text summaries led to interesting results: when looking for a specific link, users tended to focus on more search results as the summaries got longer. This effect was less notable for open-ended "informational" tasks that were not focused on a specific goal. The researcher speculated that this difference was due to the relevance of the summaries in each case: summaries that were useful in the informational task were distractions that obscured the specific link name in the other tasks (Cutrell and Guan, 2007). Other studies have examined patterns in eye movements as users interact with websites, moving both within individual pages and across multiple pages (Buscher, Cutrell and Morris, 2009; Card et al., 2001; Goldberg et al., 2002).

Other experiments have used eye tracking to understand the progression of eye focus during menu selection tasks. One study found that eye-focus patterns in tasks involving reading menu items differed significantly from selecting items. Although users fixated on each item when reading menus, they tended to use sequences of eye movements in a given direction – known as "sweeps" – when performing selection tasks (Aaltonen, Hyrskykari and Räihä, 1998). Eye tracking has also been used to study differences in how user attention differs for alternative visualizations of hierarchical structures (Pirolli, Card and Van Der Wege, 2000), to build document summaries based on eye-gaze data describing areas that were the focus of user attention (Xu, Jiang and Lau, 2009), and to explore the possibility of using gaze in immersive collaborative environments (Steptoe et al., 2008).

Eye tracking in HCI research can be a high-cost, high-reward endeavor. Equipment can be expensive and tricky to use, and data interpretation is often challenging. Rewards come in the form of insight into user activity that is often unavailable through other means. The possibility of inexpensive systems built on commonly-available hardware

(Kumar, 2006) may make eye tracking more widely accessible. Until such systems are available, researchers considering this technology should carefully consider questions of both design and analysis.

Although eye tracking has been successfully used for both top-down, hypothesis-driven experiments and bottom-up exploratory work (Jacob and Karn, 2003), appropriate experimental design may increase the odds of success. Exploratory analysis offers the possibility of generating novel, unexpected insights, at the potential cost of open-ended searching for illusive needles in haystacks of data. Hypothesis-driven experiments constrain the analysis needed, helping avoid fruitless searches down blind alleys.

A narrow focus can also help simplify exploratory work. A study of the effectiveness of browser feedback for secure websites used eye tracking to study the use of security indicators, including the secure web protocol indicator ("https://"), lock or key icons, and security certificates (Whalen and Inkpen, 2005). Focusing on these areas, researchers learned that users often looked at the lock icon on the browser window before or after looking at the HTTPS header in the web location bar. Eye tracking also identified potential confusion due to browser designs, as some users looked at the lower left-hand corner of the browser (where the lock is on Netscape/Mozilla browsers) rather than the lower right-hand corner (where it can be found on the Internet Explorer browser used in the study) (Whalen and Inkpen, 2005).

13.2   Physiological tools

Our bodies are intricate devices, with numerous inter-related systems that change their behavior as we are excited, frustrated, or otherwise aroused. Each cell in our body is part of an electrical system, with voltage levels that differ across cell membranes and change under the right conditions (Stern, Ray and Quigley, 2001). Blood flow, heart rate, rate of breathing, and electrical conductivity of various parts of the body are just a few of the measures that have been studied in an attempt to better understand these responses. The combination of these physiological measures with more traditional study of task performance and subjective responses is known as *psychophysiology* (Wastell and Newman, 1996).

Psychophysiology brings the possibility of using concrete measurements to generate fine-grained assessments of seemingly subjective measurements that can otherwise only be studied through the use of questionnaires. Imagine a study of user frustration levels with a series of alternative interface designs. You might start by asking participants to complete a series of tasks with each interface. After they complete the tasks, you could ask the users to complete one or more questionnaires aimed at understanding frustration levels. You might even ask them which features of the designs were more or less frustrating.

Even though this might be a fine design for your study, it misses some potentially important and interesting information. For example, when were the users most frustrated? Were they frustrated on the same task for each interface or did some designs cause less frustration on some tasks and more frustration on others? Post-fact questionnaires are simply too coarse-grained to address these questions. The retrospective nature of questionnaires means that you are relying on the participants' fallible and incomplete memories to get your results.

Suppose your careful and thorough reading of the appropriate literature tells you that increases in frustration lead to increases in heart rate. With some sensors, recording equipment, and appropriate training in their use, you could change your experiment to monitor heart rate during task completion time. Appropriate tools for synchronizing the physiological data with other data that you collect during the tasks – such as task completion time or fine-grained records of all activities – will let you see exactly what the participant was doing when he became most frustrated. Correlating this information with feedback from the subjective questionnaire will provide you with a much fuller picture than you would have been able to get from only the task performance data and subjective responses.

13.2.1 Physiological data

Appropriate use of physiological data for research requires an understanding of the types of data that can be collected, the tools required for data collection, and the ways in which these data sources respond to various stimuli. Skin conductivity, blood flow, and respiration rate (to name a few examples) are very different measures, each presenting a variety of challenges in terms of both collection and interpretation.

Approaches that collect data from various parts of the body require different classes of sensor for measuring responses. Broadly speaking, these sensors fall into two classes: electrodes, which directly record electrical signals, and transducers, which convert mechanical or physical measurements into an electrical form (Stern, Ray and Quigley, 2001). Once measured by sensors, these data are stored on a computer (often after having been converted to a digital form by an analog-to-digital converter), where they can be filtered and analyzed.

Complex physiological responses to different stimuli can make interpretation a challenge: there is no single, monolithic notion of arousal. The concept of *stimulus–response specificity* tells us that certain stimuli lead to identifiable response patterns that may involve increases in some measures alongside increases in others (Stern, Ray and Quigley, 2001). Although this may not be a major concern for relatively simple HCI experiments involving only one form of physiological data, you should always understand the range of potential responses that might be observed in response to stimuli introduced in your research.

The sources of physiological data that have been used in HCI research can be classified according to the type of signal involved, the location on the body, and the kinds of sensors required (see Table 13.1). The range of data sources and their applications are likely to continue to expand as researchers find creative applications for evolving technologies: one recent study suggested the use of pupil-diameter measurements from eye-tracking systems as a means of measuring user stress (Barreto, Gao and Adjouadi, 2008).

Data source	Technique	Signal type	Possible locations	Sensors
Electrodermal activity	Galvanic skin response (GSR) (Mandryk and Inkpen, 2004; Scheirer et al., 2002)	Electrical	Fingers, toes	Surface electrodes
Cardiovascular data	Blood-volume pressure (Scheirer et al., 2002)	Light absorption	Finger	Surface electrodes
	Electrocardiography (Mandryk and Inkpen, 2004)	Electrical	Chest, abdomen	Surface electrodes
Respiration	Chest contraction and expansion (Mandryk and Inkpen, 2004)	Physical	Thorax	Stress sensor
Muscular and skeletal positioning	Pressure or position sensing (Brady et al., 2005; Dunne et al., 2006a; Dunne et al., 2006b)	Physical or electrical	Varied	Pressure sensor, fiber optics, others
Muscle tension	Electromyography (Mandryk and Inkpen, 2004)	Electrical	Jaw, face	Surface electrodes
Brain activity	Electroencephalography (Lee and Tan, 2006)	Electrical	Head	Electrodes in helmet
	Evoked responses (Stern, Ray and Quigley, 2001)	Electrical	Head	Surface electrodes

Table 13.1 Types of physiological data used in HCI research.

13.2.1.1   *Electrodermal activity or galvanic skin response*

Conductivity is a measure of how well electricity flows through a substance: higher conductivity means a greater flow of electricity. Electrodermal activity is the measurement of the flow of electricity through the skin. As many science-museum exhibits demonstrate, human bodies can act as conductors for electricity. Glands in our hands and feet produce sweat in response to emotional and cognitive stimuli. The salty sweat increases conductivity, allowing more electricity to flow (Mandryk and Inkpen, 2004; Stern, Ray and Quigley, 2001). Electrodermal systems use a pair of electrodes on the skin – usually connected to fingers – to measure the conductivity between two points (Figure 13.4). Fear leads to smaller increases in skin conductance than sadness (Cacioppo et al., 2000). Conductance levels have also been linked to arousal, cognitive activity (Mandryk and Inkpen, 2004), and frustration (Scheirer et al., 2002).

Figure 13.4 Thought Technology's skin conductance sensor attaches to two fingers or toes to measure galvanic skin response (GSR) (http://www.thoughttechnology.com/sensors.htm, accessed 5 March, 2008).

13.2.1.2 Cardiovascular signals

Anyone who has ridden a roller coaster or watched a suspenseful movie has first-hand knowledge of how the heart responds to stimuli. Increased heart rate is one part of a complex set of reactions that may involve changes in the variability of the heart rate, blood pressure and blood-volume pressure (Scheirer *et al.*, 2002). Heart-rate variability has been used to measure mental effort and stress (Mandryk and Inkpen, 2004; Rowe, Sibert and Irwin, 1998; Wastell and Newman, 1996) and emotional responses including fear, happiness, and anger (Cacioppo *et al.*, 2000).

Commonly-used techniques for measuring cardiovascular activity include blood-volume pressure (BVP) monitoring and electrocardiography (EKG). Blood-volume pressure measurements are based on the light-absorption characteristics of capillaries in the finger. Changes in blood volume in a given location lead to changes in reflected light. Sensors worn on the finger can measure these changes. As blood-volume changes can be correlated with stimuli that provoke anxiety, BVP can be used as an indirect measurement of user anxiety. Heart-rate variability information can also be inferred from BVP data (Scheirer *et al.*, 2002). Electrocardiography measures the electrical current that causes the heart to pump. Using sensors placed on different places on the body, EKG can measure heart rate, the interval between heartbeats, and heart-rate variability (Mandryk and Inkpen, 2004).

13.2.1.3 Respiration

Just as certain stimuli can make our hearts beat faster, changes in mood can affect our breathing. Arousal may make us breathe faster and some emotions can cause irregular breathing (Mandryk and Inkpen, 2004). Respiratory measures are strongly linked to cardiovascular activity (Stern, Ray and Quigley, 2001).

A relatively straightforward approach to measuring respiration involves tracking the expansion and contraction of the chest cavity. Sensors that can measure how far and how rapidly the chest moves with each breath can be attached to the thorax (Mandryk and Inkpen, 2004; Stern, Ray and Quigley, 2001) and even integrated into clothing (Brady *et al.*, 2005).

13.2.1.4 Muscular and skeletal position sensing

Human bodies are constantly moving: even when we are "sitting still", our torsos move slightly with each breath. Cleverly constructed sensors using a variety of technologies can be attached to clothing or the body to sense movement and positioning. Fiber optics (Dunne *et al.*, 2006b), flexible sensors (Demmans, Subramanian and Titus, 2007), accelerometers (Arteaga *et al.*, 2008), computer vision (Jaimes, 2006), and sensors mounted on chairs (Mutlu *et al.*, 2007) have been used to assess posture. Foam sensors stitched into clothing can detect both respiration and shoulder and arm movements (Dunne *et al.*, 2006a). Countless systems that sense pressure and position have been developed over the years, with examples including a device that integrates a handgrip sensor with a mouse control (Mueller, Gibbs and Vetere, 2009) and the Nintendo Wii position sensor (Schlömer *et al.*, 2008; Voida and Greenberg, 2009). With appropriate software support, these and similar devices can measure various activities involving hand and finger movements.

13.2.1.5 Muscle tension

The contraction of muscles creates electrical signals that can be detected and measured using electromyography (EMG). Electrodes can be placed on the muscle of interest to measure activity that can indicate emotional states. Measurements on the jaw can reveal tensions associated with a clenched jaw. Sensors on eyebrows or cheeks can detect muscle movements associated with frowns or smiles, respectively. Mildly positive emotions lead to lower EMG readings over the eyebrow and mildly higher activity over the cheek, relative to mildly negative emotions. Reactions to specific emotional moods including sadness, fear, and happiness have been studied as well, with less clear results (Cacioppo *et al.*, 2000). EMG has also been used as an input modality: one project investigated the use of an EMG armband as a means of unobtrusively controlling a digital media player (Costanza *et al.*, 2007).

13.2.1.6 Brain activity

Numerous techniques for directly and indirectly measuring brain activity have been developed. Brain-imaging techniques provide detailed displays, but the expensive equipment and required medical expertise have limited their use in HCI research. Indirect measures that use changes in electrical signals on the head to measure brain activity provide less detail, but they are significantly easier to work with.

Electroencephalography involves the use of electrodes distributed across the scalp to measure brain activity in the cerebral cortex. Typically, this involves placing a helmet containing 128–256 electrodes on a participant's scalp. These electrodes are used to measure electrical activity in various locations, with differences between locations or relative to some average baseline used as indicators of various types of activity (Stern, Ray and Quigley, 2001). Evoked response measurements involve measurements of differentials between electrodes in two locations (perhaps earlobe and scalp), in response to auditory or visual responses (Stern, Ray and Quigley, 2001).

Some researchers have begun exploring the use of functional magnetic resonance imaging (fMRI), which presents the tantalizing possibility of identifying specific locations in the brain that exhibit increased activity in response to stimuli. One study used fMRI to observe an emotional response to emoticons, even when regions of the brain associated with face recognition were inactive, indicating that participants did not recognize the emoticons as faces (Yuasa, Saito and Mukawa, 2006). As they evolve, new tools for measuring brain activity are likely to be applied to HCI challenges. The fNIRS and HCI sidebar gives a taste of things to come.

Research In Practice

fNIRS and HCI

Functional near-infrared spectroscopy (fNIRS) uses the reflectivity characteristics of the skull, scalp, and brain to measure mental activity. Near-infrared light can travel 2–3 centimeters into the brain before being either absorbed or reflected. Wavelengths that are reflected by hemoglobin can be used to measure mental activity (Hirshfeld *et al.*, 2007; Izzetoglu *et al.*, 2004). An fNIR measurement system generally includes light sources and detectors, mounted on a flexible headband.

Preliminary applications to HCI research have examined the ability of fNIRS to measure mental effort. An examination of the mental effort involved in solving rotating cube puzzles found that fNIRS measured distinguishable differences when comparing tasks with a graphical cube on a screen to tasks involving a physical cube. fNIRS was able to distinguish between tasks at three different levels of difficulty, with better-than-random accuracy (Hirshfeld *et al.*, 2007). The application of fNIRS to a military command-and-control task found that fNIRS could be used to predict cognitive workload (Izzetoglu *et al.*, 2004) The results from these studies were interpreted as demonstrating the utility of fNIRS for HCI research.

13.2.2   Challenges in data collection and interpretation

Physiological data collection presents some challenges that are not generally encountered in more traditional HCI research. To make use of the data sources that literally measure the body, researchers must be in direct physical contact with their subjects. For galvanic skin response or blood volume measurements, this may be as simple as placing an electrode on a finger tip. Surface electrodes (for EKG or EMG) and chest-mounted sensors (for respiration measurements) are substantially more complicated. These electrodes must be attached carefully in the appropriate position to ensure high-quality recording of the desired data.

Measurements based on body-mounted sensors involving pressure (Brady *et al.*, 2005) or skeletal positioning (Dunne *et al.*, 2006b) present a different set of challenges. As these approaches are relatively new and the technology is rapidly-evolving, off-the-shelf tools with clear guidance may be few and far between. You may need to familiarize yourself with the pros and cons of a variety of sensors before conducting this sort of work. Before using any of these tools for measuring physiological data, you should make sure that you have appropriate training in their use. Partnering with an experienced health professional is an attractive means of ensuring correct use of sensors and other – probably expensive – equipment.

Although electrodes and sensors aren't physically invasive, they may cause some discomfort and unease for some participants in your study. You may want to take extra care to be sensitive to participant's concerns, particularly involving the placement and attachment of electrodes. Some researchers suggest that electrodes should be attached only by someone of the same gender as the participant, in order to reduce anxiety and embarrassment (Stern, Ray and Quigley, 2001). As some participants may become uncomfortable, your informed consent forms (Chapter 14) should be particularly explicit regarding potential risks. Take extra care to observe the participants' moods: when faced with a particularly distressed subject, you may wish to remind them that they can withdraw if they are uncomfortable. In addition to being considerate, this approach may save you from difficulties in data interpretation: if a participant's anxiety levels are high due to concern about the experiment, it may be difficult or impossible to identify anxiety responses caused by your stimuli.

These logistical challenges are even greater for more invasive techniques that require the involvement of a trained expert. Although surface electrodes are widely used in EMG measurements, needles placed in muscles are a possible alternative for many applications (Raez, Hussain and Mohd-Yasin, 2006). Although the needles are safe, they must be used correctly, making them a strictly "don't try this at home" proposition. HCI researchers have shied away from this approach (Mandryk and Inkpen, 2004); unless your team has an experienced EMG professional, you would be well-advised to do so as well.

As with other naturally-occurring signals, these data sources are all very noisy, containing artifacts and variability that can make interpretation difficult. EMG signals, for example, suffer from significant amounts of distortion and random noise from other muscles (Raez,

Hussain and Mohd-Yasin, 2006). Tonic activity levels measure physiological responses in the absence of specific responses. These "baseline" measurements can differ significantly from one individual to the next and sometimes within individuals, due to factors such as headaches. Furthermore, the magnitude of response to a specific condition may be influenced by the tonic levels of a given signal: the response to any given stimulus might be lesser for a heart that is already beating quickly. Habituation is another concern: the magnitude of response to a stimulus decreases after repeated presentation (Stern, Ray and Quigley, 2001). This can present a challenge for both experimental design and data interpretation.

Although a wide variety of methods have been proposed for extracting the signal from the surrounding noise (Raez, Hussain and Mohd-Yasin, 2006), their use might require additional expertise: without a basis in a solid understanding, the application of signal-processing tools to noisy data streams can become a case of "garbage-in, garbage-out".

Once you have extracted the signal in your physiological data from the noise, your next challenge is to determine the granularity of the data that you will analyze. Some experiments call for relatively coarse data: if you are interested in comparing average responses for circumstances, you can just collect streams of data in each circumstance, without worrying about specific correspondences between physiological data points and events in the computer interface.

However, if you want to use physiological data to identify arousal, frustration, or other responses to specific interactions with a computer, you need to be able to synchronize changes in physiology with user actions. Plainly speaking, if you know that the variability in a user's heart rate increased at a certain point in time, you won't be able to interpret that change unless you know what the user was doing at the time. You are likely to be keeping a textual log of user actions, tracking mouse movements, key presses, and related information about the state of the application. Your physiological data would similarly be recorded via software that would create fine-grained records containing multiple measurements per second.

The first measurement challenge involves fine-grained measurements. Whereas physiological data are essentially continuous, tracking of events on the computer may not be. Fine-grained timing information may require using system clocks which operate on the order of milliseconds. Recording the number of internal clock "ticks" between events is one way to get high-resolution event data (Scheirer *et al.*, 2002).

The next measurement challenge lies in integrating data streams that are collected separately – perhaps even on different computers. Although your application data may be fine-grained logs of individual events, physiological data streams may not have access to that information. If all data collection is done on one computer, the timestamp might be used with both data streams. When physiological data is captured on a separate computer, some clever engineering might be necessary. One set of experimenters used a modified mouse to solve this problem: in addition to sending control signals to the computer running the application, the mouse had a second wire that sent a pulse to the computer collecting

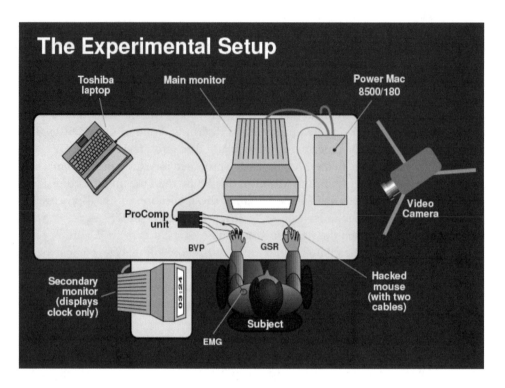

Figure 13.5 A complex experimental setup: physiological signals are collected by the ProComp analog-to-digital converter and stored on the laptop; the mouse is modified to simultaneously send control events to the computer and pulses to the analog-to-digital converter (*Source*: Scheirer *et al.*, 2002, © Elsevier).

physiological data. These pulses were used to synchronize the two streams (Scheirer *et al.*, 2002).

The possibility of using a separate computer for physiological data collection hints at another challenge: the management of a fairly complex experimental setup. Besides the two computers (one for the application and one for data collection), you have sensors, analog-to-digital converters for converting the physiological signals into a form suitable for storage on the computer, potentially modified input devices, and possibly other equipment for audio and video recording (Figure 13.5).

The granularity of the data collected can influence the process of analysis and interpretation. For simple comparisons involving overall responses to differing conditions, averages might be sufficient (Mandryk and Inkpen, 2004). More complex analyses might attempt to model and classify episodes of emotional reaction (Scheirer *et al.*, 2002). As always, you should design your data collection and management with an understanding of your analysis, and be sure to pilot test your procedures and equipment.

A final interpretive challenge lies in the difficulty of understanding physiological signals. Even if you have a clear difference in some measure that seems to come in response to a specific event, interpreting that measure may prove challenging. You may be tempted to classify a response as specific emotional state – happiness, sadness, disgust, fear, or other examples – but data for many measures are inconclusive (Cacioppo *et al.*, 2000). Mixed or incomplete measures are a very real possibility: some stimuli may lead to a response in one measure, with no change in another (Stern, Ray and Quigley, 2001).

Physiological data presents tantalizing possibilities for researchers. Although the challenges of collecting and interpreting data from these sources are considerable, the possibility of identifying fine-grained, real-time responses to interfaces is often hard to resist. Before committing your valuable human and financial resources to such an effort, you may want to ask yourself if there is an easier way to observe the phenomena of interest. You may legitimately decide that your study of user frustration requires fine-grained detail about specific events, making post-test questionnaires insufficiently detailed. Before concluding that physiological data measures are required to identify incidences of frustration in real-time, you should consider using simpler methods such as videotapes, observations, think-aloud protocols, or time diaries. You may find that simpler methods get the job done with much less headache and expense.

13.3 Examples of physiological research in HCI

Despite the challenges, numerous HCI researchers have used physiological data to observe user interactions in ways that would not otherwise be possible. An examination of some of these studies indicates the common theme of using these techniques to record real-time observations of a task in progress, as opposed to subjective, post-test response.

A study of cognitive load and multimodal interfaces used three different traffic control interfaces with three different task complexity levels to investigate the possibility of using galvanic skin response (GSR) to measure cognitive load. Participants used gesture-based, speech-based, or multimodal (speech and gesture) interfaces to complete tasks. Initial analysis of data from five participants indicated that average response levels were lowest for the multimodal interface, followed by speech and then gesture interfaces. For all three interfaces, the total response increased with task complexity. This was interpreted as providing evidence for the utility of using GSR to indicate cognitive loads. Analysis of specific recordings found GSR peaks to be correlated with stressful or frustrating events, with responses decreasing over time. Peaks were also correlated with major events that were thought to be cognitively challenging, including reading instructions and competing tasks (Shi *et al.*, 2007).

Another study used both galvanic skin response and blood-volume pressure to measure user frustration in an explicit attempt to develop methods for using multiple sensing technologies. The experimental design involved a game with several puzzles. Participants were told that the experimenters were interested in how brightly-colored graphics would influence physiological variables in an online game. Unbeknown to the participants, the game software was rigged to randomly introduce episodes of unresponsiveness. As participants were being timed and had been offered a reward if they had the fastest task completion times, these delays would presumably cause frustration.[1] Blood-volume pressure and GSR responses were used to develop models that could distinguish between frustrating and non-frustrating states (Scheirer *et al.*, 2002).

Interaction with computer games is a natural topic for physiological data. As anyone who has played video games knows, players can become excited while driving race cars, hunting aliens, or playing basketball on the computer. However, the fast-paced nature of these games limits the applicability of many techniques. Intrusive data collection techniques, such as "think-aloud" descriptions, interfere with the game-playing experience and post-test questionnaires fail to recapture all of the nuances of the playing experience (Mandryk and Inkpen, 2004).

One study used various physiological data sources – GSR, EKG, cardiovascular rate, respiration rate, and facial EMG – to measure responses to computer games played against a computer and against a friend. Starting from the premise that the physiological data would provide objective measures that would be correlated to players' subjective reports of experiences with video games, the researchers hypothesized that preferences and physiological responses would differ when comparing playing against a computer to playing against a friend. Specifically, they hypothesized that participants would prefer playing against friends, GSR and EMG values would be higher (due to increased competition), and that differences between GSR readings in the two conditions would correspond to subjective ratings (Mandryk and Inkpen, 2004).

To test these hypotheses, they asked participants to play a hockey video game, against the computer and against a friend. Participants were recruited in pairs of friends, so each person knew their opponent. The hypotheses were generally confirmed: participants found playing against a friend to be more exciting, and most had higher GSR and facial EMG levels when playing with a friend. Cardiovascular and respiratory measures did not show any differences. Investigation of specific incidents also revealed differences – participants had a greater response to a fight when playing a friend. Examination of the relationship between GSR, fun, and frustration revealed a positive correlation with fun and a negative correlation with frustration (Mandryk and Inkpen, 2004).

EEGs have been used by HCI researchers to develop brain–computer interfaces that use measurable brain activity to control computers (Millán, 2003). Machine-learning algorithms applied to EEG signals have been used to distinguish between different types of activity. Similar to the study of cooperative gaming described above (Mandryk and Inkpen, 2004), one study found that EEG signals could be used to distinguish between resting states, solo game play, and playing against an expert player (Lee and Tan, 2006). Other HCI applications

---

[1]This experimental design is an example of deception (see Chapter 14). At the end of each session, participant debriefing explained the true purpose of the experiment. Participants were offered the opportunity to withdraw their data after the debriefing (Scheirer *et al.*, 2002).

involving EEG signals include identifying images of interest from a large set (Mathan *et al.*, 2006) and measurement of memory and cognitive load in a military command-and-control environment (Berka *et al.*, 2004).

Electromyography has been used to measure a variety of emotional responses to computer interfaces. One study of web surfing tasks found strong correlations between facial EMG measures of frustration and incorrectly completed tasks or home pages that required greater effort to navigate (Hazlett, 2003). Similar studies used EMG to measure emotional responses to videos describing new software features, tension in using media-player software (Hazlett and Benedek, 2006), and task difficulty or frustration in word processing (Branco *et al.*, 2005). An experiment involving boys playing racing games on the Microsoft X-Box established the validity of facial EMG for distinguishing between positive and negative events (Hazlett, 2006). Combinations of multiple physiological measures, including EMG, have also been used to study emotional responses (Mahlke, Minge and Thüring, 2006).

Summary

Many HCI questions involve digging deeper than the level of individual tasks. Instead of simply asking whether a task was completed correctly or how quickly it was completed, these efforts hope to understand what happened during the completion of the task. Such questions may involve examination of what the user is doing (which keys they are pressing, where they are moving the mouse, where they are looking) and how they are reacting (are they happy, sad, frustrated, or excited)?

Traditional measurement and observation techniques can be used to address these questions, but they are limited in their applicability. Even the most careful observations and video-recording are very limited in determining which keys a user presses and how quickly they are pressed. Observation and video tape present similar limitations for tracking mouse movements or eye gazes. Inferring emotional states is similarly challenging: we may be able to identify excitement simply by watching someone playing a video game, but more subtle responses such as frustration may not be apparent. Asking users after the fact provides some detail, but questionnaires or interviews are limited to details that the participant remembers after the fact, making fine-grained data collection difficult, if not impossible.

Automated data collection approaches provide data that are unavailable through these more traditional approaches. For studies of mice and keyboard usage, actions that are intrinsically part of user tasks can be recorded for further analysis. Relatively simple data collection software can collect data tracking exactly what the user did (mouse press, mouse movement, key press) and when she did it. This information can be used to describe accuracy, identify problems in task completion, and classify task completion into periods of activity and inactivity. Combinations of multiple input devices – such as keyboard and mouse – can provide richer details.

Other interesting sources of human data may require a larger investment, both in time and expertise. Eye-tracking systems that can identify areas of an interface that draw attention may be intriguing, but hardware costs are significant and the resulting data may require some interpretation. These concerns are even more pronounced for physiological measurements, which require equipping participants with electrodes, sensors, gauges, headbands, or even helmets. Interpreting the resulting noisy data is another challenge that requires substantial experience in signal processing.

You might want to start with simpler, less expensive techniques before you commit to the expense and difficulty associated with eye-tracking or physiological approaches. You might try simpler measures such as observation, video recording, or interviews, to see if they can be used to generate the insights that you need. Another approach would be to find proxies: although you might be tempted to use eye gaze to track a user's attention, tracking mouse movements might be a workable alternative.

For some research problems, the temptation of fine-grained physiological data is too great to resist. If you find yourself faced with such a question, be sure to work with experts: the assistance of collaborators who are familiar with both the equipment and the data interpretation challenges will be crucial to your success.

Discussion Questions

1. Physiological data-measurement tools present an interesting dilemma for researchers. Electrodes, helmets, chest-mounted sensors and other tools used to measure these signals may be unfamiliar to many participants in research studies. Particularly for head-mounted equipment, the unfamiliarity and potential discomfort associated with these data collection tools may cause some individuals to become nervous, upset, or otherwise ill at ease. These responses might create a problem for studies aimed at understanding emotional responses to computer tasks. How would you go about distinguishing between measurable physiological responses that result from the use of unfamiliar, and potentially uncomfortable, monitoring hardware from responses to the task in question? How might factors such as the length of the experimental session and characteristics of the tasks complicate the challenge of distinguishing between these types of reactions?

2. Collaborative systems have the potential for generating a wide range of emotional reactions. When two or more people use a single computer system to work together on a problem of common interest (known as "co-located, synchronous collaboration"), some tasks may cause conflict, tension, excitement, or a variety of other emotional reactions. System behavior can also influence user reactions, as technical glitches and encouraging or discouraging feedback may lead to feelings of frustration. Technical concerns are even greater for collaboration between users at different locations ("distributed collaboration"), as network latencies, dropped connections, and slow responses are just a few of the problems that might be encountered. How would you go about measuring these emotional responses? Discuss the advantages and disadvantages of physiological data in this context, as opposed to self-reports, observation, or video-recording. How might you use physiological data to study frustration in distributed collaboration?

Research Design Exercise

Commonly available, inexpensive heart-rate monitors used for monitoring exercise might be usable for measuring physiological responses to computer use. Use one of these monitors to measure your pulse while you do a variety of computer tasks. First, measure your pulse while you are relaxed. Then, try some increasingly demanding and stressful tasks. You might try performing a simple task, such as completing an email message, a more complex task involving an advanced tool, such as a photo editor, a mentally-challenging task, such as a math puzzle, and a fast-paced, exciting video game. How does your pulse change with each of these activities? As the act of pausing to read the display of the monitor may change your activity level, you might want to ask a friend to do the measurement and take notes.

References

Aaltonen, A., Hyrskykari, A., and Räihä, K.-J. (1998) 101 spots, or how do users read menus? *Proceedings of the ACM Conference on Human Factors in Computing Systems,* 132–139.

Arteaga, S., Chevalier, J., Coile, A., et al. (2008) Low-cost accelerometry-based posture monitoring system for stroke survivors. *Proceedings of the ACM Conference on Assistive Technology (ASSETS),* 243–244.

Ball, R., North, C., and Bowman, D.A. (2007) Move to improve: Promoting physical navigation to increase user performance with large displays. *Proceedings of the ACM Conference on Human Factors in Computing Systems,* 191–200.

Barreto, A., Gao, Y., and Adjouadi, M. (2008) Pupil diameter measurements: Untapped potential to enhance computer interaction for eye tracker users? *Proceedings of the ACM Conference on Assistive Technology (ASSETS),* 269–270.

Berka, C., Levendowski, D., Cvetinovic, M., Petrovic, M., Davis, G., Lumicao, M., Zivkovic, V., Popovic, M., and Olmstead, R. (2004) Real-time analysis of EEG indexes of alertness, cognition, and memory acquired with a wireless EEG headset. *International Journal of Human–Computer Interaction,* **17**(2):151–170.

Bieg, H.-J. (2009) Gaze-augmented manual interaction. *Proceedings of the ACM Conference on Human Factors in Computing Systems,* 3121–3124.

Brady, S., Dunne, L.E., Tynan, R., et al. (2005) Garment-based monitoring of respiration rate using a foam pressure sensor. *Proceedings of the 9th IEEE International Symposium on Wearable Computers.*

Branco, P., Firth, P., Miguel, E.L., and Bonato, P. (2005) Faces of emotion in human–computer interaction. *Extended Abstracts of the ACM Conference on Human Factors in Computing Systems,* 21–30.

Buscher, G., Cutrell, E., and Morris, M.R. (2009) What do you see when you're surfing? Using eye tracking to predict salient regions of web pages. *Proceedings of the 27th international conference extended abstracts on Human Factors in Computing Systems.*

Cacioppo, J.T., **Bernston, G.G.**, **Larsen, J.T.**, *et al.* (2000) The psychophysiology of emotion. In M. Lewis and J.M. Haviland-Jones (eds), *Handbook of Emotions*, 173–191. New York: The Guilford Press.

Card, S.K., **Pirolli, P.**, **Van Der Wege, M.M.**, *et al.* (2001) Information scent as a driver of Web behavior graphs: Results of a protocol analysis method for Web usability. *Proceedings of the ACM Conference on Human Factors in Computing Systems*, 498–505.

Costanza, E., **Inverso, S.A.**, **Allen, R.**, and **Maes, P.** (2007) Intimate interfaces in action: Assessing the usability and subtlety of EMG-based motionless gestures. *Proceedings of the ACM Conference on Human Factors in Computing Systems*, 819–828.

Crowe, E.C. and **Narayanan, N.H.** (2000) Comparing interfaces based on what users watch and do. *Proceedings of the 2000 symposium on Eye Tracking Research and Applications*, 29–36.

Cutrell, E. and **Guan, Z.** (2007) What are you looking for? An eye-tracking study of information usage in web search. *Proceedings of the ACM Conference on Human Factors in Computing Systems*, 407–416.

Demmans, C., **Subramanian, S.**, and **Titus, J.** (2007) Posture monitoring and improvement for laptop use. *Extended Abstracts of the ACM Conference on Human Factors in Computing Systems*, 2357–2362.

Dunne, L.E., **Brady, S.**, **Tynan, R.**, *et al.* (2006a) Garment-based body sensing using foam sensors. *Proceedings of the 7th Australasian User Interface Conference*, 165–171.

Dunne, L.E., **Walsh, P.**, **Smyth, B.**, and **Caulfield, B.** (2006b) Design and evaluation of a wearable optical sensor for monitoring seated spinal posture. *Proceedings of the IEEE International Symposium on Wearable Computers*, 65–68.

Goldberg, J., **Stimson, M.**, **Lewenstein, M.**, **Scott, N.**, and **Wichanky, A.** (2002) Eye tracking in web search tasks: Design implications. *Proceedings of the 2002 symposium on Eye Tracking Research and Applications*, 51–58.

Guan, Z. and **Cutrell, E.** (2007) An eye tracking study of the effect of target rank on web search. *Proceedings of the ACM Conference on Human Factors in Computing Systems*, 417–420.

Hazlett, R.L. (2003) Measurement of user frustration: A biologic approach. *Extended Abstracts of the ACM Conference on Human Factors in Computing Systems*, 734–735.

Hazlett, R.L. (2006) Measuring emotional valence during interactive experiences: Boys at video game play. *Proceedings of the ACM Conference on Human Factors in Computing Systems*, 1023–1026.

Hazlett, R.L. and **Benedek, J.** (2006) Measuring emotional valence to understand the user's experience of software. *International Journal of Human–Computer Studies*, **65**(4):306–314.

Hirshfeld, L.M., **Girouard, A.**, **Solovey, E.T.**, *et al.* (2007) Human–computer interaction and brain measurement using functional near-infrared spectroscopy. *Proceedings of the ACM Conference on User Interface Software and Technology*.

Hornof, A., Cavender, A., and Hoselton, R. (2004) Eyedraw: A system for drawing pictures with eye movements. *Proceedings of the ACM Conference on Assistive Technology (ASSETS),* 86–93.

Izzetoglu, K., Bunce, S., Onaral, B., *et al.* (2004) Functional optical brain imaging using near-infrared during cognitive tasks. *International Journal of Human–Computer Interaction,* **17**(2):211–231.

Jacob, R.J.K. and Karn, K.S. (2003) Commentary on Section 4. Eye tracking in Human–Computer interaction and usability research: Ready to deliver the promises. In J. Hyona, R. Radach **and** H. Deubel (eds), *The Mind's Eyes: Cognitive and Applied Aspects of Eye Movements.* Oxford: Elsevier Science.

Jaimes, A. (2006) Posture and activity silhouettes for self-reporting, interruption management, and attentive interfaces. *Proceedings of the ACM Conference on Intelligent User Interfaces,* 24–31.

Kumar, M. (2006) Reducing the cost of eye tracking systems. Technical Report CSTR 2006-08, Stanford University. Retrieved on August 21, 2009 from http://hci.stanford.edu/cstr/reports/2006-08.pdf.

Kumar, M., Paepcke, A., and Winograd, T. (2007) EyePoint: Practical pointing and selection using gaze and keyboard. *Proceedings of the ACM Conference on Human Factors in Computing Systems,* 421–430.

Lee, J.C. and Tan, D.S. (2006) Using a low-cost electroencephalograph for task classification in HCI research. *Proceedings of the ACM Symposium on User Interface Software and Technology,* 81–90.

Mahlke, S., Minge, M., and Thüring, M. (2006) Measuring multiple components of emotions in interactive contexts. Extended Abstracts of the ACM Conference on Human Factors in Computing Systems, 1061–1066.

Mandryk, R.L. and Inkpen, K.M. (2004) Physiological indicators for the evaluation of co-located collaborative play. *Proceedings of the ACM Conference on Computer-Supported Cooperative Work,* 102–111.

Mathan, S., Whitlow, S., Erdogmus, D., *et al.* (2006) Neurophysiologically driven image triage: A pilot study. Extended Abstracts of the ACM Conference on Human Factors in Computing Systems, 1085–1090.

Millán, J. d. R. (2003) Adaptive brain interfaces. *Communications of the ACM,* **46**(3):74–80.

Mueller, F.F., Gibbs, M.R., and Vetere, F. (2009) The mousegrip. *Extended Abstracts of the ACM Conference on Human Factors in Computing Systems,* 3199–3204.

Murata, A. (2006) Eye-gaze input versus mouse: Cursor control as a function of age. *International Journal of Human–Computer Interaction,* **21**(1):1–14.

Mutlu, B., Krause, A., Forlizzi, J., Guestrin, C., and Hodgins, J. (2007) Robust, low-cost, non-intrusive sensing and recognition of seated postures. *Proceedings of the ACM Symposium on User Interface Software and Technology,* 149–158.

Pirolli, P., Card, S.K., and Van Der Wege, M.M. (2000) The effect of information scent on searching information: Visualizations of large tree structures. *Proceedings of the Working Conference on Advanced Visual Interfaces,* 161–172.

Raez, M.B.I., Hussain, M.S., and Mohd-Yasin, F. (2006) Techniques of EMG signal analysis: Detection, processing, classification and applications. *Biological Procedures Online*, **8**.

Rowe, D.W., Sibert, J., and Irwin, D. (1998) Heart rate variability: Indicator of user state as an aid to human–computer interaction. *Proceedings of the ACM Conference on Human Factors in Computing Systems*, 480–487.

Scheirer, J., Fernandez, R., Klein, J., and Picard, R.W. (2002) Frustrating the user on purpose: A step toward building an affective computer. *Interacting with Computers*, **14**:93–118.

Schlömer, T., Poppinga, B., Henze, N., and Boll, S. (2008) Gesture recognition with a Wii controller. *Proceedings of the ACM International Conference on Tangible and Embedded Interaction*, 11–14.

Shahabi, C., Marsh, T., Yang, K., Yoon, H., Rizzo, A., McLaughlin, M., and Mun, M. (2007) Immersidata analysis: Four case studies. *IEEE Computer*, **40**(7):45–52.

Shi, Y., Ruiz, N., Taib, R., Choi, E., and Chen, F. (2007) Galvanic skin response (GSR) as an index of cognitive load. *Extended Abstracts of the ACM Conference on Human Factors in Computing Systems*, 2651–2656.

Steptoe, W., Wolff, R., Murgia, A., Guimaraes, E., Rae, J., Sharkey, P., Roberts, D., and Steed, A. (2008) Eye-tracking for avatar eye-gaze and interactional analysis in immersive collaborative virtual environments. *Proceedings of the ACM Conference on Computer-Supported Cooperative Work*, 197–200.

Stern, R.M., Ray, W.J., and Quigley, K.S. (2001) *Psychophysiological Recording*. Oxford: Oxford University Press.

Voida, A. and Greenberg, S. (2009) Wii all play: The console game as a computational meeting place. *Extended Abstracts of the ACM Conference on Human Factors in Computing Systems*, 1559–1568.

Wastell, D.G. and Newman, M. (1996) Stress, control and computer system design: A psychophysiological field study. *Behaviour & Information Technology*, **15**:183–192.

Whalen, T. and Inkpen, K.M. (2005) Gathering evidence: Use of visual security cues in web browsers. *Proceedings of Graphics Interface Conference* 2005, 137–144.

Xu, S., Jiang, H., and Lau, F.C.M. (2009) User-oriented document summarization through vision-based eye-tracking. *Proceedings of the ACM Conference on Intelligent User Interfaces*, 7–16.

Yuasa, M., Saito, K., and Mukawa, N. (2006) Emoticons convey emotions without cognition of faces: An fMRI study. *Extended Abstracts of the ACM Conference on Human Factors in Computing Systems*, 1565–1570.

Zhai, S., Morimoto, C., and Ihde, S. (1999) Manual and gaze input cascaded (MAGIC) pointing. *Proceedings of the ACM Conference on Human Factors in Computing Systems*, 246–253.

Working with human subjects

Research into human–computer interaction (HCI) almost invariably involves the participation of human subjects. Whether you are running a focus group, leading a collaborative design process, running a controlled study, or conducting an ethnographic investigation, you need to engage people in your work.

Although this may sound simple, it isn't. As anyone who has done so can tell you, working with human subjects involves many challenges. Finding the right subjects is often difficult and time-consuming, especially for evaluations of systems designed for specific populations or situations.

The real fun can begin when the subjects are ready to begin participating in your study. Research ethics require that participants must be treated fairly and with respect. This means that they must be provided with information about the nature of the study that they can use to make a meaningful decision as to whether or not they really want to be involved. This notion of *informed consent* is a critical component of modern research on human subjects.

Although some of the details may differ, the general problems in finding and informing research subjects apply to any form of research involving human participants, regardless of the type of person involved. The additional challenges that online research presents in each of these areas is described in Section 14.4. This chapter uses the terms "subject" and "participant" interchangeably.

14.1   Identifying potential participants

You've just built an interactive system for two-handed input to an architectural modeling system and you'd like to run some summative tests to help find usability problems. This leaves you with a problem: who should participate in your study? There are plenty of potential users with two hands, but having the physical ability to manipulate your tool is just a start. People without the appropriate training and experience will be unable to tell you if your tool succeeds in its primary goal – supporting the work of an architect. Narrowing your pool of potential participants to architects would be your next logical step, but even this limitation may not be fine-grained enough. Are you willing to accept architecture students? This might help if there is a school of architecture nearby, but students may lack real-world experience. This might lead you to insist upon professional architects, who may be hard to find. HCI researchers are familiar with these and related challenges in finding appropriate study participants.

In the early days, in the late 1970s and early 1980s, many of the participants in HCI research were workers in corporate computing environments. This population of relatively early users was professionally motivated to participate in studies aimed at improving the systems that they used. As computer use spread more broadly into society and academic groups became active centers of HCI research, student bodies became available (often just walking down the hall) and easily motivated (via cash or food) pools of participants. Countless studies involving computer science or psychology undergraduates have been published over the years.

So, what's wrong with recruiting undergraduate students – or other easily found subjects – in HCI research? Often, nothing. If you are interested in evaluating interfaces intended for use by undergraduate students, this approach is perfect. However, tests that draw on a homogeneous group of participants may be open to criticism: results may not apply to users from a different demographic group. Even if a specific menu arrangement in a word-processing program works well for (predominantly young, male) computer science students, it may not work well for retired women. In a case like this, the mismatch may simply limit the extent to which you can claim that your study answers the problem.

The number of participants is another crucial factor. Different forms of research require different numbers of participants. Studies with too few participants may not yield generalizable results, while studies with too many participants are unnecessarily expensive and time-consuming.

14.1.1 Which subjects?

In selecting participants, you should strive to find people with *personal attributes* and *goals* appropriate for your study. By personal attributes, we mean demographic, educational, vocational and avocational details. Some studies may simply need computer users, while others need participants of a certain gender, age range, education level, professional background, or any combination of these characteristics.

Each individual's goals, background, and motivations may play a role in determining how appropriate they are for your study. Insufficiently interested subjects may be unlikely to contribute constructively, no matter how well they match your other criteria. Even with the right physical attributes, an architect who is strongly opposed to the use of computers for modeling would probably not make a good subject for studying the architectural tool described above. On the other hand, some studies might benefit from the perspective of less-motivated participants, who might be more critical and less forgiving of shortcomings than enthusiasts. The participation of these less-motivated users can be particularly useful when studying tools that may be used by a broad range of users in non-voluntary circumstances, such as mandatory workplace timesheet reports. Unmotivated users can also be useful for studies aimed at understanding the factors that might influence reluctance to adopt new technology.

Expertise is always an important consideration: study participants should have expertise that is comparable to that of the expected users. We usually define expertise in terms of two largely separable dimensions: computer expertise and domain expertise – knowledge of the problems, systems, goals, and tools used in a specific line of work. If you are testing a tool that is built for highly trained professionals who rarely use complex computer applications, you'll be looking for users who may be computer novices, even though they have significant domain expertise. In other cases, you might be looking for sophisticated computer users who are using a new type of software: computer experts but domain novices. Any differences in expertise between your target population and the participants in your study may lead to results that are hard to interpret. You may be left wondering why your population of computer experts failed to successfully complete tasks with your interface for domain experts: was it because the interface failed or because the users lacked the required experience in the domain?

Interfaces that are intended for use by a broad audience present relatively little difficulty in terms of user characteristics. General-purpose desktop computing tools and interfaces on widely used communications devices are likely to be used by many motivated users, so study participants do not need to meet many specific criteria and can often (but not always) be similar to each other.

The need for appropriate participants becomes more apparent with tools that are de-signed for specific populations. Children and adults have vastly different cognitive and physical abilities, which directly influence their ability to act as useful study participants. Similarly, cultural differences between users may play a significant role in task performance for communication systems. Whenever possible, studies of tools designed for specific ages, genders, social backgrounds, and physical or cognitive abilities should involve participants who fit the appropriate category. Ethnographic studies of specific users and situations are also sensitive to the appropriateness of the participants. If study participants are not the intended users of a system, you can only make limited claims about the utility of the system for the intended population.

Systems designed for domain experts can be particularly challenging in this regard. As the construction of tools for highly specialized tasks requires a detailed understanding of domain-specific work practices, there is a natural tendency to use techniques such as participatory design to involve users in system design. This inclusion may lead to valuable insights, but domain experts who were involved in the design of a tool may have biases in favor of the resulting design, making them inappropriate candidates for subsequent usability tests or other summative evaluations.

Difference between users can also be an important part of study design. Investigations of potential gender differences in organizing certain forms of information would require both male and female participants. Similarly, an experiment exploring the role of user motivation in understanding the effectiveness of a given interface design may need participants who are highly motivated, as well as those who are not at all motivated.

Additional care is necessary when study designs require multiple groups that differ in some dimension. Ideally, the groups would differ in the relevant attribute but be compara-ble in all others. Any other differences would be possible confounding variables – factors that could be responsible for observed differences. In the study of gender differences in information management, the male and female groups should be comparable in terms of education, age, income, professional experience, and as many other factors as possible. If the women were significantly younger than the men, it might be hard to determine whether any performance differences were due to age or gender: further experimentation may be necessary.

Although these issues may be most important for controlled experiments, the identification of an appropriately general group of participants is always a challenge. Appropriate recruiting methods can help, but there are no guarantees. Despite your best efforts to find a representative population, you always face the possibility that your group of participants is insufficiently representative in a way that was unanticipated. As this bias is always possible, it's best to explicitly state what steps you have taken to account for potentially confounding variables and to be cautious when making claims about your results.

14.1.2   How many subjects?

Determining the number of participants to involve in a research study is subject to a trade-off between the information gained in the study and the cost of conducting it. Studies with a very large number of participants – say, tens of thousands – probably involve many people of different ages, educational backgrounds, and computer experience. Any outcome that you see consistently from this population may therefore not be something that can be explained away by the specific characteristics of the individual participants: it is likely to be a "real" effect. Huge studies like this are particularly helpful for controlled experiments in search of statistically significant results. Even subtle differences can be statistically significant if the populations are sufficiently large.

Unfortunately, large studies are difficult and expensive to run. Each participant involves substantial costs for recruiting, enrolling, conducting the study, and managing data. If the participants are not at your workplace, there may be travel involved, and many studies pay people for their time. If your study allows you to involve many people at once – perhaps 20 people in a roomful of computers – you may be able to achieve some efficiencies in terms of the time involved. However, research that involves one-on-one interactions between a researcher and a participant may have costs that grow linearly with the number of participants.

At the other extreme, a study with one individual has very real limitations. This study would be relatively inexpensive, but also very limited. Because this study would not have a range of users with different characteristics, any results would run the risk of telling you more about the participant than they did about the research question at hand. If you're conducting an ethnographic study with one person, you may learn a great deal about how that person performs certain types of work, but you have no idea about how representative her habits are: you may get unlucky and find someone who is completely unlike colleagues in the field. As studies with few participants rarely, if ever, produce statistically significant results, the conclusions that you can draw from these small studies are extremely limited.

Controlled experiments or empirical studies require a sample group of participants large enough to produce statistically significant results. The research design (the number of independent variables, within or between subjects) will play a role as well. Experiments involving larger numbers of independent variables and between-subjects (as opposed to within-subjects) analysis can require more participants (see Chapter 3). Limitations on resources can often lead researchers to substitute the feasible experiment – the design that requires fewer participants – for the experiment they'd prefer to be doing. In some cases, statistical techniques can be used to determine the minimum number of subjects necessary for a result of a given significance (Chapter 3). Usually, you want at least 15–20 participants: smaller studies may miss potentially interesting results.

The inclusion of more participants gives you more statistical power. As each participant comes with costs in time, energy, and money, there are always good arguments in favor of limiting the size of the study. However, larger populations – ranging from several dozen to several hundred participants – offer the possibility of stronger statistical significance or the identification of subtle effects that would not be significant in smaller populations.

Statisticians have developed a range of techniques for determining the number of participants necessary for establishing statistically significant effects with differing degrees of confidence: Cook and Campbell, (1979) is a classic text in this area. These techniques can help you understand how many participants you need *before* your study starts, thus minimizing the chances for painful problems further down the line.

By contrast, case studies and ethnographic studies (Chapters 7 and 9) can often be conducted with a small number of users. If your goal is to gather requirements from domain experts, in-depth discussions with two or three motivated individuals may provide a wealth of data. The length of the session also plays a role here: ethnographic observations generally take more time per participant – and therefore place more demands upon the participants – than controlled experiments.

Usability studies can also be successfully conducted with a small set of participants. These studies use guidelines, heuristics, and a variety of techniques to identify potential usability problems with proposed interface designs (Chapter 10). While some authors state that as few as five usability experts could find 80% of the usability problems in an interface, there is a healthy debate about this (Nielsen, 1994). Of course, identification of an appropriate set of five usability experts might be a challenge, particularly since colleagues working on your project would not be good candidates.

The nature of the participants required for your study often play a role in this decision. Studies that involve systems for general use by a broad range of users should be able to attract a suitably large pool of participants, even if hundreds of people are needed. On the other hand, research aimed at studying very specific populations may need to rely on substantially smaller pools of participants: there simply aren't tens of thousands of potential participants for the study of a tool for space-shuttle astronauts. Studies of domain experts often face challenges in this regard.

Finding a suitably large participant pool can be particularly challenging for research involving people with disabilities. In addition to being an often-overlooked segment of society, people with disabilities often face significant challenges in transportation, making trips to research labs difficult. Studies with these users are often smaller, tending towards observational case studies with two or three users (Steriadis and Constantinou, 2003), rather than controlled experiments, see Chapter 15 for more details.

The time required for each participant is another important factor. Studies that require a single session of limited length (perhaps a few hours) can enroll larger numbers of participants than ethnographic observations that may involve several days or controlled experiments that require multiple sessions conducted over a period of weeks. As the time required from each participant – both in terms of direct involvement and the elapsed interval from start to finish – increases, it becomes more difficult to recruit and retain people who are willing to commit to that level of involvement.

How many participants should your study have? You should start by using your design as a guide. Ethnographies and case studies can be successfully completed with as few as two or three people. Numbers vary wildly for controlled experiments: although studies with as few as 12 users are not uncommon in HCI, results with 20 or more users are more convincing. From that base, you might expand to involve as many subjects as you can reasonably afford to include. You should then add a few more for pilot tests, replacements for participants who drop out, and a margin for error. Investigation of related work in the research literature can help in this regard: basing your population on a population used in similar prior work can be a good strategy. If there is no clearly related work, you might be able to use a smaller population.

14.1.3   Recruiting participants

Once you have determined *who* your participants are and *how many* you need, you must find them and convince them to participate.

If you work for a large corporation that frequently performs user studies, you may be able to draw upon the expertise of a dedicated group that maintains rosters of people interested in user studies and generates participant pools for research. Those who don't have such resources available (i.e., most of the professionals who conduct HCI studies) generally must do their own legwork.

The characteristics of your desired participants play an important role in determining how you will go about finding them. If you have relatively few constraints, recruiting is relatively simple. Advertisements and flyers on your college, university or corporate bulletin boards (both physical and electronic) can entice users. However, this must be done carefully: if you wish to get participants with a wide range of ages and education by recruiting on a university campus, you should be careful to explicitly recruit faculty and staff, as well as students. Notices in local newspapers and on community-oriented websites can be useful for recruiting an even broader group of participants.

More specific requirements are likely to require more focused recruiting efforts. Increased specificity in advertisements is a starting point: you might specifically indicate that you are looking for female college students. Community groups, professional organizations, and similar groups can be helpful for finding people with other, more specific characteristics. Many of these groups will be willing to pass messages along to members, particularly if the research may be of interest to them. If you can find a group of people that meet your specific needs, it may help to go to them. If you can give a short presentation at a meeting and make yourself available for questions afterwards, you may encourage otherwise reluctant people to participate. Email lists and online groups can be helpful in this regard as well, but these tools should be used carefully: sending out messages that don't comply with posted group or lists policies is inappropriate. Sending unsolicited email messages directly to individuals is almost certainly a bad idea. Although an email message that comes from a trusted mailing list might be well-received, the same message sent directly by an individual might be seen as annoying junk email.

Focused ethnography and long-term case studies require fewer subjects, but the effort involved in enrolling each participant may be greater. These projects may require building cooperative arrangements with companies, schools, other organizations, and individuals in order to identify appropriate subjects. Many academic researchers address these challenges by bringing in outside organizations as collaborators. In addition to creating a formal agreement, collaboration can also provide funds that support the efforts of the cooperating organizations.

Incentives can often motivate people to participate. Many undergraduates have been lured into research sessions by promises of cash or pizza. If you can pay your subjects for their time, do so. Gifts can be more appropriate for some participants – particularly children. If you don't have enough funds to pay all participants, you can offer to enter them in a raffle for an MP3 player or similar desirable prize. Compensation can also be a motivator that can elicit desired behavior: in one study on interruption, researchers asked participants to both complete a memory task and respond to interrupting signals. In order to entice participants to complete both tasks, extra payment was given to the subjects with the best performance (Gluck, Bunt and McGrenere, 2007). Incentives for organizations that assist in recruiting can also be useful. In addition to the research collaborations described above, you might pay groups as consultants (see the Menu Task Performance Studies with Blind Users sidebar for an example).

Research In Practice

Menu Task Performance Studies with Blind Users

Task performance with hierarchical menus has been the subject of many studies over the years, leading to a general consensus that menus with many choices at each of a few levels (broad, shallow trees) lead to faster task completion than menus with a few choices at each of many levels (narrow, deep structures), see Chapter 1. As these studies have generally been conducted with sighted users, who could rely upon a visual scan to quickly identify items in a long list, we were interested if these results would hold for blind users who rely upon the serial presentation of items by screen readers. To address this question, we designed a study based on an early experiment that looked at breadth vs. depth in web-based choices from an encyclopedia (Larson and Czerwinski, 1998).

Experimental studies involving blind people can be particularly challenging to run. As blind people often face challenges in transportation, expecting them to come to us would have been unrealistic. We also knew that we wanted a particular population: experienced users of a particular screen-reader package, who did not have any residual vision.

We enlisted the help of the National Federation of the Blind (NFB), who helped identify potential participants and provided us with access to space in their offices, where we were able to run the study. NFB was paid as a consultant on the project and study participants were compensated as well. Due to the specific nature of the participants, compensation was significantly higher than is customary for similar studies.

Compensation should be commensurate with the amount of time requested and the type of participant involved. Busy professionals may command a higher fee than students or children. For longer ethnographic or case studies, particularly with domain experts, direct payment for study participation is unlikely to account for the value of their time. In these cases, collaboratively funded research may be the best approach. For formative studies aimed at capturing requirements for systems to be used by domain experts, the ability to use the software being developed in their daily work might be a powerful enticement.

Special populations may require creative incentives and accommodations. If you are working with children, you might give them small toys as gifts for participating (cash compensation for accompanying parents is probably always welcome). Elderly people or others without easy access to transportation may be interested in participating but may be unable to make the trip to your lab or office. You might consider trying to conduct your study in participants' homes, community centers, or other locations that would be easy for interested participants to travel to.

Some studies may have additional requirements that require screening of interested participants to determine whether or not they meet important criteria. For example, tools designed for novices should probably not be evaluated by people who work professionally with similar interfaces. Initial questions and interviews with potential subjects can be important tools for ensuring that an individual is appropriate for your study. Specific questions about education, age, experience, and other important attributes can be asked to verify that there is indeed a good match. If you take this approach, you might also consider asking whether they are willing to be contacted in the future for subsequent studies. People who agree to future contact can form the basis for a home-grown database of study participants. Maintaining such a database may involve a fair amount of work, but it can be potentially very useful if you plan to run many studies.

Your database of potential subjects can be an important safety net in the event of difficulties along the way. You may start out with 15 (or 20, 30, or 60) participants with confirmed appointments, only to find that several cancel at the last minute or simply fail to show up. Other problems associated with participant characteristics may force you to dig deeper for a wider range of ages, skills, or backgrounds. If the participants in your study of a general-purpose tool for managing personal photos are all men between 35 and 40 years old (or women over 60), you might have a hard time arguing that your results are indeed general. It's easy to argue that better planning and participant screening might help with this problem, but such details are often not obvious from the beginning. If you're faced with this dilemma, your best option might be to dig deeper into your list, inviting more participants to form a larger (and hopefully more representative) study.

Experiments that involve multiple experimental conditions may require dividing participants into roughly equal-sized groups. If you are comparing performance across user attributes – such as age or gender – your groups must differ in the relevant attributes, while remaining as comparable as possible for other characteristics. If your potential pool of participants is large, you need to select participants in a manner that minimizes any potential bias in selection: selecting the first names from a list that is sorted by gender may get you a group of subjects that is entirely male or female. See Chapter 4 for more discussion of these and related issues in population sampling.

14.2   Care and handling of research participants

Studies with human participants put researchers in a privileged position. As "scientific experts", researchers have expertise, experience, and contextual knowledge that make them well-equipped to understand the reasons for conducting the experiment and the potential costs and benefits involved in participation in a study. Potential participants may lack some or all of this relevant background.

Research studies should be designed to protect participants. Informed consent – the notion that research participants should be provided with the information needed to make a meaningful decision as to whether or not they will participate – is the cornerstone of this protection. Academic and industrial organizations that conduct human subjects research generally rely on institutional review boards to review proposed research for any possible risks and to guarantee that appropriate procedures for informed consent are being followed.

14.2.1   Protecting participants

Participation in a research study involves multiple agreements between the participant and the researcher. The participant agrees to perform certain tasks as needed by the experiment and the experimenter frequently agrees to provide some incentive or compensation to the participant. Perhaps more importantly, experimenters agree to conduct responsible research that protects participants' rights, health, and safety.

Risks to participants are often most pronounced in medical research, where investigation of new drugs, devices, and procedures can lead to health risks, particularly when things don't work as intended (or hoped). However, physical harm is not necessarily the only relevant concern. Famous psychology experiments have shown how research that places people in uncomfortable situations can cause significant emotional distress (see the Milgram's Experiment and Stanford Prison Experiment sidebars). Although some HCI experiments might raise these concerns, most of the studies in our field are low risk. Some studies may lead to fatigue (from mouse movements) or eye strain, but these risks are minor. Regardless of the level of risk involved, researchers must treat human subjects appropriately.

Research In Practice

Milgram's Experiment

Perhaps the most famous example of deception in psychology research, Stanley Milgram's obedience experiment illustrates one possible extreme of human subjects research.

In this study, subjects were told that they were participating in a study of the effect of punishment on learning. They were asked to administer tests to another subject – a "learner" – who would have to identify a word that had previously been associated with a stimulus word. Subjects were told that they had to administer an electric shock to the learner if incorrect answers were given and that the voltage of the shock should be increased after each incorrect answer. Shocks were described as being "extremely painful", but incapable of causing permanent damage (Milgram, 1963).

This description was an elaborate deception aimed at concealing the true goal of the experiment: a study of the limits of obedience. As the "learner" was in fact a colleague of the experimenter's, no actual shocks were administered. However, the subject did receive a mild shock to provide evidence of the authenticity of the equipment and the learner acted as if shocks had been applied. The experimenter participated actively in the deception, urging subjects to continue with the experiment even when they expressed reluctance.

The results of the study were intriguing: of 40 participants, all continued giving shocks until after the point where the "learner" kicked on the wall and stopped responding to the test questions. Most (26 out of 40) of the participants administered the maximum level of shock – two steps beyond "Danger: Severe Shock." Participation caused discomfort including nervous laughter, embarrassment, and seizures for several subjects.

This experiment would not have worked without deception: had the subjects known that they were not actually administering potentially painful shocks, they presumably would have been even less reluctant to participate. The deception created a scenario in which obedience had a real cost, in terms of the distress associated with inflicting harm on a fellow human being.

Milgram's experiment would probably not be considered appropriate human subjects research in most current research environments. The extreme nature of the psychological distress involved in these experiments and the strong reactions experienced by some of the participants raise serious questions as to whether such research can be conducted responsibly (Milgram, 1963).

Virtual environments provide interesting possibilities for subsequent investigations of similar phenomena without raising the ethical concerns associated with Milgram's experiment as originally executed. In a "virtual reprise" of those experiments, subjects were asked to administer shocks to a female virtual human in an immersive environment. The use of a computer-generated character eliminated the need for deceit, thus removing some of the possible ethical objections. Although participants knew that they were interacting with a computer-generated avatar, they responded to the situation as if they were working with a real person, particularly if they could see the avatar (as opposed to communicating via a text chat interface) (Slater *et al.*, 2006).

The Stanford Prison Experiment

Research In Practice

Many interesting and important questions about human behavior in difficult situations can only be examined by conducting studies that expose participants to the risk of significant psychological distress. As interesting as these questions may be, the risks are substantial enough to make this research effectively off limits.

The Stanford prison experiment, conducted by Philip Zimbardo and his colleagues during the summer of 1971, provides an example of both the risks and insight potentially associated with research that exposes participants to significant emotional distress. In order to examine the social forces associated with prisons, the researchers divided a group of Stanford undergraduates (all males) into "guards" and "prisoners". Prisoners were arrested at their homes, blindfolded, placed in uniforms, and incarcerated in a makeshift prison constructed in the basement of Stanford's psychology building. Guards were not given training – they were simply told to do what was necessary to maintain order.

The researchers and participants were all surprised by their responses. Both guards and prisoners completely fell into their roles. Guards humiliated prisoners, using tactics such as awaking prisoners throughout the night for "counts" and placing people in solitary confinement to establish their authority and prevent rebellion. Prisoners temporarily lost their personal identity, thinking of themselves only by their prisoner number. They were passive, depressed, and helpless. One prisoner suffered significant stress, including crying and rage. Both the guards and the researchers responded like real prison staff, believing that he was faking. Dr. Zimbardo – the professor in charge of the experiment – found himself acting like a prison warden, bristling at concerns for the well-being of the prisoners – who were, after all, innocent bystanders. Originally planned for two weeks, the study was terminated after six days, out of concern for the participants (Haney, Banks and Zimbardo, 1973; Zimbardo, 2008).

The observation that seemingly ordinary people would quickly assume the role of sadistic prison guards raises serious questions about the role of context in determining human behavior. Although we would all like to think that we would not behave abusively in such contexts, the Stanford Prison Experiment raises the concern that environment and expectations can play a huge role in encouraging seemingly inhuman behavior. This lesson continues to have significant relevance: Philip Zimbardo has been an oft-quoted commentator on the behavior of guards at the Abu Ghraib prison in Iraq (Zimbardo, 2008).

The Stanford prison experiment also provides a cautionary tale regarding the evolution of research ethics. Despite the known potential for harm, this study was approved by Stanford's Human Subjects Review Board, participants signed an informed consent form, and a 1973 review from the American Psychological Association determined that the study had been consistent with existing ethical guidelines (Zimbardo, 2008). Changing views on responsible research – influenced at least in part by this – have led to a much more conservative view of appropriate research. Philip Zimbardo publicly apologized for his role in the study (Zimbardo, 2008) and the establishment of beneficence – maximizing of benefits while minimizing harm (National Commission, 1979) – argued for research that would strive to avoid the harms seen in the prison experiment. It's hard to imagine a study with this degree of potential harm being approved by any modern institutional review board.

Specific definitions of the responsibilities of researchers grew out of concerns about inappropriate medical procedures conducted during the mid-20th century (see the Informed Consent: Origins and Controversies sidebar). In 1979, the National Commission for the Protection of Human Subjects of Biomedical and Behavioral Research published the Belmont Report (National Commission, 1979). This document established three principles for the treatment of research participants: respect for persons, beneficence, and justice. Respect for persons involves allowing individuals to make independent and autonomous decisions regarding their participation in research. Researchers must allow participants to make judgments and must provide the information necessary for making those judgments. Special consideration must be given in cases of illness or disability that may limit an individual's ability to make independent decisions. Beneficence refers to the need to minimize possible harm while maximizing possible benefits. Justice requires that neither the burdens of participating in research nor the benefits of the research should be limited to certain populations, particularly when some groups of people may be easily manipulated (National Commission, 1979). These principles form the basis for informed consent.

Informed Consent: Origins and Controversies

Famous (or infamous) medical research experiments conducted during the mid–20th century led to the development of modern concepts of informed consent and appropriate treatment of research participants. Nazi Germany's use of concentration camp prisoners in often brutal and barbaric medical experiments led to the Nuremberg code, which established some of the principles behind informed consent (National Cancer Institute, 2001).

The US Public Health Service Syphilis Study at Tuskegee involved hundreds of black men with syphilis over 40 years. Although they were told that they were being treated, no treatment was in fact given, and efforts were actively made to prevent participants from getting treatment (Centers for Disease Control and Prevention, 2007). Several other studies in the US involving administration of drugs or treatment without consent were conducted in the US after the end of World War II (Pellegrino, 1997). More recently, drug trials conducted by Western companies in countries such as India have raised concerns about the nature of informed consent across such cultural and financial divides (Sharma, 2005).

The costs associated with these studies are not limited to the substantial harm inflicted upon the subjects. These unethical experiments reflect poorly on science and scientists in general, harming public trust and increasing reluctance to participate. One study of both white and black residents of Detroit found that black residents were more likely to have heard of the Tuskegee experiments. They were also more likely to be distrustful of researchers and less likely to participate in research (Jones, 1993; Shavers, Lynch and Burmeister, 2000).

Participants should also be assured that their privacy will be protected. Work in the field of privacy protection provides guidance that can help HCI researchers protect the privacy of study participants (Patrick, 2007b). Researchers should obtain consent for the collection and storage of personal information; limit the information collected to that which is necessary; identify the uses that will be made of any information; limit the use, disclosure, and retention of the information; securely protect any information; disclose policies and procedures; provide a means for addressing concerns regarding compliance with information practices; and be accountable for those practices (Patrick, 2007b). Patrick (2007b) provides questions that can be asked in each of these areas to guide privacy practices.

The use of photography and video or audio recording presents special challenges regarding the privacy of participants. Photos, videos, and audio recordings can be very useful tools for illustrating the use of an interface, but they can also unambiguously identify individuals as having participated in a research project. There are several steps that you should take in any project before you start the shutters snapping or cameras rolling. You should clearly tell participants what you are recording and why. If you are going to consider using images of participants in any publications or reports, participants should be fully informed of this possibility. These practices should be mentioned in your informed consent forms (Section 14.2.2) and discussed with participants. If you are video-recording, you might consider recording a portion of the discussion, taking care to include footage of the participants explicitly agreeing to be video-recorded. You should plan your photos or videos carefully: if you are really interested in what is going on with the interface, take pictures and video of the inputs and display – not the faces of the participants. You might be able to shoot over the users' shoulders to get a fuller view without identifying your participants. Similarly, audio recordings captured for potential distribution should minimize use of the participant's voices – record the voices of the research staff if necessary. If you must show people in action, you might consider using image-manipulation techniques, such as blurring or black bars over the eyes to hide the identity of the participants. Pictures or videos of the research staff might be more appropriate for distribution. Finally, you should provide an alternative for participants who are concerned about their privacy: you probably don't need video or audio recordings of every individual in your study.

14.2.2 Informed consent

The notion of informed consent has two parts. "Informed" means that study participants must understand the reason for conducting the study, the procedures that are involved, potential risks, and how they can get more information about the study. Without this information, participants do not have the information necessary to make a truly meaningful decision as to whether or not they wish to participate. If potential participants are not told that the use of a specific virtual-reality environment can occasionally cause nausea, particularly sensitive individuals may agree to participate without being aware that they might be subjecting themselves to an unpleasant experience. For these reasons, researchers should strive to clearly provide information that is relevant and necessary for appropriate decision-making. Truly informing potential participants means that the information must be provided in a manner that is comprehensible (National Cancer Institute, 2001). The reason for the study, the procedures being used, and other details should be provided in a manner that is clear, accessible, and free from professional jargon.

The second, equally important notion is "consent": participation in research studies should be entirely voluntary and free from any implied or implicit coercion. Potential participants should not be given any reason to believe that a decision not to participate will lead to repercussions or retaliation, whether in the form of punishment by employers; withholding of medication or the use of a system; or disapproval from the researcher. Researchers in academic settings should be very careful about giving students credit for coursework in exchange for their participation in studies: if an alternative means of earning the credit are not provided, some students may feel that their grades will suffer if they decline to participate. In such circumstances, participation would be coerced, not consensual.

In most cases, researchers provide participants with an informed consent document that contains several sections (National Cancer Institute, 2001).

- *Title and Purpose*: Why is the study being done?
- *Description of Procedures:* What will be asked of participants? For HCI studies, this probably involves using one or more interface variants, discussing goals and needs, commenting on design proposals, and other related tasks.
- *Duration:* How long will each participant be involved in the study? This should tell the user how much time will be involved. If there are multiple sessions, the number of sessions, the length of each session, and the elapsed interval required should all be specified.
- *Risks:* What risks might be involved in participation? Medical trials may involve the risks of unknown drug side-effects, but the risks are generally less severe in HCI studies. Fatigue, boredom, and perhaps slight discomfort due to repetitive motion are possible risks for studies involving desktop computers. Virtual-reality systems may involve some risk of nausea or disorientation. Studies involving mobile devices, computers in cars, or other interfaces in non-traditional settings may involve additional health or safety risks. Evaluation of the potential distractions caused by computing devices in cars should probably not be conducted in cars driving on public roads! Other interfaces involving social interactions may pose emotional risks, if tasks or content may prove upsetting to participants (see Milgram's Experiment sidebar). The privacy risks of photography and video or audio recording are discussed above; projects involving online-conferencing or ongoing use of online chat systems may present similar concerns. Experimenters should, of course, design studies to minimize all risks. Any remaining risks should be described in detail in informed consent forms and then discussed honestly and thoroughly with study participants.
- *Benefits:* What are the benefits of participation? Some researchers may provide participants with ongoing access to software that is being evaluated. In other cases, financial or material compensation is the main benefit.
- *Alternatives to Participation:* What other options are available? For most HCI studies common alternatives include simply not participating and continuing to use the software that was being used before the study.
- *Confidentiality:* Participants' privacy should be respected. This section of the form generally includes comments indicating that personally identifying information will not be used or published in any way. Confidentiality is a particularly important issue for HCI research involving observation of user behavior such as search or information use activity. Web search, email organization, and other activities may reveal sensitive personal information that could compromise confidentiality. Proper protection of participant privacy involves limiting the use, disclosure, and retention of data; taking appropriate measures

to protect data, including encryption and secure storage; openly describing policies and practices; providing avenues for challenging compliance with data protection procedures; and providing for training and related measures to ensure accountability (Patrick, 2007b).

- *Costs/Additional Expenses:* Are there any financial expenses or other costs associated with participation? Although such costs may not be inappropriate, they may discourage some users from participating. If you are going to ask participants to make costly trips to travel to your location, to purchase software for their computer, or to spend significant amounts of time entering data into diaries, you need to make sure that they are aware of these costs.
- *Participant's Rights:* This section should make three important points:
  - Participation is voluntary.
  - Participants can choose to stop participating at any time, without penalty.
  - Participants have the right to be informed of any new information that will affect their participation in the study (National Cancer Institute, 2001).
- *Contact Information:* Who should participants contact if they have questions or concerns? This section should contain names and contact information for the researchers in charge of the study, as well as for representatives of the institutional review board or other appropriate body.
- *Supplemental Information:* Where should participants go for further information? This section should list resources that can be used for additional information, including (but not limited to) descriptions of the research program and institutional policies and procedures for research involving human subjects.
- *Signature:* Participants should sign a copy of the consent form. The signature should be accompanied by a statement indicating that the participant:
  - has volunteered to participate;
  - has been informed about the tasks and procedures;
  - has had a chance to ask questions and had questions answered;
  - is aware that he/she can withdraw at any time;
  - consented prior to participation in the study (Shneiderman and Plaisant, 2009).

The researcher should provide a copy of the consent form to each participant for reference, while retaining the signed copies as documentation of the consent.

Construction of an informed consent document can be a useful step in ensuring that your research meets accepted ethical standards. If you have accounted for the risks, benefits, alternatives, and confidentiality measures associated with your project, the relevant sections of the document should be relatively straightforward to put together. Similarly, difficulty in construction of these sections may indicate the need to rethink proposed practices in procedures.

Writing clear, concise informed documents is not trivial. One study of informed consent forms for medical research studies found that users preferred simpler statements written at a seventh-grade level (as opposed to at a college graduate level) but the simpler statements did not lead to greater comprehension (Davis *et al.*, 1998). Pilot testing of the consent forms, either as part of a pilot test for an experiment or via reviews by potential participants or collaborators can help identify confusing language or areas that may need clarification. An example informed consent form is given in Figure 14.1.

Informed consent requires affirmative agreement from an individual who is capable of understanding the implications of agreeing to participation in the research. Research involving participants who are not able to interpret informed consent forms may require additional measures. When children participate in research studies, parents or legal guardians are generally asked to consent to the participation. When possible, children may also be asked to "assent" – to agree to participate – even if they are not capable of giving informed consent (Society for Research in Child Development, 1991). This assent would be in addition to – not instead of – parental consent. Considerations of informed consent and users with disabilities are discussed in Chapter 15.

Local or national legislation may place additional constraints on the content of an informed consent document. In the United States, federal regulations prohibit language in informed consent forms that would waive legal rights or absolve researchers of legal responsibility (National Cancer Institute, 2001).

The use of informed consent forms – even those that are approved by institutional review boards (see Section 14.2.3) should not be seen as a green light to move forward with research that may otherwise raise questions regarding respect for the rights and concerns of participants.

14.2.3 Institutional review boards

Universities, hospitals, corporations, and other organizations that conduct research often have standing committees that review and approve projects involving human subjects. These institutional review boards (IRBs) examine proposed studies for appropriate practices, procedures, goals, and disclosures. By conducting this review prior to the start of human subjects research, IRBs protect all of the groups and individuals that may be affected by the research. Participants are protected by examination of proposed research for any elements that may be manipulative, coercive, or otherwise abusive. Proposals that contain any such elements should not be approved by IRBs. Researchers and institutions benefit from the knowledge that the proposed research has been reviewed for issues that may cause embarrassment or legal liability. Although this review is certainly not foolproof, it generally works well in practice.

IRB review and approval for proposed research generally begins when a researcher submits materials relating to proposed research. A description of the proposed research, draft informed consent forms, instructions to be provided to users, questionnaires, and materials to be used during the course of the research are some of the items that might be required. Upon receipt of these materials, the IRB will review them for completeness and content. The board may approve the research, request additional information, require revision of materials, or take other steps as appropriate.

INFORMED CONSENT FORM

Evaluating Menu Selection Task Performance

PRINCIPAL INVESTIGATOR: A. Researcher
Department of Computer and Information Sciences
Research University
Phone: 555-555-5555
Email: researcher@research.edu

Purpose of the Study: The goal of this study is to understand how computer interfaces might be customized to best suit the needs of users. Participants will be asked to use a menu interface to find items in various multi-level hierarchy designs. Task completion times and subjective responses will be used to determine which (if any) design is most suitable for these users.

Procedures: Participation in this study will involve two phases. In the first phase, you will be asked to use a web browser to make selections from a menu of choices, in order to locate a specified entry. You will be given the opportunity to try a sample task, and then you will have to complete multiple tasks with different menu structures. This study should take about one hour to complete.

After you have completed the experimental tasks, we may ask you some questions about the various interfaces. These questions will be designed to help us understand which (if any) of the interfaces you preferred, and why. We may also ask some general questions about your habits and practices with respect to computer use.

Risks/Discomfort: You may become fatigued during the course of your participation in the study. You will be given several opportunities to rest, and additional breaks are also possible. There are no other risks associated with participation in the study. Should completion of either the task or the interview become distressing to you, it will be terminated immediately.

Benefits: It is hoped that the results of this study will be useful for the development of guidelines for the design of user interfaces that will help people use computers more effectively.

Alternatives to Participation: Participation in this study is voluntary. You are free to withdraw or discontinue participation at any time.

Cost and Compensation: Participation in this study will involve no cost to you. You will be paid for your participation.

Confidentiality: All information collected during the study period will be kept strictly confidential. You will be identified through identification numbers. No publications or reports from this project will include identifying information on any participant. If you agree to join this study, please sign your name below.

_____ I have read and understood the information on this form.
_____ I have had the information on this form explained to me.

_____   _____
Subject's Signature   Date

_____   _____
Witness to Consent Procedures   Date

_____   _____
Principal Investigator   Date

If you have any questions regarding this study please contact Dr Researcher at (555) 555-5555 or the Institutional Review Board Chairperson, Dr Chair Person, Research University, (555) 555-6666.

Figure 14.1 Informed consent form.

As research cannot begin until the IRB approval is complete, it is generally best to start this process early. Some research funding agencies will not release any funds until appropriate IRB approvals have been obtained. As each IRB has its own rules, it is important that researchers understand and follow the appropriate procedures for their institution. Many IRBs have websites that describe policies and provide relevant forms. It's a good idea to familiarize yourself with this material. Although some boards consider applications on a rolling basis, others have scheduled meetings, with published submission deadlines for consideration at each meeting. Attention to detail is particularly important for boards that meet on a set schedule: if your IRB meets bi-monthly, minor omissions in a proposed package may lead to a two-month delay in acquiring the necessary approval.

Some IRBs – particularly those at large research institutions with affiliated medical schools – may spend much of their time focusing on drug or treatment studies. If your IRB falls into this category, board members may not be aware of the techniques used in HCI research (as described in this book). You may have to spend some time and effort explaining ethnography, research based on online data sources, or other techniques that they are not familiar with. If you run into this sort of challenge, you should stress the widespread application of these techniques, and the existing body of research from groups such as the Association of Internet Researchers (www.aoir.org) or the Ethnographic Praxis in Industry Conference (EPIC). It's best to approach such discussions from a collegial, not confrontational, perspective.

Although the paperwork required by some IRBs may feel like a nuisance, you should consider your IRB as an ally. By insisting upon procedures, IRBs protect researchers and institutions from problems associated with research that goes wrong. IRBs can also provide helpful feedback in situations that may raise questions. Some projects may blur the lines between participating in the research and acting as a collaborative partner. For example, projects involving participatory design may involve ethnographic observation of users in the workplace. Is informed consent necessary in this case? Although the conservative approach of requiring informed consent is unlikely to be inappropriate, discussing this question with a member of your IRB might provide insight into your institution's policies regarding such research. Many IRBs require researchers to take training courses before conducting any studies involving human subjects research. These courses may not seem exciting, but they can provide valuable information that might prove helpful when you are preparing informed consent materials.

Organizations that infrequently engage in human subjects research may not have an established institutional review board. This may be particularly true for small companies that run occasional user studies. If you find yourself in such a situation, it may be helpful to discuss matters with appropriate professionals in your organization, including community relations staff and legal counsel. IRBs from nearby research institutions may be willing to provide feedback as well. The use of informed consent forms and proper procedures is always appropriate, even in the absence of a formal review from an IRB.

14.2.4 Potentially deceptive research?

Researchers may occasionally have legitimate reasons to be less than forthcoming about the goals and procedures of their research. The practice of potentially deceptive research involves asking a user to perform a set of tasks that are described as relating to a particular goal, when the researcher is actually interested in addressing a different question unrelated to the goal presented to the user. Although concealing the true nature of the study does present some concerns regarding the validity of informed consent, this practice is often necessary, particularly in situations where full disclosure might compromise the realism of the study.

A study involving security and usability provides an example of the use of deception in HCI research (Schechter et al., 2007). This study had two goals: to determine the influence of security feedback and to see if participants using their own data would behave more or less securely than those who were role-playing using someone else's data. As the researchers were concerned that study participants would not behave naturally if they were told that usability was being studied, they were told that the purpose of the study was to "help make online banking better" (Schechter et al., 2007). Participants were asked to perform online banking tasks. Some participants were "role-playing" – they were asked to pretend that they were a specific individual with specific goals in mind; others used their own bank accounts. In addition to finding that security indicators were not particularly helpful, this study found that people using their own data behaved more securely than those who were role-playing (Schechter et al., 2007).

Schecter et al. (2007) used deceit as a means of setting up conditions that maximized the realism of the experiment. By presenting users with real online banking tasks, they focused the experiment on how actual users might behave when using online banking on their own. If participants had been told that the experiment was examining their behavior regarding security and privacy, they might have paid extra attention to their behavior in these areas. This use of deception may be useful and valid, but it does have its limits. These limits arise from the established psychological concept of demand characteristics (Orne, 1962), which states that participants in a research study may act in a manner that attempts to validate the hypotheses being tested. In this study, participants may have taken the goal of improving online banking to heart, perhaps acting more insecurely than they otherwise might have (Patrick, 2007a).

Deception in HCI research should be used carefully and sparingly. As deception pushes at the limits of the concept of informed consent, researchers should be careful to frame deceptions clearly, justify their use, and minimize any risks – particularly regarding discomfort and distress – that may be involved (See the Milgram's Experiment sidebar for a famous example of deceptive research). Participants in studies involving deception should be thoroughly debriefed at the end of their participation. Debriefing has been shown to help deceived participants eliminate negative effects and even to have experiences that were more positive than those of participants who have not been deceived (Smith and Richardson, 1983).

14.2.5 General concerns

Participants are crucial to our studies – without them, HCI research would be all but impossible. We should make every effort to treat participants in a manner that reflects this importance. Compensation for time and effort is certainly helpful, but researchers should also take concrete steps to make participation convenient and enjoyable. Comfortable surroundings may put participants at ease. Ample opportunities for rest or bathroom breaks should be provided, particularly for studies that involve longer research sessions. Flexibility in scheduling and location can be particularly important for some users: enrolling professionals in your study may require that you travel to their workplace or allow for sessions outside of traditional working hours. If your study is fun and convenient, participants may be more likely to help your recruiting efforts by urging friends and colleagues to join in.

These concerns are particularly important for special cases that place a significant burden on participants. Longitudinal studies require participants to make a huge time commitment – many hours over weeks or months. Research on people with disabilities may require enrolling participants who have significant difficulty traveling. You may find that engaging the required range of participants requires traveling to participants' home or workplace, at times of their choosing.

When working with human participants in any form of HCI research, you must pay careful attention to your role as a researcher. Participants may be impressed or intimidated by your presence, your use of language, your technical skills, the context of the experiment, or any of a variety of related factors. This is particularly true for observations and contextual-inquiry, where you will spend a great deal of time in close contact with one or more participants. Although you should make every reasonable effort to help participants feel as at ease as possible, you should also be aware that your presence may have an impact on observed performance. In some cases, participants may exhibit the "demand characteristics" described above, trying to behave in the manner that they think you are looking for.

Others have claimed that the mere act of participating in an experiment will influence user behavior, in the so-called "Hawthorne effect". Although this effect has been the subject of significant debate among scientists, some suggested responses are clear and appropriate. Researchers should never give feedback regarding user performance during the course of a study and experiments involving the comparison of multiple interfaces should be controlled and "blind" – participants should not know if one of the alternatives is favored by the researchers (Macefield, 2007).

More generally, these concerns about the influence of researchers on experimental results point towards a need to be modest about the results of our research. All experiments have flaws and no single study establishes incontrovertible facts on its own. When reporting results and drawing conclusions, we should avoid overstatement, admit the flaws in our research, and point the way for future work that will bring greater understanding.

14.3 Online research

Working with human subjects is often challenging. Scheduling sessions, recruiting participants, finding appropriate space, and managing other logistical details require time and energy, neither of which ever seems to be available in abundance.

Online HCI research presents the tantalizing prospect of a way out of these challenges but, as you might have guessed, there is no silver bullet. This section outlines research issues including appropriate topics for online research, recruiting, study design, ethical concerns, and methods for data collection.

14.3.1 Appropriate topics for online research

Although it may seem somewhat obvious to note that online research will involve working with participants who are online, this helps point us toward the insight that online HCI research may be most appropriate for studies about the tools that people use online and the uses that they make of those tools. Participants in online studies will probably be working with web browsers, chat tools, and related online software as they read instructions, provide informed consent, perform tasks, and otherwise complete your experimental protocol. Research that works within this realm may be most successful.

As far as tools are concerned, this implies that studies involving web applications or online tools may be particularly well suited for online research. If you are interested in testing the usability of website design or using a dynamic website to collect data on task performance, an online study may be very appropriate. If you are running the website on your own servers, web logs (Chapter 12) can provide useful feedback regarding timing, tasks, and errors. Conversely, studies of other application software, mobile devices, or novel interaction devices may be harder to do online: data collection is likely to be more difficult, incompatibilities between software versions may pop up, etc.

That's not to say that online studies of website designs are easy. Good design practice certainly calls for cross-platform testing, but there is no guarantee that you won't run into versioning and compatibility problems, even with seemingly straightforward web pages. If your test involves dynamic Javascript and HTML combinations, bugs and plug-ins could cause all sorts of trouble.

Investigation of the uses that people make of online tools might involve ethnographic analysis of online bulletin boards for various communities of interest (Maloney-Krichmar and Preece, 2005) and other studies that attempt to understand online socialization, resource usage, and other behavior. The Association of Internet Researchers (www.aoir.org) hosts an annual conference with numerous studies along these lines, many of which are of direct interest to the HCI community.

14.3.2 Recruiting

By opening your research up to the Internet, you provide yourself with access to a much larger pool of participants. Recruiting can be easier, as emails to appropriate lists and postings on various websites can go a long way towards identifying potential subjects. As online research generally involves the use of a website or other online software, participants do not need to be local. Self-driven website or study tools allow participants to complete tasks at their leisure, eliminating the need for scheduling.

Just as the use of undergraduates as study participants introduces a bias that may not be appropriate for some studies, online recruitment limits your subject pool to a particular segment of the larger population: Internet users who are interested enough to participate. This may mean that you do not attract relatively inexperienced individuals or participants who limit their time online to relatively focused activities. Whether or not this poses a problem depends on the specifics of the study in question.

In some cases, online research can give you access to pools of participants that otherwise would have been unavailable. This is particularly true for people with disabilities, who may find traveling to a researcher lab to be logistically unfeasible (Petrie et al., 2006), and domain experts, who may be hard to find in sufficient numbers in some locales (Brush, Ames and Davis, 2004). See Chapter 15 for more details on HCI research involving people with disabilities. Collaborative research involving distant partners can also be substantially aided by online tools for communicating and gathering data.

One important difference between online and in-person research is the potentially complete anonymity of participants in online studies. When you meet a participant face-to-face, you can usually make a pretty good guess about their age, gender, and other demographic characteristics. The lack of face-to-face contact with online participants makes verification of such details harder – you have no way of verifying that your participants are male or female, old or young. This presents some recruiting challenges, particularly if your research requires participants that meet certain demographic constraints such as age or gender. If your only contact is via email or other electronic means, you may not be able to verify that the person with whom you are communicating is who he or she is claiming to be. Online studies that don't require the participants to reveal their true identity (relying instead on email addresses or screen names) are highly vulnerable to deception. Certain incentives, such as offering to enter participants in a draw for a desirable prize, might compound this problem. For example, a survey aimed at a specific demographic group might draw multiple responses from one individual, who might use multiple email addresses to appear as if inquiries were coming from different people. Possible approaches for avoiding such problems include eliminating incentives; requiring proof of demographic status (age, gender, disability, etc.) for participation; and initial phone or in-person contact in order to provide some verification of identity. Since payment or other delivery of incentives often requires knowing a participant's name and address, verification of identity is often not an added burden.

Online research involves giving up a certain amount of control over both the participants and the process. When you meet participants face-to-face, you can gain a great deal of information by observing their actions and behavior. To varying extents, you can tell if they are being truthful about demographic information, observe their subjective reactions to their participation, provide assistance when appropriate, and make note of any cues or observations that may seem pertinent. The contextual feedback associated with online research is much less limited. Even if you are doing synchronous research with video chat and screen capture, you will still be somewhat limited in the information that you will be able to observe during the course of the session.

14.3.3 Study design

Surveys (Lazar and Preece, 1999), usability evaluations (Brush, Ames and Davis, 2004; Petrie *et al.*, 2006), and ethnographic studies of support groups (Maloney-Krichmar and Preece, 2005) have all been successfully completed online. Recent examples of online usability studies have shown that both synchronous studies with domain experts (Brush, Ames and Davis, 2004) and asynchronous studies with disabled users (Petrie *et al.*, 2006) have yielded results comparable to those that were found in traditional usability studies. Perhaps due to difficulties in sampling and controls, online empirical studies of task performance are less common. One study of the influence of informal "sketch-like" interfaces on drawing behavior used an online study as a means of confirming the results of a smaller, traditional study. Results from the 221 subjects in the online study were highly consistent with the results from the 18 subjects in the traditional, controlled study in the lab. The agreement between the two sets of results provides a more convincing argument than the lab study on its own (Meyer and Bederson, 1998).

Opinions differ on the appropriateness of online research for different types of data collection. The lack of controls on the participant population might be seen as a difficulty for some controlled, empirical studies. Others have argued that as online research does not allow for detailed user observation, it is more appropriate for quantitative approaches (Petrie *et al.*, 2006). In the absence of any clear guidelines, it is certainly appropriate to design studies carefully and to clearly describe and document the reasoning behind any designs that are adopted. When possible, hybrid approaches involving both in-person and online research may provide additional data and avoid some of the downsides associated with each approach.

14.3.4 Ethical concerns

Although the usual guidelines regarding protection of participants apply to online research, numerous confounding factors can create some interesting and challenging dilemmas.

Studies of online communities must consider questions of privacy and online consent. What is the expectation of privacy when participants in an online forum post messages publicly? Are such messages fair game for researchers? Is informed consent required before messages can be used? What if the site is only accessible to users who register and login? These questions have generated debate, discussions, and some guidelines (Bruckman, 2002; Frankel and Siang, 1999), but specific issues vary from case to case. Creating communities specifically for research purposes can be a successful – if not always practical – strategy (Bruckman, 2002).

Debriefing and informed consent online can also be tricky. Providing important information for either of these tasks via online text may not be sufficient. In-person studies provide the possibility of direct feedback: experimenters know if participants have any questions or if there is any post-experiment distress. These factors are much harder to gauge online (Azar, 2000). Although one study indicated that comprehension of informed consent forms online may be comparable to comprehension of forms on paper, poor recall in both cases illustrates the general challenge of constructing effective consent forms (Varnhagen *et al.*, 2005). These studies should not be undertaken without careful attention to IRB processes and approval.

Further complications in informed consent and debriefing arise with online studies involving deception. A series of studies of "phishing" – the use of forged emails to attempt to entice users to login to fraudulent websites, thus giving attackers access to their user names, passwords, and related credentials – used social network analysis and related means to identify potential participants, who were sent phishing emails. These emails effectively enrolled recipients in the study, without any prior knowledge or informed consent. Although the methods received IRB approval, these studies raised many concerns and controversies, including legal ramifications, potential for harm due to online debriefing, and technical issues relating to Internet hosting of study materials (Finn and Jakobsson, 2007).

The considerable challenges and headache associated with deceptive online research provide a strong argument against this sort of approach. If you find yourself tempted to try this sort of study, consider a lab-based study instead. You may still use deception in this case but the use of prior informed consent can help you avoid many difficult questions.

As with any HCI research, online research can be particularly challenging if there is potential harm involved or when dealing with special cases, such as research involving children. Technical measures such as encryption of transmitted data may be useful for privacy protection and for verifying parental consent in the case of minors (Kraut *et al.*, 2004). Laws such as the Children's Online Protection Act in the United States may limit the amount of information that can be collected from minors. Researchers working in these areas should construct study materials carefully; consult with IRBs and external experts to review proposed procedures; and use traditional studies as opposed to online studies when appropriate (Kraut *et al.*, 2004).

14.3.5   Data collection

Web logs or other software designed to collect appropriate data and send it back to a server can be a powerful means of collecting experimental data in a manageable and accessible format. In addition to indicating which pages were visited and when, logs can provide information regarding the browser that was used and the "referring site" (where the user came from). Particularly when used with tools designed to extract and analyze patterns from such logs, this data can provide a useful picture of how websites are used. Commercial packages for remote usability evaluation provide similar functionality.

Similar techniques can be used with other software packages. In a process known as "instrumentation", custom software tools can be extended to collect data and send it back to a remote server via a network connection. For example, a browser plug-in might be used to track mouse paths on a web page. This information might be sent to a server and correlated with web logs to provide an understanding of where a user's mouse went on a given page. Other tools might be augmented with "talk-back" mechanisms, which might periodically send data back to a server – either silently or after alerting a user. Many of the automated data collection techniques discussed in Chapter 12 can be applied to online research.

Used appropriately – that is, with relevant disclosures to participants and safeguards to protect privacy – remote data collection tools can provide a wealth of data for online research.

Summary

Working with human subjects is one of the most challenging and informative aspects of HCI research. Finding appropriate participants; informing them of their rights; protecting their privacy; and answering their questions can be time-consuming and often tedious, but the results are more than worth the effort. Even when study participants criticize our designs or fail to confirm our cherished experimental hypotheses, they provide invaluable insight that provides a rigorous foundation for our work.

Whatever type of study you are running, it is never too early to plan for recruiting, informed consent documentation, and other aspects of human participation. Proper planning will keep your study from becoming one of the many that have been delayed by unforeseen circumstances including difficulty in finding participants, or delays in IRB approval.

Recruiting entails finding the right number of the right kinds of participants. For usability studies, ethnographic observations of users, interviews, focus groups, and other approaches aimed at gathering requirements or evaluating design proposals, this may mean understanding the audience of users and identifying a sample of participants that is broad enough to reflect the needs and behavior of potential users. *Designers* and *professional developers* conducting research of this sort might work with collaborators, marketing teams, professional organizations, or others with appropriate understanding and context to identify both the range of viewpoints that would be needed and possible sources of the appropriate individuals.

Empirical studies require consideration of both the diversity of potential participants and any confounding factors that might contribute to performance differences. Characteristics of desirable participants might both be informed by and influence experimental hypotheses. *Students* and *researchers* conducting these studies should be careful to plan their data analysis and recruiting together, to ensure that the participants will be selected to increase the power of the statistical analysis.

Appropriate respect for participants is a cornerstone of all research involving human subjects. Although *designers* and *developers* may not be required to secure the approval of institutional review boards, they should still endeavor to protect their subjects from any form of harm and to treat them with respect and dignity.

These issues are particularly relevant for studies that involve deception. Even when not required by institutional policy to do so, designers and developers would be advised to use formal informed consent forms to help participants make informed decisions. *Students* and *researchers* should take the time – again, as early in the process as possible – to understand the regulations in force in their institution, and to make sure that their approvals are in order before starting any project.

Designers and *developers* may find online studies to be an attractive means of evaluating proposed interface designs. *Students* and *researchers* will undoubtedly continue to find the prospect of online research too enticing to resist. Before moving studies online, HCI professionals should be careful to validate that their proposed designs will provide the desired information. Pilot tests may be particularly useful in these cases.

Human subjects research in HCI can be an unpredictable and often unsettling process. Unforeseen problems, including misinterpreted tasks and goals, systems failures and missed appointments, are routine: it's rare that a study (of any sort) goes off completely without a hitch. These matters can complicate data collection and interpretation: if a user chooses an interpretation of a written task that differs from your intent and then completes the task correctly, how do you interpret the result – is it correct or not? What should be done with results from a user who decides to withdraw from a study after completing only a portion of the tasks? As hard and fast rules for handling situations like these are few and far between, you may have to handle each issue on a case-by-case basis. The specific decisions that you make may be less important than how they are enforced: consistent application of policies and procedures will ensure your ability to make meaningful comparisons.

All participants in HCI research study should be well-treated and approached with an open mind. Participating in HCI studies should be fun and engaging whenever possible: by making our studies positive experiences, we encourage people both to participate and to provide useful feedback. As researchers, we should "expect the unexpected": software will crash, devices won't work, and (perhaps most distressingly) users will hate our beloved inventions. High-quality HCI research takes these setbacks in its stride, all the while striving to observe carefully while maintaining respect for the people who give a bit of their time to help our studies along. By watching and listening carefully, we can learn from what they do and how they do it. That, after all, is the point of conducting user studies.

Discussion Questions

1. University researchers occasionally ask students in a class to participate in research studies. However, this practice may involve elements of coercion, as students may be concerned that refusal to participate may negatively impact their grade. Is voluntary informed consent possible in such a situation? What steps might be taken to reconcile the researcher's need for subjects with the students' right to decline to participate?

2. The virtual reprise of Milgram's experiment (see Section 14.2.1) asked participants to inflict harm upon a computer-generated avatar. This approach eliminates some of the potential ethical concerns associated with the original experiment, but may raise additional questions. As user behavior was similar to what was observed in the original experiments, it is possible that participants in the "virtual" versions would experience similar patterns of nervousness and distress. Do you consider this sort of research to be appropriate? What might be done to protect participants in this sort of experiment?

3. As part of a larger study of how various aspects of interaction in online worlds, such as Second Life, impact the offline lives of participants, you are interested in observing participants both online and offline. As you know, participants in online games such as these may not represent a broad cross-section of society. The race and sex of online characters may not reflect those of the real individuals involved and some may choose to hide their "real" identity. Given these challenges, how might you go about finding a group of participants that would be interesting to work with? How might these challenges affect the conclusions that you might be able to draw from your observations and your ability to generalize from those conclusions?

Research Design Exercises

1. You are designing a study to evaluate the effectiveness of a new text-entry method for messaging on cell phones. Due to the popularity of messaging among college students, you decide that the undergraduate student body at your school would be an appropriate pool of potential participants. What would you want to know about the habits of these students regarding text messaging? You might be interested in comparing the performance of computer science students against students from other fields. Are there any other attributes of the students that might make for interesting comparisons? Given the male–female imbalance in computer science, what problems might this comparison involve?

2. Your research design for the study of text-entry on cell phones involves asking users to perform a set of tasks in a laboratory. As they will not be using their own phones, there is little, if any, privacy risk. What other risks might this study pose, and how would you inform users about them?

3. Find the website or other information about your institutional review board. Examine the policies and procedures specific to your institution, and write a draft informed consent form for the study described in Exercise 1.

4. Studies of how users respond to events that interrupt their work (Gluck, Bunt and McGrenere, 2007) present a challenge in design. If participants are told that the study is investigating reactions to

interruptions, they may be more sensitive to those events than they would otherwise be. A deceptive study, in which the subjects were provided with an alternative description of the goals of the study, might be one way to get around this problem. How might you describe a deceptive study for examining reactions to interruptions? How would you describe this study in an informed consent form? What would you discuss in the debriefing sessions?

References

Azar, B. (2000) Online experiments: Ethically fair or foul? *Monitor on Psychology*, **31**(4).

Bruckman, A.S. (2002) Ethical guidelines for research online. Retrieved July 2, 2007, from http://www.cc.gatech.edu/~asb/ethics/.

Brush, A.J., Ames, M., and Davis, J. (2004) A comparison of synchronous remote and local usability studies for an expert interface. *Extended Abstracts of the ACM Conference on Human Factors in Computer Systems*, 1179–1182.

Centers for Disease Control and Prevention (2007) *US Public Health Service Syphilis Study at Tuskegee.* Retrieved May 31, 2007, from http://www.cdc.gov/nchstp/od/tuskegee/.

Cook, T.D. and Campbell, D.T. (1979) *Quasi-Experimentation: Design and analysis issues for field settings.* Boston: Houghton Mifflin Company.

Davis, T.C., Holcombe, R.F., Berkel, H.J., *et al.* (1998) Informed consent for clinical trials: A comparative study of standard versus simplified forms. *Journal of the National Cancer Institute*, **90**(9):668–674.

Finn, P. and Jakobsson, M. (2007) Designing ethical phishing experiments. *Technology and Society Magazine, IEEE*, **26**(1):46–58.

Frankel, M.S. and Siang, S. (1999) Ethical and legal aspects of human subjects research on the Internet. American Association for the Advancement of Science. Retrieved July 2, 2007, from http://www.aaas.org/spp/sfrl/projects/intres/report.pdf.

Gluck, J., Bunt, A., and McGrenere, J. (2007) Matching attentional draw with utility in interruption. *Proceedings of the ACM Conference on Human Factors in Computing Systems*, 41–50.

Haney, C., Banks, C., and Zimbardo, P. (1973) Interpersonal dynamics in a simulated prison. *International Journal of Criminology and Penology*, **1**: 69–97.

Jones, J.H. (1993) *Bad Blood: The Tuskegee syphilis experiment.* New York: Free Press.

Kraut, R., Olson, J., Banaji, M., *et al.* (2004) Psychological research online: Report of Board of Scientific Affairs' Advisory Group on the Conduct of Research on the Internet. *American Psychologist*, **59**(2):105–117.

Larson, K. and Czerwinski, M. (1998) Web page design: Implications of memory, structure and scent for information retrieval. *Proceedings of the ACM Conference on Human Factors in Computing Systems*, 25–32.

Lazar, J. and Preece, J. (1999) Designing and implementing web-based surveys. *Journal of Computer Information Systems*, **39**(4):63–67.

Macefield, R. (2007) Usability studies and the Hawthorne Effect. *Journal of Usability Studies*, **2**(3):145–154.

Maloney-Krichmar, D. and Preece, J. (2005) A multilevel analysis of sociability, usability, and community dynamics in an online health community. *ACM Transactions on Computer–Human Interaction*, **12**(2):201–232.

Meyer, J. and Bederson, B. (1998) *Does a Sketchy Appearance Influence Drawing Behavior?* University of Maryland, Human-Computer Interaction Lab. Retrieved October 15, 2009 from http://hcil.cs.umd.edu/trs/98-12/98-12.pdf.

Milgram, S. (1963) Behavioral study of obedience. *Journal of Abnormal and Social Psychology*, **67**(4):371–378.

National Cancer Institute (2001) A guide to understanding informed consent. Retrieved June 4, 2007, from http://www.cancer.gov/clinicaltrials/conducting/informed-consent-guide/.

National Commission (1979) The Belmont Report: Ethical principles and guidelines for the protection of human subjects of research. National Commission for the Protection of Human Subjects of Biomedical and Behavioral Research. Retrieved June 27, 2007, from http://ohsr.od.nih.gov/guidelines/belmont.html.

Nielsen, J. (1994) *Usability Engineering*. San Francisco: Morgan Kaufmann.

Orne, M.T. (1962) On the social psychology of the psychological experiment: With particular reference to demand characteristics and their implications. *American Psychologist*, **17**(11):776–783.

Patrick, A. (2007a) Commentary on research on new security indicators. Retrieved June 22, 2007, from http://www.andrewpatrick.ca/essays/commentary-on-research-on-new-security-indicators/.

Patrick, A. (2007b) Privacy practices for HCI research. Retrieved June 4, 2007, from http://www.andrewpatrick.ca/essays/privacy-practices-for-hci-research/.

Pellegrino, E.D. (1997) The Nazi doctors and Nuremberg: Some moral lessons revisited. *Annals of Internal Medicine*, **127**(4):307–308.

Petrie, H., Hamilton, F., King, N., and Pavan, P. (2006) Remote usability evaluations with disabled people. *Proceedings of the ACM Conference on Human Factors in Computing Systems*, 1133–1141.

Schechter, S., Dhamija, R., Ozment, A., and Fischer, A. (2007) The emperor's new security indicators: An evaluation of website authentication and the effect of role playing on usability studies. *Proceedings of the IEEE Symposium on Security and Privacy*, 51–65.

Sharma, K. (2005) Can clinical trials ever be truly ethical? *The Hindu*.

Shavers, V.L., Lynch, C.F.L., and Burmeister, L.F. (2000) Knowledge of the Tuskegee study and its impact on the willingness to participate in medical research studies. *Journal of the National Medical Association*, **92**(12):563–572.

Shneiderman, B. and Plaisant, C. (2009) *Designing the User Interface*, 5ᵗʰ edition. Boston: Pearson Addison-Wesley.

Slater, M., Antley, A., Davison, A., *et al.* (2006) A virtual reprise of the Stanley Milgram obedience experiments. *PLoS ONE*, **1**(1).

Smith, S.S. and Richardson, D. (1983) Amelioration of deception and harm in psychological research: The important role of debriefing. *Journal of Personality and Social Psychology*, **44**(5):1075–1082.

Society for Research in Child Development (1991) Ethical standards for research with children. Retrieved June 22, 2007, from http://www.srcd.org/ethicalstandards.html.

Steriadis, C.E. and Constantinou, P. (2003) Designing human–computer interfaces for quadriplegic people. *ACM Transactions on Computer–Human Interaction*, **10**(2):87–118.

Varnhagen, C.K., Gushta, M., Daniels, J., *et al.* (2005) How informed is online informed consent? *Ethics & Behavior*, **15**(1):37–48.

Zimbardo, P. (2008) Stanford prison experiment. Retrieved June 2, 2008, from www.prisonexp.org.

Working with research participants with impairments

15.1 Introduction

Chapter 14 talks about approaches for and issues that arise when working with human participants in research. As the number of research projects involving users with impairments grows, it is important also to examine the specific concepts, issues, and challenges of doing human–computer interaction (HCI) research with users with various impairments. Computer technology is now being used everywhere, by everyone, on a daily basis, for work, for pleasure, for communication, and for overall living. This includes users with perceptual impairments (e.g. hearing and visual), motor impairments (e.g. limited or no use of hands, arms, legs, or mouth) and cognitive impairments (whether lifelong impairments, such as Down Syndrome and autism, impairments that develop over time, such as dementia and Alzheimer's Disease, or event-based impairments, such as aphasia).

The grouping of "users with impairments" is itself somewhat artificial. It encompasses lots of different individuals with different impairments, abilities, and strengths; all they may have in common is that they have the label "impairment" or "disability" attached to them. For instance, individuals who are blind, and individuals who have Alzheimer's Disease may have practically nothing in common. And people that are often grouped together in research may be exact opposites. For instance, in evaluating technologies for people with cognitive impairment, some researchers have grouped together young adults with autism and Down Syndrome, when they are polar opposites in social skills, motor skills, and intellectual skills. This is important to remember: you can't just group together people with different impairments under that one large umbrella. While research on users with perceptual and motor impairments has existed since the 1970s, only recently have researchers tackled the challenges of designing computer interfaces for users with cognitive impairments (Lazar, 2007b) and only rarely have researchers worked with individuals with multiple impairments.

The goals of HCI research on users with impairments are the same as research with other users, to understand the phenomena surrounding computer interfaces and usage patterns. Because the users have a complex story, it is important to involve those individuals in HCI research, design, and evaluation. You can't just take guidelines from the research on interface design for people with impairments, and you can't just take proxy users that represent the users with impairments. You must work with users with impairments themselves. The overall research methods (experimental design, surveys, time diaries, case studies, etc.) are the same as for other users. However, the logistics of performing this type of research are what makes it different. There are differences in the number of participants, how you recruit participants, where you perform your research, how you get them to sign IRB forms, and how you pay users with impairments for their participation. These differences in logistics are covered in this chapter. Due to these complex logistics, it is realistic to say that it may take more time to do research involving participants with impairments. It is intensive, but you should do it anyway! In addition, some technologies that start out as assistive technology for a specific impairment population wind up later becoming popular among the general population. So, research that leads to improved interface and design experiences for people with impairments may eventually lead to interfaces that are better for the general population!

15.2 How many participants?

One of the greatest challenges of doing research with users with impairments is access to the participants themselves. Historically, many general research studies utilize computer users that are easy to gain access to. This includes students at universities, local business professionals, and children in schools (Lazar and Norcio, 2000). Finding appropriate users with the specific impairment that is the focus of the study can be a challenge. In doing research with the general population of users, it is often expected that a research study would have a minimum of 20–30 users, to be considered valid (see Chapters 2 and 3 for more information on sample sizes). These expectations may not be realistic for users with impairments, as it might be impossible to get access to so many users in one geographic area with a specific impairment.

The generally accepted approaches for dealing with the issue of access to appropriate participants for research focusing on users with impairments are small sample sizes, distributed research, and in-depth case studies. Choosing the most appropriate approach will depend on the nature of the research questions. For instance, controlled studies often use small sample sizes or in-depth case studies. Research of a more exploratory nature (with fewer controls) can use distributed research.

15.2.1 Small sample sizes

For research focusing on users with impairments, it is generally acceptable to have 5-10 users with a specific impairment take part in a study. This is due to a number of factors discussed later in the chapter. For example, in the recent proceedings of the ASSETS conference (well-accepted as a high-quality conference on this topic), most of the research studies in which blind users had to be physically present to take part in the research had 15 or fewer blind individuals taking part in the research. This means that if a classic experimental design is used, that there will often be no more than one control group and one treatment group, as the number of participants does not allow for empirical tests for multiple treatment groups (see Chapters 2 and 3 for more information on experimental design). However, this is fine, as research on users with impairments is often not of a traditional control-group–treatment-group nature; instead, it is often exploratory, a hybrid of quantitative and qualitative research, or primarily qualitative.

15.2.2 Distributed research

A different approach for users with impairments is to do distributed research, where the users do the research in their own home or office, without researchers present, and data is collected via time diaries, surveys, or keystroke logging. While this lowers the control that the researchers have over the study, it generally allows for higher numbers of users (100 users or more) to take part. In addition, a number of the challenges discussed later in the chapter (such as scheduling and transportation) may not be present for distributed research. To see an example of this, see the Time Diary to Study User Frustration sidebar in Section 6.1.

15.2.3   In-depth case studies

Yet another approach is to do in-depth case studies, in which fewer users (say, between three and 10) take part in a more intensive way. These studies might involve data collection over several days or users being trained, or longitudinal studies. This is most appropriate when data cannot be appropriately collected in a short amount of time (say, two to three hours). For instance, for many complex software applications or devices, users really do need a period of training, as well as time to familiarize themselves with the tool. So, a two-day period of research for each user can be seen as a minimum for a case study. Ideally, longitudinal studies would examine how users adapt to and utilize a new application over 3–6 months. For an example of a case study that included training, see the iSonic Evaluation Case Studies sidebar. Due to the complex nature of this software/hardware application, an in-depth case study was the most appropriate form of research.

Research In Practice

iSonic Evaluation Case Studies

A software tool called iSonic was developed to allow blind users to explore coordinated maps and tables, using sonification on the maps. The goal of this project was to create an accessible equivalent to information visualization for blind users, which would allow for coordinated data views using both tables and maps, along with the ability to filter and zoom in on items of interest.

In sonification, different non-textual tones represent different values. Specifically in iSonic, users could listen to a "map sweep": the users would hear various tones to represent, for example, the population of various states in the US (or counties), starting from the northwest, crossing to the northeast, and then going from the southwest to the southeast. After the iSonic tool was developed, a series of case studies took place to evaluate the tool.

Seven blind users took part in the research study and three sets of data were used: one for training (data on the 50 states in the US), one for actual evaluation (data on the 24 counties of Maryland, where the evaluation study was taking place), and one for post-evaluation free exploration (data on the 44 counties of Idaho). For each user that took part, there were two separate sessions on two days. On the first day, the users interacted with a tutorial on iSonic and practiced using all of the features and sample tasks. On the second day, the user attempted a series of tasks, using both Excel and the iSonic tool, to compare the performance of those tools. For instance, these tasks included "Name the five counties [in Maryland] with the lowest housing unit value" and "What is the population of Dorchester County [Maryland]?" After the tasks were completed, there was a short period of interviewing users. Finally, the users were then encouraged to freely explore a new map (the map with data for Idaho). Between the seven users, a total of 42 hours of data was collected (Zhao et al., 2008).

15.3   Proxy users

In the past, some researchers would use "proxy users", where individuals without impairment would represent individuals with impairment during design or research. This could include people with no connection to the impairment and people with some knowledge of the impairment. Examples of people with no connection to the impairment include blindfolding people who can see or tying people's hands behind their back to simulate users with motor impairments. These "simulations" are generally not encouraged for any type of research as, over time, users with perceptual or motor impairments learn to compensate by improving the use of their other senses or body parts. Someone who is blind has learned to rely more on their hearing than someone who can see. Even if the users of interest and users without any impairments are considered to have equal skill in some area (for instance, good quality speech), the impairment makes users perceive the technology differently. So, it is inappropriate to test speech-recognition solutions for users with spinal cord injuries, by using users without any impairment, based on the claim that they have similar quality speech (Feng, Sears and Law, 2005). Since users often compare a new technology to a previously used technology or option, the comparisons are very different.

There are some situations where it is appropriate to use people who are familiar with the users and impairments to represent the users themselves. These are generally situations where users are unable to communicate, or are unable to process information due to their impairment. For instance, one study used speech–language pathologists who work closely with individuals with aphasia, instead of the actual users themselves, to get an understanding of user needs (Boyd-Graber *et al.*, 2006). In another study, caregivers and family members were used as the primary information sources for designing technology for individuals with Alzheimer's Disease (Cohene, Baecker and Marziali, 2005). In both of these cases, the users of interest were themselves unable to communicate. In another study, parents answered questions about the computer usage of their children with Down Syndrome (see sidebar).

Research In Practice

Children with Down Syndrome

There has been almost no research into the computer usage of children and young adults with Down Syndrome. Two of the co-authors of this book created a survey study, to learn more about the computer usage patterns of children and young adults with Down Syndrome.

The goal was to establish some baseline data about how children with Down Syndrome used computers, and what challenges they faced. Since the project was geared towards individuals with Down Syndrome between the ages of five and 21, asking the children and young adults themselves to fill out the survey would not have been feasible. While the older individuals (teenagers and up) might have been capable of filling out the survey, they might not have had the level of reflection and language required to understand and explain exactly what they do on the computer. Certainly, the younger children would not have been able to respond to the survey.

Furthermore, since most participants were under 18 years old, their parents would have been required to provide the informed consent to participate. Therefore, parents, as individuals who could give consent for participation and were most familiar with the computer habits and skills of their children, were considered appropriate proxies for their children with Down Syndrome (Feng et al., 2008).

Note that, even with cognitive or motor impairment, many users can communicate by using some form of assistive and augmentative communication (AAC) device. You should never use proxy users when users can communicate but the researchers don't speak their language (such as people who are deaf and use sign language or blind–deaf users who use Braille or finger-spelling). In those cases, you need to access individuals who can communicate and translate with the users in their own language.

Another situation where proxy users might be appropriate is when a specific application or tool is being developed and it is undergoing multiple iterations before a proof-of-concept is complete. If users with the specific impairment would not be available to take part in all stages and all iterations of design, then proxy users might be suitable in limited stages and limited circumstances, for testing purposes. However, they should closely be followed up by evaluations with users who actually do have the impairment.

15.4   Multi-Population Studies

Given that users with impairments are really a mosaic of different communities with different needs, it is sometimes important to test an interface with either multiple impairment groups, or a combination of impairment groups and users without impairment. There are generally two approaches for developing interfaces for users with impairments (Lazar, 2007a):

- Try to make an interface (for a website, digital library, or operating system) that works well for a majority of users with impairments, especially perceptual and motor impairments. Usually, this is the scenario where the users have the same end task goal as users without impairments (such as accessing an article or purchasing a song online), and they are simply utilizing alternative input or output devices (Slatin and Rush, 2003).
- Design an interface that is optimized for a specific user group. This is the approach that tends to be used for people with severe cognitive impairment, including children with autism and adults with Alzheimer's Disease or aphasia (Cohene, Baecker and Marziali, 2005; Moffatt et al., 2004; Tartaro, 2007). The needs of the population are so specific,

that the interface, and the corresponding task scenarios and applications, are so focused on the specific needs of the user population that they are unlikely to meet the need of other populations.

For the first approach, interfaces are generally designed for a combination of the general user population without impairments and a few targeted user groups (such as users with hearing impairment, visual impairment, and spinal cord injuries). In these cases, it is generally important to make sure that an interface that is easy to use for users without impairments is also easy to use for users with certain impairments. Therefore, it is necessary to test the interfaces with two or three different user groups (users without impairments and the targeted two user groups). While we often talk about the goal of universal usability, the reality is that you can never test an application or interface with every possible existing user population. Often, an application is labeled "universally usable" when it is evaluated with three or four user populations.

It might make sense, for instance, to test a new form of CAPTCHA (a web-based security tool to differentiate between a software program and a human being) using both blind users and users without any impairments. While a CAPTCHA that works for blind users is nice, it will only be used in practice if it is also easy to use for the typical user without impairments (Holman *et al.*, 2007). In reality, if an interface works well for users with perceptual or motor impairments, that's wonderful, but companies and organizations will not implement those interfaces if they in any way degrade the user experience for users without impairments. In these situations, where an interface must be easy to use for users with and without impairments, multi-population studies are needed to involve both the general user population and a few selected impairment populations. In those cases, the general user population is NOT serving as a proxy user, but rather, is part of the targeted user population for an interface.

15.5 Recruiting users through community partners

At this point, it should be clear that recruiting actual users with impairments is necessary for all forms of research, including usability testing. The next question is, how is this done? You can't just place signs in the computer department or on campus saying, "we want users with spinal cord injuries to take part in our research study," as there are often not a sufficient number of individuals with impairments on university campuses. The target population may not see the signs (if they have a visual impairment) or have access to the spaces where the signs are posted. The best way to recruit users is usually to partner with a community-based group that focuses on the impairment of interest to the research. Most people with impairments have some sort of organization, support group, or coordination point. For instance, there are organizations for people with visual and hearing impairment, organizations for people with spinal cord injuries, and organizations for people with Alzheimer's Disease. In cases where the impairment impacts on the ability to live an independent life, these organizations often include caregivers and family members. Many university campuses have an office that provides support to people with impairments.

It is usually good to approach these organizations for help in recruiting users. However, simply saying, "we want to do some research, and we need your help in recruiting users" is not sufficient, and it is hard to establish immediate trust (Feng, Sears and Law, 2005). If you really care about these user populations, then you need to become involved with the community-based group for the long term. Most of these organizations get multiple requests for help, and they may be leery of "drive-by research," where you ask for their help, do the research, and then never show up or contact them again.

Some organizations are geographically based and you may want to contact their national offices. For instance, the Royal National Institute of Blind People in the United Kingdom and the National Federation of the Blind in the United States are leading organizations for blind individuals. Similarly, there are many other groups, such as the National Down Syndrome Congress in the United States and the Down Syndrome Association in the United Kingdom. While national organizations are common, other organizations may work at the grassroots, with local city-based groups that do not coordinate with each other. If possible, you should become a part of these organizations: go to their meetings, meet people, get involved in their community, and take part in fundraisers. If there is a regional or national convention, it is important to attend that gathering. At these gatherings, it is possible to better understand the logistics and challenges involved for that population, which can help with the planned research in the future. But it isn't sufficient to go to the meetings just to learn about issues such as Braille handouts or physical room limitations for individuals in wheelchairs. The end goal should not simply be to further your research, but to further the cause of these individuals and their quality of life. Your research is simply a piece of that long-term goal. As such, your partnership needs to be a two-way street. If you are asking for their help, then they should be able to expect your help. You should find a way to compensate the organization for their assistance to you. When your research is complete, you should make sure that the organization receives copies of any final reports.

Rehabilitation centers that are often sponsored by local governments or industry provide training and modifications to help adults with certain impairments move into the workforce. These organizations can often be sources of participants for research.

If you are working with a community-based organization that specializes in a certain impairment, the goal of your research is to further their cause and improve the quality of life for individuals with the specific impairment by improving understanding of HCI issues for the user population. If the only goal you have is to further your own professional career, with little concern for the needs of the population, look elsewhere. Working with users with impairments is a long-term, emotional, involved process, with great societal benefit and long-term payoffs in the quality of life for individuals. Expect that the organizations involved will come to count on you and consider you a part of their cause. Invest in the long term or get out of the game. End of sermon.

When recruiting users, it is important to understand their preferred method of communication and any related challenges. For instance, e-mail may not be the preferred option for users with spinal cord injuries, as it may be harder for users with SCI to generate text. Instead, phone calls might be the preferred option (Feng, Sears and Law, 2005). Obviously, phone calls might not work well for deaf people, who may prefer e-mail or text messaging. Other user populations may have different challenges in communication. For instance, e-mail is often a preferred method of communication for blind users. However, due to the large amount of time required for them to process spam e-mail, blind users tend to have very strong filtering on their e-mail. E-mails sent to multiple blind users using the BCC option will not make it through the spam filter to most users (Lazar *et al.*, 2005). So for blind users, it is important to place the recipients' e-mail address in the To line, not in the CC line or BCC lines. Another approach might be to use the phone, but it is important to ask permission in advance before doing so. For users with some types of cognitive impairment, it may be necessary to contact caregivers.

15.6 Pilot studies

Due to the logistics involved, it is often very necessary to do pilot studies before beginning any real data collection. Your simulation in the lab, or your expectations of how a user will interact, are likely to be very different from the reality. While this is true in any type of HCI research, it is especially true in working with users with impairments. Since you may have access to a limited number of users and you won't have any opportunity to do the data collection a second time, you need to confirm or address your perceptions early on in the process by doing a pilot study with one or two users.

Pilot studies can uncover a number of problems. For instance, is the documentation accessible for the specific user population? Users with spinal cord injuries can't physically handle documentation, and blind users may not be able to use printed materials or even Braille materials (approximately 10–20% of blind individuals are fluent in Braille). Users in wheelchairs will need physical settings, including computer desks, that can accommodate their wheelchairs. Other technical problems may arise. For instance, any text documents for blind users must work under multiple screen readers (Window-Eyes and JAWS), multiple operating systems (OS X, Win XP), and multiple text editors (MS-Word, Word Perfect, and Notepad), as well as various combinations of screen reader, operating system and text editor (Lazar *et al.*, 2005). Sometimes the file format that works best is Rich Text Format, which tends to work with most text editors. In doing a pilot study, you may find out that the participants expect to use aids (such as a portable notetaker, voice recorder, or electronic device) or expect you to have aids available to them (Sauer *et al.*, 2009). Generally, you need to be aware if all participants are using certain aids; if only some of them do, you need to find a way to compensate for that in your data collection.

One or two users in the pilot study are generally enough, just to confirm that you are on the right track and that there are no major problems with logistics. If you have worked with a specific user population for a long time, you may have a few users that you collaborate with regularly, who are comfortable with you, and are willing to help you test out materials and serve as your "reality check." Whatever flaws or problems are discovered during the pilot study should be modified and accounted for before the main study begins.

15.7   Scheduling users with impairments

It is important to remember that users with perceptual, cognitive, or motor impairments frequently do not drive a car. They may rely on rides from others, public transportation, taxis, and scheduled services to get from point A to point B. Therefore, these users must typically be scheduled in advance. It is often not possible for these participants to make transportation plans, or change them, at the last minute.

Rather than asking participants to come to a university or remote location, it is far better for researchers to offer to go to a home or workplace location. To help ensure the safety and security of researchers entering participant homes, it is preferable to go in teams of at least two researchers. By visiting users in their home or workplace, it alleviates the need for the user with an impairment to schedule transportation to a new location. In addition, getting a glimpse of the user in their own environment, using their own technical setup, is likely to lead to a more ecologically valid data collection effort. Many blind users have a screen reader (such as JAWS or Window-Eyes) customized to their specific needs. The speed of speech, how links are read, and even the type of voice (e.g. American English vs. British English) are personal preferences that may not be obvious to the researcher, but can be very important to the user. Visiting the user in their natural environment allows the user to be most relaxed and productive and yields the most ecologically valid data.

The major drawback of visiting users in their work or home environment is that you tend to have less control over the environment (Feng, Sears and Law, 2005). If users are able to come to a research lab, this offers the researchers more control over the layout and noise in the environment. However, aside from the transportation challenge, there is another major challenge: the accessibility of the building. Researchers must be completely certain that the building that they expect users to come to is accessible. This means that the doors must be wide enough, restrooms must have accessible stalls, elevators must be present, and Braille must be available on all signs. In addition, some users may have service animals working with them (Feng, Sears and Law, 2005).

It is also important to note that a large number of users with an impairment do not have a job; those who are employed may be very sensitive about missing work for an outside research project. They are unlikely to let a research study interfere with their job performance (Lazar, Feng and Allen, 2006). So when possible, visit them on-site, either at their workplace or their home (which is sometimes preferable because it won't interfere with work). Also, note that it may be necessary to schedule research sessions during evenings or weekends.

It is important for researchers to understand that the variety of users and the various levels of severity of the impairment (see Section 15.9) mean that the time involved for a user to take part in a research study might be relatively unpredictable. The researcher's schedule should be left flexible enough that it is not a problem if a user takes much longer for data collection than is expected. In addition, many users with impairments are determined to prove that they can accomplish tasks. This means that if the time period is limited for the specific user's data collection, they may still want to continue and feel the need to complete the task. For a researcher to tell the user that "time is up" may be met with resistance. This is not generally a problem, except that it needs to be accounted for in the scheduling of users.

15.8   Documentation for users with impairments

Often, there are a number of documents that are required for participation in a research study. These include human subjects forms (also known as institutional review board (IRB) forms – see Chapter 14 for more information), instructions, task lists, and questionnaires. In traditional paper format, these forms may pose a problem for users that are print-disabled (blind or with low vision or dyslexia) or that can read but may have problems handling forms (such as users with spinal cord injuries). It's also important to note that in some cases, if children with impairments are involved in the research, then the researchers themselves may be required to submit their own approval paperwork related to criminal record background checks.

15.8.1   Human subjects forms

To start with, nearly all research projects involving humans require that participants be informed of their rights, and this usually takes the form of a human subjects or IRB form (see Chapter 14 for more information on what rights human participants have). Most human subjects forms require handwritten signatures, as per university or institutional requirement. This may be a problem for a number of user populations.

Users with motor impairments, especially those that are unable to use their arms, may not be able to use a pencil to sign a form or handle a form. An audio recording, or a video of the user, agreeing to take part in the study, hopefully will be acceptable to the institutional review board. For users with certain types of cognitive impairment, it's questionable whether they would be able to sign a legal document. A caregiver, who has legal standing, might need to provide the signature. For children with an impairment, often the parents need to give their approval for participation in the research project. Blind users may be able to sign the form, however, they will need guidance on where to sign the form (in addition, it's questionable whether we should ask participants to sign a form that they cannot read first). For users that either cannot read or handle the form, it is good practice to send an electronic version of the form beforehand, so that the user can read and be comfortable with it. Be sure to understand the specific policies relating to IRB forms from the organization that approved the research study (usually a university). For instance, many universities accept nothing but a signed, paper-based form. Some universities are beginning to accept electronic versions of informed consent (see Chapter 14). It is helpful to check if your institutional review board can accept some modified form of informed consent, which is more appropriate to the user population. If the institutional review board will not accept audio or video recording of a user giving consent, there are work-arounds that can be utilized.

If a sponsoring organization requires signed forms from blind users, there are two popular ways of guiding blind users to the appropriate place to sign on the form. One method is to provide a signature guide (a small piece of plastic with a window in the middle, to indicate where the signature should be – see Figure 15.1). The other method is to attach a Braille label right below the signature line. The Braille label could say something along the lines of "sign above" (Lazar *et al.*, 2005). While this might not be meaningful for the majority of blind individuals who are not able to read Braille, the tactile information provided by the top line of the label can provide useful information on where the signature should be placed. Careful attention to details such as these can help build trust and confidence with participants, as they may appreciate that you've made the effort to make things work for them.

The discussion of blind users and Braille brings up another important issue. You must be aware of the diversity within user populations. For instance, print forms are relatively useless for blind users, unless they have a scanner available. So it might seem that forms in Braille would be the appropriate alternative. You first need to check that all of your user population can read Braille and that your university or other sponsoring organization will accept forms written in Braille. Most individuals who are blind cannot read Braille; if you want to test screen reader usage, by having forms printed in Braille, you would limit yourself to the estimated 10–20% of blind individuals that are fluent in Braille (National Federation of the Blind, 2006). And, of course, you would also need access to some form of Braille printer to print good-quality Braille. If you are not very familiar with the characteristics of a certain population and are working with them for the first time, you really should get advice on all of your research plans from someone who has years of experience working with that user population.

15.8.2 Research documentation

Once the issue of human subjects forms has been addressed, there are issues surrounding the other documentation in the research study. For instance, participants in research studies must often either read material, or record their responses, on paper. If users are unable to read printed documents or have trouble handling physical documents, then there are other options. One option is to provide all of the materials in electronic format, which can be used both for reading and for recording responses. Plain text versions of all documentation can be made available to the users, at the time of the research study. Only the IRB form should be made available beforehand, as providing actual study documents could lead to learning effects. Electronic forms introduce another complicating factor into the research study. For instance, what happens if some users are more experienced with text readers or word processors than other users? Will that difference, even though it is not being measured or controlled for, make a difference in the outcome of the research?

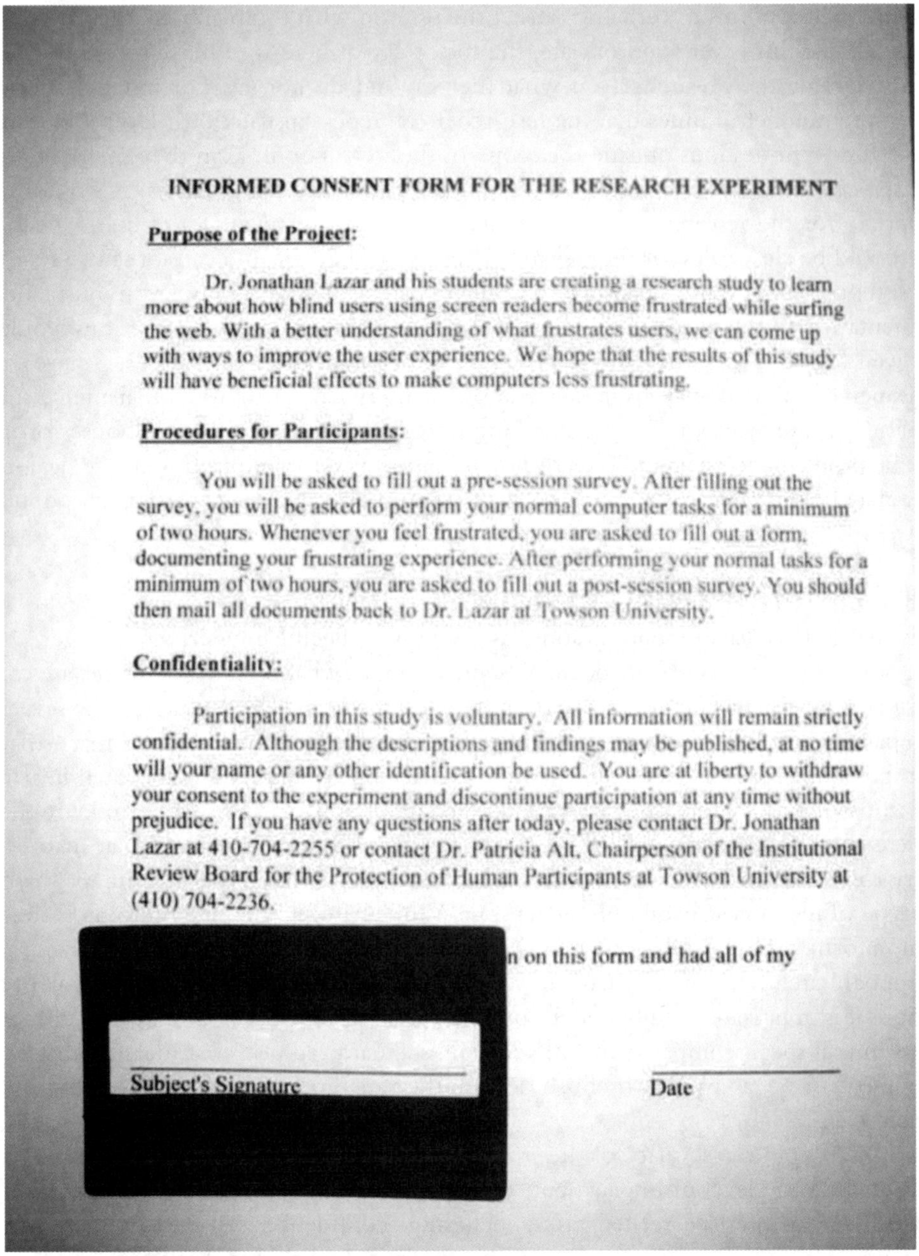

INFORMED CONSENT FORM FOR THE RESEARCH EXPERIMENT

Purpose of the Project:

Dr. Jonathan Lazar and his students are creating a research study to learn more about how blind users using screen readers become frustrated while surfing the web. With a better understanding of what frustrates users, we can come up with ways to improve the user experience. We hope that the results of this study will have beneficial effects to make computers less frustrating.

Procedures for Participants:

You will be asked to fill out a pre-session survey. After filling out the survey, you will be asked to perform your normal computer tasks for a minimum of two hours. Whenever you feel frustrated, you are asked to fill out a form, documenting your frustrating experience. After performing your normal tasks for a minimum of two hours, you are asked to fill out a post-session survey. You should then mail all documents back to Dr. Lazar at Towson University.

Confidentiality:

Participation in this study is voluntary. All information will remain strictly confidential. Although the descriptions and findings may be published, at no time will your name or any other identification be used. You are at liberty to withdraw your consent to the experiment and discontinue participation at any time without prejudice. If you have any questions after today, please contact Dr. Jonathan Lazar at 410-704-2255 or contact Dr. Patricia Alt, Chairperson of the Institutional Review Board for the Protection of Human Participants at Towson University at (410) 704-2236.

n on this form and had all of my

_____   _____
Subject's Signature   Date

Figure 15.1 An IRB form with a signature guide for blind users.

The other option is to verbally instruct the user on what to do and ask them to respond verbally. While this is very appropriate, the major caveat here is to make sure that rules are created to guide the researchers on what they do and do not say. For instance, is there a limit on the number of times that the researcher can repeat instructions? Do the researchers refuse to answer questions outside the scope of the instructions? Can they spell out words? For instance, if the research study was investigating web searching habits, it would not be appropriate for the researchers to give hints or provide guidance to the users. Therefore, there should be clear rules for the researchers on what they can and cannot say, so that there is consistency across all users taking part in the research study. Obviously, you must tailor the documentation to the needs of the participants. For instance, verbal instructions would not work well for users with hearing impairment or who are deaf. If those users have vision, then paper documents may be preferred. But if users have a motor impairment, such as a spinal cord injury, in which case handling documents and recording responses on paper might be problematic, then audio recording might be a good option. If users are deaf–blind, Braille may be the preferred option. As always, you must know your participant population very well.

15.9   Differing levels of ability

Ability levels may vary widely among users with a specific impairment (Jaeger, 2009). Assumptions should never be made, for instance, about "what users with aphasia are capable of." Since many impairments are due to underlying medical or health causes, the severity of the impairment will vary among different users. Most impairments are not binary, that you either have them or don't. People can have partial impairments (such as partial hearing or visual impairment). People can have varying severity of impact (for instance, mild, moderate, or severe aphasia, Alzheimer's Disease, or dementia). Even impairments that at first seem to be very clear and binary are not. For instance, there are different types of amnesia, based on what type of memory capability has been lost. While trisomy Down Syndrome is the most common form, there is another type of Down Syndrome, called "mosaic Down Syndrome", that is much rarer, but generally has a lower impact on cognitive performance. In all of these situations it is important to fully understand the nature of the population, by consulting with experts in that specific impairment. In addition, standardized tests that measure the severity of the impairment can be very useful, as long as they are properly conducted and interpreted (Moffatt et al., 2004).

Not only does the severity of the impairment influence interface design, but even for people at the same level of impairment, there are a number of other factors that influence performance on interface-related tasks, including: confidence, self-efficacy, and previous experience with using computers. The results are not always what they seem and it takes a lot of experience with a specific user population to understand this.

For instance, research tasks that might take user A only one hour might take user B 3.5 hours. In a typical population without impairments, this would lead the researcher to believe that either users B's performance is lower, or maybe there is a problem with the equipment that user B is utilizing (e.g. it is older equipment or network connections). However, this would not necessarily hold true for populations with disabilities. For instance, newer users of a certain application or tool (such as head tracking) might be satisfied with completing a series of tasks in 3.5 hours. This same amount of time might be frustrating to someone who has utilized the equipment for years. Each user with an impairment (or a combination of impairments) is a unique individual, with a unique performance speed that they alone consider to be their average "default speed". The "default speed" should be taken into consideration to determine individual usability. However, the "default speed" can also be a complication when trying to compare the performance of a group of users with a specific impairment. For instance, typical data input and output speeds vary more greatly for users with impairments than for the general user population. As an example, blind users listen to their screen readers at varying rates, and tend to think that any speed that is not their pre-set speed is either too fast or too slow. Often in studies with blind users, you want to remove the potential confounding factor of having various screen reader speeds in the mix by using one screen reader speed for every participant. This is a very good thing for your research design, but may frustrate the individuals who participate.

In another example of the complexity of user differences within a specific impairment population, for a screen reader user who listens to JAWS at a very rapid rate, they may be frustrated if a task takes more than five minutes to complete. Another user, who listens to the screen reader at a much slower speed, may be very satisfied if the same task takes 20 minutes to complete. Their personal expectations of performance may not always be obvious to the researcher and this may be hard to measure. Experience with the computer and confidence may also play a role. For instance, imagine three blind users, all of whom are attempting the same task. User A may give up after two minutes of attempting the task, because they know that they typically can only find information using four different navigation methods, and once they have attempted all four navigation methods, it is pointless to continue, as they are confident that they would not be able to use any other method and succeed. User B may also give up after two minutes, but because they have low confidence. They are not confident in their abilities and think it is unlikely that they will be able to complete a task. User C does not give up, even after 45 minutes of attempting a task. While the computing skill set of user C might be high or low, they are confident in their abilities, and they repeatedly say, "I am not a quitter. I will keep going until I am able to complete the task." In this example, time is not directly correlated to experience or confidence, but rather, is influenced by both. The authors of this book have personally witnessed all three behaviors.

15.10 Bringing extra computer parts

When visiting users with impairments in their home or workplace, it's important to understand that their setup may not be what most researchers are used to, and that technical setup will be out of the researcher's control. For instance, blind users may not have a working monitor, deaf users may not have working speakers, and users with motor impairments may not have a working mouse. Since many of these users have purchased a "standard package" of CPU, monitor, and peripherals from a computer company, if pieces of hardware that are useless to them break, there is no real incentive for the users to replace them. However, researchers often rely on these tools to understand the user interaction. For instance, often researchers who are visual will need to see the screen to understand what the screen reader is reading. If this is the case, you need to carry extra computer parts in your car when you visit the users. For instance, bring a monitor with you if you are visiting blind users in their workplace or home. Also bring standard cables (such as video and USB cables). If doing multiple on-site visits, it is good practice to take extra parts (monitors, cables, speakers, mice, external keyboards) with you at all times, and simply leave them in the car, as you never know when you may need them.

Research
In
Practice

Participants Getting Frustrated

What happens if a user with an impairment is taking part in a study, is not successful at completing any of the tasks, and is getting frustrated? This person is getting agitated, is still trying to complete the tasks, but clearly is not making any progress. What happens next? This is a realistic question.

For the researcher who is monitoring this user, it is an upsetting time. Although our research studies in HCI typically do not endanger health or leave lasting emotional effects, it is certainly possible that a situation of this nature could occur which could leave the user angry and upset. Aside from a few rare studies designed to frustrate people on purpose, such as (Riseberg et al., 1998), HCI research is generally not designed to aggravate the user.

There are a few options. The researcher can remind the user that they have the right to end their participation in the experiment, at any time, with no adverse consequences (which is typically a standard requirement in IRB forms). As part of this reminder, the researcher should note that whatever payment is due to the user for participation will be given to the user, regardless of when they end their participation. But if the user does not want to end the session, what happens next? Perhaps the user can be offered a short break or a period of rest, which would allow them a few minutes to calm down. The researcher technically has the right to end the experiment if they feel that someone is starting to be harmed. However, for the researcher to unilaterally end the participation of the user also sets some bad precedents. If researchers frequently end user participation, there could be some bias injected into the research study. This is a tricky situation. Especially when working with users with impairments, who are often hard to recruit and replace.

15.11 Payment

When paying users for taking part in research, it is important to make sure that the form of payment will be useful to the users. For instance, gift cards for a specific store (such as a local bookstore) may not be useful for some people if they cannot use standard print materials. Also, gift cards that only work at a certain store may not be useful, if transportation is required to visit the store and use the gift cards. Gifts that are typically used to recruit university students for research, such as iPods, may also not be appropriate, as many users with impairments have very specific technical needs and may not want to use new devices. The best forms of payment are either cash or cash equivalents, such as cash cards. If those are not viable options, than at least a gift card should be given at a store that has online ordering options and an accessible website (such as Amazon) or that has many local branches and many types of merchandise. It is also important to note that users with impairments are typically paid more than users without impairments for their participation in HCI research.

Summary

Research involving participants with impairments can be challenging but it offers many rewards. The computer usage of many of these users has not been explored in as much depth as with the general population of users, so there are many great research questions that remain unexamined. And these topics need attention! With appropriate planning and attention to logistics, HCI research involving users with impairments can be very successful.

Review Questions

1. What are the three generally accepted approaches for dealing with the challenge of access to participants with a certain impairment?
2. What is an advantage of doing distributed research with participants with impairments and what is a disadvantage?
3. What is a proxy user? Why is the use of proxy users in research discouraged? What are the rare circumstances in which proxy users would be acceptable?
4. What are the two general approaches for developing computer interfaces for users with impairments?
5. Why is it important to make sure that an interface designed for a user with a perceptual or motor impairment is also maximized for the general user population?
6. What are some good places to look for potential participants with impairments ?
7. Is e-mail always the best way to contact potential participants with impairments?
8. Pilot studies can be helpful in identifying potential challenges in logistics. Name at least three logistical challenges that a pilot study can uncover.

9. Why is transportation a challenge to participation for users with impairments and how can researchers address that?
10. What is a major challenge in using IRB forms for blind users? What about for users that are paralyzed?
11. Why are standardized tests of the severity of impairment useful in research studies?

Research Design Exercise

Imagine a research study that involves users who have both slurred speech and severe arthritis. These users do not have any cognitive impairment and their vision is average. The goal of this research study is to examine various input devices and determine which one is most effective for this user population. As hearing and vision is intact for most of these users, output is not a problem, only input is a problem. What might the transportation issues be for this population? What might the scheduling issues be? What might be the best way to communicate with these users? Would it be better to go out to their homes or have them come to the research lab at the university? How would you handle IRB forms? How would you give them the documentation on the tasks to be performed? How would you have them record responses (since, due to the arthritis, they may have trouble with writing)? How might these users like to be paid for their participation?

References

Boyd-Graber, J.L., Nikolova, S.S., Moffatt, K.A., *et al.* (2006) Participatory design with proxies: Developing a desktop-PDA system to support people with aphasia. *Proceedings of the ACM Conference on Human Factors in Computing Systems*, 151–160.

Cohene, T., Baecker, R., and Marziali, E. (2005) Designing interactive life story multimedia for a family affected by Alzheimer's Disease: A case study. *Proceedings of the ACM Conference on Human Factors in Computing Systems*, 1300–1303.

Feng, J., Lazar, J., Kumin, L., and Ozok, A. (2008) Computer usage and computer-related behavior of young individuals with Down Syndrome. *Proceedings of the ACM Conference on Assistive Technology (ASSETS)*, 35–42.

Feng, J., Sears, A., and Law, C. (2005) Conducting empirical experiments involving participants with spinal cord injuries. *Proceedings of the Universal Access in Human–Computer Interaction Conference*.

Holman, J., Lazar, J., Feng, J., and D'Arcy, J. (2007) Developing usable CAPTCHAs for blind users. *Proceedings of the ACM Conference on Assistive Technologies (ASSETS)*, 245–246.

Jaeger, P. (2009) Persons with disabilities and intergenerational universal usability. *interactions*, **16**(3):66–67.

Lazar, J. (2007a) Introduction to universal usability. In J. Lazar (ed.), *Universal Usability: Designing computer interfaces for diverse user populations*, 1–12. Chichester, UK: John Wiley & Sons

Lazar, J. (ed.) (2007b) *Universal Usability: Designing Computer Interfaces for Diverse User Populations*. Chichester, UK: John Wiley & Sons.

Lazar, J. and Norcio, A. (2000) Service research: Community partnerships for research and training. *Journal of Informatics Education and Research*, **2**(3):21–25.

Lazar, J., Allen, A., Kleinman, J., and Lawrence, J. (2005) Methodological issues in using time diaries to collect frustration data from blind computer users. *Proceedings of the 11th International Conference on Human–Computer Interaction (HCI)* (on CD-ROM).

Lazar, J., Feng, J., and Allen, A. (2006) Determining the impact of computer frustration on the mood of blind users browsing the web. *Proceedings of the ACM Conference on Assistive Technology (ASSETS)*, 149–156.

Moffatt, K., McGrenere, J., Purves, B., and Klawe, M. (2004) The participatory design of a sound and image enhanced daily planner for people with aphasia. *Proceedings of the ACM Conference on Human Factors in Computing Systems*, 407–414.

National Federation of the Blind (2006) *Braille Usage: Perspectives of legally blind adults and policy implications for school administrators*. Baltimore, MD: National Federation of the Blind.

Riseberg, J., Klein, J., Fernandez, R., and Picard, R. (1998) Frustrating the user on purpose: Using biosignals in a pilot study to detect the user's emotional state. *Proceedings of the ACM Conference on Human Factors in Computing Systems*, 227–228.

Sauer, G., Holman, J., Lazar, J., Hochheiser, H., and Feng, J. (2009) Accessible privacy and security: A universally usable human-interaction proof. *Universal Access in the Information Society*, In press.

Slatin, J. and Rush, S. (2003) *Maximum Accessibility*. New York: Addison-Wesley.

Tartaro, A. (2007) Authorable virtual peers for children with autism. *Proceedings of the ACM Conference on Human Factors in Computing Systems*, 1677–1680.

Zhao, H., Plaisant, C., Shneiderman, B., and Lazar, J. (2008) Data sonification for users with visual impairment: A case study with geo-referenced data. *ACM Transactions on Human–Computer Interaction*, **15**(1):1–28.

Index